Official Guide
to Mini SQL 2.0

Brian Jepson and David J. Hughes

WILEY COMPUTER PUBLISHING

John Wiley & Sons, Inc.
New York • Chichester • Weinheim • Brisbane • Singapore • Toronto

Publisher: Robert Ipsen
Editor: Cary Sullivan
Assistant Editor: Pam Sobotka
Managing Editor: Angela Murphy
Electronic Products, Associate Editor: Mike Sosa
Text Design & Composition: Benchmark Productions, Inc.

Designations used by companies to distinguish their products are often claimed as trademarks. In all instances where John Wiley & Sons, Inc., is aware of a claim, the product names appear in initial capital or ALL CAPITAL LETTERS. Readers, however, should contact the appropriate companies for more complete information regarding trademarks and registration.

This book is printed on acid-free paper. ∞

Library of Congress Cataloging-in-Publication Data:

Jepson, Brian
    Official guide to Mini SQL 2.0 / Brian Jepson. David Hughes
      p.   cm.
    Includes index.
    ISBN 0-471-24535-6 (pbk. : CD-ROM : alk. paper)
    1. SQL (Computer program language) I. Hughes, David, 1968-
  II. Title.
  QA76.73.S67J47 1998
   005.75'85--dc21   97-37927

Printed in the United States of America
10 9 8 7 6 5 4 3 2 1

Contents

Acknowledgments

Some people start working on a book because they think it fills a general need. That sort of person, when he or she is right on the money, is a true visionary. Other people work on a book because they believe it will solve someone else's specific problem. That lot derives their content from the experience of others, and are true empaths. Some people start working on a book because they think it will sell well. Those sort of people are realists. In my case, I started working on this book because I wanted to write about Mini SQL. I suppose I'm a romantic, then. I've always been enamored of Mini SQL, and I believe its simplicity and elegance has always captured and always *will* capture the hearts of its users.

When I started putting a proposal together for this book, I sent it off for review to David Hughes, the creator of Mini SQL. Although such an arrangement had not crossed my or David's mind, Cary Sullivan, our editor at Wiley, suggested that I try to get David as a co-author. To my delight, he agreed to do it. The result is the book that you now hold in your hand. Developed in parallel with release 2.0 of Mini SQL, this book aims to be the definitive resource for Mini SQL development.

I owe a great deal of thanks to David, who not only wrote a good chunk of this book, but who at the same time developed Mini SQL 2.0. Without his work, this book would never have happened. I'd like to also thank Cary Sullivan, Pam Sobotka, and Angela Murphy at Wiley, who put up with a random flow of semi-finished writing, and who saw this book through to its completion. Jim Bray (jb@cs.wcu.edu) put in numerous hours as a technical reviewer, and helped shape this book into its final form. Finally, I'd like to thank my cat Oscar for giving up his habit of stalking and pouncing on the nearest human (usually me, but sometimes unsuspecting passersby who have been drawn in by Oscar's alien mind screens) during the development of this book.

—Brian Jepson

Well, it's done. Although my input to this book pales next to Brian's effort, I now have an understanding and a heightened appreciation of the toil of the humble author. It has been said that the written word is the greatest expression of man. I think an appropriate subnote to that sentiment would be that it is not only a great expression, but also a great exertion. To those who make the art of composition their career, I take my hat off.

When Brian approached me with the idea of helping him with this endeavor, I was strangely excited. The thought of an official guide to Mini SQL being penned by someone of Brian's reputation and published by a house such as Wiley was another peak in the phenomenon that is mSQL. If someone had told me in 1994 when mSQL 0.1 was made available to some fellow researchers in academia, that in a few short years it would be the topic of such sustained interest, licensed by some of the world's largest computer companies, talked about, written about and used by thousands of people, I would have had a hearty chuckle. I look back now on what would then have been fantasy but has since become reality with a sense of awe, encouragement, and thankfulness.

The success of mSQL has proven two important points. Firstly that the global community is in fact a reality rather than a political or financial thesis. The power of the Net in bringing work from all corners of the globe into the hands of those who can use it best is astonishing. I have always, and will always, believe strongly in the sharing of ideas and tools with those who will create the next generation of ideas and tools—the academic and research community. Never before has a medium had such a profound impact on the assembly of disparate minds.

The second point proven was that the spirit of fair play is alive and well. When I have explained the distribution mechanism of mSQL to others they have laughed. "You trust Joe Public enough to give him the complete product expecting him to pay if he uses it?", they question. Well, I'm very happy to say that Joe is an honorable man. To those of you reading this book that accepted our cooperative approach to software distribution and licensing, I thank you.

Finally, I must follow in the time honored tradition of offering thanks to those who have helped. Mainly, I must thank the cast of thousands that have used mSQL during the past few years of continual development. In particular I owe a debt of gratitude to the small but vocal group of maniacs that worked with the mSQL 2.0 code during the pre-alpha, alpha and beta stages. Others who have provided either reasoned input or at the very least a damn fine sounding board (I'll let them determine which :) include Mr. Birkenstocks, Miss Pedantic, paf, and Paul "now I'm really mentally contaminated" Reithmuller.

Naturally, Brian Jepson deserves more credit than you can imagine for pulling this together while I was bashing on code (or whatever else it was that took me away from the book)—thanks, mate. Also the crew at Wiley, namely Cary Sullivan and Pam Sobotka, for dealing with a somewhat trying and often A.W.O.L. author.

A final note to my family, and those close to me. I'll call you soon just to make sure you remember what I look like—I promise ;-)

—David J. Hughes

(also known as Bambi)

Introduction

Getting into a client-server SQL database can be expensive and complicated, especially if you're thinking about publishing data using Internet technology. Inexpensive single-tier engines like dBase, FoxPro, or Access are generally out of the question. Although these database packages are inexpensive, each remote or local connection to the database usually consumes a large amount of system resources, unless a third-party solution is introduced. Client-server packages such as Oracle or Sybase are not only much more expensive, but generally require one or more full-time employees to maintain each installation.

Fortunately, there is a mid-level database package that meets the needs of users who don't want the expense and headache of more expensive client-server systems. That package, Mini SQL (also known as mSQL), is available for $US250, and is quite sufficient for many applications. This book will introduce you to the fundamentals of Mini SQL, and then explore many of the ways in which you can use it.

Mini SQL has been around long enough that it is a tested and stable product, and can be integrated with a number of programming languages, such as Perl, Java, C, PHP/FI, and others. It comes bundled with a scripting language, Lite. Lite can be used with the W3-mSQL package to generate dynamic Web pages that are derived from information in the database.

How This Book Is Organized

Since Mini SQL is supported in a variety of programming languages, this book has been divided in such a way that the reader can pick and choose the elements he or she feels will be of the most use. Section One is for everyone; it introduces Mini SQL, the SQL language itself, and W3-mSQL. Section Two is for Java programmers. It includes a brief introduction to Java, and goes on to cover the two Java APIs (Application Program Interfaces) available for mSQL development: MsqlJava and mSQL-JDBC. Perl is covered in Section Three, which includes an introduction to Perl and goes on to cover the ways Mini SQL can be used from Perl, including MsqlPerl and DBD::mSQL. Section Four covers some other topics, such as PHP/FI and the Apache Web server. Finally, a collection of appendices rounds out the book, which includes some mSQL internals information as well as annotated source code for some of the longer example programs.

Who Should Read This Book

This is not one of those books that tries to be everything to everyone. There are two groups of people who will benefit most from this book. If you are a database developer, and you are looking for a robust, fast, and lightweight SQL engine for Unix and Unix-like operating systems, then Mini SQL is most definitely for you. Most of the examples will apply equally well to other operating systems on which mSQL is available, such as Windows NT, Windows 95, and OS/2.

In addition to being suitable for many client-server applications, Mini SQL is inexpensive and versatile. The other group to whom this book will appeal consists of you Web developers who are looking to step into the realm of database-enabled Web pages. No longer satisfied with storing information in flat files or Unix DBM files, you crave the power of a relational database to bring dynamic content to your users. If this description fits you, then Mini SQL is definitely for you, and this book will be an indispensable companion in your travels.

Even if you don't fit into one of those two groups, this book may still be of value to you. While you can download Mini SQL from the Web, this book includes a single user/developer's license. If you're a programmer who has realized that it's time to learn SQL, you'd do yourself a service to pick up this book. If you take this book home and install the software included on the CD-ROM, you will have a complete SQL engine and a host of connectivity options. Although it does not support all of the features that Oracle and Sybase offer, Mini SQL is an excellent tool for many applications, and this book and CD combination supplies everything you need to get up and running. Even if you already know SQL, this book can be useful in learning how to interact with SQL from Perl or Java. Although there are many differences between Mini SQL and high-end dataservers, a lot of what you learn in this book will apply to other SQL environments, so it's safe to think of this book as an "SQL Classroom Between Two Covers."

What You Will Need To Use This Book

On Unix platforms, Mini SQL is distributed as source code. In order to compile Mini SQL, you should have an ANSI C compiler and programming tools such as the GNU compilation tools and binary utilities, or equivalent compilation tools supplied by your operating system vendor. The Perl examples included with this book have been tested with version 5.004, although they should work with 5.002 or later. The Java examples require JDK 1.1 or later.

About the Single User/Developer's License

This book comes with a single-user/developer's license, which allows you to use it for development purposes. This version carries the restriction that only five concurrent users may be logged into the database, which should be sufficient for testing and development. A site license may be purchased, which is suitable for use on a Web server, and allows a much larger number of concurrent users. A coupon is provided at the back of this book, which allows you to purchase the full version of Mini SQL at a discounted rate.

Mini SQL is available free of charge for certain noncommercial purposes in unrestricted form, so if you fall into this category, you can grab a copy off the Net and use it. This applies to education institutions (with the exception of commercial training outfits), noncommercial research organizations, registered charities, registered not-for-profit organizations, and full-time students.

Please note that you can download the full version of Mini SQL from the Internet at any time. Unless you fall into one of the categories listed earlier, this version is only available for a limited evaluation period, after which you must register it. The developer's version included on the CD, while limited by the number of concurrent users, may be used indefinitely. As new versions of Mini SQL 2.0 are released, patches will be made available for users of the developer's version.

An Introduction to Mini SQL 2.0

Mini SQL 2.0, the second generation of the mSQL database system, is a lightweight database engine optimized for both large and small data sets. The main focus of the second-generation development has been to extend the capabilities of the database engine and to provide new tools to simplify the development and delivery of mSQL-based applications. The large acceptance of mSQL 1.x and widespread implementations thereof highlighted several shortcomings of the original product. As developers pushed the envelope of mSQL's capabilities, applications managing databases with up to a million records were being reported. Naturally, the performance of the 1.x engine was not appropriate for the task.

The database engine in mSQL 2.0 has been designed to handle large data sets and to provide consistent and rapid access to large data sets in the million-record size. In doing so it has in no way compromised the outstanding performance shown by the 1.x engine in handling small data sets. The performance increase for large applications has been achieved by the incorporation of flexible and powerful indexing to the database as well as sophisticated query execution optimization.

One of the major applications of mSQL has been as a back-end database for World Wide Web (WWW) sites. With this fact in mind, mSQL 2.0 includes the new W3-mSQL WWW interface package. Using W3-mSQL, Web-based applications can be rapidly developed by embedding mSQL and other programmatic constructs directly into the HTML code. This removes the need to write a multitude of small CGI scripts for every Web page with dynamic content.

Also included in the 2.0 distribution is the Lite scripting language. Lite is a stand-alone version of the language used by W3-mSQL. By including Lite in the distribution, a developer has a consistent language that can be used to develop stand-alone or Web-based applications that utilize mSQL. Chapter 3, "Lite and W3-mSQL," covers this in great detail.

Installing Mini SQL

For the eager reader, an overview of the compilation and installation process can be found in the *Express Setup* section later in the chapter.

Mini SQL is generally distributed in source code form to enable the widest possible use of the software. It is not feasible for binary distributions to be generated for every Unix platform for each release of mSQL. Instead, the software and the installation tools have been made as portable as possible. In general, the software will automatically configure itself to the capabilities of the operating system on which it is being compiled. Typing four commands can complete the process of compiling and installing mSQL on most Unix platforms. Only under extreme situations will the software not compile "out of the box." Hints for getting the software compiled on troublesome operating systems is available in the *Installation Troubleshooting* section later in the chapter.

Mini SQL is distributed in binary form for Windows NT and Windows 95, although source is available. This distribution includes a graphical installation utility that installs Mini SQL and the Mini SQL ODBC driver.

Getting Ready to Compile

The software is distributed as a gzipped (i.e., compressed) tar file. Tar is a standard Unix facility for combining many files and directories into a single archive file. The tar utility should be available on any modern Unix system. If your system does not provide the tar utility then a freely available version of tar has been produced by the Free Software Foundation (the GNU project). The GNU version of tar can be found on any GNU archive site. Similarly, the gzip compression tools are produced by the Free Software Foundation. If your system does not provide the gzip or gunzip utility you will need to obtain these from your nearest GNU archive site.

Table 1.1 shows a selection of commonly used GNU archive sites. To access these sites use anonymous FTP (or the URL provided). A complete list of GNU software mirror sites can be found at:

```
www.gnu.org/order/ftp.html
```

Table 1.1 A Partial List of GNU Software Sites

Country	Hostname	Directory	URL
Australia	archie.au	/gnu	ftp://archie.au/gnu
United States	prep.mit.edu	/pub/gnu	ftp://prep.mit.edu/pub/gnu
United States	ftp.uu.net	/systems/gnu	ftp://ftp.uu.net/systems/gnu
United States	gatekeeper.dec.com	/pub/GNU	ftp://gatekeeper.dec.com/pub/GNU
United Kingdom	ftp.mcc.ac.uk	/pub/gnu	ftp://ftp.mcc.ac.uk/pub/gnu

Before the software can be compiled, the contents of the archive file must be extracted. This involves decompressing the archive file with gunzip and then using the tar utility to extract the file. If, for example, the file containing the mSQL distribution is called msql-2.0.3.tar.gz, the following commands will extract the files (two methods are outlined):

```
gunzip msql-2.0.3.tar.gz
tar -xvf msql-2.0.3.tar
```

or

```
gzcat msql-2.0.3.tar.gz | tar -xvf -
```

This process will create a new directory called msql-2.0.3 in the current directory. Within that directory you will find the entire mSQL distribution. Along with various other files and directories there will be directories containing the source code (the src directory) and the documentation (the doc directory). Although it is tempting to just enter the src directory and type "make" it is not the correct way to compile mSQL and doing so will cause problems.

The mSQL distribution is structured to allow it to be compiled on multiple machines using the same copy of the source code (source tree). For example, the source tree can be shared between various machines using NFS, and versions for each machine type can be compiled in the same source tree. To achieve this, mSQL uses target directories for each machine type (hardware platform and operating system combination). To create a target directory for your machine simply type the following from the top directory of the distribution:

```
make target
```

This process will create a new directory called targets in the top-level directory. In the targets directory you will find a target directory for your machine (e.g., targets/SunOS-4.1.4-Sparc or targets/FreeBSD-2.2.2-i386). It is in this newly created target directory that you will compile the mSQL applications.

To continue the compilation process, change directory to your target directory using the cd command (e.g., cd targets/SunOS-4.1.4-Sparc). Once you are in the target directory you can configure the source tree, which prepares it for the compilation process. The configuration process is totally automatic and will determine what system calls, library functions, and header files your operating system provides. To configure the compilation process simply type:

```
./setup
```

While the setup utility is executing you will see various pieces of information about your operating system being displayed as it is determined. This output is informative only. The results are automatically placed in files used by mSQL.

Once the automatic configuration is complete, you may either compile the software using the default configuration settings or change the configuration settings from their default value. There are two configuration items located in the site.mm file in the targets directory that you may consider modifying. The configuration utility will try to determine the best C compiler to use on your system. If you have multiple C compilers (e.g., a system compiler and gcc) you may wish to modify the CC entry in site.mm.

The only other option in site.mm that may require modification is the INST_DIR entry. This entry defines the default installation directory. This setting is not only used during installation of the software but also as the directory containing the run-time configuration file. If you intend to run mSQL from a directory other than the default /usr/local/Hughes directory, you should modify the INST_DIR entry in site.mm to reflect your installation directory.

Compilation and Installation

Once the setup utility has completed, you may compile the software by typing:

```
make all
```

The compilation process will traverse all the directories of the mSQL distribution and compile the C source code in those directories. Status information is displayed to you as the compilation process proceeds. If the compilation process stops with an error at any stage then you must consult the *Installation Troubleshooting* section included later in this chapter. If the compilation has completed properly you will see a message on your screen informing you that you are ready to install mSQL.

Installation of mSQL can also be achieved using a single command, although you may need to have special permissions on your Unix system (usually root access). By default, mSQL will be installed in a directory called /usr/local/Hughes on your system. If /usr/local is owned by root on your system (as it is on most systems), you will either need root access or you will have to get your system administrator to complete the installation for you. If you have root privileges, you may use the su command to assume those privileges before you install mSQL. If you are using a nondefault installation directory make sure that you have the required permissions to create the directory you specified. To complete the installation, simply type:

```
make install
```

Mini SQL Configuration

mSQL 1.x offered several configuration options, including such details as the user the server should run as, the location of the TCP and Unix sockets for client/server communications, location of the database files, and so on. The problem with configuring mSQL 1.x was that all these details were hard-coded into the software at compile time. Once the software was compiled and installed you couldn't easily change those settings.

To overcome this problem, mSQL 2.0 utilizes an external run-time configuration file for definition of all these values. The file is called msql.conf and is located in the installation directory (usually /usr/local/Hughes). All standard mSQL applications and utilities provide a command-line flag, -f ConfFile, which allows you to specify a nonstandard configuration file. Any values that are specified in that file will override the normal operating parameters used by mSQL. If no configuration file is found (or certain items are not set), the default values (listed later in the chapter) will be used.

The Mini SQL config File

The configuration file is a plain text file organized into sections. The file can contain blank lines and comments. A comment is a line that begins with the # character. Each section of the configuration file has a section header, which is written as the section name enclosed in square brackets (e.g., [general]).

Configuration values within a section are presented using the configuration parameter name followed by an equals sign and then the new value. There can only be one entry per line, and if an entry is defined multiple times in the one config file the last value defined will be used. If a parameter is not defined in the config file then an internal default value will be used at run time.

The General Section

The following configuration parameters (Table 1.2) are available in the general section of the config file. Please note that %I may be used in configuration entries to signify the mSQL installation directory (e.g., /usr/local/Hughes).

Table 1.2 Parameters from the General Section of the config File

Parameter	Default Value	Definition
Inst_Dir	/usr/local/Hughes	The full path to the installation directory. This is the directory in which all the mSQL files are located (such as the program files, the database files, etc).
mSQL_User	msql	The user that the mSQL server should run as. If a user other than this user starts the server (e.g., it is started as root from a boot script) it will attempt to change UID so that it runs as the specified user.
Admin_User	root	The user that is allowed to perform privileged operations such as server shutdown, creation of databases, etc.
Pid_File	%I/msql2.pid	The full path of a file in which the PID of the running mSQL server process will be stored.
TCP_Port	1114	The TCP port number on which the mSQL server will accept client/server connections over a TCP/IP network. If this value is modified, it must be modified on the machine running the client software as well.
UNIX_Port	%I/msql2.sock	The full pathname of the Unix domain socket created by the mSQL server for connections from client applications running on the same machine.

Table 1.3 Parameters from the W3-mSQL Section of the config File

Parameter	Default Value	Definition
Auth_Host	NULL	The machine on which the mSQL database containing W3-Auth data is located. See the W3-Auth section for further details. If set to NULL (the default value), the database is assumed to be on the local host.
Hughes_Footer	True	Controls the appending of the standard Hughes Technologies footer to Web pages.
Private_Only	False	If set to True, the W3-mSQL interface will only process private pages (see the W3-mSQL section for information on private pages). This may be used to enforce strict security on your system, stopping remote users accessing normal HTML pages via the W3-mSQL cgi program.

Table 1.4 Parameters from the System Section of the config File

Parameter	Default Value	Definition
Msynch_Timer	30	Defines the interval in seconds at which the memory mapped data regions maintained in the mSQL server process will be synched with the on-disk images. Setting this value to 0 will disable forced synchronization of the data and rely on the kernel's synching of the mmap regions.
Host_Lookup	True	Determines whether ip address to hostname lookups are required. If set to True, connections by hosts that do not resolve to a hostname will be rejected.
Read_Only	False	Forces the server to operate in read-only mode. Any attempts to modify the database will be rejected (the only commands accepted are *select* queries).
		This option can be used if multiple database servers are to be run using the same data files. In such a case only one server should be running in read-write mode with all others running in read-only mode. This can easily be achieved by using different configuration files (specifying different TCP and Unix ports as well) and loading the appropriate config file in the client application.

The W3-mSQL Section

The configuration parameters shown in Table 1.3 are available in the W3-mSQL section of the config file. These items impact the operation of the W3-mSQL Web interface package.

The System Section

The configuration parameters shown in Table 1.4 are available in the System section of the configuration file and determine the values of various system-level configuration items.

Sample Configuration File

Next is a sample configuration file. This file just sets the parameters to their default values.

```
#
# msql.conf - Configuration file for Mini SQL Version 2.0
#
# This configuration sets all options to their default values.
# Note : %I is expanded to the value of the Inst_Dir element
#

[general]
Inst_Dir = /usr/local/Hughes
mSQL_User = msql
Admin_User = root
Pid_File = %I/msql2.pid
TCP_Port = 1114
UNIX_Port = %I/msql2.sock

[w3-msql]
Auth_Host = NULL
Hughes_Footer = True
Private_Only = False

[system]
Msynch_Timer = 30
Host_Lookup = True
Read_Only = False
```

The msql.acl File

Access control is managed by the msql.acl file in the installation directory. This file is split into entries for each database to be controlled. If the file doesn't exist or details for a particular database aren't configured, access reverts to global read/write. An example ACL entry is included here:

```
# Sample access control for mSQL
database=test
read=bambi,paulp
write=root
host=*.Bond.edu.au,-student.it.Bond.edu.au
access=local,remote
```

Using this definition, database `test` can be accessed by both local and remote connections from any host in the `Bond.edu.au` domain except for the machine `student.it.Bond.edu.au`. Read access is only granted to `bambi` and `paulp`. Nobody else is allowed to perform selects on the database. Write access is only available to `root`.

Control is based on the first match found for a given item. So, a line such as `read=-*,bambi` would not do the desired thing (i.e., deny access to everyone other than `bambi`) because `-*` will also match `bambi`! In this case the line would have to be `read=bambi,-*` although the `-*` is superfluous as that is the default action.

Note that if an entry isn't found for a particular configuration line (such as `read`) it defaults to a global denial. For example, if there is no `read` line (i.e., there are no `read` tokens after the data is loaded) no users will be granted read access. This is in contrast to the action taken if the entire database definition is missing, in which case access to everything is granted.

Another thing to note is that a database's entry must be followed by a blank line to signify the end of the entry. There may also be multiple config lines in the one entry (such as `read =bambi,paulp read=root`). The data will be loaded as though it was concatenated onto the same `read` line (i.e., `read=bambi,paulp,root`).

Wildcards can be used in any configuration entry. A wildcard by itself will match anything whereas a wildcard followed by some text will cause only a partial wildcard (e.g., `*.Bond.edu.au` matches anything that ends in `Bond.edu.au`). A wildcard can also be set for the database name. A good practice is to install an entry with `database=*` as the last entry in the file so that if the database being accessed wasn't covered by any of the other rules a default site policy can be enforced.

The ACL information can be reloaded at run time using `msqladmin reload`. This will parse the file before it sends the reload command to the engine. Only if the file is parsed cleanly is it reloaded. Like most msqladmin commands, it will only be accepted if generated by the `root` user (or whoever the database was installed as) on the localhost.

Express Setup

Here we present a rough outline of the process of compiling, installing, and configuring mSQL. It is intended as a guide for those who are familiar with installing software on a Unix machine. If you are not familiar with any of the steps mentioned, then please read the complete installation guide from the start of this section.

Step 1. Unpack the software distribution using gunzip and tar.

```
gunzip msql-2.0.3.tar.gz
tar -xvf msql-2.0.3.tar
```

or

```
gzcat msql-2.0.3.tar.gz | tar -xvf -
```

Step 2. Create a target directory for your hardware platform.

```
cd msql-2.0.3
make target
```

Step 3. Configure the compilation process.

```
cd targets/YourTargetDirectory
./setup
```

Step 4. Check the default values of INST_DIR and CC in the site.mm file.

Step 5. Compile the software.

```
make all
```

Step 6. Install the software.

```
make install
```

Step 7. Configure the software by editing the msql.conf file in the installation directory.

Troubleshooting

The next sections present some common problems encountered while installing mSQL. If you continue to have problems compiling or installing mSQL after you have checked the following sections, please e-mail support@Hughes.com.au with details of your system (operating system version, the C compiler you used to compile Mini SQL, and other pertinent information) and an explanation of the error you are experiencing.

mmap()

mSQL 2.0 requires a fully functional mmap() implementation. Some operating systems either provide no mmap() support at all or provide a limited subset of mmap(). At this point in time, mSQL cannot operate on these operating systems. The most common operating systems displaying this problem are Digital Ultrix, Cray UNICOS, and Linux versions earlier than 1.3 (newer versions of Linux are fine).

Dynamic Loading

Some of the mSQL tools utilize dynamic loading of object modules (most notably the Lite and W3-mSQL tools). The setup utility will try to determine how to perform dynamic loading on your platform automatically. If you encounter link problems with references to functions such as dl_open, then the automatic configuration has failed. You can safely remove the dynamic-loading functionality by editing the site.mm file and removing the HAVE_DYNAMIC option.

Linux

Some distributions of Linux, including the Slackware distribution, do not include all the required C header files by default. If you did not include the kernel sources when you installed your version of Linux you may not be able to compile the mSQL software. Installing the kernel sources will solve this problem.

bitypes.h

On some systems, the compilation of mSQL will fail with errors relating to the `bitypes.h` header file. This is commonly due to the installation of BIND 4.9 nameserver software. BIND replaces some of your header files during installation but fails to reinstall the `bitypes.h` and `cdefs.h` files. The problem is solved by copying these header files from the compat/include directory of the BIND distribution to the /usr/include/sys directory of your system.

Irix

Some installations of Irix include duplicate versions of several system routines in separate C libraries. The setup utility will recognize these libraries and automatically include them in the link process. This can cause errors relating to "weak definitions" and also unresolved symbols. To overcome this problem, edit the `site.mm` file and remove anything included on the `EXTRA_LIBS` line (i.e., set it to `EXTRA_LIBS=`).

Standard Programs and Utilities

The mSQL distribution contains several programs and utilities to allow you to use and manage your databases. The tools provided allow you to communicate with the database server, import data, export data, submit queries, and view your database structures. The following sections provide detailed descriptions on the various tools provided in the distribution.

The Monitor—mSQL

The mSQL monitor is an interactive interface to the mSQL server. It allows you to submit SQL commands directly to the server. Any valid mSQL syntax can be entered at the prompt provided by the mSQL monitor. For example, by typing a "`create table`" statement at the mSQL monitor prompt you can instruct the database server to create the specified table. The mSQL monitor is intended to be used as a mechanism for creating your database tables and for submitting ad-hoc SQL queries to the server. It is not intended to be used for client application development other than for testing queries before they are coded into your applications.

Control of the monitor itself is provided by four internal commands. Each command is comprised of a backslash followed by a single character. The available commands are:

\q   Quit (also achieved by entering Ctrl-D)

\g   Go (Send the query to the server)

\e   Edit (Edit the previous query)

\p   Print (Print the query buffer)

Usage

```
msql [-h host] [-f confFile] database
```

Options

-h   Specify a remote hostname or IP address on which the mSQL server is running. The default is to connect to a server on the localhost using a Unix domain socket rather than TCP/IP, yielding improved performance.

-f   Specify a nondefault configuration file to be loaded. The default action is to load the standard configuration file located in INST_DIR/msql.conf (usually `/usr/local/Hughes/msql.conf`).

Schema Viewer—relshow

The relshow utility is used to display the structure of the contents of mSQL databases. If no arguments are given, relshow will list the names of the databases currently defined. If a database name is given it will list the tables defined in that database. If a table name is also given then it will display the structure of the table (i.e., field names, types, lengths, etc.).

If an index name is provided along with the database and table names, relshow will display the structure of the specified index including the type of index and the fields that comprise the index.

Usage

```
relshow [-h host] [-f confFile] [database [rel [idx] ] ]
```

Options

-h   Specify a remote hostname or IP address on which the mSQL server is running. The default is to connect to a server on the localhost using a Unix domain socket rather than TCP/IP.

-f   Specify a nondefault configuration file to be loaded. The default action is to load the standard configuration file located in INST_DIR/msql.conf (usually `/usr/local/Hughes/msql.conf`).

Admin Program—msqladmin

msqladmin is used to perform administrative operations on an mSQL database server. Such tasks include the creation of databases, performing server shutdowns, and so forth. The available commands for msqladmin are:

create db_name	Creates a new database called `db_name`.
drop db_name	Removes the database called db_name from the server. This will also delete all data contained in the database!
shutdown	Terminates the mSQL server.

reload	Forces the server to reload ACL information.
version	Displays version and configuration information about the currently running server.
stats	Displays server statistics.
copy fromDB toDB	Copies the contents of the database specified as the fromDB into a newly created database called toDB. If the toDB already exists an error will be returned. This command provides a simple mechanism for creating a backup copy of a data for use as a test or development environment.
move fromDB toDB	Renames an existing database called fromDB to toDB. The data is not modified in any way.

Usage

```
msqladmin [-h host] [-f confFile] [-q] Command
```

Options

-h   Specify a remote hostname or IP address on which the mSQL server is running. The default is to connect to a server on the localhost using a Unix domain socket rather than TCP/IP.

-f   Specify a nondefault configuration file to be loaded. The default action is to load the standard configuration file located in INST_DIR/msql.conf (usually /usr/local/Hughes /msql.conf).

-q   Put msqladmin into quiet mode. If this flag is specified, msqladmin will not prompt the user to verify dangerous actions (such as dropping a database).

> **TIP** Most administrative functions can only be executed by the user specified in the run-time configuration as the admin user. They can also only be executed from the host on which the server process is running (e.g., you cannot shut down a remote server process).

Data Dumper—msqldump

msqldump produces an ASCII text file containing valid SQL commands that will recreate the table or database dumped when piped through the mSQL monitor program. The output will include all CREATE TABLE commands required to recreate the table structures, CREATE INDEX commands to recreate the indices, and INSERT commands to populate the tables with the data currently contained in the tables. If sequences are defined on any of the tables being dumped, a CREATE SEQUENCE command will be generated to ensure the sequence is reset to its current value.

Usage

```
msqldump [-h host] [-f confFile] [-c] [-v] database [table]
```

Options

-h Specify a remote hostname or IP address on which the mSQL server is running. The default is to connect to a server on the localhost using a Unix domain socket rather than TCP/IP.

-f Specify a nondefault configuration file to be loaded. The default action is to load the standard configuration file located in INST_DIR/msql.conf (usually /usr/local/Hughes /msql.conf).

-c Include column names in `INSERT` commands generated by the dump.

-v Run in verbose mode. This will display details such as connection results, etc.

Data Exporter—msqlexport

msqlexport produces an ASCII export of the data from the specified table. The output produced can be used as input to other programs such as spreadsheets. It has been designed to be as flexible as possible. The user may specify the character to use to separate the fields; the character to use to escape the separator character if it appears in the data; and whether the data should be quoted, and if so, what character to use as the quote character. The output is sent to stdout with one data row per line.

An example use of msqlexport would be to create a Comma Separated Values (CSV) file to be imported into a popular spreadsheet application such as Microsoft Excel. The CSV format uses a comma to separate data fields and quotation marks to quote the individual values. If a value contains a quotation mark, it is escaped by prefixing it with another quotation mark. To generate a CSV representation of a table called staff in the company database, the following msqlexport command would be used:

```
msqlexport -s , -q " -e " company staff
```

Usage

```
msqlexport [-h host] [-f conf] [-v] [-s Char] [-q Char] [-e Char] database
table
```

Options

-h Specify a remove hostname or IP address on which the mSQL server is running. The default is to connect to a server on the localhost using a Unix domain socket rather than TCP/IP.

-f Specify a nondefault configuration file to be loaded. The default action is to load the standard configuration file located in INST_DIR/msql.conf (usually `/usr/local/Hughes /msql.conf`).

-v Verbose mode.

-s Use the character Char as the separation character. The default is a comma.

-q Quote each value with the specified character.

-e Use the specified `Char` as the escape character. The default is `\`.

Data Importer—msqlimport

msqlimport loads a flat ASCII data file into an mSQL database table. The file can be formatted using any character as the column separator. When passed through msqlimport, each line of the text file will be loaded as a row in the database table. The separation character, as specified by the -s flag, will be used to split the line of text into columns. If the data uses a specific character to escape any occurrence of the separation character in the data, the escape character can be specified with the -e flag and will be removed from the data before it is inserted. Some data formats (such as the CSV format) will enclose an entire value in quotation marks. The -q option can be used to indicate such a format and to specify the character being used for quoting.

To import a file formatted in the Comma Separated Values format (CSV) into a table called staff in the company database, the following msqlimport command would be used:

```
msqlimport -s , -q " -e " company staff
```

Usage

```
msqlimport [-h host] [-f conf] [-v] [-s Char] [-q Char] [-e Char] database
table
```

Options

-h   Specify a remote hostname or IP address on which the mSQL server is running. The default is to connect to a server on the localhost using a Unix domain socket rather than TCP/IP.

-f   Specify a nondefault configuration file to be loaded. The default action is to load the standard configuration file located in INST_DIR/msql.conf (usually /usr/local/Hughes /msql.conf).

-v   Verbose mode.

-s Char   Use the character Char as the separation character. The default is a comma.

-q Char   Remove quotes around field values if they exist (the specified character is the quote character).

-e Char   Use the specified Char as the escape character. The default is \.

A Quick Tour of Mini SQL

This tour assumes that you have installed Mini SQL successfully. In order to run this, you will first need to assume the userid of the mSQL admin user (please see your msql.conf file). As this tour progresses, you will see a shell prompt that shows the commands that you should issue (in **bold**), and the output of the system. You will be seeing some SQL commands that you might not recognize at this point, but they will be explained in the next chapter. The mSQL admin user is typically root. If you have permission to become the root user, you can assume that user's permissions with the su command. If you are the mSQL admin user, you can log in as yourself. If another user is the mSQL admin user, you can either log in as that user or use the su command to become that user.

```
bash-2.00$ su
Password:
```

After you have become the root user (or whoever the mSQL admin user is on your system), you should create a database called `testdb` with the msqladmin utility. If you installed mSQL in a location other than the /usr/local/Hughes directory, you will need to change the path (and the paths in all the other examples in this tour) when you issue this statement yourself.

```
# /usr/local/Hughes/bin/msqladmin create testdb
Database "testdb" created.
```

It's not a good idea to interact with your operating system as a privileged user, except for cases where it is absolutely necessary. Before you return to your previous user id, you will need to ensure that you have access to the database that was just created. In order to do this, you should edit the msql.acl (access control list) file in the /usr/local/Hughes directory. If you just performed a fresh install of mSQL, you will have a file called msql.acl.sample. You should rename this to msql.acl, but only do this if there is no msql.acl file already! You can rename it with the `mv  -i` command. However, if you try it, and see a warning message, you should answer "no," and you can safely skip this step.

```
# mv -i /usr/local/Hughes/msql.acl.sample /usr/local/Hughes/msql.acl
mv: overwrite /usr/local/Hughes/msql.acl (y/n)?
```

Once you have a working msql.acl file, you should edit it, and add the following lines, substituting your user id for the one in the example (`bjepson`):

```
database=testdb
read=bjepson
write=bjepson
access=local
```

The access permissions in this example will allow the user `bjepson` to read or write to the database, but that user must connect from the local machine. After you change the permissions, you must invoke the msqladmin program to reload the acl file.

```
# /usr/local/Hughes/bin/msqladmin reload
```

Once you have reloaded the permissions, you should exit the shell that was created when you used the `su` command.

```
# exit
```

At this point, you have returned to your original user id. This should be the id of the user you granted read-and-write permission to. In order to enter the msql monitor program, which allows you to interactively execute SQL commands, you should type the following:

```
bash-2.00$ /usr/local/Hughes/bin/msql testdb
Welcome to the miniSQL monitor.  Type \h for help.

mSQL >
```

Now you'll create a table with the CREATE TABLE command. This statement will create a table named employee, with three columns. The first column is for the employee's first name, and will be 25 characters wide. The second is for the employee's last name, and is also 25 characters wide. The last column is an integer column that should contain an employee id.

```
mSQL > CREATE TABLE employee
    -> (first_name CHAR(25),
    -> last_name  CHAR(25),
    -> empl_id    INT)
    -> \g
```

Query OK. 1 row(s) modified or retrieved.

Next, we'll insert some rows into the table:

```
mSQL > INSERT INTO employee VALUES ("Japhy", "Ryder", 1)
    -> \g
mSQL > INSERT INTO employee VALUES ("Irwin", "Garden", 2)
    -> \g
mSQL > INSERT INTO employee VALUES ("Lester", "Bangs", 3)
    -> \g
```

Now that there is some data in the database, you can issue a query that will retrieve the rows.

```
mSQL > SELECT first_name, last_name, empl_id
    ->      FROM employee
    ->      ORDER by last_name, first_name
    -> \g
```

Query OK. 3 row(s) modified or retrieved.

```
+--------------+--------------+------------------------------+------------+
| first_name   | last_name    | empl_id                      |
+--------------+--------------+------------------------------+------------+
| Lester       | Bangs        | 3                            |
| Irwin        | Garden       | 2                            |
| Japhy        | Ryder        | 1                            |
+--------------+--------------+------------------------------+------------+
```

Mini SQL For You, Mini SQL For Me

Mini SQL is a very simple and straightforward tool, and it offers powerful ways to manipulate information. The quick tour in this chapter showed you how easy it can be to get data in and out of Mini SQL. The following chapter will provide an exhaustive introduction to the dialect of the SQL language used by Mini SQL, and the full power offered by Mini SQL will become clearer. Throughout the rest of the book, we will concentrate on the ways in which Mini SQL can work with various languages and APIs, including Perl, Java, and others.

SQL Programming with mSQL

When you work with the SQL language, you will be working with magical creatures such as tables, rows, and columns. It may not be a land of make-believe that, in the words of Homer Simpson, is filled with "flowers and bells and leprechauns and magic frogs with funny little hats," but it's a fun place nonetheless. Before you can play with any of these, some hard and fast definitions are in order. A table is a collection of rows (sometimes called records). Each row is broken down into one or more columns (sometimes called fields). It might be easiest to think of a table as a list.

Database Design

The examples in the beginning of this chapter will be concerned with the database system belonging to a fictional collectors' club. Each member owns a vintage Atari home computer system, and they collect video game cartridges for that system. They lead exciting lives, and the club's list of members, systems, and games looks like Table 2.1.

Table 2.1 The Vintage Atari Collector's Club Master List

Collector	System	Defender	Miner 2049er	Missile Command	Pacman	Star Raiders
E. Wood	800	Yes	No	Yes	Yes	No
B. Jepson	1200XL	No	Yes	No	Yes	Yes
J. Lee	65XE	No	No	Yes	Yes	Yes
T. Johnson	800	No	Yes	Yes	No	No

17

Of course, there are probably a lot more games in each person's collection, but you get the idea. At first glance, this list looks somewhat well designed, and perhaps even suited to practical use. However, experience shows that tables organized in this fashion are difficult to work with. If you were to design your table to look exactly like this list, you would start running into trouble when someone obtained a cartridge that wasn't already on the list.

The Relational Model and the First Normal Form

In 1970, a mathematician, Dr. E. F. Codd, established a theory for data modeling that formed the foundation for design methodology in relational database management systems (RDBMSs) such as Mini SQL, SQL Server, and Oracle. In a paper entitled "A Relational Model of Data for Large Shared Data Banks" (Communications of the ACM 13, No. 6, June 1970; available on the Web at www.acm.org/classics/nov95/), he established key guidelines of *data normalization*. Data normalization is a process that optimizes the way your data is represented in tables. Each step in normalization takes your data to what is called a *normal* form. Most people tend to concern themselves with three normal forms, and this chapter will explore the steps needed to normalize a database to the third normal form.

In order for the database design to adhere to the first normal form, it is necessary to *eliminate repeating columns*. In Table 2.1, there is a column for the person's name, the computer system he or she owns, and a column for each cartridge. That collection of cartridges is a perfect candidate for elimination, as it is a repeating group of columns. This is a remarkably inefficient way to store data. For one, storage space is wasted; for each person there must be a column for each possible cartridge, whether that person has 0 or 10 cartridges. Also, if a new cartridge is added to the list, the table structure must be physically modified. This is a big no-no, for if specifications have been adequately drawn up for a system, no modification to table structure should be necessary unless significant new requirements arise.

In order for this table to conform to the first normal form, it needs to be split into two tables. A new table will be created, called `cartridge`. This table will contain the name of the cartridge, and two new columns. The first will be a Cartridge Id, and the second will be a Collector Id. The original table, which will be referred to as `collector`, will lose all of the cartridge columns, but gain a new one: Collector Id. The Collector Id will link the list of cartridges to the collector. Here's the "new look" for the `collector` table (Table 2.2).

Table 2.2 The Vintage Atari Collector's Club `collector` Table

Collector	System	Collector Id
E. Wood	800	1
B. Jepson	1200XL	2
J. Lee	65XE	3
T. Johnson	800	4

Table 2.3 The Vintage Atari Collector's Club `cartridge` Table

Cartridge Name	Cartridge Id	Collector Id
Defender	1	1
Missile Command	2	1
Pacman	3	1
Miner 2049er	4	2
Pacman	3	2
Star Raiders	5	2
Missile Command	2	3
Pacman	3	3
Star Raiders	5	3
Miner 2049er	4	4
Missile Command	2	4

The `cartridge` table will look like Table 2.3.

Organizing the table in this fashion may make it harder for humans to read, but it really makes things easy for the computer. The new columns that were added reveal some of the method in normalized data design. Each table in a well-designed *schema* (a schema is a collection of tables that are connected to each other in some way) should have a column that acts as a *primary key*. A primary key is a unique identifier, a column or group of columns whose values are unique for each row in which it appears. The `collector` table has the Collector Id as primary key; there must be no two rows that share the same Collector Id in that table. The primary key in the `cartridge` table consists of two columns: Collector Id + Cartridge Id. There can be no two rows that have the same Collector Id + Cartridge Id. We can see some of you raising your hands back there. "What's that? What if one collector has more than one of the same cartridge?" Hmmm. In that case, it's a matter of adding another column: Quantity. Here's the revised `cartridge` table (Table 2.4), to satisfy the nitpickers among this crowd (we can even let T. Johnson have two copies of Missile Command).

Far out! The schema, which started out containing one horrible *denormalized* table, now consists of two tables, which are in the first normal form. Unfortunately, our work is far from done. It's traditional to take the tables in a schema at least to the third normal form before you try to write any programs that manipulate it.

Second Normal Form

The primary key for the `cartridge` table (Collector Id + Cartridge Id) satisfies the requirement of the definition of a primary key; the value of the two columns will be different for each

Table 2.4 The Revised Vintage Atari Collector's Club `cartridge` Table

Cartridge Name	Cartridge Id	Collector Id	Quantity
Defender	1	1	1
Missile Command	2	1	1
Pacman	3	1	1
Miner 2049er	4	2	1
Pacman	3	2	1
Star Raiders	5	2	1
Missile Command	2	3	1
Pacman	3	3	1
Star Raiders	5	3	1
Miner 2049er	4	4	1
Missile Command	2	4	2

row. You may have noticed that the Cartridge Name repeats; it is a dependent value, and it is only dependent upon one of the components (the Cartridge Id) of the multivalued primary key. The application of the second normal form seeks to eliminate this type of relationship, and in doing so, it eliminates redundant data. Right now, the Cartridge Name appears wherever a cartridge is owned by a member. If one of the Cartridge Names is misspelled, it can cause reporting anomalies, and you might not get the right count of cartridges. Even worse, if an error had been introduced into the system at an early date, such as the repeated misspelling of a Cartridge Name, it would require updating all of the records in the `cartridge` table, which is doing double duty as a cross-reference table. For people whose greatest passion is collecting old videogames, the results of such errors can cause massive psychological trauma.

In order to bring the tables in this schema up to snuff with the second normal form, it is necessary to create yet another table. This will be called the `cartridge_xref` table, and will contain the Cartridge Id, Quantity, and Collector Id. The `cartridge` table will now only contain the Cartridge Name and Cartridge Id. The `cartridge` table will look like Table 2.5.

Table 2.5 The Revised (Again) Vintage Atari Collector's Club `cartridge` Table

Cartridge Name	Cartridge Id
Defender	1
Missile Command	2
Pacman	3

Continues

Table 2.5 *Continued*

Cartridge Name	Cartridge Id
Miner 2049er	4
Star Raiders	5

The `cartridge_xref` table will look like Table 2.6.

Table 2.6 The Vintage Atari Collector's Club `cartridge_xref` Table

Cartridge Id	Collector Id	Quantity
1	1	1
2	1	1
3	1	1
4	2	1
3	2	1
5	2	1
2	3	1
3	3	1
5	3	1
4	4	1
2	4	2

Third Normal Form

The third normal form has some things in common with the second normal form, but it is a little pickier. It seeks to eliminate any columns that are not dependent upon the key. Looking back at the `collector` table, note that there are three columns: Collector Name, System, and Collector Id. Of these, only Collector Name is dependent upon the Collector Id. The System name is independent of that. As proof, you can see that two collectors have the same system: Jones and Johnson both own 800s. Again, it is necessary to split tables. A new table will be created: `system`. This will contain a System Name and a System Id. Also, another cross-reference table will be created: `system_xref`. As a bonus of satisfying the conditions of the third normal form, Collectors may now own more than one system. Won't they be happy to hear that!

The `system` table is shown in Table 2.7.

Table 2.7 The Vintage Atari Collector's Club `system` Table

System Name	System Id
800	1
1200XL	2
65XE	3

The `system_xref` table is shown in Table 2.8.

Table 2.8 The Vintage Atari Collector's Club `system_xref` Table

System Id	Collector Id
1	1
2	2
3	3
1	4

Finally, the `collector` table can be modified as shown in Table 2.9.

Table 2.9 The Revised Vintage Atari Collector's Club `collector` Table

Collector	Collector Id
E. Wood	1
B. Jepson	2
J. Lee	3
T. Johnson	4

The Collection schema started out with one table. After taking it to the third normal form, it now consists of five tables: `collector`, `cartridge`, `cartridge_xref`, `system`, and `system_xref`.

The mSQL Query Language

The mSQL language offers a significant subset of the features provided by ANSI SQL. It allows a program or user to store, manipulate, and retrieve data in table structures. It does not support some relational capabilities such as views and nested queries. Although it does not support all the relational operations defined in the ANSI specification, mSQL provides a significant subset of the ANSI SQL standard and is capable of supporting the vast majority of applications. The definitions and examples in the next section depict mSQL keywords in uppercase, but mSQL is not case-sensitive, so you can utilize the keywords in upper- or lowercase.

The Create Statement

The CREATE statement as supported by mSQL 2 can be used to create tables, indices, and sequences. The three valid constructs of the CREATE statement are shown here:

```
CREATE TABLE table_name
    ( col_name col_type [ not null ]
  [, col_name col_type [ not null ] ]... )

CREATE [ UNIQUE ] INDEX index_name
    ON table_name ( field_name [ , field_name ]...)

CREATE SEQUENCE
    ON table_name [ STEP step_val ] [ VALUE initial_val ]
```

An example of the creation of a table is shown here:

```
CREATE TABLE emp_details (
    first_name char(15) not null,
    last_name char(15) not null,
    comment text(50),
    dept char(20),
    emp_id int )
```

The available types are shown in Table 2.10.

Table 2.10 Mini SQL 2.0 Data Types

Type	Description
char (len)	String of characters (or other 8-bit data).
text (len)	Variable length string of characters (or other 8-bit data). The defined length is used to indicate the expected average length of the data. Any data longer than the specified length will be split between the data table and external overflow buffers. Note: Text fields are slower to access than char fields and cannot be used in an index nor in LIKE tests.
int	Signed integer values.
real	Decimal or Scientific Notation real values.
uint	Unsigned integer values.
date	Date values in the format of DD-Mon-YYYY; e.g., 1-Jan-1997.

Continues

Table 2.10 Mini SQL 2.0 Data Types (*Continued*)

Type	Description
time	Time values stored in 24-hour notation in the format of HH:MM:SS.
money	A numeric value with two fixed decimal places.

Since one of the primary missions of a database system is to allow applications to retrieve data, it's best that the data be retrieved as efficiently as possible. Since the tables in mSQL can become quite large if they are filled with data, it can be quite slow to process a query if thousands or millions of rows must be retrieved. In order to remedy this, mSQL offers you the ability to create an index on a given column or group of columns.

The table structure shown in the example would benefit greatly from the creation of some indexes. It is assumed that the emp_id field would be a unique value that is used to identify an employee. Such a field would normally be defined as the *primary key*. A primary key is a column that has been identified as being the unique identifier for a given table. No two rows in the table may have the same value for a column that has been designated as a primary key. In mSQL, unique indexes are used to enforce the integrity of a primary key.

Users may wish to query the employee table based on the combination of the first and last names. A *compound index* is an index that is constructed from more than one field, and would improve performance for such queries. Naturally, such a compound index may have multiple entries with the same value (if more than one person called John Smith works for the same company), so a non-unique index would be required. We could construct a unique and a non-unique index using:

```
CREATE UNIQUE INDEX idx1 ON emp_details (emp_id)
CREATE INDEX idx2 ON emp_details (first_name, last_name)
```

These indices will be used automatically whenever a query is sent to the database engine that uses those fields in its WHERE clause. The user is not required to specify any special values in the query to ensure the indices are used to increase performance.

Sequences provide a mechanism via which a sequence value can be maintained by the mSQL server. Sequences are a numeric value that can be used as serial numbers, staff identifiers, invoice numbers, or any other application that requires a unique numeric value. Having the server maintain the index allows for atomic operations (such as getting the next sequence value) and removes the concerns associated with performing these operations in client applications. A client application would need to send two queries (one to read the current value and one to update the value), which introduces a "race condition" and the potential for the same sequence value to be assigned to multiple items.

A sequence is associated with a table and a table may contain at most one sequence. Once a sequence has been created it can be accessed by SELECTing the _seq system variable from the table in which the sequence is defined. Here is an example of a statement to create a sequence, followed by one that retrieves the sequence:

```
CREATE SEQUENCE ON test STEP 1 VALUE 5
SELECT _seq FROM test
```

The CREATE operation in the preceding example would define a sequence on the table called *test* that had an initial value of 5 and would be incremented each time it is accessed (it is said to have a step of 1). The SELECT statement would return the value 5. If the SELECT was issued again, a value of 6 would be returned. Each time the _seq field is selected from *test* the current value is returned to the caller and the sequence value itself is incremented.

Using the STEP and VALUE options, a sequence can be created that starts at any specified number and is increased or decreased by any specified value. The value of a sequence would decrease by 5 each time it was accessed if it was defined with a step of –5.

The Drop Statement

The DROP statement is used to remove a definition from the database. It is most commonly used to remove a table from a database but can also be used for removing several other constructs. It can be used to remove the definition of an index, a sequence, or a table. It should be noted that *dropping* a table or an index removes the data associated with that object as well as the definition. Dropping a table removes any indices or sequences defined for the table.

> **TIP** The DROP statement cannot be used to remove an entire database. Dropping a database is achieved by using the msqladmin utility program that is included in the software distribution.

The syntax of the DROP statement as well as examples of its use are given here:

```
DROP TABLE table_name
DROP INDEX index_name FROM table_name
DROP SEQUENCE FROM table_name
```

Examples of the use of the DROP statement for removing an entire table, an index, and a sequence are shown here:

```
DROP TABLE emp_details
DROP INDEX idx1 FROM emp_details
DROP SEQUENCE FROM emp_details
```

The Insert Statement

The INSERT statement is used to insert or add data to the database. When you insert data, you may either specify a list of fields that you wish to provide values for, or you may omit the field names if you are providing values for every field. If you do not specify the field names they will be used in the order in which they were defined—you must specify a value for every field if you use this form of the INSERT statement. If you provide the field names then the number of data values provided must match the number of fields specified. Each column that is not specified will receive a NULL value. A NULL value is not really a value, but a special state in which a column may be. It indicates that the column has no value for a particular row.

```
INSERT INTO table_name
    [ ( column [ , column ]... ) ]
    VALUES ( value [ , value ]... )
```

For example:

```
INSERT INTO emp_details
    ( first_name, last_name, dept, salary)
    VALUES ( "David", "Hughes", "Development", 12345.00)

INSERT INTO emp_details
    VALUES ("David", "Hughes", "Development", 12345.00)
```

The Select Statement

The SELECT statement is used to extract data from the database. It allows you to specify the particular columns you wish to retrieve as well as a condition that identifies the records or rows that are of interest. Two features defined by the ANSI SQL standard that are not supported by mSQL are nested SELECT statements and aggregate functions such as COUNT() or AVG().

Here is a list of the features that are supported by mSQL:

- Relational joins between multiple tables
- Table aliases
- DISTINCT row selection for returning unique values
- ORDER BY clauses for sorting
- Normal SQL regular expression matching
- Enhanced regular expression matching including case insensitive and soundex
- Column-to-column comparisons in WHERE clauses
- Complex conditions

The formal definition of the syntax for mSQL's SELECT statement is:

```
SELECT [table.]column [, [table.]column ]...
    FROM table [ = alias] [ , table [ = alias] ]...
 [ WHERE [table.] column OPERATOR VALUE
 [ AND | OR [table.]column OPERATOR VALUE]... ]
 [ ORDER BY [table.]column [DESC] [, [table.]column [DESC]... ]
```

OPERATOR can be <, >, =, <=, =, <>, LIKE, RLIKE, CLIKE, or SLIKE. VALUE can be a literal value or a column name.

You may use parentheses within the WHERE clause to force the grouping of conditions separated by AND or OR, as in:

```
WHERE (age <20 OR age >30) AND sex = "male"
```

A simple select that returns the first and last names of anybody employed in the Finance department would be:

```
SELECT first_name, last_name FROM emp_details
    WHERE dept = "finance"
```

To sort the results of the query we would add an ORDER BY clause to the SELECT statement. mSQL supports sorting on multiple values in either ascending or descending order for each value. If a direction is not specified it defaults to ascending order. To sort the data from the previous query in ascending order by last_name and descending order by first_name we could use the query shown next. Note that the two sorting values are separated by a comma and that the first_name field includes the DESC attribute to indicate that sorting is required in descending order.

```
SELECT first_name, last_name FROM emp_details
    WHERE dept = "finance"
    ORDER BY last_name, first_name DESC
```

A query such as the one just presented may return multiple rows having the same value. If, for example, there were two people named John Smith working in the Finance department, the name "John Smith" would be returned twice from the query. You may remove any duplicates from the returned data by providing the DISTINCT attribute with the query. An example of using the DISTINCT attribute to remove duplicates from the above query is given here:

```
SELECT DISTINCT first_name, last_name FROM emp_details
    WHERE dept = "finance"
    ORDER BY last_name, first_name DESC
```

mSQL provides four regular expression operators for use in *where* comparisons. These operators may be used to perform "fuzzy" matching on the data if you do not know the exact value for which you are searching. An example of such a search would be if you were looking for any employee with a last_name starting with "Mc" such as McCormack or McDonald. In such a situation, you cannot provide a complete value for the last_name field as you are only interested in part of the value.

The standard SQL syntax provides a very simplistic regular expression capability that does not provide the power nor the flexibility to which UNIX programmers or users will be accustomed. mSQL supports the "standard" SQL regular expression syntax, via the LIKE operator, but also provides further functionality if it is required. The available regular expression operators are:

- LIKE—The standard SQL regular expression operator
- CLIKE—A standard LIKE operator that ignores case
- RLIKE—A complete Unix regular expression operator
- SLIKE—A "soundex" matching operator (i.e., phonetic matching)

NOTE CLIKE, RLIKE, and SLIKE are not features of standard SQL and may not be available in other implementations of the language. If you choose to use them you may have problems porting your application to other database systems. They are, however, very convenient and powerful features of mSQL.

LIKE and CLIKE utilize the regular expression syntax as specified in the ANSI SQL standard. As mentioned earlier, the ANSI standard regular expression feature provides only a very simplistic implementation of regular expressions. It provides for only single- and multiple-character wildcards. It does not include enhanced features such as value ranges, value exclusions, or value groups. The syntax of the LIKE and CLIKE operators is provided in Table 2.11.

Two examples of using the LIKE operator are provided next. In the first, we are searching for anyone in the Finance department whose last name consists of any letter followed by "ughes," such as Hughes. The second example shows the query for the "Mc" example mentioned earlier in this section.

```
SELECT first_name, last_name
   FROM emp_details
   WHERE dept = 'finance'
   AND   last_name like '_ughes'

SELECT first_name, last_name
   FROM emp_details
   WHERE dept = 'finance'
   AND   last_name like 'Mc%'
```

The RLIKE operator provides access to the power of the Unix standard regular expression syntax. The Unix regular expression syntax provides far greater functionality than SQL's LIKE syntax. The Unix regex syntax does not use the _ or % characters in the way SQL's regex does (as outlined earlier), but provides enhanced functionality such as grouping, value ranges, and value exclusion. The syntax available in the RLIKE operator is shown in Table 2.12. Tutorials for using Unix regular expression matching are available in the manual pages of any Unix system (such as the manual pages for grep or ed).

Table 2.11 LIKE and CLIKE Special Characters

Operator	Description
_	Matches any single character.
%	Matches 0 or more characters of any value.
\	Escapes special characters (e.g., \% matches % and \\ matches \). All other characters match themselves.

Table 2.12 RLIKE Special Characters

Operator	Description
.	The dot character matches any single character.
^	When used as the first character in a regex, the caret character forces the match to start at the first character of the string.
$	When used as the last character in a regex, the dollar sign forces the match to end at the last character of the string.
[ ]	By enclosing a group of single characters within square brackets, the regex will match a single character from the group of characters. If the] character is one of the characters you wish to match you may specify it as the first character in the group without closing the group (e.g., []abc] would match any single character that was], a, b, or c). Ranges of characters can be specified within the group using the "first-last" syntax (e.g., [a-z0-9] would match any lowercase letter or a digit). If the first character of the group is the ^ character, the regex will match any single character that is *not* contained within the group.
*	If any regex element is followed by a *, it will match *zero or more* instances of the regular expression. To match any string of characters you would use .* and to match any string of digits you would use [0-9]*.

> **TIP** Because `RLIKE` utilizes a complete Unix regex implementation, the evaluation of a condition containing the `RLIKE` operator is quite complex. The performance of searches using the `RLIKE` operator will be slower than those using the `LIKE` or `CLIKE` operators. You should only use the `RLIKE` operator if you cannot achieve your desired matching using the more simplistic `LIKE` or `CLIKE` operators.

The `SLIKE` operator provides soundex matching of values (i.e., one value sounds like another value). It does not use an explicit syntax in the same way as the other `LIKE` operators. You simply provide the word you wish to match. If you wished to search for any name that sounded like "Hughes," such as "Hues" you could use `SLIKE` "Hughes."

Relational *joining* is one of the most powerful features of a relational query language. The concept of "joining" relates to "merging" multiple database tables together and extracting fields from the merged result. As an example, if you had two tables defined, one containing employee details and another containing a list of all current projects, you may wish to extract a list of the projects that each employee was working on. Rather than duplicating the employee details in the projects table you could simply include the employee's staff ID number in the projects table and use a join to extract the first and last names.

The query shown next is an example of such an operation. The logic behind the query is that we want to extract the first and last names of the employee, plus the name of the project on which the employee is working. We can identify which combinations of the merged table we are look-ing for as they will have a common value for the employee's staff ID value. Because we are ref-erencing multiple tables in the query, we must include the table name for each field when it is included in the query (e.g., emp_details.first_name rather than just first_name).

```
SELECT emp_details.first_name, emp_details.last_name,
       project_details.project
   FROM emp_details, project_details
   WHERE emp_details.emp_id = project_details.emp_id
   ORDER BY emp_details.last_name, emp_details.first_name
```

TIP It is important to understand the inner workings of a join. If we are joining table A with table B, a merged row will be created for all possible combinations of the rows of both tables. If table A contains only two rows and table B contains 10 rows, then 20 merged rows will be generated and evaluated against the WHERE condition. If no WHERE condition is specified then all 20 rows will be returned. If this example is extended so that table A contained 1000 rows and table B contained 2500 rows then the result would be 1000 * 2500 merged rows (that's two and a half million rows!). Whenever a join is used there should normally be a common value in both tables (such as the employee ID in our example), and the condition must include a direct comparison between these two fields to ensure that the result set is limited to only the desired results.

---

mSQL places no restriction on the number of tables "joined" during a query so if there were 15 tables all containing information related to an employee ID in some manner, and each table included the employee ID field to identify the employee, data from each of those tables could be extracted, by a single query. As mentioned before, a key point to note regarding joins is that you must qualify all field names with a table name. Remember that you must qualify every column name as soon as you access more than one table in a single SELECT.

mSQL also supports table aliases so that you can perform a join of a table onto itself. This may appear to be an unusual thing to do but it is a very powerful feature if the rows within a single table relate to each other in some way. An example of such a table could be a list of people including the names of their parents. In such a table, there would be multiple rows with a parent/child relation-ship. Using a table alias you could find out any grandparents contained in the table using the query shown next. The logic is to find any person who is the parent of someone's parent.

```
SELECT t1.parent, t2.child
   FROM parent_data=t1, parent_data=t2
   WHERE t1.child = t2.parent
```

The table aliases t1 and t2 both point to the same table (parent_data in this case) and are treated as two different tables that just happen to contain exactly the same data. Like any other join, the possible result set size is the multiplication of the number of rows in each table. If a table is joined with itself, this equates to N^2 rows where N is the number of rows in the original table. Care must be taken to ensure that the result set is limited by the condition specified; otherwise, the query can take a very long time to complete and has the potential to fill your disk drive with temporary data as the query is processed.

The Delete Statement

The SQL DELETE statement is used to remove one or more rows from a database table. The selection of rows to be removed from the table is based on the same WHERE clause as used by the SELECT statement. In the SELECT statement, the WHERE condition is used to identify the rows to be extracted from the database. In the DELETE statement, the WHERE condition identifies the rows that are to be deleted from the database. As with all SQL queries, if no WHERE condition is provided, then the query applies to *every row in the table* and the *entire contents of the table will be deleted*. The syntax for mSQL's DELETE statement is shown here:

```
DELETE FROM table_name
    WHERE column OPERATOR value
    [ AND | OR column OPERATOR value ]...
```

OPERATOR can be <, >, =, <=, =, <>, LIKE, RLIKE, CLIKE, or SLIKE.

An example of deleting a specific employee (identified by the employee ID number of the person) and also deleting every employee within a particular salary range is given here:

```
DELETE FROM emp_details
    WHERE emp_id = 12345

DELETE FROM emp_details
    WHERE salary > 20000
    AND   salary < 30000
```

The Update Statement

The SQL UPDATE statement is used to modify data that is already in a table. The operation is carried out on one or more rows as specified by the WHERE condition. If the condition provided in the WHERE clause matches multiple rows in the database table then each matched row will be updated in the same way. The value of any number of fields in the matched rows can be updated. The syntax supported by mSQL is shown here:

```
UPDATE table_name
    SET column=value [ , column=value ]...
    WHERE column OPERATOR value
    [ AND | OR column OPERATOR value ]...
```

OPERATOR can be <, >, =, <=, =, <>, LIKE, RLIKE, CLIKE, or SLIKE.

The next example will set the salary of each employee to $30,000 whose emp_id is 1234. The second example will subtract $5,000 from the salary of each employee whose salary is greater than $50,000 and transfer them to the Audit department. Haw, haw, haw! Serves them right for making more than the rest of us!

```
UPDATE emp_details
    SET salary=30000
    WHERE emp_id = 1234

UPDATE emp_details
    SET salary = salary - 5000, dept='Audit'
    WHERE salary > 50000
```

It's No Hanging Matter

It's hoped that this chapter has offered enough of an introduction to SQL and relational databases for even the most inexperienced reader to hit the ground running. There's no doubt that dealing with relational databases is a "new head," as we used to say in the 1980s. The techniques used in structured or object-oriented programming certainly are different from the techniques for dealing with relational data. As a result, there will often be a conceptual mismatch between SQL and the language that you are using to develop end-user software. A thorough understanding of both SQL and that language will help immensely. In the remainder of this book, we'll explore applications in various languages that involve SQL.

Lite and W3-mSQL

The fact that mSQL can be accessed from virtually every popular scripting language used on Unix and Win32 systems has been one of the factors that contributes to its popularity. To overcome the need to add mSQL support to an existing language, such as Perl or Tcl, mSQL 2.0 includes its own scripting language preconfigured with support for the mSQL API. The scripting language, called *Lite*, is the same language used by W3-mSQL, the WWW-to-mSQL interface package. People wishing to access mSQL from standalone scripts or via the Web now have to learn only one simple yet powerful language. However, mSQL can still be integrated with many popular scripting languages, so many options exist for those who express a preference toward one language or another.

The Basics

Lite has been designed to mimic the syntax and semantics of the C language while reducing some of the complexities and error-prone features of C. This is intentional as most programmers working on Unix machines have a working knowledge of C but look for a more "easy-to-use" language for scripting. The main changes from C are:

- All memory management (i.e., allocation and deallocation of memory for variables) is taken care of by the Lite Virtual Machine. Your script does not need to perform any memory management operations.

- A variable has no fixed type. It will contain whatever is stored in it (e.g., char value, numeric value). When you perform an operation on a variable, such as a math operation or character comparisons, the contents of the variable are checked to ensure they are of the correct type. This concept will become clearer as we progress through this chapter.

- There is a dynamic array type. Each element of the array is a variable as previously described. The elements are accessed as they are in C (i.e., variable[offset]), but they need not be declared before use. That is, the array element is created when a value is stored in it without a predefinition of the array.

- Variables are not pre-declared. They are created when they are first used.

- Variable names must start with a $ character. This will be familiar to shell script programmers.

Variables, Types, and Expressions

Variables consist of a $ sign followed by alphanumeric characters and the _ character. The only restriction placed upon the name of a variable is that the first character of a user-defined variable must not be an uppercase character. There is no need to pre-declare variables as you do in a language such as C. A variable is created the first time you assign a value to it. Similarly, the type of the variable is defined by the value that you assign to it. There are four types of scalar variables: char, integer, unsigned integers, and real numbers.

The following example code illustrates the creation of variables. Note that the second example makes an explicit cast from an integer value to an unsigned integer type.

```
$int_value = 9;
$uint_value = (uint)240983;
$char_value = "Some text value";
$real_value = 12.627;
```

At any point in time, the type of a value can be changed by using the type cast notation, which is identical to that of the C language. If, for example, you wished to include a numeric value from an integer variable in a text string, you would simply cast the integer value to the char type. The following code would result in a char variable that contained the string 1234:

```
$int_val = 1234;
$char_val = (char) $int_val;
```

The valid type casts are listed in Table 3.1 (note that uint casts are valid wherever an int cast would be).

Table 3.1 Valid Type Casts in Lite

From	To	Result	Example
int	char	Text representation of numeric string	12 = 12
int	real	Real representation of integer value	12 = 12.0
real	char	Text representation of real value	123.45 = 123.45
real	int	Integer representation of real value	123.45 = 123

Array variables are supported by Lite but there is no fixed type for the array. Each element of the array can hold data from any of the available data types. An array is created by assigning a value to one of the array elements such as:

```
$arrayval[3] = "Foo";
$arrayval[4] = 5;
$arrayval[6] = 1.23 + 5.38;
```

Lite expressions are formed from mathematical equations incorporating the values of variables and values returned from function calls. Lite is a little more flexible than other languages such as C. It will allow you to do mathematic operations on all data types including the char type. Adding two char values together results in the concatenation of the two strings. You can also perform mathematic operations on values of different types by casting the value to the correct type within the expression. Examples are given here:

```
$charval = "Hello" + " there!";
$intval = 8 + 1;
$charval = (char)$intval + " green bottles";
```

The first expression would result in the char value `"Hello there!"`. The second would result in the integer value 9. The final expression would result in the char value `"9 green bottles"` using the text representation of the value of `$intval` from the previous line. Mathematic expressions of any complexity, including any number of subexpressions enclosed in ( ) characters, are supported.

Table 3.2 lists the available mathematic operators and the data types to which they may be applied.

A special operator supported by Lite is the count operator written as the # sign. The count operator is used to determine the size of certain variables. If you apply the count operator to a char value it will evaluate to the length of the string (the number of characters in the string). If you apply it to an array it will evaluate to the number of elements in that array. In the first example shown here, `$intval` would contain the value 5. In the second example, it would contain 3.

Table 3.2 Lite's Mathematic Operators

Operator	Description	Int	Text	Real
+	Addition	Yes	Yes	Yes
-	Subtraction	Yes	No	Yes
/	Division	Yes	No	Yes
*	Multiplication	Yes	No	Yes

```
$charval = "Hello";
$intval = # $charval;
$array[0] = 0;
$array[1] = 1;
$array[2] = 2;
$intval = # $array;
```

Conditions and Loops

Conditions are provided by Lite using the same syntax as C. That is, the conditional block is started by an `if (condition)`. The blocks of code are defined using the `{` and `}` characters. Unlike C, you must always wrap code blocks in `{ }` characters (in C you don't have to if the code block is only one line long). After the initial code block, an optional `else` block may be defined.

Multiple parts of the conditional expression may be linked together using logical ANDs and ORs. Like C, the syntax for an AND is `&&` while the syntax for an OR is `||`. As you will see in the example following, Lite provides more flexibility than C in conditions containing text values. You can compare two text values using the `==` equality test or the `!=` inequality test rather than having to use a function such as `strcmp()`.

```
if ($intval > 5 && $intval < 10){
    echo("The value is between 5 and 10\n");
} else {
    echo("The value is not between 5 and 10\n");
}
if ($charval == "") {
    echo("The variable contains no value!!!\n");
}
```

Lite supports only one form of looping—a `while` loop. The syntax and operation of the `while` loop is identical to the `while` loop offered by the C language. This includes the use of `continue` and `break` clauses to control the flow of execution within the loop.

```
while ($intval < 10) {
    $intval = $intval + 1;
}
while ($charval != "") {
    $charval = readln($fd);
    if ($charval == "Hello")
    {
        break;
    }
}
```

Comments

As in C, you can include comments in Lite files. Comments are delimited with `/*` and `*/`, as in:

```
/* if it's greater than 5 and less than 10, let the user know */
```

```
if ($intval > 5 && $intval < 10){
    echo("The value is between 5 and 10\n");
} else {
    /* It must have been in another range of values, which is a
        pity of sorts, although it does let us use this multi-
        line comment! */
    echo("The value is not between 5 and 10\n");
}
```

User-Defined Functions

As with most modern programming languages, Lite allows you to write user-defined functions. The definition of a Lite function is:

```
funct functName ( type arg, type arg ...)
{
    statements
}
```

As the definition dictates, a function must be started with the `funct` label. The remainder looks like a C function declaration in that there is a function name followed by a list of typed arguments. Any type may be passed to a function and any type may be returned by a function. All values passed to a function are passed by value rather than by reference. A few example functions are given here:

```
funct addition ( int $value1, int $value2 )
{
    $result = $value1 + $value2;
    return ( $value );
}

funct merge ( array $values, int $numVals)
{
    $count = 0;
    $result = "";
    while ( $count < $numValues) {
        $result = $result + $values [ $count ];
        $count = $count + 1;
    }
    return ( $result );
}

funct sequence ( int $first, int $last )
{
    $count = 0;
    while ( $first < $last ) {
        $array [$count] = (char) $first;
        $first = $first + 1;
    }
    return ( $array );
}
```

It must be noted that function declarations can only be made before any of the actual script code of the file. That is, all functions must be defined before the main body of the script is reached.

TIP Lite enforces a strict scope on variables used in user-defined functions. Any variable referenced by the function is defined as a local variable in that function even if there is a global variable by the same name. Parameters are passed by value, not by reference, so any modification of the parameter variables is not reflected outside the scope of the function. The only way to modify the value of variables outside the scope of the function is by returning a value from the function or by explicitly referencing global variables as outlined next.

Lite supports the concept of explicitly accessible global variables by using a different syntax when referencing the variable. If a variable is referenced as $variable then it is a variable within the current scope (a local variable if it is referenced in a function, a global variable if referenced from the main code). If a variable is to be explicitly referenced as a global variable then it can be referenced as @variable rather than $variable (a preceding @ character rather than a $ character). This will force the Lite symbol table management routines to access the global symbol table rather than the symbol table associated with the current execution scope.

User-Defined Libraries

To help provide an efficient programming environment, Lite (and W3-mSQL) allows you to build a library of functions and load the library into your script at run time. This allows for effective reuse of code in the same way that languages such as C allow you to reuse code by linking against libraries. The main difference is that the library is not "linked" into the script, it is loaded on request at run time (a little like a C shared library). If the functions that were defined previously were placed into a library called "mylib," a script could access those functions by loading the library as depicted here:

```
load "mylib.lib";

/*
** Now we can use the functions from the "mylib" library
*/
$array = sequence(1,10);
$count = 0;
while ($count < # $array) {
    printf("Value %d is '%s'\n", $count, $array);
    $count = $count + 1;
}
```

The power and convenience of Lite libraries is most obvious when writing large WWW-based applications using W3-mSQL. Like any application, there will be actions that you will need to perform several times. Without the aid of libraries, the code to perform those actions would need to be recoded into each W3-mSQL-enhanced Web page (because each HTML file is a stand-alone program). By placing all these commonly used functions into a library, each Web page can simply load the library and have access to the functions. This also provides a single place at which modifications can be made that are reflected in all Web pages that load the library.

Library files are not like normal Lite script files. A Lite script file is a plain ASCII text file that is parsed at run time by Lite. A library file contains precompiled versions of the Lite functions that will load faster as they do not need to be reparsed every time they are used. A Lite library file is created by using the -1 flag of the Lite interpreter. If a set of functions was placed in a file called mylib.lite, a compiled version of the library would be created using the syntax shown here:

```
lite -lmylib.lib mylib.lite
```

The -1 flag tells Lite to compile the functions and write the binary version of the functions to a file called mylib.lib. This is similar to the concept of using the C compiler to create an object file by using the -c flag of the compiler.

There are three points that should be noted about the use of Lite libraries. First, it should be noted that a Lite library can only contain functions (i.e., it cannot contain any "main body" code that you would normally include in a script file). Second, like functions themselves, a library can only be loaded into a Lite script prior to the start of the main body code. Finally, the path given to the load command within the script does not enforce a known location for the library file. If you specify the library file as mylib.lib then Lite will expect the library file to exist in the current directory. You can, of course, provide a complete pathname rather than just a filename to the load command.

Lite's Standard Module

The standard module is to Lite as the standard C library is to C. It is a library of functions that are available to all Lite programs. It provides basic functionality for string manipulation, file IO, and other normal expectations of a programming language. Outlined next is a description of each of the functions available within the standard module.

Input-Output Routines

The following Lite routines are all concerned with input and output. These include routines to display information to the HTML page, as well as routines for opening files and reading their contents.

echo ( )

```
echo ( string )
char * string
```

echo() outputs the content of string to the standard output of the Lite script (or as text to be included in the generated HTML of a W3-mSQL page). Any variables that are included in string are evaluated and expanded before the output is generated.

```
$name = "Bambi";
echo("My name is $name\n");
```

printf ( )

```
printf ( format [ , arg ... ] )
char * format
```

`printf()` produces output in a manner similar to the echo function (i.e., sent to the standard output or included in the generated HTML). The semantics of the function are the same as those of `printf()` in C. The `printf()` format can include field width and justification information. Specification of a format field as `%17s` will generate a right-justified value 17 characters wide. Prefixing the field width definition with the – character will produce a left-justified result.

> **TIP** It should be noted that unlike `echo()`, any variables included in the format string passed to `printf()` are not expanded before the output is generated. The only way to include variable values in the output is to use C-styled format definitions (such as `%s` for a string value, etc).

Example:

```
$name = "Bambi";
printf("My name is also %s\n", $name);
```

fprintf ( )

```
fprintf ( fd , format [ , arg ... ] )
int fd
char * format
```

Like `printf()`, `fprintf()` produces text output based on the content of the format string and the arguments passed to the function. Unlike `printf()`, `fprintf()` sends the output to a file rather than including it in the HTML sent to the browser. The first argument is a file descriptor as returned by the `open()` function. See the description of `open()` in the next section for more information.

Example:

```
$name = "Bambi";
$fd = open("/tmp/name","");
fprintf($fd, "My name is $name\n");
close($fd);
```

open ( )

```
int fd = open ( path , access )
char * path
char * access
```

open() opens the object (usually a file) pointed to by path for reading and/or writing as specified by the access argument, and returns a file descriptor for that newly opened file. The possible values for the access flags are shown in Table 3.3.

An error is indicated by a returned value of −1. In such a case, the system variable $ERRMSG will contain the error message.

> **TIP** It should be noted that both the named pipe-related modes create the pipe prior to accessing it. If the pipe exists in the file system prior to the call, open() will fail.

Example:

```
$fd  = open("/tmp/output", ">");
if ($fd < 0) {
    echo("Error : $ERRMSG\n");
} else {
    fprintf($fd,"This is a test\n");
    close($fd);
}

$fd = open("ls -l /etc", "<|");
$line = readln($fd);
printf($line);
close($fd);
```

Table 3.3 Flags for the open() Function

Flag	Description
<	File is opened for reading.
>	File is opened for writing.
<>	File is opened for reading and writing.
<P	Create a named pipe in the file system and open it for reading.
>P	Create a named pipe in the file system and open it for writing.
<|	The contents of the path argument is a shell command. The command is executed and the output of the new process is available to be read from the returned file descriptor.
>|	The contents of the path argument is a shell command. The command is executed and any data written to the returned file descriptor is passed as input to the new process.

close ( )

```
close ( fd )
int fd
```

close() closes an open file descriptor. If the descriptor relates to a file or a pipe, the file or pipe is closed. If the descriptor is a process, the stdin of the process is closed (and the process should terminate when it reads an EOF from its input).

TIP Please note that if you do not close all file descriptors you open, you will eventually run out of file descriptors.

Example:

```
$fd = open("/tmp/input", "<");
close ($fd);
```

read ( )

```
read ( fd , numBytes )
int fd
int numBytes
```

read() reads numBytes bytes of data from the specified file descriptor and returns the data. It returns the empty string "" when on end of file or error. $ERRMSG will be set if an error occurred.

Example:

```
$fd = open("/etc/passwd","<");
$buf = read($fd, 80);
if ($buf == ""){
    if ($ERRMSG != "") {
        printf("Read Error : $ERRMSG\n");
    } else {
        printf("Read : End Of File\n");
    }
} else {
    printf("$buf\n");
}
close($fd);
```

readln ( )

```
readln ( fd )
int fd
```

readln() reads a line of text from the specified file descriptor and returns the data. The new-line value is not removed from the data returned. Like read(), the return of an empty string indicates EOF or an error. $ERRMSG will be set to a non-empty string on error.

Example:

```
$fd = open("/etc/passwd","<");
$line = readln($fd);
```

readtok ( )

```
readtok ( fd , token )
int fd
char * token
```

`readtok()` reads data from the file descriptor until it finds the character specified as the token in the input data. Only the data read prior to the token is returned; the token character itself is not.

TIP Please note that the token is a single-character value. If more than one character is passed in the token argument, only the first character is used.

Example:

```
$fd = open("/etc/passwd", "<");
$username = readtok($fd, ":");
printf("Username is '$username'\n");
close($fd);
```

String Manipulation Routines

The following routines offer means of manipulating strings. These include simple routines to extract a portion of the string, as well as routines that offer regular expression manipulation features.

split ( )

```
split ( str , token )
char * str ,   * token
```

`split()` splits the contents of a variable into multiple substrings using the value of token as the separator character. The result of splitting the string is returned as an array. If more than one character is passed as the token, all but the first character are ignored.

Example:

```
$line = "bambi:David Hughes:Hughes Technologies";
$info = split($line,":");
printf("Username = $info[0]\n");
printf("Full name = $info[1]\n");
printf("Organisation = $info[2]\n");
```

strseg ( )

```
strseg ( str , start, end )
```

```
char * str
int start , end
```

strseg() returns a segment of the string passed as the str argument. The segment starts at start characters from the start of the string and ends at end characters from the start of the string. In the example following, $sub will contain the string "is a".

Example:

```
$string = "This is a test";
$sub = strseg($string, 5, 8,);
```

chop ( )

```
char * chop ( str )
char * str
```

chop() removes the last character from the text string str and returns the new value. The primary use of this function is for chopping end-of-line characters off strings read from files with readln().

Example:

```
$line = readln($fd);
$line = chop($line);
```

tr ( )

```
char * tr ( str , expr1 , expr2 )
char * str ,  * expr1 ,  * expr2
```

tr() performs text translations on the string argument str based on the contents of expr1 and expr2 and returns the modified string value. expr1 and expr2 are sets of characters. Any character that is found in str that matches a character in expr1 is translated to the corresponding character from expr2. The character sets can be defined by listing individual characters or by providing character ranges (such as A–Z to indicate all characters between A and Z). The example following will translate any uppercase characters to lowercase and translate any exclamation marks (!) found in the string with a period, or full stop (.).

Example:

```
$str = "Hello There!";
$str = tr($str, "A-Z!", "a-z.");
```

sub ( )

```
char * sub ( str , expr1 , expr2 )
char * str ,  * expr1 ,  * expr2
```

sub() performs string substitutions on the string argument str based on the contents of expr1 and expr2. If the string value passed as expr1 is found anywhere in str it is substituted for the value of expr2. The example following would leave the value "This was a test" in $str. Note that unlike tr(), the length of the string can be modified by sub() as there is no restriction on the content or length of the value of expr2.

Example:

```
$str = "This is a test";
$str = sub($str, "is", "was");
```

substr ( )

```
char * substr ( str , regexp , pattern )
char * str ,   * regexp , * pattern
```

substr() extracts substrings from str based on the regular expression regexp and the extraction template pattern. Any parts of the string that are matched by parts of the regular expression enclosed in parentheses are made available to the extraction template. The first such substring is available as $1, the second as $2, and so on. The string value created by expanding any such variables in pattern is returned. The example following would produce the string "Who's Jack?" as the regular expression enclosed in parentheses will match a word containing a leading capital letter followed by lowercase letter.

Example:

```
$str = "well, Jack is alright.";
$new = substr($str, ".* ([A-Z][a-z]*) .*", "Who's $1?");
```

File Manipulation Routines

The following routines offer the ability to get information on or manipulate a given file. These include many functions that have counterparts in Unix shell utilities, such as test and chmod.

test ( )

```
test ( test, filename )
char * test
char * filename
```

test() offers functionality similar to the test program provided by the shell. Given a filename and a test, it will determine if the file matches the test specification. If it matches, 1 is returned; otherwise, 0 is returned. Table 3.4 outlines the available tests.

Example:

```
if (test("b", "/tmp/foo") == 1) {
    echo("/tmp/foo is a block device\n");
}
```

Table 3.4 Tests Available to the `test()` Function

Test	File Type
"b"	Block mode device
"c"	Character mode device
"d"	Directory
"p"	Named pipe
"s"	Non-empty regular file
"f"	Regular file
"u"	File is setuid
"g"	File is setgid

unlink ( )

```
unlink ( path )
char * path
```

`unlink()` removes the named file from the file system. If the file does not exist or another error occurs, a negative value is returned and the $ERRMSG variable is set to an appropriate error message.

Example:

```
if (unlink("/tmp/foo") < 0) {
    echo("ERROR : $ERRMSG\n");
}
```

umask ( )

```
umask ( mask )
int mask
```

`umask()` sets the umask for the current process (see the system manual page for a description of a umask). As with any numeric value, the mask can be given in decimal, hex, or octal.

Example:

```
umask(0227);
```

chmod ( )

```
chmod ( path , mode)
char * path
int mode
```

chmod() changes the mode of the specified file to the specified mode.

Example:

```
if (chmod("/tmp/foo", 0700) < 0) {
    echo("ERROR : $ERRMSG\n");
}
```

mkdir ( )

```
mkdir ( path )
char * path
```

mkdir() creates the directory specified by path.

Example:

```
if (mkdir("/tmp/myDirectory") < 0) {
    echo("ERROR : $ERRMSG\n");
}
```

chdir ( )

```
chdir ( path )
char * path
```

chdir() changes directory to the specified path.

Example:

```
if (chdir("/tmp/myDirectory") < 0) {
    echo("ERROR : $ERRMSG\n");
}
```

rmdir ( )

```
rmdir ( path )
char * path
```

rmdir() removes the specified directory from the file system.

Example:

```
if (rmdir("/tmp/myDirectory") < 0) {
    echo("ERROR : $ERRMSG\n");
}
```

rename ( )

```
rename ( old , new )
char * old
char * new
```

`rename()` renames the specified file from the old name to the new name. You cannot rename files over the boundary of a file system.

Example:

```
if (rename("/tmp/foo", "/tmp/baa") < 0) {
    echo("ERROR : $ERRMSG\n");
}
```

truncate ( )

```
truncate ( path , length)
char * path
int length
```

`truncate()` will set the length of the file to the specified length.

Example:

```
if (truncate("/tmp/foo", 0) < 0) {
    echo("ERROR : $ERRMSG\n");
}
```

link ( )

```
link ( path , new )
char * path
char * new
```

`link()` will create a new link named new to the file specified by path. You cannot create a link over a file system boundary.

Example:

```
if (link("/tmp/foo", "/tmp/baa") < 0) {
    echo("ERROR : $ERRMSG\n");
}
```

symlink ( )

```
symlink ( path , new)
char * path
char * new
```

`symlink()` will create a symbolic link called new to the file specified by path.

TIP It should be noted that this function will not be available if the installation process determined that your operating system does not support the `symlink()` system call.

Table 3.5 Elements of the Array Returned by `stat()`

Field	Description
0	Inode number
1	File mode
2	Number of links to file
3	UID
4	GID
5	Size of file
6	atime
7	mtime
8	ctime
9	Block size of file system
10	Number of file system blocks used

Example:

```
if (symlink("/tmp/foo", "/tmp/baa") < 0) {
    echo("ERROR : $ERRMSG\n");
}
```

stat ( )

```
stat ( path )
char * path
```

`stat()` provides an interface to the `stat()` system call. The information from `stat()` is returned as an array. The elements of the array are shown in Table 3.5.

Example:

```
$sbuf = stat("/tmp/foo");
if ( #$sbuf == 0) {
    echo("ERROR : $ERRMSG\n");
} else {
    echo("/tmp/foo is $sbuf[5] bytes long\n");
}
```

Process-Oriented Routines

Please note that system facilities such as `fork()` and `exec()` are not available in the standard module. As this module is shared by both Lite and W3-mSQL, it is not appropriate for such calls to be included here (having Web pages fork child processes is not a sound idea). A supplementary module called `mod_proc` will be made available to provide these facilities.

sleep ( )

```
sleep ( time )
int time
```

`sleep()` will suspend operation of the script for a length of time in seconds.

system ( )

```
system ( command )
char * command
```

`system()` will execute the command line specified by command in a subshell. Any output generated by the command is included in the HTML output. The exit status of the command is returned to the caller.

Example:

```
if (system("ls -l") != 0) {
    echo("Error running ls! \n");
}
```

getpid ( )

```
getpid ( )
```

`getpid()` returns the process ID of the process running Lite.

getppid ( )

```
getppid ( )
```

`getppid()` returns the process ID of the process that is the parent of the process running Lite.

kill ( )

```
kill ( pid , signal )
int pid
int signal
```

`kill()` sends the specified signal to the specified process.

Example:

```
if (kill(1, 9) < 0) {
    echo("ERROR : $ERRMSG\n");
}
```

Date/Time Related Routines

The following routines are concerned with obtaining and formatting various time values.

time ( )

```
time ( )
```

`time()` returns the time since 00:00:00 GMT, January 1, 1970, measured in seconds as an integer value.

Example:

```
$time = time();
echo("The number of seconds since Jan 1 1970 is $time\n");
```

ctime ( )

```
ctime ( time )
int time
```

`ctime()` converts a value returned by `time()` into the standard Unix text representation of the date and time.

Example:

```
$time = time();
printf("The date and time is '%s'\n",
ctime($time));
```

time2unixtime ( )

```
time2unixtime ( sec, min, hour, day, month, year )
int sec , min , hour , day , month , year;
```

`time2unixtime()` provides a facility by which you can create a standard Unix time value (i.e., the time since 00:00:00 GMT, January 1, 1970, measured in seconds) for any specified date/time.

Example:

```
$time = time();
$time2000 = time2unixtime(0,0,0,1,1,2000);
printf("The number of seconds before the end of the century is %d\n",
$time2000 - $time);
```

unixtime2* ( )

```
unixtime2* ( time )
int time;
```

The functions just shown take a Unix time value (i.e., seconds since January 1, 1970) and return an integer value representing part of the time information. A list of the functionality provided by the individual routines is shown here:

`unixtime2year()` The year in which time falls

`unixtime2month()`	1 to 12 representing the month in which time falls
`unixtime2day()`	1 to 31 representing the day in which time falls
`unixtime2hour()`	0 to 23 representing the month in which time falls
`unixtime2min()`	0 to 59 representing the minute in which time falls
`unixtime2sec()`	0 to 59 representing the second from the start of the minute in which time falls

Example:

```
$time = time();
$year = unixtime2year($time);
$month = unixtime2month($time);
$day = unixtime2day($time);

echo("The date is $day/$month/$year\n");
```

strftime ( )

```
time ( fmt, time )
char * fmt; int time;
```

`strftime( )` returns a text representation of the Unix time value based on the format string passed as fmt. The available formatting options are shown in Table 3.6.

Table 3.6 Formatting Options for `strftime()`

Option	Description
%a	Day of week, using locale's abbreviated weekday names
%A	Day of week, using locale's full weekday names
%b	Month, using locale's abbreviated month names
%B	Month, using locale's full month names
%d	Day of month (01–31)
%D	Date as %m/%d/%y
%e	Day of month (1–31 with single digits preceded by a space)
%H	Hour (00–23)
%I	Hour (00–12)
%j	Day of year (001–366)
%k	Hour (0–23, blank padded)

Continues

Table 3.6 *Continued*

Option	Description
%l	Hour (1–12, blank padded)
%m	Month number (01–12)
%M	Minute (00–59)
%p	AM or PM
%S	Seconds (00–59)
%T	Time as %H:%M:%S
%U	Week number in year (01–52)
%w	Day of week (0–6, Sunday being 0)
%y	Year within the century (00–99)
%Y	Year including century (e.g., 1999)

Example:

```
$time = time();
$message = strftime("The time is %H:%M:%S on %A, %e %B", $time);
echo("$message\n");
```

Password File Related Routines

This section enumerates the password file related routines, which can be used to obtain information from the password file, such as group id, home directory, shell, and other information.

getpwnam ( )

```
getpwnam ( uname )
char * uname
```

getpwnam() returns the passwd file entry for the user specified by uname. The result is returned as an array, with the array elements defined in Table 3.7.

Example:

```
$pwinfo = getpwnam("bambi");
if ( # $pwinfo == 0) {
    echo("User "bambi" does not exist!\n");
    exit(1);
}
printf("Bambi's home directory is %s and his uid is %d\n",
$pwinfo[5], (int)$pwinfo[2]);
```

Table 3.7 Elements of the Array Returned by `getpwnam()`

Element	Contents
0	Username
1	Password
2	UID
3	GID
4	GECOS
5	Home directory
6	Shell

getpwuid ( )

```
getpwuid ( UID )
int UID
```

`getpwuid()` returns the same information as `getpwnam()` but uses a UID to identify the user rather than a username. See the definition of `getpwnam()` for details of the return format and usage.

Network-Related Routines

The following routines offer some network-related functionality that you may find useful.

gethostbyname ( )

```
gethostbyname ( host )
char * host
```

`gethostbyname()` returns an array of information about the specified host. Element 0 of the array contains the hostname while element 1 contains the host's IP address.

Example:

```
$info = gethostbyname("www.Hughes.com.au");
if ( # $info == 0) {
    echo("Host unknown!\n");
} else {
    echo("IP Address = $info[1]\n");
}
```

gethostbyaddress ( )

```
gethostbyaddress ( addr )
char * addr
```

gethostbyaddr() returns an array of information about the specified host. Element 0 of the array contains the hostname while element 1 contains the host's IP address.

Example:

```
$info = gethostbyaddr("127.0.0.1");
if ( # $info == 0) {
    echo("Host unknown!\n");
} else {
    echo("Host name = $info[0]\n");
}
```

Routines Available Only in W3-mSQL

The routines described in this section are only available in W3-mSQL. These are web-related routines that deal with such things as URL encoding and setting the correct content type for the browser.

urlEncode ( )

```
urlEncode ( str )
char str
```

urlEncode() returns a URL-encoded version of the specified string. The returned data can then be used in GET method operations without any potential problems of not conforming to the data encoding standard.

Example:

```
$value = urlEncode("This is a test");
```

setContentType ( )

```
setContentType ( str )
char *str
```

setContentType() can be used to override the default content type sent to the browser in the HTTP header before any HTML output is sent. If it is to be used, it must be the first line of the script. Note: Not even a blank line may precede a call to setContentType().

Example:

```
setContentType("image/gif");
```

includeFile ( )

```
includeFile ( filename )
char *filename
```

includeFile() may be used to include the contents of the specified file in the HTML output sent to the browser. The contents of the file are not modified or parsed in any way. If the first

character of the filename is a /, then the filename is an absolute pathname from the root directory of the machine. If the first character of the filename is not /, the filename is a relative path
from the location of the script file.

Example:

```
includeFile("standard_footer.html");
```

Lite's mSQL Module

The Mini SQL module is a library of routines for communicating with a Mini SQL database. The
functions provided by this module mimic the functions provided by the mSQL C API. Outlined
next is a description of each of the functions available within the Mini SQL module.

msqlConnect ( )

```
int msqlConnect ( host )
char *host
```

msqlConnect() connects to the mSQL server on the specified host. If no host is specified, it
connects to the local mSQL server.

Example:

```
$sock = msqlConnect("research.Hughes.com.au");
if ($sock < 0) {
    echo("ERROR : $ERRMSG\n");
}
```

msqlClose ( )

```
msqlConnect ( sock )
int sock
```

msqlClose() closes a connection made using msqlConnect().

Example:

```
msqlClose($sock);
```

msqlSelectDB ( )

```
int msqlSelectDB ( sock , db )
int sock
char *db
```

msqlSelectDB() tells the mSQL server which database you wish to use.

Example:

```
if (msqlSelectDB($sock,"my_db") < 0) {
    echo("ERROR : $ERRMSG\n");
}
```

msqlQuery ( )

```
int msqlQuery ( sock , query )
int sock
char *query
```

`msqlQuery()` submits a query to the mSQL server connected to the specified socket.

Example:

```
if (msqlQuery($sock, "select * from foo") < 0) {
    echo("ERROR : $ERRMSG\n");
}
```

msqlStoreResult ( )

```
msqlStoreResult ( )
```

`msqlStoreResult()` stores any data that was a result of the previous query.

Example:

```
$res = msqlStoreResult();
```

msqlFreeResult ( )

```
msqlFreeResult ( res )
int res
```

`msqlFreeResult()` frees any memory allocated to the specified result.

Example:

```
msqlFreeResult($res);
```

msqlFetchRow ( )

```
msqlFetchRow ( res )
int res;
```

`msqlFetchRow()` returns a single row of the data stored in the specified result.

Example:

```
$row = msqlFetchRow($res);
if ( # $row == 0) {
    echo("ERROR : $ERRMSG\n");
} else {
    echo("Field 0 is $row[0]\n");
}
```

msqlDataSeek ( )

```
msqlDataSeek ( res , location )
int res
```

```
int location
```

`msqlDataSeek()` allows you to move the data pointer within the result table. Specifying a location of 0 will rewind the result. The next call to `msqlFetchRow()` will return the first row of the result table again.

Example:

```
msqlDataSeek( $res, 0);
```

msqlListDBs ( )

```
msqlListDBs ( sock )
int sock
```

`msqlListDBs()` returns an array of the names of the databases available on the specified server.

Example:

```
$dbs = msqlListDBs($sock);
$index = 0;
while ($index < # $dbs) {
    printf("Database = %s\n", $dbs[$index]);
    $index = $index + 1;
}
```

msqlListTables ( )

```
msqlListTables ( sock , db )
int sock
char *db
```

`msqlListTables()` returns an array of the names of all the tables available in the current database of the specified server.

Example:

```
$tabls = msqlListTables($sock);
$index = 0;
while ($index < # $tabls) {
    printf("Table = %s\n", $tabls[$index]);
    $index = $index + 1;
}
```

msqlInitFieldList ( )

```
msqlInitFieldList ( sock , db , table )
int sock
char *db
char *table
```

`msqlInitFieldList()` generates an internal result handle containing details of all the fields in the specified table of the specified database. The result handle is used in conjunction with the functions discussed next to access the field structure information. Note that the result handle is held as a static variable inside the mSQL module, and further calls to `msqlInitFieldList()` will free the result.

msqlListField ( )

```
msqlListField ( )
```

`msqlListField()` returns an array of information about a single field of the current field list result that was generated using `msqlInitFieldList()`. The elements of the array contain information shown in Table 3.8.

Example:

```
$res = msqlInitFieldList($sock,"my_db","my_table");
$field = msqlListField($res);
while( # $res != 0) {
    echo("Name $field[0]\n");
    $field = msqlListField($res);
}
```

msqlFieldSeek ( )

```
msqlFieldSeek ( res , location )
int res
int location
```

`msqlFieldSeek()` acts upon the result of a call to `msqlInitFieldList()` in the same way `msqlDataSeek()` acts upon the result of a call to `msqlStoreResult()`. It allows you to move the internal result pointer to the specified location.

msqlNumRows ( )

```
int msqlNumRows ( res )
int res
```

`msqlNumRows()` returns the number of rows contained in the result handle `res`.

Table 3.8 Elements of the Array Returned by `msqlListField()`

Element	Description
0	Field name
1	Table type
2	Type
3	Length
4	Flags

Example:

```
msqlQuery($sock, "select * from foo");
$res = msqlStoreResult();
$cnt = msqlNumRows($res);
printf("There are %d rows in foo\n", $cnt);
```

msqlEncode ( )

```
msqlEncode ( string )
char *string
```

msqlEncode() is passed a string value that may contain characters that can cause errors in mSQL query strings (such as the ' character in text values). It returns a modified version of the string with all such characters escaped.

Example:

```
$name = "O'Mally";
$newName = msqlEscape($name);
```

W3-mSQL: The WWW Interface Package

W3-mSQL version 2.0 represents the second generation of HTML scripting products developed by Hughes Technologies Pty Ltd. The first-generation product provided a simple programmatic interface to the mSQL database system from within an HTML document. W3-mSQL 2.0 goes beyond the functionality provided by the first-generation W3-mSQL product to enable the development of entire programs within a WWW page while offering comprehensive access control and security features.

W3-mSQL achieves this by providing a complete programming language embedded within an HTML document. The language, called Lite, is similar in style and syntax to the C programming language and the ESL scripting language. Using W3-mSQL and the embedded Lite language, you can generate HTML code on-the-fly in the same way you do when you write custom CGI programs. What's more, you can mix normal HTML code with W3-mSQL code so that you only need to use the CGI-styled approach where you actually have to.

Scripting Tags

To facilitate the W3-mSQL extensions to normal Web pages, Lite code is included in your HTML code. It is differentiated from normal HTML code by including it inside < ! > tags. As an example, a W3-mSQL version of the legendary "Hello World" program is provided here:

```
<HTML>
<HEAD>
<TITLE>Hello World from W3-mSQL</TITLE>
<HEAD>
```

```
<BODY>
<CENTER>
<H1>Introduction to W3-mSQL<H1>
<P>
<! echo("Hello World\n"); >
<\CENTER>
<BODY>
<HTML>
```

As you can see, there is a line of code in the middle of the HTML page, enclosed in `< !  >` tags. When the page is loaded through the W3-mSQL CGI program, anything enclosed in `< !  >` tags is parsed and executed as an embedded program. Any output generated by the program is sent to the user's browser. In this case, the string "Hello World" would be sent as part of the HTML page to the browser. The remainder of the page is sent to the browser unmodified.

There can be any number of W3-mSQL tags within a single page, and there can be any number of lines of code within a single W3-mSQL tag.

To execute the script just shown, do not specify the path to the file in the URL as you would normally do as your browser will just be sent the unprocessed HTML document. To execute the script you must specify a URL that executes the W3-mSQL binary and tells it to load and process your script. The W3-mSQL binary is called w3-msql and will usually be located in the /cgi-bin directory (if it isn't there, contact your system administrator). If the normal URL of a W3-mSQL-enhanced Web page is `/staff/lookup.html`, you would load it using the following URL:

`/cgi-bin/w3-msql/staff/lookup.html`

This URL instructs the Web server to execute the W3-mSQL binary and tells it to load the `/staff/lookup.html` script file. Some Web servers can be configured to execute a CGI based on the suffix of the requested file. Such a server could be configured to automatically execute the w3-msql CGI program for every file with a suffix of `.msql`.

Form Data

One thing virtually all CGI-type programs have in common is that they process the contents of an HTML form. The form data is passed to the CGI program via either a GET or a POST method by the HTTP server. It is then the responsibility of the CGI script to decipher and decode the data being passed to it. W3-mSQL greatly simplifies this process by converting any form data passed to a script into global Lite variables within the Lite Virtual Machine. These variables can then be accessed by your script code.

When an HTML form is defined, a field name is given to each of the elements of the form. This allows the CGI to determine what the data values being submitted actually mean. When the data is passed to W3-mSQL, the field names are used as the variable names for the global variables. Once a set of variables has been created for each form element, the values being passed to the script are assigned to the variables. This is done automatically during start-up of the W3-mSQL program.

As an example, imagine that the following form was defined in an HTML page:

`<FORM ACTION=/cgi-bin/w3-msql/my_stuff/test.html METHOD=POST>`

```
<INPUT NAME=username SIZE=20>
<INPUT NAME=password SIZE=20 TYPE=PASSWORD>
<SELECT NAME=user_type>
<OPTION VALUE="casual">Casual User
<OPTION VALUE="staff">Staff Account
<OPTION VALUE="guest">Temporary Guest Account
</SELECT>
</FORM>
```

In the example we have defined three fields within the form: two text entry fields called username and password, and a menu called user_type. We have also specified that the action for the form is to call W3-mSQL and tell it to process /my_stuff/test.html passing the form data via the POST method. When the data is submitted, the values entered for the three form fields are passed to W3-mSQL. It then creates three global variables called $username, $password, and $user_type, and assigns the user's data to those variables. The values can then be accessed within the Lite script code embedded in test.html by referencing the variables.

Security-Related Features

W3-mSQL tries to address security-related issues from several points of view. The most obvious security problem is the management of access to data contained in Web pages. A good solution to this problem provides both authentication of the users and access control to restrict access based on where the user is located. W3-mSQL solves this problem with a built-in authorization scheme known as W3-auth.

When building "real" applications with a scheme such as W3-mSQL, other security-related issues become apparent. Because the actual program code is embedded in the HTML code, anyone wishing to obtain a copy of your source code would just need to access the W3-mSQL-enhanced Web page directly rather than accessing it via the W3-mSQL CGI program. If a user did this, the source code would not be processed and would appear in the HTML sent to the browser. If a user saved the source of the page from his or her browser, he or she would have a full copy of your source code on his or her machine. Naturally, this is a major problem for people who write proprietary applications.

To overcome this problem, W3-mSQL provides two features: private scripts and precompiled libraries. Your Web server may also provide a feature that can overcome this problem. All three options are discussed next.

Private Scripts A problem associated with embedding your source code in an HTML document is that by pure definition an HTML document is a public document (available to anyone via your Web server). The software we write with W3-mSQL is safe as long as the user only accesses it via the W3-mSQL CGI program (because it will be processed and removed from the HTML source before it is sent to the browser). So the problem is not that the source code is in the HTML file, it is that a user may access the HTML file directly by specifying the URL and bypassing the W3-mSQL CGI program.

The obvious solution to this problem would be if the HTML file was not available directly from the Web server. If that was the case, the user couldn't specify the URL directly, and as such could not download your source code. But how is this possible if the W3-mSQL expects to find the enhanced HTML file in the Web document space? The solution is to install your enhanced Web pages as *private scripts*.

A private script is an HTML file that is installed outside the Web document tree (i.e., it is not directly available through your web Server). When a page is requested via W3-mSQL, it looks for the file based on the URL specified. For example, if you requested the page `/cgi-bin/w3-msql/test/myfile.html`, W3-mSQL would try to load and process `WEB_ROOT/test/myfile.html`, where `WEB_ROOT` is the directory in which you install Web pages (such as `/usr/local/etc/htdocs` or similar). If it finds the file at that location, it will load and process it. If it doesn't find the file at that location, W3-mSQL assumes it must be a private script.

When W3-mSQL determines that the request references a private script (i.e., it didn't find the page in the Web tree), it looks in an external directory for the page. The default location for private scripts is `/usr/local/Hughes/www`. In the previous example, W3-mSQL will try to load `/usr/local/Hughes/www/test/myfile.html` and process it. In short, it will use the private script directory as a second Web document tree. Your Web server does not know that documents are stored in that directory so it is not able to send them without the help of W3-mSQL.

In the previous example, if someone tried to load `/test/myfile.html` directly, the Web server would report an error because the file does not exist in the Web tree. If the user then requested it using the W3-mSQL CGI program, a check for the file in the Web tree would fail so the file installed in the private script directory would be loaded, processed, and sent back to the user. This eliminates the possibility of a user directly accessing your file and downloading your source code.

Precompiled Lite Libraries   Lite libraries are precompiled versions of Lite functions that are loaded into Lite scripts and W3-mSQL-enhanced Web pages at run time. See the *Lite* section of this manual for a complete description of Lite libraries.

From a security point of view, libraries can be used to hide your Lite source code from a user. A library is a binary version of the Lite code in the same way that an object file is a binary version of C code after it has been compiled. If all of your "sensitive" functions are placed in a library then they are totally hidden from the remote users (the binary file will be of no use to anyone as you cannot reverse the process and turn the library back into source code).

Using libraries in this way also increases the performance of your W3-mSQL applications because the source code does not need to be compiled every time the page is requested (it is compiled once and the binary version is then loaded directly into the Lite Virtual Machine when needed). Please see the section of the Lite documentation covering libraries for further information.

HTTP Server Support   Some HTTP servers provide a mechanism via which you can map a file extension to a specific action (Apache is an example of such a Web server). If your Web server provides this feature you can configure it to force the processing of your W3-mSQL enhanced files automatically.

For example, let us assume that all your enhanced Web pages are stored in files with a suffix of `.msql` (e.g., `/test/myfile.msql`). You could then configure your Web server to process any request for a file ending in `.msql` through the W3-mSQL CGI program. The Web server will ensure that no user can access your enhanced HTML document without it being processed by the W3-mSQL CGI program. Configuring your Web server to do this is specific to the Web server you are using. For users of the Apache Web server, please see the "Using W3-mSQL with Apache" document in the library section of the Hughes Technologies Web site at: `www.Hughes.com.au`.

W3-Auth: User Authentication for W3-mSQL

A major problem associated with delivering "real" applications over the World Wide Web is controlling access to the application. A database application will probably have the facility to modify the data contained in the database as well as simply viewing the information. Naturally, access to the update facilities must be controlled. Most Web servers provide a username/password facility for controlling access to areas of the document tree. Configuring such access control usually requires editing files on the server machine itself and running utilities from the shell prompt. Such a scheme is not appropriate for large-scale applications or organizations that host a large number of Web-based applications.

To overcome these problems, the W3-mSQL package includes an *authentication* facility. This facility utilizes the HTTP authorization protocol to determine the user's username and password (via the familiar popup username box in most Web browser packages). When enabled, W3-mSQL will automatically check the username and password of any user accessing a page that is generated by W3-mSQL. W3-Auth does not use files on the Web server machine nor does it require utilities to be run from the shell prompt. All configuration of W3-Auth-based access control is performed via a Web interface with the data stored in an mSQL database.

Web Server Requirements

To determine the username and password of the client, W3-Auth uses the HTTP authorization protocol. This protocol will force the browser to prompt the user for a username and password and then return the information to the Web server. The Web server software must then make this information available to the W3-mSQL and W3-Auth CGI programs so that the information can be validated. If the authorization information is not passed through to the CGI programs, access to the protected pages will never be granted as a username and password can not be validated.

The usual (and expected) method for passing this information to CGI programs is via a Unix environment variable. In general, the Web server will create a variable of a predefined name containing this information before calling the CGI program. Unfortunately, some Web server developers have viewed the passing of authorization information as a potential security problem. The grounding for this view is that a malicious user could install a rogue program on the server and capture people's passwords. We do not view this as a problem due to the implied security of a Unix server. If a user can overwrite a valid CGI program with a rogue "Trojan Horse," then the general security of the server machine is not acceptable. In simple terms, it is similar to saying that keeping a spare set of keys at home is a security risk because if someone breaks into your home he or she could take a key. Naturally, if he or she has already broken into your home a key wasn't needed, and other areas of your security need to be improved.

Web servers that are known not to provide this information are those based on the NCSA HTTP server code (most notably the popular Apache Web server). To aid in determining whether or not a server provides this information, we have written a simple test program. The program is available from the software section of the Hughes Technologies Web site (www.Hughes.com.au). To overcome this limitation in the Apache server, we also provide a software patch for Apache on our server. The patch and a complete distribution of Apache that has already been patched can be found in the software section of our Web site.

Terms and Concepts

W3-Auth uses several new terms and concepts for managing the access control of your applications. The definitions of these terms and concepts are provided next.

Namespace   A *namespace* is a logical group of usernames. If, for example, a company provides Web-hosting services and wishes to allow clients to use W3-Auth-based access control for their application, a namespace could be defined for each client. If client A has a user called "fred" and client B also has a user called "fred," they would be viewed as the same person (with the same password).

By using multiple namespaces, each client can have a user called "fred" and they will be viewed as separate people. It is common to define a namespace for each client or for each W3-mSQL-based application on your server (allowing people to have different passwords for different applications).

Area   An *area* is a segment of your Web document tree that you wish to secure. An area is defined in terms of the URL used to access the pages. For example, if an application called Trident was developed and installed as "http://your.web.server/trident/," a secure area could be defined covering the /trident section of the Web tree. Any URL that includes /trident as a prefix will be included in the area.

Secure areas can be nested to provide greater control. If, for example, the Trident application contained sections for viewing data and also for editing data, access to the editing features could be restricted using a nested area. If all the pages associated with editing the database are located in the /trident/edit directory, then a second area could be defined to cover /trident/edit. When a URL is requested, the longest defined prefix that matches the URL indicates the area (e.g., /trident/edit is longer than /trident).

Configuring W3-Auth

The first step in configuring W3-Auth is to create the database required for its configuration information. A Lite script is included in the mSQL distribution to help in this process. The script is called setup_w3auth and is located in the misc directory. The script assumes that Lite is located in /usr/local/Hughes/bin. If you have installed mSQL in a nondefault location, then you will need to edit the first line of the script to reflect the location of Lite on your machines.

During the execution of the script, several tables will be created in a new database called w3-msql. It will also set up a "super user" for the initial configuration of the W3-mSQL access control. You will be prompted for user details of this newly created super user.

Once the database has been created, the configuration process of W3-Auth can begin. To start the configuration, simply load the following URL in your Web browser:

```
http://your.machine.name/cgi-bin/w3-auth
```

As the CGI executes, you will be prompted for a username and password. Enter the username and password of the super user you created with the setup_w3auth script. Once you have logged in you will be prompted to select a namespace in which you will work. The only available option will be the SuperUser namespace. This namespace is the "master" namespace in which new namespaces are defined. A user who has management capabilities in any namespace must be a user of the SuperUser namespace.

Case Study

The easiest way to document the configuration process of W3-Auth is by using an example. In this example, the original SuperUser is a user called bambi. Using the bambi account we will create a new namespace called Trident and set up a secure area for it. In our example we will use several users: bambi is the system administrator, bill is the customer who is responsible for maintenance of the new namespace, and fred and john are users of the new namespace.

Step 1 is to create a new SuperUser. This SuperUser will not have complete control of the W3-Auth system. We will create a SuperUser with limited power who will be responsible for the addition and deletion of users from the new namespace (bill in our example). To create the new SuperUser, enter the SuperUser namespace management area by selecting the SuperUser namespace from the main menu. You will be presented with the SuperUser Management menu depicted in Figure 3.1. By selecting the User Management option from the menu you will be presented with a list of the currently defined users in the namespace (only bambi at this time). Select the Add option and then click Execute to add a new user. You will be prompted for the new user's details (for bill in this case). Enter the details and click Execute to create the new user.

Step 2 is to create the new namespace. To do this we again enter the SuperUser namespace from the main menu. From the menu select the "Namespace Management" option. The browser will now show you a list of currently defined namespaces (just the SuperUser namespace in this case). To create a new namespace, select Add and then click the Execute button. You will be prompted for the name of the new namespace, a description, and a list of namespace administrators. In our example, the name of the namespace is "Trident," a description could be "Hughes Tech. Trident System," and the administrator would be bill.

Now that the new namespace has been defined we must define what privileges our administrator, bill, has over the namespace. To do this, enter the SuperUser namespace menu, choose Privilege Management, and then choose to edit bill's privileges. At this time you will be presented with a list of namespaces of which bill is an administrator (only "trident" in our example). Select trident from the list to edit the privileges bill has for that namespace. You will see that bill currently has no privileges in the trident namespace. You can enable individual privileges by selecting the checkbox associated with the privilege.

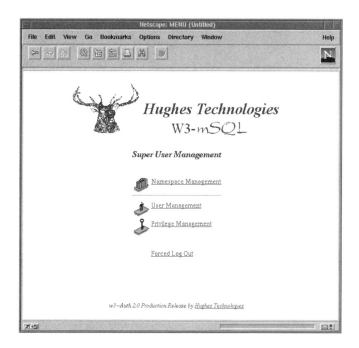

FIGURE 3.1 The SuperUser management form.

In our example, we want `bill` to be able to manage users and user groups within the `trident` namespace. To achieve our goal, select User Management and Group Member Management from the list. Your screen should look like Figure 3.2. `Bill` can now run the w3-auth program and add users to the Trident namespace.

We have stated that `bill` can manage the users of the trident namespace but that is all. There are other operations that need to be performed on the namespace that `bill` is not allowed to do (such as defining a secure area). As `bambi` is the system administrator, it is up to her to perform these tasks. Currently, `bambi` has no privileges for the trident namespace. To enable them, use the Namespace Management option from the SuperUser menu to edit the definition of the trident namespace and add `bambi` as a namespace administrator.

Once that is complete, use the Privilege Management option to edit `bambi`'s privileges for the `trident` namespace and enable all privileges. Now that `bambi` has permission to modify the `trident` namespace, return to the main menu and enter the `trident` namespace (it will now be visible to `bambi` as she is listed as an administrator).

The Authentication Management menu shown in Figure 3.2 will be displayed in your browser. Before we can proceed much farther we must define a couple of user groups. User groups are used in the definition of the access control to define which users defined in the namespace have access to the secure area.

FIGURE 3.2 The Edit Privilege form.

In our example we want to define two groups, a general user group and an admin group. To do this, select the Group Management option and add a group called "users" with `bill` as the administrator. Repeat the process and create another group called "admin" also with `bill` as the administrator. Even though `bill` was given group member management privileges, he can only manage group members in groups for which he is defined as an administrator.

Once the groups are created we can define the secure area for our W3-mSQL-based application. Our application offers two classes of access. Primarily, the application allows a general user to query the data contained in the database. Secondly, it offers a set of pages that allow the database to be modified. The main application is installed in a directory called /trident in our Web document tree (i.e., `http://your.host/trident`), while the administrative pages are located in `/trident/admin`. We wish to view these as separate areas in terms of access control even though they are part of the same application. A general user will be allowed to access the query pages, but only a restricted set of users will be allowed to access the administrative pages.

To tighten the security even further, we have decided to incorporate host-based access control as well. Access to the administrative pages should only be granted if the access request comes from a machine in our domain (`Hughes.com.au`) regardless of the identity of the user attempting the access.

Now that we have decided the access control policy for our application, implementing it is as easy as clicking the mouse a few times. To start the process we must enter the `trident` namespace from the main menu and select Area Management from the Authentication Management menu. The Area Management facility provides the same familiar interface as the other management options. To create the new area we simply select the Add option and click Execute. We will be prompted for an area name, an area URL, and some access control options. For this example we will create the general access area first and give it a name of "Trident User." The URL field requires only the path element of the URL, not the entire URL. In this case we would specify `/trident` as the URL.

The next step is to add the access control elements to the area definition. The area definition screen is shown in Figure 3.3. The form shown on the screen allows us to specify up to five elements of the access control list for the area. By default, each element is flagged as being Inactive. To enable an element, simply change the Index value from Inactive to the numeric value on the menu. You should define access control elements from the top of the list without leaving any inactive elements between active elements, so simply activate the first element for this example.

For our example we want to allow access to the area to anyone in the "users" group. Unlike the admin area, we are not going to place any restriction on the originating host of the connection. To achieve this configuration we simply select the "users" group from the Group menu and set the host field to * (indicating any host). The complete form is shown in Figure 3.3.

FIGURE 3.3 The Add Area form.

The access control field of the element can contain either a hostname-based expression or an IP address-based expression (including a wildcard in either form of expression). To restrict access to machines in the `Hughes.com.au` domain (as was the policy for the `admin` section), we would set the value of the Access Control field to `*.Hughes.com.au`. Similarly, if we wished to restrict access to machines on a particular IP subnet, we could use something like `192.168.1.*`

In a similar manner, we could allow access to any person if he or she is coming from a specified location. To do this, simply leave the Access Group as "** Public **" and set the Access Control to the correct hostname or IP address expression. In such a configuration, the user will only be prompted for a username and password if he or she attempts to access the pages from a machine not matching the Access Control expression. If we activate no other Access Control elements, the user would always be rejected as no user groups were specified in the Access Control Elements.

By using a combination of access control elements we can achieve very fine-grained control over who accesses the pages. If, for example, there was a group of people at a remote location that required access to the pages from their company network (`foo.com`), you could define a new group called remote and activate a second access control element with an access group of remote and an access control of `*.foo.com`. Such a configuration would allow access if the connection attempt matched either of the entries.

Once the Trident User area has been created the process should be repeated for the Trident Admin area. For the `admin` area, we would define the URL as `/trident/admin` and set a single Access Control element setting the Access Group to "admin" and the Access Control to `*.Hughes.om.au`.

The only remaining task is the creation of the actual users: `fred` and `john` in our example. The responsibility for user management was assigned to `bill` and his privileges were set so that he could create users and also add users to groups (group member management). `Bill` can now complete the job by accessing the W3-Auth program, entering the `trident` namespace, and using the User Management and Group Member Management menu options. If either of the new users is allowed to access the admin features of our application then they should be added to the "admin" group as well as the normal "users" group. Simply adding them to the admin group will provide them access to the admin pages.

A final note to remember about W3-Auth access control is that access control must be enabled on a per-directory basis. To enable access control you must create a file called ".w3-auth" in every directory within the area that is to be protected. The reason for this requirement is to boost performance. W3-mSQL simply checks for the file while it is loading the requested page. If the file exists, it then starts querying the database for W3-Auth configuration details and tries to match the requested URL with an area definition. If the directory is not being covered by W3-Auth, this is a waste of valuable time.

mSQL and Java

If you've been near a computer in the last couple of years, you probably couldn't help hearing something about Java. You may feel that you've heard a little too much about it, so this chapter will either overload you with more information or, if you're very lucky, it may filter out some of the noise that's been hurled your way. One of us remembers the day that he decided to stop ignoring all the hype about Java. I downloaded the HotJava browser and what was then an alpha-release JDK. I learned that Java incorporates a lot of good ideas that have been around for a long time, including an object-oriented nature, platform independence through compilation to generic bytecode, and execution within a "virtual machine." It also bundled these features with a generous helping of multimedia, network features, and graphical user interface (GUI) components. It did so at a very opportune time, just when people were getting excited about multimedia networked applications with sexy GUIs.

By no means should this be construed as a jab against Java. The designers of Java came up with a relevant product at a relevant time; the icing on the Java cake is that Java can be embedded within other applications, such as a Web browser. The first browser that supported this was Sun's HotJava browser. It wasn't long before Java could run within Netscape and Microsoft Internet Explorer. Java has gone far beyond browsers, and is now embedded in many other applications, from Web servers to operating systems. Java is also available on a chip, so it won't be long before Java is embedded within consumer devices.

Scope and Purpose of This Section

In the next couple of chapters, we'll see ways that you can interact with Mini SQL using Java. Java is an inherently extensible language, and it didn't take too long for developers to stop playing with silly animations and try to put Java to work. The first mSQL interface for Java, MsqlJava, was written by Darryl Collins (darryl@minmet.uq.oz.au), and provides a Java version of the mSQL C API. Not too long after the release of Java, JavaSoft released a database access specification for Java, known as JDBC (http://splash.javasoft.com/jdbc for more information). mSQL was the first through the gate with JDBC support; George Reese (borg@imaginary.com) released a JDBC driver for Mini SQL that was built "on top of" Darryl's MsqlJava API. Being the first JDBC driver with freely redistributable source, George's driver became a reference implementation for people who wanted to write their own JDBC drivers.

This chapter will show you enough Java to begin working with the examples in the chapters that follow. It is not intended as a comprehensive introduction to the language, but should give you enough of a bearing to make sense of what follows and build some of your own tools and applications.

Obtaining and Installing Java

JavaSoft's Java can be freely downloaded from:

```
www.javasoft.com
```

for Windows NT and 95, Solaris for SPARC and Intel architecture, and the Macintosh. The Linux port of Java is available from:

```
www.blackdown.org
```

Ports are available for other operating systems; you should consult your vendor for information on obtaining it. Java is typically packaged as a compressed tar file, zip file, or self-extracting archive. These archives will either automatically install the software, or you will need to extract the files yourself. Typically, the site you download Java from will include installation instructions, or they may be included with the distribution as a README file.

Programs that are written in Java are compiled to files with a .class extension. All programs you write will make use of prepackaged classes, classes you install, or classes you write. A class is simply a definition that determines the properties and behavior of objects that are created at run time. All programming in Java is done in this fashion; you define the behavior and properties of a class, and when you wish to use (invoke) the behavior, you must instantiate an object, which uses the class as a definition. This can be as simple as creating a class definition that corresponds to a real-world object like an employee. You could define properties such as height, weight, salary, IQ, and shoe size.

Additionally, you could create methods for the employee, which may cause external events or affect the employee's properties. Methods correspond to the behavior that real-world entities exhibit, and could include such things as "go on a diet," "take a pay cut," "grovel," and so forth. It is important to remember that the class definition of an employee doesn't refer to any *particular* employee. When you create a new employee, you use the class definition to produce a generic employee, and customize him or her by manipulating properties and methods.

When you install Java, it includes the base Java classes and specialized APIs (Application Program Interfaces), such as JDBC, RMI (Remote Method Invocation), and Serialization. These are all packed up into an uncompressed zip file, often called classes.zip; in order to add an optional kit such as mSQL-JDBC or MsqlJava, you will need to extract the distribution of the kit. After you've extracted it, you will need to locate the directory containing the class files. The README that accompanies each package should tell you where to find it. Your CLASSPATH is an environment variable that needs to be set before you can use the classes.

The CLASSPATH variable should include an entry for the classes.zip file that comes with Java, and you will need to add an entry for the top-level directory of each package you install. In the case of mSQL-JDBC, it needs to be the name of the directory containing the COM directory; in the case of MsqlJava, it needs to be the directory containing the msql directory. Depending upon the platform you are using (Unix, Win32, OS/2, etc.), you will need to set your CLASSPATH differently. On Win32, the CLASSPATH is an environment variable that can be set within your AUTOEXEC.BAT (Windows 95) or under the System control panel (Windows NT). It might look something like this:

```
D:\JDK1.1.1\LIB\classes.zip;D:\CLASSES;.
```

The . allows you to tell Java to include whatever your current directory happens to be. Under Unix, it is likely to look like this:

```
/usr/local/java/lib/classes.zip;/usr/local/java/lib/classes;.
```

If you are using another operating system, or a third-party Java development environment, you will need to consult the relevant documentation for instructions on setting your CLASS-PATH environment variable.

Compiling and Running Java Programs

In order to run a Java program, it must first be compiled. A Java program is a text file that contains valid Java source code, and usually ends in a .java extension. Compiling it creates a class file, which can be executed using the Java interpreter. This file always ends in a .class extension. Here's a sample Java application, which is included on the accompanying CD in the directory that contains the Chapter 4 examples:

```
// Hello.java
//
// A simple Java application that says hi.
//

public class Hello {

    String greeting; // a String object to hold our greeting.

    /**
```

```
 *
 * The constructor for this class. This constructs and
 * returns an object of the Hello class. It also takes
 * care of initializing the greeting String.
 *
 */
public Hello() {
    greeting = "Hello World";
}

/**
 *
 * The greet() method. This prints the greeting string
 * out to the console.
 *
 */
public void greet() {
    System.out.println(greeting);
}

/**
 *
 * This is a static method, meaning it isn't invoked through
 * an object, but can be invoked through the class itself,
 * without having to construct an object from the class. In
 * fact, the java interpreter will look for a main() method
 * in any class you feed to it from the command line. This
 * one happens to construct a new Hello object and call its
 * greet() method.
 *
 */
public static void main (String argv[]) {
    Hello hello_object = new Hello();
    hello_object.greet();
}

}
```

To execute this or any other class, you must first compile it. If you have installed Java correctly, and if the Java binaries (javac, java, javap, etc.) are in your PATH, you can issue the following command from your shell or command prompt (you may need to add Java's bin directory to your path):

```
javac Hello.java
```

javac is the Java compiler and, if it succeeds, will generate a file called Hello.class. You can execute this new class by issuing the following command:

```
java Hello
```

TIP It's important to type these commands exactly as shown. In the case of `javac`, you must include the `.java` extension. In the case of `java`, you must *not* include the `.class` extension.

You can use this technique to execute other examples in this chapter. If you are using a third-party development environment, such as Visual J++ or Café, please consult the accompanying documentation for instructions regarding compilation and execution of your Java classes.

The Java Language

Java may not be so foreign a language to anyone who's been programming for some time. At first glance, it looks a lot like C. In fact, the similarities continue, even as you dig deep into the language. The ideas that Java puts forth are not so unusual. First of all, the language is object oriented; every program must be a Java class, and unless methods and variables are declared as *static*, they belong solely to an instance of that class. The `static` keyword doesn't have the same meaning in Java that it does in C. In Java, as is the case with other object-oriented languages, there are two varieties of properties and methods. Static methods and properties can be manipulated through the class itself (static methods and properties are sometimes referred to as *class* methods and properties). *Instance* methods and properties must be accessed through an instance of that class (instance methods and properties are sometimes referred to as *virtual* methods and properties). It's possible to write a Java program that's made up entirely of static methods and properties, but it feels weird to do that, to say the least.

Classes and Objects

What is meant by the "class itself" versus an instance of a class? It's best to see this by example. A class in Java consists of all the methods and variables (also known as *properties* or *fields*) found in the program. The class is merely a description of what properties an *object* has and how it should behave. An object is a specific instance of a class. Here's a very simple class called `Truffle`. It includes a constructor (the method named `Truffle`) that takes a `String` as an argument. Every time our `main()` method calls `new Truffle(String)`, it gets back a new `Truffle` object. The `Truffle` object "remembers" the string that was passed in, and so each one is different, in a way.

```
// Truffle.java
//
// Another basic Java example.
//

public class Truffle {

    // a String to hold the name of the flavor.
    //
    String flavor;
```

```
/**
 *
 * The constructor for this class. It should be
 * invoked with the flavor as an argument.
 *
 */
public Truffle(String f) {
    flavor = f;
}

/**
 *
 * A method that prints out the flavor of this
 * Truffle.
 *
 */
public void what_flavor() {
    System.out.println(
        "This is a " + flavor + " flavored Truffle.");
}

/**
 *
 * A static method to construct a bunch of new Truffles
 * and invoke their what_flavor() methods.
 *
 */
public static void main (String argv[]) {

    Truffle s = new Truffle("smokey");
    Truffle l = new Truffle("salmon");
    Truffle c = new Truffle("caviar");

    s.what_flavor();
    l.what_flavor();
    c.what_flavor();

}
```

}

One of the words you'll hear a lot is "this"; phrases like "this" object, "this" Truffle, and "this" instance are important in the context of Java, and object-oriented programming languages in general. The class only defines a pattern by which an object should be built; you need to call a constructor to "create" an instance of a class that you can work with. Until that time, it's just code in your computer's memory, and nothing happens. When you instantiate an object, the appropriate constructor method is called (the method with the same name as the class), and whatever program invoked the constructor gets an object back. It is through this object that the instance methods, such as what_flavor(), can be invoked. Static methods, on the other hand, can be invoked through the class, and can manipulate static properties. A common example of this is a counter to keep track of how many instances of an object there are. For this, we'll define a static variable and a method to display that number. We'll also change the constructor to increment this variable each time the constructor is invoked.

```java
// Truffle2.java
//
// Static vs. virtual methods and variables.
//

public class Truffle2 {

    // a String to hold the name of the flavor.
    //
    String flavor;

    // a static variable to count how many Truffles
    // there are.
    //
    static int count = 0;

    /**
     *
     * The constructor for this class. It should be
     * invoked with the flavor as an argument.
     *
     */
    public Truffle2(String f) {

        flavor = f;

        // increment the count
        //
        count++;
    }

    /**
     *
     * A method that prints out the flavor of this
     * Truffle.
     *
     */
    public void what_flavor() {
        System.out.println(
            "This is a " + flavor + " flavored Truffle.");
    }

    /**
     *
     * a static method to display the count of
     * the Truffles.
```

```
    *
    */
public static void count_truffles() {
    System.out.println(
        "There are " + count + " truffle(s).");
}

/**
 *
 * A static method to construct a bunch of new Truffles
 * and invoke their what_flavor() methods.
 *
 */
public static void main (String argv[]) {

    Truffle2 s = new Truffle2("smokey");
    Truffle2 l = new Truffle2("salmon");
    Truffle2 c = new Truffle2("caviar");

    s.what_flavor();
    l.what_flavor();
    c.what_flavor();

    Truffle2.count_truffles();

}


}
```

In case there's "too much static" for this to make sense, remember that a static method is invoked through the class, and not through a specific instance of a class. The methods `main()`, `count_truffles()`, and even the constructor, `Truffle2()`, are invoked through the class, and are therefore static methods. You don't need to create a specific `Truffle` before you start using these methods. The `main()` method is special; the Java interpreter knows to invoke it if you feed it the compiled class file. The `Truffle2()` method is also special; although it does not specify a return type, it returns a `Truffle2` object, and through it, you can access the `what_flavor()` method, which is an instance, or virtual method. Like static and instance methods, there are also static and instance properties (variables and objects). The `String` object known as `Flavor` is an instance property; each instance of the `Truffle2` object gets its own flavor. The `count` variable, however, is different; it belongs to the class, so whether we increment it within the constructor for our salmon, caviar, or smoky-flavored truffle, it's the same variable.

Filling in the Cracks: Objects versus Variables

We went a little too quickly through the previous material to say we've covered enough about Java. You've been introduced to objects and variables such as `String` objects and `int` (integer) variables. These look pretty similar; you can throw them around in Java the same way, but there are differences.

In order to assign a value to an object or variable, you must use the assignment operator, which is the equals sign (=). Here is an example where a string value (shown within quotes) appears to be assigned to a `String` object:

```
String s = "This is a string.";
```

But that's very deceptive. Strings are actually objects and not variables. When you use the assignment operator with an object, you are actually assigning a reference—the identifier `s` is a reference to the String object. Because of this, it's entirely possible for multiple identifiers to refer to the same object. It is correct to say that `s` is an identifier, and that it refers to a `String` object, and one of that object's attributes is the value "This is a string". The line of code shown previously is actually a shortcut for constructing a new String. A full-blown String constructor looks like:

```
String s = new String("This is a string.");
```

In Java, `Strings` are objects, although characters, integers, and floating-point values, among others, are simply primitive variables. Variable assignment looks a lot like the first form of the String constructor:

```
int i = 10;
```

This assigns the value of 10 to an integer variable `i`. There is no special magic here. While `i` is still an identifier, it can be used synonymously with the variable to which it corresponds. Objects, on the other hand, are not so simple. Identifiers can be created that refer to objects, and more than one identifier can refer to the same object.

Filling in the Cracks: Return Types

You've been introduced to the `static` keyword, which is used to differentiate methods and variables that "belong to" the class itself, rather than to an instance of the class.

TIP You've probably noticed the liberal use of the word "`void`." `void` is a keyword borrowed from the C language, which indicates that the method is not expected to return a value.

When someone's program invokes a method, the programmer will expect one of two things: either the method will return a value, or the method will *not* return a value. The value can be any of Java's primitive types, or the value can be a reference to an object. In any case, it is required that the method's declaration includes the type of its return value. The following program, `Return.java`, demonstrates this:

```
// Return.java
//
// A simple Java application that demonstrates return
// values.
//

// import all class definitions in the java.lang.* package.
```

```java
// In this example, we use java.lang.Math.random, which is a
// static method that is part of the java.lang.Math class
// definition. We also use java.lang.String, which is the
// class definition for String objects. Notice that we don't
// have to specify the full name of each class definition.
//
import java.lang.*;

public class Return {

    /**
     *
     * The constructor for this class. Besides constructing
     * a 'Return' object, it also calls methods to create a
     * double variable and a String object. It also
     * constructs a Hello object and invokes its greet()
     * method.
     *
     */
    public Return() {

        // Demonstrate a call to a method which returns an
        // integer value (primitive type).
        //
        double ret1 = get_a_double_val();
        System.out.println("double value: " + ret1 + ".");

        // Demonstrate a call to a method which returns a
        // String object (java.lang.String).
        //
        String ret2 = get_a_String();
        System.out.println("String object: " + ret2 + ".");

        // Demonstrate a call to a method which returns a
        // Hello object (see Hello.java). Instead of
        // printing it ourselves, we'll invoke its greet()
        // method.
        //
        Hello hello_object = new Hello();
        hello_object.greet();

    }

    /**
     *
     * The get_a_double_val() method. Gets a random number
     *
     */
    public double get_a_double_val() {

        double random_value = Math.random();
        return random_value;
```

```
    }

    /**
     *
     * The get_a_String() method.
     *
     */
    public String get_a_String() {

        return new String("this is some text");

    }

    /**
     *
     * This is a static method, meaning it isn't invoked
     * through an object, but can be invoked through the
     * class itself, without having to construct an object
     * from the class. In fact, the java interpreter will
     * look for a main() method in any class you feed to it
     * from the command line. This one happens to construct
     * a new Return object.
     *
     */
    public static void main (String argv[]) {
        Return return_object = new Return();
    }

}
```

Vectors

There are two types of "growable" data structures that we're going to look at here; they are the classes `Vector` and `Hashtable`. A `Vector` is a data structure that is similar to an array, except that it can grow and shrink at the programmer's whim. The `java.util.Vector` class definition offers methods for discovering and accessing the elements, as well as adding and deleting elements. The following program is a very simple example that inserts `String` objects into the `Vector`, performs some manipulations on the objects, and then displays the objects. When you retrieve a specific element from a `Vector`, it returns an object of type `Object`.

The `Object` is so named since it is a totally generic class definition. In any object-oriented system, the definition of a new class derives characteristics from another class. This "other class" is known as the *superclass*. The new class definition is said to be a subclass of the "other class." These definitions can be deeply nested, and you can define classes that are subclasses of existing classes or new classes.

Every class you define in Java has `Object` as its superclass definition somewhere along the way. The classes you define will automatically inherit only the properties and methods of `Object`, unless you specify another superclass using the `extends` keyword, as in `public` class myFrame extends Frame. The class you inherit from either is a subclass of Object, or a subclass of something that is a subclass of Object, and so on.

Since the object we're retrieving is really a String object, we need to *cast* it to a String, which tells Java to treat the Object that the Vector returned as though it were a String object. If it's not a String object, or not an object that is a subclass of String, you will receive an exception. Exceptions are an important part of Java's error-handling mechanism; they can be delivered (thrown) by any object, or handled (caught) by any block of code. Here's an example that shows some ways to manipulate a Vector:

```
//
// TestVector.class - a simple example program that
// demonstrates one way of working with the Vector
// object.
//

import java.util.*;
import java.lang.*;

public class TestVector {

    // declare test to be a Vector object
    //
    Vector test;

    public TestVector() {

        // instantiate the new Vector object
        //
        test = new Vector();

        // add several strings to the Vector
        //
        test.addElement( new String("Breads"));
        test.addElement( new String("Meat"));
        test.addElement( new String("Fruit & Vegetables"));
        test.addElement( new String("Dairy"));

        // display the whole vector
        //
        displayElements();

        // remove an element
        //
        System.out.println("\nDeleting element two...");
        test.removeElementAt(2);

        // display the whole vector
        //
        displayElements();
    }
```

```
public void displayElements() {

    System.out.println("\nHere's the Vector now:");

    // iterate over each element of the Vector
    //
    int i;
    for (i = 0; i < test.size(); i++) {

        // create an identifier called item, that
        // refers to the String object in the Vector.
        // Notice that we need to explicitly cast it
        // to a String, since elementAt() returns
        // an Object
        //
        String item = (String) test.elementAt(i);

        // display the Vector index and the actual
        // string
        System.out.println("Item " + i + ": " + item);

    }

}

// a static constructor, main, which will
// get automatically invoked when we run
// this class through the java interpreter.
//
public static void main(String argv[]) {
    TestVector foo = new TestVector();
}

}
```

Hashtables

Another type of growable and shrinkable data structure is a Hashtable. A Hashtable, like a Vector, is a collection of objects. You can add or delete objects, and you can also retrieve them. However, where the Vector is indexed, or keyed, by the position of the element within the Vector (much like an array), elements within the Hashtable are actually keyed by another object, usually a String. This offers you the ability to create associations between objects, or to simply maintain a list of data that is indexed by a String, much like Perl's hashes, also known as associative arrays. The next example shows a Hashtable that contains four arrays, each of which is a list of food items. Each array is keyed by the corresponding food group, and can be retrieved using the String that corresponds to it. The arrays are declared and initialized in one go, using an array initializer, set off by the curly braces.

```java
//
// TestHashtable.class - a simple example program that
// demonstrates one way of working with the Hashtable
// object.
//

import java.util.*;
import java.lang.*;

public class TestHashtable {

    // declare test to be a Hashtable object
    //
    Hashtable test;

    public TestHashtable() {

        // instantiate the new Hashtable object
        //
        test = new Hashtable();

        // add several String arrays to the Hashtable,
        // keyed by related Strings - remember that a
        // bare String, such as "sometext", can be
        // shorthand for:
        //
        //   new String("sometext")
        //

        String[] breads = { "baguette",
                            "wheat",
                            "rye",
                            "multi-grain" };

        String[] meat   = { "pork",
                            "beef",
                            "chicken",
                            "ostrich" };

        String[] fruit  = { "apples",
                            "cucumbers",
                            "squash",
                            "melon" };

        String[] dairy  = { "chevre",
                            "2% milk",
                            "cheddar cheese",
                            "spray cheez" };

        test.put( "Breads",             breads);
        test.put( "Meat",               meat);
        test.put( "Fruit & Vegetables", fruit);
```

```java
        test.put( "Dairy",                    dairy);

        // display just the meat
        //
        displayArray("Meat");

        // display just the fruit and vegetables
        //
        displayArray("Fruit & Vegetables");

    }

    // display the array associated with a given key
    //
    public void displayArray( String key ) {

        // display the name of the key
        //
        System.out.println("\n" + key + ":");

        // get the array associated with this key from
        // the Hashtable
        //
        String[] array = (String[]) test.get(key);

        // iterate over each array element
        //
        int i;
        for (i = 0; i < array.length; i++) {

            // display each String
            //
            System.out.println("Item " + i + ": " + array[i]);

        }

    }

    // a static constructor, main, which will
    // get automatically invoked when we run
    // this class through the java interpreter.
    //
    public static void main(String argv[]) {
        TestHashtable foo = new TestHashtable();
    }


}
```

Summary

The examples shown in this chapter are meant as a basic introduction to Java programming, and have exposed you to many of the concepts and techniques that will be used to work with the sort of dynamic data that is found in databases. Java works quite well with databases such as mSQL. For example, the JDBC API offers a database-independent means of issuing queries and processing results from within Java. The MsqlJava API is a set of Java classes that provide access to mSQL in a way that resembles the mSQL C API. Java is an intensely rich language, with many subtle aspects that can be grasped with a little sweat and time. There are many books that cover Java in more detail; *Java in a Nutshell* by David Flanagan, published by O'Reilly and Associates, is a good start. *The Java Developer's Toolkit* by Josh Marketos, published by John Wiley & Sons, is a good follow-up to *Java in a Nutshell*, as Joshua's book contains many applied examples that cover specific aspects of the Java language.

MsqlJava

Darryl Collins' (darryl@minmet.uq.oz.au) MsqlJava is a Java API for Msql development that allows you to write Java programs that interact with a Mini SQL server. It provides a very simple API, which can be learned quite quickly by anyone with Java experience. This chapter will begin with an introduction to MsqlJava, illustrated by some basic examples that demonstrate common tasks, and will end with a nifty little Java program that lets you visually create and modify tables in your database.

MsqlJava History

MsqlJava was the first ever 100 percent Java database interface. A computer systems manager at the University of Queensland in Australia, Darryl Collins has a long history with computing, having cut his teeth on Basic programming in his teenage years. While that may be a familiar story for people who had access to early micro- and home computers, Darryl's experience is a little different than most peoples'. The students at the school he attended had access to a computer, there was no doubt about that. The only hitch was that it was 50 miles away at a nearby college. The students at Darryl's school had the opportunity to submit one program a week; neither debugging nor testing was possible.

Darryl's career has followed the emergence of the Australian Internet closely, as he was involved in setting up PC networks in the early stages using KA9Q. As time went on, he developed skills in Perl and Java, eventually developing and releasing MsqlJava. As someone who has always benefited from the spirit of sharing that has permeated the computing community, it was natural for Darryl to give away MsqlJava at no charge. MsqlJava is not the only software that Darryl has given away; back in 1991, he wrote a DLL for Windows 3.0 called NETBIOS.DLL. As people have still found it to be useful under Windows 95, he still receives a steady stream of requests for it. Darryl can be reached at darryl@minmet.uq.edu.au, and his home page is available at:

```
http://mama.minmet.uq.oz.au/~darryl/
```

MsqlJava or mSQL-JDBC?

One of the questions we hear a lot is "When should I use MsqlJava and when should I use mSQL-JDBC?" Chapter 6 will introduce mSQL-JDBC, which is a driver for JavaSoft's JDBC API that gives developers the ability to interact with mSQL servers. You'll notice that its mission is no different than that of MsqlJava. MsqlJava defines its own API; when you use it, you'll be working with methods and properties that are unique to the MsqlJava classes. mSQL-JDBC, on the other hand, adheres to the JDBC API.

When you work with mSQL-JDBC, you'll be using the same methods and properties that you would use with PostgreSQL, Sybase, ODBC, or any other data source supported by a JDBC driver. JDBC defines the API; while the SQL that you use to converse with your database will differ depending upon your database back end, you can use the same Java techniques regardless of what JDBC driver you are using. This may have a great deal of appeal for some people, especially if you are developing programs that need to function across a wide range of database back ends. Nevertheless, MsqlJava is a very simple, easy-to-learn API, as is JDBC. You should familiarize yourself with both APIs, and use whichever one suits your needs.

Obtaining MsqlJava

MsqlJava is distributed as a collection of Java classes, complete with source code. These classes occupy a package that is appropriately called msql. In order to use the MsqlJava classes, you need to issue an import msql.*; statement in your Java program. You can get the MsqlJava kit from:

```
www.minmet.uq.oz.au/msqljava
```

This is the master site for MsqlJava, and includes information about using MsqlJava, including a FAQ and other documents. Once you download and extract the MsqlJava kit, you should ensure that the top-level msql directory resides in a directory that is included in your CLASS-PATH environment variable. For example, if your CLASSPATH is:

```
/usr/local/java/lib:/usr/local/classes:.
```

you could move the msql directory into either /usr/local/java/lib or /usr/local/classes, which would create either of these new directories: /usr/local/java/lib/msql or /usr/local/classes/msql. If your CLASSPATH is:

```
C:\JDK1.1.1\CLASSES;C:\CLASSES;.
```

you could move the msql directory into either C:\JDK1.1.1\CLASSES or C:\CLASSES, yielding C:\JDK1.1.1\CLASSES\msql or C:\CLASSES\msql as a new directory. Of course, you could always put them anywhere you want, so long as your CLASSPATH includes the directory that contains the msql directory, but your CLASSPATH should not include the msql directory itself. Therefore, the following CLASSPATHs would be bogus, even if you had put msql into either C:\CLASSES (Win32) or /usr/local/classes (Unix variants):

```
C:\JDK1.1.1\CLASSES;C:\CLASSES\msql;.
/usr/local/java/lib:/usr/local/classes/msql:.
```

> **TIP** If you're using MsqlJava in an applet, you will need to make sure the msql directory is sitting in the same directory that contains your applet, since the applet will try to load the msql.* classes over the network.

Connecting to the Server

Once you've got the MsqlJava classes installed, you can begin writing Java programs that use the classes. As we mentioned earlier, you will need to import the classes, using the following line of code at the top of your program along with any other import statements:

```
import msql.*;
```

The constructor for the Msql class will allow you to specify the name of a server to connect to, by simply supplying a String with the name of the mSQL host. Many of the methods supplied by the Msql class can throw MsqlExceptions, so they must be caught appropriately. The examples shown later in this chapter will show how this is done, but here is the line of code that will instantiate an Msql object and connect to the database server:

```
Msql msql;
msql = new Msql("localhost");
```

If you'd like, you can also use the form of the constructor that takes no parameter, and use the Connect() method to make a connection to the database server at your convenience.

```
Msql msql;
msql = new Msql();
msql.Connect("localhost");
```

The Connect() method can also take a user name, or a port name, in cases where you are not using one of the default ports that Mini SQL uses.

```
// example with a custom port number
msql.Connect("localhost", 7777);

// example with a user name specified
msql.Connect("localhost", "bjepson");

// example with both a user name and port number specified
msql.Connect("localhost", "bjepson", 7777);
```

Issuing Queries

Once you have made a connection to the database server, you can use the Query() method to issue queries. A query can be a string of SQL code that's passed to the Query() method as a parameter. There are basically two types of queries: queries that return data, such as those involving the SELECT statement, and queries that don't return data, such a DELETE, INSERT, CREATE TABLE, and DROP TABLE. Before you can issue a query, you need to select a database on the database server using the SelectDB() method. Since databases contain tables, upon which these SQL statements can operate, you must select a database before you can work with any of its tables.

Here's a complete example that shows the use of the Msql constructor to instantiate an object and connect to a database server, select a database, and issue a CREATE TABLE statement. This example requires that there be a database called "sample" in your database server; it can be created with the msqladmin utility. Also, this example assumes that the mSQL server is on the same machine (localhost) as the machine on which you are running this Java application. If the mSQL server is running on another machine, you can substitute the name of the appropriate server in place of localhost. Here's the example, which is named MsqlQuery.java, and is contained in the eg/ch05 directory in the sample code distribution:

```
import msql.*;

/**
 *
 * MsqlQuery.java
 *
 * A simple example that shows how to connect to a Mini SQL
 * database and issue a query that produces no results.
 *
 */

public class MsqlQuery {

    public static void main ( String argv[] ) {

        // Instantiate a new Msql object, and pass the
        // host name in. This will connect to the Msql
        // server on the localhost; you can change the
        // hostname to a different name if necessary.
        //
        // Since the constructor can throw an exception,
        // it's necessary to catch it here.
        //
        Msql msql = null;
        try {

            msql = new Msql();
            msql.Connect("localhost");
```

```
} catch (MsqlException e) {

    System.err.println(
        "Connection to database failed.");
    e.printStackTrace();
    System.exit(0);

}

// Now, let's select a database to work in. If you
// haven't created this database, you can do so by
// making sure you are logged in as the "admin
// user," usually root, and running the command:
//
//     msqladmin create sample
//
// This can throw an exception, so MsqlException is
// caught here.
//
try {

    msql.SelectDB("sample");

} catch (MsqlException e) {
    System.err.println(
        "Could not select the sample database; " +
        "try running:\n" +
        "    msqladmin create sample");
    e.printStackTrace();
    System.exit(0);
}

// At this point, we can issue a query. We're
// going to create a table called 'frobnitz'
// here. If it already exists, you'll get an
// exception at this point. If this occurs, you
// may want to drop the table first using the
// mSQL monitor.
//
try {
    msql.Query("CREATE TABLE frobnitz " +
                " (frotz_name CHAR(25), " +
                "  frotz_id    INT)");
} catch (MsqlException e) {
    System.err.println(
        "Could not create the table. " +
        "Does it exist already?");
    e.printStackTrace();
    System.exit(0);
}

System.out.println(
```

```
                "The CREATE TABLE statement succeeded.");

    }

}
```

This next example, `MsqlInserts.java`, uses the same technique to issue three INSERT statements. It adds records to the table created in the previous example. You should take care when running these programs more than once. The previous example will throw an Exception if the table already exists, and running the next example more than once will add duplicate records to the table. You can always drop the table using the `msql` monitor program before running the examples again.

```java
import msql.*;

/**
 *
 * MsqlInserts.java
 *
 * A simple example that issues several INSERT statements
 * to the table created in the MsqlQuery example.
 *
 */

public class MsqlInserts {

    public static void main ( String argv[] ) {

        // Instantiate a new Msql object. See MsqlQuery.java
        // for more details.
        //
        Msql msql = null;
        try {

            msql = new Msql();
            msql.Connect("localhost");

        } catch (MsqlException e) {

            System.err.println(
                "Connection to database failed.");
            e.printStackTrace();
            System.exit(0);

        }

        // Select the sample database. See MsqlQuery.java
        // for more details.
        //
        try {

            msql.SelectDB("sample");
```

```
        } catch (MsqlException e) {
            System.err.println(
                "Could not select the sample database; " +
                "try running:\n" +
                "     msqladmin create sample");
            e.printStackTrace();
            System.exit(0);
        }

        // Now, we'll issue several INSERT statements
        // to populate the table we created in the
        // MsqlQuery example. If you haven't run this
        // example yet, this portion will get an error.
        //
        try {
            msql.Query("INSERT INTO frobnitz " +
                       "  (frotz_name, frotz_id) " +
                       "  VALUES ('mumble', 1)");

            msql.Query("INSERT INTO frobnitz " +
                       "  (frotz_name, frotz_id) " +
                       "  VALUES ('bumble', 2)");

            msql.Query("INSERT INTO frobnitz " +
                       "  (frotz_name, frotz_id) " +
                       "  VALUES ('hum', 3)");

        } catch (MsqlException e) {
            System.err.println(
                "Could not issue the INSERTS; " +
                "Did you run MsqlQuery?");
            e.printStackTrace();
            System.exit(0);
        }

        System.out.println(
            "The INSERT statements succeeded.");

    }

}
```

Processing the Results of a Query

So far, you've seen how to send SQL statements to the Mini SQL server, but you haven't seen how to process the results. That's not a big problem, since none of the examples so far have returned any results. The `Query()` method returns an `MsqlResult` object, which provides methods for traversing the results of the query and retrieving the values. Here's a sample line of code that will obtain an `MsqlResult` object:

```
MsqlResult r =
    msql.Query("SELECT frotz_name, frotz_id " +
               "FROM frobnitz");
```

You can find out the number of rows in the result set with the NumRows() method. In relational database jargon, the term *row* is often used as a synonym for *record*. However, the term *record* actually refers to a physical unit of storage, and SQL provides a very high level of abstraction from the physical storage of the data. Similarly, the terms *column* and *field* are often used interchangeably. Like *record*, *field* is a term that refers to the physical unit of storage, while a *column* is a logical unit of data. Since most database developers work with databases using a high-level language, such as SQL, that hides the underlying physical organization of the data, it is not uncommon for the terms *row* and *record*, or the terms *field* and *column*, to be used interchangeably.

When you work with the result set, you're no longer working with an Msql object, but a different object, known as MsqlResult. Here's an example of using the NumRows() method with the object we just created:

```
int number_of_rows = r.NumRows();
```

In order to process each row, you must invoke the FetchRow() method. You can keep doing this until you run out of rows. When you run out of rows in the result set, the call to FetchRow() returns null (not to be confused with an SQL NULL column value). The FetchRow() method returns an array of Strings, which correspond to the columns in the result set. Any INT or REAL values are converted to a String. The following code, MsqlQueryResults.java, demonstrates the use of the MsqlResult object:

```
import msql.*;

/**
 *
 * MsqlQueryResults.java
 *
 * In this example, we'll query the table that was
 * created in MsqlQuery.java and was populated with
 * data in the MsqlInserts.java example.
 *
 */

public class MsqlQueryResults {

    public static void main ( String argv[] ) {

        // Instantiate a new Msql object. See MsqlQuery.java
        // for more details.
        //
        Msql msql = null;
        try {

            msql = new Msql();
            msql.Connect("localhost");
```

```
    } catch (MsqlException e) {

        System.err.println(
            "Connection to database failed.");
        e.printStackTrace();
        System.exit(0);

    }

    // Select the sample database. See MsqlQuery.java
    // for more details.
    //
    try {

        msql.SelectDB("sample");

    } catch (MsqlException e) {
        System.err.println(
            "Could not select the sample database; " +
            "try running:\n" +
            "    msqladmin create sample");
        e.printStackTrace();
        System.exit(0);
    }

    // Now, we'll issue a SELECT statement to
    // fetch some data from the table.
    //
    try {

        // Issue the query; the Query() method returns
        // an MsqlResult object.
        //
        MsqlResult r =
            msql.Query("SELECT frotz_name, frotz_id " +
                       "FROM frobnitz");

        // The MsqlResult object offers a FetchRow()
        // method, which returns an array of Strings,
        // converting INT and REAL values as appropriate
        //
        String row[];

        // Print out a header for the name and id
        // columns; since we'll separate them with
        // tabs in the output, we'll do the same
        // here as well.
        //
        System.out.println("name\tid");
        System.out.println("====\t==");
        while ( (row = r.FetchRow()) != null) {
```

```
                System.out.println(row[0] + "\t" + row[1]);
            }

        } catch (MsqlException e) {
            System.err.println(
                "Could not issue the query; " +
                "Did you run MsqlQuery and MsqlInserts?");
            e.printStackTrace();
            System.exit(0);
        }

    }

}
```

Obtaining Metadata

Without being able to get information about the databases, tables, and columns from the server, you are flying somewhat blind. Fortunately, there are ways to obtain information about how the data is stored on the server. This information is called *metadata*, and is basically data that concerns data. This includes information such as the names of the databases on the server, the names of tables within the current database, and information about columns contained within a given table.

For starters, you can get an array of `Strings`, each element of which contains the name of one of the databases on the server, by using the `ListDBs()` method.

```
String[] db;
db = msql.ListDBs();
```

Similarly, the `ListTables()` method will provide an array of `Strings` that holds all of the tables for the currently selected database.

```
String[] tables;
msql.SelectDB("sample");
tables = msql.ListTables();
```

The `ListFields()` method is a little different. It returns an array of `MsqlFieldDesc` objects. An `MsqlFieldDesc` object supplies methods to get information about each field (or column) for the given table. This example, `MsqlInfo.java`, shows `ListFields()` in action, along with `ListTables()`. Figure 5.1 shows an example of the output from this program.

```
import msql.*;
import java.util.*;

/**
 *
 * MsqlInfo.java
 *
 * A simple example that issues several INSERT statements
```

```
 * to the table created in the MsqlQuery example.
 *
 */

public class MsqlInfo {

    public static void main ( String argv[] ) {

        // This is a lookup table for the different
        // data types supported by mSQL
        //
        Hashtable fieldinfo = new Hashtable();
        fieldinfo.put(new Integer(Msql.CHAR), "CHAR");
        fieldinfo.put(new Integer(Msql.INT),  "INT");
        fieldinfo.put(new Integer(Msql.REAL), "REAL");
        fieldinfo.put(new Integer(Msql.TEXT), "TEXT");

        // Instantiate a new Msql object. See MsqlQuery.java
        // for more details.
        //
        Msql msql = null;
        try {

            msql = new Msql();
            msql.Connect("localhost");

        } catch (MsqlException e) {

            System.err.println(
                "Connection to database failed.");
            e.printStackTrace();
            System.exit(0);

        }

        // Select the sample database. See MsqlQuery.java
        // for more details.
        //
        try {

            msql.SelectDB("sample");

        } catch (MsqlException e) {
            System.err.println(
                "Could not select the sample database; " +
                "try running:\n" +
                "    msqladmin create sample");
            e.printStackTrace();
            System.exit(0);
        }

        // In this block, we'll try to get a list of
```

```
// tables from the selected database. For each
// table, we will invoke the ListFields method,
// which gives us information about each field.
//
try {

    // Get a String array holding all the table
    // names.
    //
    String table_name[] = msql.ListTables();
    if (table_name != null) {

        // Walk the array of table names.
        //
        for(int i = 0; i < table_name.length; i++) {

            // Get the field description object
            // from the ListFields() method.
            //
            MsqlFieldDesc mfd[] =
                msql.ListFields(table_name[i]);

            // Display the name of the table.
            //
            System.out.println(
                "\nTable: " + table_name[i]);

            // These are used to pad out the
            // column headers and data.
            //
            String pad = "                        ";
            int plen = pad.length();

            // Print out headers for the name, type,
            // and size columns. They'll be padded
            // out to the length of the pad String.
            //
            System.out.println(
                "Name" + pad.substring(0, plen - 4) +
                "Type" + pad.substring(0, plen - 4) +
                "Size" + pad.substring(0, plen - 4));
            System.out.println(
                "====" + pad.substring(0, plen - 4) +
                "====" + pad.substring(0, plen - 4) +
                "====" + pad.substring(0, plen - 4));

            for (int j = 0; j < mfd.length; j++) {

                // Get the name of the field.
                //
                String name = mfd[j].FieldName();
```

```
                    // Get the data type - it comes from
                    // the MsqlFieldDesc object as an
                    // integer, so it needs to be
                    // looked up in the fieldinfo
                    // Hashtable.
                    //
                    int itype = mfd[j].FieldType();
                    String type = (String)
                      fieldinfo.get(new Integer(itype));

                    // Get the column width and convert
                    // it to a String.
                    //
                    int isize = mfd[j].FieldLength();
                    String size = String.valueOf(isize);

                    // Figure out the length of each
                    // item for padding.
                    //
                    int nlen = name.length();
                    int tlen = type.length();
                    int slen = size.length();

                    // Print out the name, type, and
                    // size of each field. They'll be
                    // padded out to the length of the
                    // pad String.
                    //
                    System.out.println(
                      name +
                        pad.substring(0, plen - nlen) +
                      type +
                        pad.substring(0, plen - tlen) +
                      size +
                        pad.substring(0, plen - slen));
                }

            }

        }

    } catch (MsqlException e) {
        System.err.println(
            "Could not get table information!");
        e.printStackTrace();
        System.exit(0);
    }

    }

}
```

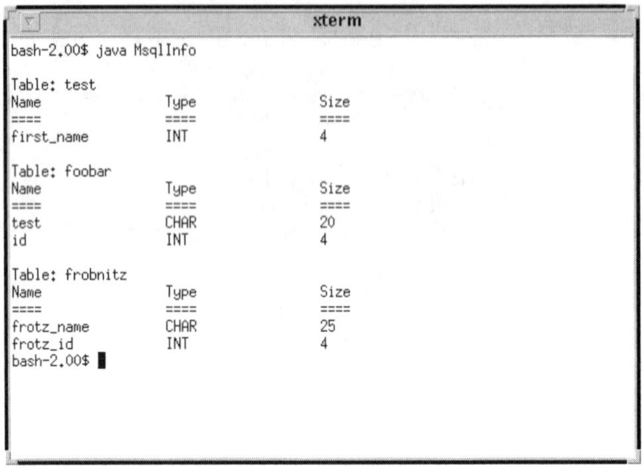

```
                              xterm
bash-2.00$ java MsqlInfo

Table: test
Name                    Type            Size
====                    ====            ====
first_name              INT             4

Table: foobar
Name                    Type            Size
====                    ====            ====
test                    CHAR            20
id                      INT             4

Table: frobnitz
Name                    Type            Size
====                    ====            ====
frotz_name              CHAR            25
frotz_id                INT             4
bash-2.00$ █
```

FIGURE 5.1 The output of the `MsqlInfo.java` program.

Putting It All Together

In my eternal quest to make things interesting, we put together a little Java application, shown in action in Figure 5.2, that allows you to manipulate table definitions on a Mini SQL server. This program, `MsqlTables.java`, uses many of the techniques shown in the previous examples, especially the methods that are used to retrieve metadata from the database server. It also creates a simple user interface, using features of the AWT (The Abstract Window Toolkit, Java's graphical user interface API) that are included with JDK 1.1.

MsqlTables.java

Most of this program is included in the `MsqlTables.java` program, but the `Alert.java` and `YesNoAlert.java` programs supply some additional functionality. This example provides an exhaustive investigation of MsqlJava; it is hoped that it will even provide a useful means of creating and modifying Mini SQL tables in the real world.

At the top of the program, we issue some `import` statements. Naturally, the `msql.*` package is imported to make the Mini SQL classes available. The `java.awt.*` package is imported to supply all of the user-interface components offered by the AWT. In order to make use of the AWT's event-handling mechanism, the `java.awt.event.*` package is imported. Also, `java.util.*` offers many useful classes, in particular the `Hashtable` and `Vector` classes.

This class extends the `java.awt.Frame` class, which is basically a window that the programmer can use to display user interface components. A Java user interface is governed by a layout manager, which controls the placement of objects in the container object. In this case, `MsqlTables`, which is a subclass of `Frame`, is the container in question.

```
import java.awt.*;
```

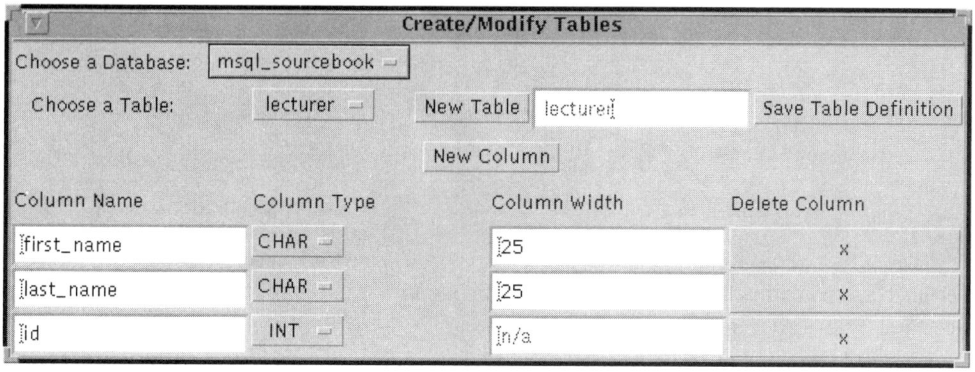

FIGURE 5.2 Editing the structure of the lecturer table using `MsqlTables`.

```java
import java.awt.event.*;
import java.util.*;
import msql.*;

/**
 * MsqlTables.java
 *
 * A simple tool to help you create and modify table
 * structures in Mini SQL
 *
 */
public class MsqlTables extends Frame {

    Button save_table;      // a button to save tables
    Choice db_name;         // list of databases
    Choice table_name;      // list of tables
    String curr_db;         // name of the current database
    String curr_table;      // name of the current table

    TextField nm_table;     // the table's name
    FieldPanel field_panel; // a component that lets you
                            // modify column info

    Msql msql;                  // the Msql object, our
                                // connection to the database

    YesNoAlert save_yesno = null; // a yes/no dialog
    Alert alert = null;           // an alert dialog

    /**
     *
     * Constructs a new MsqlTables object.
     *
     */
```

```
public MsqlTables() {

    super("Create/Modify Tables");

    GUI_init(); // user interface initialization
    DB_init();  // database initialization

}
```

The `MsqlTables` class is a subclass of `Frame`. As a result, when it comes time to add a user interface component to it, we can simply invoke the `add()` method, which is not actually defined in `Frame` but in its parent class, `Container` (actually, `Frame`'s immediate parent is `Window`, but `Window` is a subclass of `Container`).

In order to neatly arrange things in the `MsqlTables` object, the object's layout is governed using a layout manager known as `GridBagLayout`. This layout manager allows you to place components in a grid, and the grid's cells adjust to the size that the component needs. A `GridBagLayout` object works in conjunction with a `GridBagConstraints` object. The `GridBagConstraints`' properties (row, column, etc.) are first adjusted for the component you wish to add. When you are ready to add the component, you simply invoke the `setConstraints()` method of the `GridBagLayout` object with the component and the `GridBagConstraints` object as parameters, and then add the component.

The `GridBagLayout` and `GridBagConstraints` classes are very complex, and a complete discussion of their use would be outside the scope of this chapter. However, the HTML documentation that is available for the Java Core API provides a detailed discussion of these classes. This documentation is available on the www.javasoft.com Web site, and is also available for download from the same place that you obtained your copy of the JDK (Java Development Kit).

The `GUI_init()` method shown next takes care of displaying the user interface components that control such things as the currently selected database, the currently selected table, and other related components.

```
/**
 *
 * GUI_init - Prepare the user interface.
 *
 */
protected void GUI_init() {

    // Use the dreaded GridBagLayout and its evil
    // minion, the GridBagConstraints.
    //
    GridBagLayout gb       = new GridBagLayout();
    GridBagConstraints c = new GridBagConstraints();

    // Set the layout manager for this MsqlTables object
    // to be the gb object.
    //
```

```
        setLayout(gb);

        // Turn off horizontal and vertical fill for the
        // next objects we add.
        //
        c.fill = GridBagConstraints.NONE;

        // Add a label for the database chooser.
        // start out with x=0 and y=0 in the grid.
        //
        c.gridx = 0; c.gridy = 0;
        Label db_label = new Label("Choose a Database:");
        gb.setConstraints(db_label, c);
        add(db_label);

        // Increment the x axis of the grid, and add a
        // Choice object for the database names. The
        // database names will get added in DB_init().
        //
        c.gridx++;
        db_name = new Choice();
        gb.setConstraints(db_name, c);
        add(db_name);

        // Attach a listener to the database Choice object
        // so we can process events. Listeners are a core
        // piece of AWT event handling. They are simply objects
        // that are associated with a given GUI control, and
        // "come alive" when some sort of event, such as a mouse
        // click, "disturbs" the GUI control.
        //
        db_name.addItemListener(new dbWatcher());

        // Increment the y axis of the grid, set the x axis
        // to zero (starting a new row...) and add a label
        // for the table chooser.
        //
        c.gridx = 0; c.gridy++;
        Label table_label = new Label("Choose a Table:");
        gb.setConstraints(table_label, c);
        add(table_label);

        // Increment the x axis of the grid, and add a
        // Choice object for the table names. The
        // database names will get added in chooseDB().
        //
        c.gridx++;
        table_name = new Choice();
        gb.setConstraints(table_name, c);
        add(table_name);

        // Attach a listener to the database Choice object
```

```
// so we can process events.
//
table_name.addItemListener(new tableWatcher());

// Increment the x axis of the grid, and add a
// Button that lets them create a new table.
//
c.gridx++;
Button new_table = new Button("New Table");
gb.setConstraints(new_table, c);
add(new_table);

// Attach a listener to the Button so we can process
// events.
//
new_table.addActionListener(new newTableWatcher());

// Increment the x axis of the grid, and add a
// textfield for the table name.
//
c.gridx++;
nm_table = new TextField(16);
nm_table.setEnabled(false);
gb.setConstraints(nm_table, c);
add(nm_table);

// Increment the x axis of the grid, and add a
// button to save the table.
//
c.gridx++;
save_table = new Button("Save Table Definition");
gb.setConstraints(save_table, c);
add(save_table);

// Attach a listener to the Button so we can process
// events.
//
save_table.addActionListener(
    new saveTableWatcher());

// Prepare the GridBagConstraints object to accept
// the FieldPanel - this will contain the definition
// of each column, so the user can add, change, or
// delete column definitions.
//
c.gridx = 0; c.gridy++; // new row
c.gridwidth = GridBagConstraints.REMAINDER;
c.weightx = 1.0;
c.fill = GridBagConstraints.BOTH;

// Create the new FieldPanel, set its constraints,
// and add it to the MsqlTables object.
```

```
        //
        field_panel = new FieldPanel();
        gb.setConstraints(field_panel, c);
        add(field_panel);

        // Attach a listener that will be used to intercept
        // calls to close the MsqlTables object.
        //
        addWindowListener(new WinEventHandler() );

    }
```

The following method, DB_init(), retrieves the list of databases from the mSQL server. Then, it adds the name of each database to the AWT Choice menu shown in Figure 5.3.

```
    /**
     *
     * DB_init - Initialize the Msql object and retrieve
     * database information.
     *
     */
    protected void DB_init() {

        // Create a new Msql object, and connect to the
        // database server on the localhost. If it's on
        // another machine, supply the name of that
        // machine instead of "localhost."
        //
        try {
            msql = new Msql();
            msql.Connect("localhost");
        } catch (MsqlException e) {
            System.out.println(
                "Connection to database failed.");
            e.printStackTrace();
            System.exit(0);
```

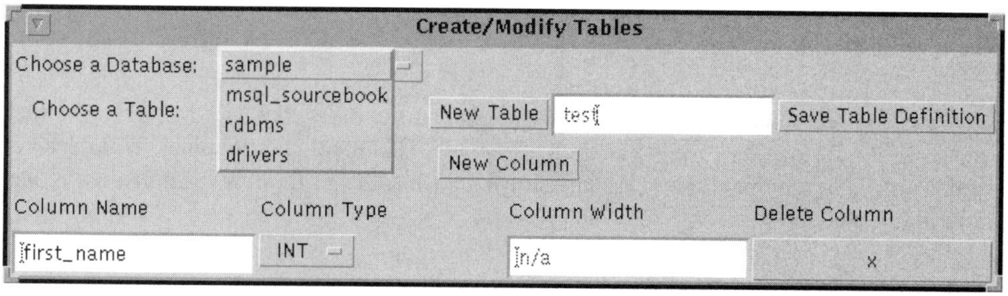

FIGURE 5.3 The database Choice menu.

```
    }

    // Get all the database names, and add them to the
    // table_name object
    //
    String[] db = null;

    // Try to get all the database names.
    //
    try {
        db = msql.ListDBs();
    } catch (MsqlException e) {
        System.out.println(
            "Could not retrieve list of databases.");
        e.printStackTrace();
        System.exit(0);
    }

    // If there are no databases, let the user know
    // and terminate the program.
    //
    if (db == null) {
        System.out.println(
            "No databases found on the server.");
        System.exit(0);
    }

    // Add each database name to the db_name Choice
    // object.
    //
    for (int i = 0; i < db.length; i++) {
        db_name.add( db[i] );
    }

    // Set option zero as the selected option, and
    // invoke chooseDB().
    //
    db_name.select(0);
    chooseDB();

}
```

When the user makes a selection from the database chooser, the `ItemListener` that's assigned to it (dbWatcher) invokes `chooseDB()`. This method determines the tables contained within that database, and adds an item for each table to the AWT Choice component shown in Figure 5.4.

```
/**
 *
 *
 * chooseDB - Process the selection of a database name.
 *
 * There are two versions of the chooseDB()
 * method, and each version is referred to
```

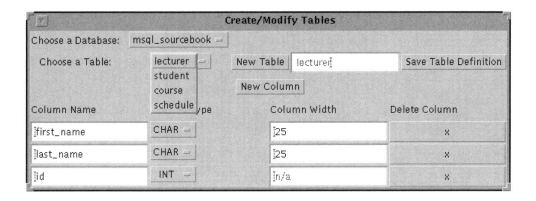

FIGURE 5.4 The AWT Choice menu that contains a list of tables within the selected database.

```
     * by its "signature". A signature refers to the
     * arguments required by the method. This is
     * the means by which Java offers a feature known
     * as method overloading.
     *
     * This method signature doesn't take a table
     * name to select, so it passes null to the
     * other method signature, which tells it to
     * choose the first table in the list.
     *
     */
    public void chooseDB() {
        chooseDB(null);
    }

    /**
     *
     * chooseDB - Process the selection of a database name.
     *
     * @param table_to_choose the table name to select
     *
     */
    public void chooseDB(String table_to_choose) {

        // Figure out the name of the currently
        // selected database.
        //
        curr_db = db_name.getSelectedItem();

        // Get all the table names.
        //
        String[] tables = null;
        try {
            msql.SelectDB(curr_db);
```

```
        tables = msql.ListTables();
    } catch (MsqlException e) {
        System.out.println(
            "Could not retrieve list of tables.");
        e.printStackTrace();
        System.exit(0);
    }

    // First, remove all of the names from table_name
    // Choice object.
    //
    table_name.removeAll();

    // If there are any tables to add, add each one in
    // turn to the table_name Choice object.
    //
    if (tables != null) {

        boolean chose_a_table = false;
        for (int i = 0; i < tables.length; i++) {
            table_name.add( tables[i] );
            if (tables[i].equals(table_to_choose)) {
                table_name.select(i);
                chose_a_table = true;
            }
        }

        // Set item 0 as the selected item if the
        // table_to_choose name was not matched.
        //
        if (!chose_a_table) {
            table_name.select(0);
        }

        chooseTable(); // invoke the chooseTable method.

    } else {

        // if there are no tables in this database,
        // clear the table name, remove all the columns
        // from the FieldPanel, and add one blank column
        // description.
        //
        nm_table.setText("");
        field_panel.removeAllFields();
        field_panel.addField();

    }

}
```

When the user selects a table from the `table_name Choice` object, the `chooseTable()` method is invoked. This method retrieves an `MsqlFieldDesc` object for the table that the user selected. For each field in the table, the `addField()` method in the `field_panel` object is invoked. The `field_panel` object, as we'll see later, is an instance of the *inner class* `FieldPanel`, which comprises the bottom portion of the display (an inner class is a class that's defined *within another* class). For every field in the table, `field_panel` shows its name, its data type, its length, and a Delete button (labeled with an "x"), which lets you drop the field from the table.

```java
/**
 *
 * chooseTable - Handle the selection of a table name.
 *
 */
public void chooseTable() {

    // This MsqlFieldDesc object will hold information
    // about the columns (aka fields) in the currently
    // selected table.
    //
    MsqlFieldDesc[] mfd = null;

    // Get the table name.
    //
    curr_table = table_name.getSelectedItem();

    // Set the text of the nm_table TextField to the
    // name of this table. Make sure the user can't
    // edit it.
    //
    nm_table.setText(curr_table);
    nm_table.setEnabled(false);

    // Try to get the field descriptions for the
    // currently selected table.
    //
    try {
        mfd = msql.ListFields(curr_table);
    } catch (MsqlException e) {
        System.out.println(
            "Could not retrieve field info.");
        e.printStackTrace();
        System.exit(0);
    }

    // Remove all of the fields from the FieldPanel,
    // and add in all the fields associated with the
    // currently selected table.
```

```
        //
        field_panel.removeAllFields();
        for (int i = 0; i < mfd.length; i++) {

            field_panel.addField(mfd[i].FieldName(),
                                  mfd[i].FieldType(),
                                  mfd[i].FieldLength());

        }

    }
```

The saveTable() method is invoked when the user presses the button marked "Save Table Definition." Unfortunately, when it changes a table definition, it trashes all the data in the table. For this reason, the user is presented with an alert that makes sure he or she really wants to perform the action. If the user wants to go ahead and modify the table definition, then this method issues a DROP TABLE statement, and then constructs a CREATE TABLE statement to send to the database server. Since the field_panel keeps track of all the information that comprises each field definition, it's natural that it would also have a method to return information about those columns. Rather than have it simply return the raw data (name, size, datatype), it returns the portion of the CREATE TABLE statement that defines all of the columns. So, this method takes care of constructing the "CREATE TABLE table_name ( )" part, and inserts the output of the field_panel's getFieldDefString() in between the parentheses.

```
    /**
     *
     * saveTable - Save the table definition, overwriting
     * the existing table, if it exists.
     *
     */
    protected void saveTable() {

        // Warn the user that this action could
        // destroy existing data.
        //
        if (save_yesno == null) {

            save_yesno = new YesNoAlert(this,
                "Are you sure you wish to create\n" +
                "this table? If it already exists,\n" +
                "*all* data in it will be lost!");

        }
        save_yesno.setVisible(true);

        // If the user said "No", then return without
        // making any changes.
        //
        if (save_yesno.getState() == YesNoAlert.NO) {
```

```
        save_yesno.dispose();
        return;
    }
    save_yesno.dispose();

    // Get the name of the new table from the
    // nm_table TextField.
    //
    String new_table_name = nm_table.getText();

    // Try to drop the table; if it doesn't exist,
    // an exception will be raised that we will
    // ignore.
    //
    try {
        msql.Query("drop table " + new_table_name);
    } catch (MsqlException excp) {
        // ignore!
    }

    // Try to create the table. If it fails, put
    // an alert up that displays the error message.
    // To create the table, we just construct a
    // string that includes the column definitions;
    // we get these from the FieldPanel object.
    //
    try {

        msql.Query(
            "create table " + new_table_name +
            " (" +
                field_panel.getFieldDefString() +
            ")");

    } catch (MsqlException excp) {

        // Let them know if there was an error.
        //
        if (alert == null) {
            alert = new Alert(this,
                "An error occurred creating\n" +
                "the table:\n" + excp.getMessage());
        }
        alert.setVisible(true);
        alert.dispose();
        return;
    }

    // Invoking chooseDB() will cause the list of
    // tables to get refreshed, and will include
    // this table if it was created successfully.
    //
```

```
        chooseDB(new_table_name);

    }
```

As with any Java class, if you want to be able to run it from the command line (rather than invoking it from another class), you must have a static method called `main()`.

```
    // This static initializer will create a new instance
    // of MsqlTables, and start it up.
    //
    public static void main( String argv[] ) {

        MsqlTables test = new MsqlTables();
        test.pack();
        test.setVisible(true);

    }
```

Before we come to the definition for the `FieldPanel` inner class, there are a few inner classes defined here that are used to handle events for various user interface components.

```
    // This is the event handler that deals with cases
    // where a user closes the MsqlTables object (a subclass
    // of Frame) by using a window control.
    //
    class WinEventHandler extends WindowAdapter {
        public void windowClosing(WindowEvent e) {
            System.exit(0);
        }
    }

    // This is the event handler that waits for the user
    // to select a database; when the database picklist
    // changes, this event handler calls chooseDB().
    //
    class dbWatcher implements ItemListener {
        public void itemStateChanged( ItemEvent e ) {
            chooseDB();
        }
    }

    // This is the event handler that waits for the user
    // to select a table; when the table picklist changes,
    // this event handler calls chooseTable().
    //
    class tableWatcher implements ItemListener {
        public void itemStateChanged( ItemEvent e ) {
            chooseTable();
        }
    }

    // This event handler watches the "Save Table" button,
```

```
// and calls the saveTable() method when the button
// is pressed.
//
class saveTableWatcher implements ActionListener {
    public void actionPerformed ( ActionEvent e ) {
        saveTable();
    }
}

// This event handler watches the "New Table" button,
// and gets the form ready for the user to enter a
// new table when the button is pressed.
//
class newTableWatcher implements ActionListener {

    public void actionPerformed ( ActionEvent e ) {

        // Enable editing of the table name, and set
        // its text to blank.
        //
        nm_table.setEnabled(true);
        nm_table.setText("");

        // Remove all the fields currently in the
        // FieldPanel, and add a blank field.
        //
        field_panel.removeAllFields();
        field_panel.addField();

    }

}
```

While the `MsqlTables` class takes care of some of the user interface, the `FieldPanel`, which is a subclass of `Panel`, is defined as an inner class within `MsqlTables`, and is responsible for managing a `Panel` that contains user interface components for each field. Rather than use a `GridBagLayout`, this subclass of Panel simply uses a `GridLayout`, which, like the `GridBagLayout`, lays out components in a grid. Unlike the `GridBagLayout`, the `Grid Layout` uses the same size cell for each component. A `FieldPanel` is shown in Figure 5.5.

```
/**
 *
 * class FieldPanel
 *
 * An inner class of MsqlTables that provides a
 * component for manipulating column (aka field)
 * definitions.
 *
 */
```

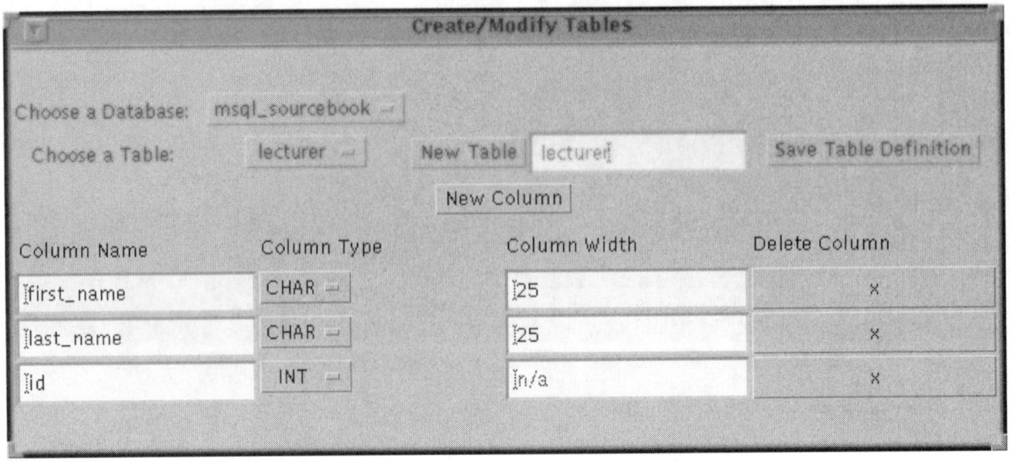

FIGURE 5.5 The `FieldPanel` is a separate Panel component within the Frame. It includes controls for each field, and a New Column button.

```java
class FieldPanel extends Panel {

    // a Panel to hold the column definitions
    Panel column_panel;
    GridLayout field_gl; // the layout for that Panel

    // Each column in the table is represented by
    // several GUI components in the FieldPanel.
    // This Vector is used to keep track of each
    // column's collection of components. This offers
    // us the ability to delete an entire set of
    // components for a given column, or to check the
    // state of each component, which lets us determine
    // what the user has selected.
    //
    Vector field_components;

    // An array of possible data types.
    //
    String[] types = { "CHAR",
                       "TEXT",
                       "INT",
                       "REAL" };
    // A lookup table to correlate data type
    // names with their corresponding constants
    // in the Msql class definition.
    //
    Hashtable typeHash;
```

```
/**
 *
 * FieldPanel - Constructs a new FieldPanel.
 *
 */
public FieldPanel() {

    // Initialize the Vector that we're
    // using to keep track of each row we
    // add to the grid of column definition
    // components.
    //
    field_components = new Vector();

    // Set the layout manager for the
    // FieldPanel.
    //
    setLayout( new BorderLayout() );

    // Set up the lookup table that correlates
    // the Msql constants to String values.
    //
    typeHash = new Hashtable();
    typeHash.put(new Integer(Msql.CHAR), "CHAR");
    typeHash.put(new Integer(Msql.TEXT), "TEXT");
    typeHash.put(new Integer(Msql.INT),  "INT");
    typeHash.put(new Integer(Msql.REAL), "REAL");

    // Add a panel to this FieldPanel which will
    // contain the "New Column" button.
    //
    Panel button_panel = new Panel();
    button_panel.setSize(new Dimension(50, 100));
    add(button_panel, "North");

    // Add the "New Column" button.
    //
    Button new_field = new Button("New Column");
    button_panel.add(new_field);

    // Add an actionListener to deal with users
    // pressing the button.
    //
    new_field.addActionListener(
        new newFieldWatcher() );

    // Create a panel to hold the field
    // definition components, and give it
    // a GridLayout with 1 row and 4 columns,
    // which will hold the initial column
    // headers.
    //
```

```
column_panel = new Panel();
field_gl = new GridLayout(1, 4);
column_panel.setLayout(field_gl);

// Add the column headers.
//
column_panel.add(new Label("Column Name"));
column_panel.add(new Label("Column Type"));
column_panel.add(new Label("Column Width"));
column_panel.add(new Label("Delete Column"));

// Add one blank field.
//
addField();

// Add the column panel to this FieldPanel.
//
add(column_panel, "Center");

}
```

The addField() method has two signatures; one is used to add a blank field, and the other to add a field with values. This is one of the weak spots of the program; when an MsqlTables object calls this in rapid succession, such as when adding all of the fields for a given table, the Frame flashes quite a bit, since addField() packs the Frame each time.

```
/**
 *
 * addField - This method signature adds a blank
 * field by invoking the other method with blank
 * values.
 *
 */
public void addField() {
    addField("", Msql.CHAR, 0);
}

/**
 *
 * addField - Add a new column (aka field)
 * definition to the list of columns.
 *
 * @param col_name the column name
 * @param col_type the column data type
 * @param col_len the column length
 *
 */
public void addField(String col_name,
                     int col_type,
                     int col_len) {
```

```
// Create a vector that will hold all
// of the components that make up this
// field definition.
//
Vector this_field = new Vector();

// Create a TextField for the column
// name.
//
TextField t = new TextField(16);
t.setText(col_name);

// Create a Choice component so the user can
// choose the data type.
//
Choice c = new Choice();

// Add each of the data types to the Choice
// object.
//
for (int i = 0; i < types.length; i++) {
    c.add(types[i]);
}

// Set the selected item in the Choice
// object to whatever was passed in as
// col_type.
//
c.select((String)
  typeHash.get(new Integer(col_type)));

// Create a TextField to let the user
// supply the column width.
//
TextField s = new TextField(4);
s.setText(Integer.toString(col_len));

// Column width is only applicable for
// TEXT or CHAR data types. If it's not
// one or the other, make it 'n/a' and
// disable it.
//
if (col_type != Msql.TEXT &&
    col_type != Msql.CHAR)
{
    s.setText("n/a");
    s.setEnabled(false);
}

// Create a button that the user can press to
// delete the column.
//
```

```
Button d = new Button("x");

// Increase the number of rows in the
// column_panel's layout manager.
//
field_gl.setRows( field_gl.getRows() + 1);

// Add each component to the column_panel,
// and also to the this_field Vector.
//
column_panel.add(t);
this_field.addElement(t);
column_panel.add(c);
this_field.addElement(c);
column_panel.add(s);
this_field.addElement(s);
column_panel.add(d);
this_field.addElement(d);

// Add the Vector (this_field) to the
// field_components Vector. this_field holds
// each component of this column, and now
// field_components can be used to retrieve
// them.
//
field_components.addElement(this_field);

// Add an actionListener to the delete button,
// passing in this_field, which the
// removeField() method can use to remove
// the column definition components from the
// column_panel.
//
d.addActionListener(
    new deleteFieldWatcher(this_field) );

// Invoke validate() and set the size of this
// FieldPanel and its parent to their preferred
// sizes. This is pretty sloppy, but it works.
//
validate();
setSize(getPreferredSize());
MsqlTables p = (MsqlTables) getParent();
if (p != null) {
    p.pack();
}

}
```

A FieldPanel keeps track of every component that is on the screen using a Vector called field_components. For every field, there's a Vector stored within the field_components Vector, so it's a Vector of Vectors, which is really no big deal. Basically, all this means is that there's a Vector for each field on the screen. This Vector contains references to each of the components that corresponds to a given field: the TextField with the name, the Choice with the data type, and the TextField with the size. These are the same components that are displayed on the screen, and the Vector simply contains references to them so their values can be easily retrieved when we build part of the CREATE TABLE statement here:

```
/**
 *
 * getFieldDefString - This method returns a field
 * definition string, suitable for insertion in a
 * CREATE TABLE statement.
 *
 */
public String getFieldDefString() {

    // Set up a StringBuffer to hold the text
    // of the field definition.
    //
    StringBuffer field_def = new StringBuffer();

    // Walk the field_components Vector, and add
    // each column definition.
    //
    for (int i = 0;
         i < field_components.size();
         i++)
    {

        // Each element of field_components is
        // yet another Vector that consists of
        // three components; the column name, the
        // data type, and the column width.
        //
        Vector field =
            (Vector) field_components.elementAt(i);

        // Retrieve each component and its
        // associated value
        //
        TextField t = (TextField) field.elementAt(0);
        String fieldname = t.getText();

        Choice c    = (Choice) field.elementAt(1);
        String fieldtype = c.getSelectedItem();

        TextField s = (TextField) field.elementAt(2);
        String fieldlen  = s.getText();
```

```
                    // Since other datatypes have a width that is
                    // determined by the data engine, we are only
                    // interested in what the user supplied as the
                    // width if we're dealing with a TEXT or CHAR
                    // datatype.
                    //
                    if (fieldtype.equals("CHAR") ||
                        fieldtype.equals("TEXT"))
                    {

                        field_def.append(fieldname + " " +
                                            fieldtype +
                                    " (" + fieldlen + ")");

                    } else {

                        field_def.append(fieldname + " " +
                                            fieldtype);

                    }

                    // put a comma between each column
                    // definition, unless we're on the
                    // last element.
                    //
                    if (i+1 < field_components.size()) {
                        field_def.append(", ");
                    }
                }

                // return the StringBuffer as a String object.
                //
                return field_def.toString();

        }
```

The `removeAllFields()` method traverses the `field_components` Vector, and invokes `removeField()` for each field it finds in the `Vector`.

```
        /**
         *
         * removeAllFields - Walk through the
         * field_components Vector and delete every column
         * component.
         *
         */
        public void removeAllFields() {
            while (field_components.size() > 0) {
                removeField(
                    (Vector) field_components.elementAt(0));
            }
        }
```

The `removeField()` method not only removes the component that corresponds to a given field from the display, but also removes it from the `field_components Vector`.

```
/**
 *
 * removeField - remove one of the column
 * definitions.
 *
 * @param field_vector components to remove
 *
 */
public void removeField (Vector field_vector) {

    // Walk the Vector, and remove each Component
    // from the column_panel.
    //
    for (int i = 0; i < field_vector.size(); i++) {
        column_panel.remove(
            (Component) field_vector.elementAt(i) );
    }

    // Remove the field_vector from the
    // field_components Vector.
    //
    field_components.removeElement(field_vector);

    // Reduce the number of rows in the
    // column_panel's GridLayout manager by one.
    //
    field_gl.setRows( field_gl.getRows() - 1);
}
```

The remaining methods in `FieldPanel` are event handlers for the New Field and Delete (the "x" button) buttons.

```
// An ActionListener for the "New Field" button;
// it calls addField() each time it's pressed.
//
class newFieldWatcher implements ActionListener {
    public void actionPerformed ( ActionEvent e ) {
        addField();
    }
}

// An ActionListener for each column's 'x' button.
// it deletes the corresponding column definition
// components.
//
class deleteFieldWatcher implements ActionListener {

    // The Vector containing all the components.
```

```
        Vector field_vector;

        // This class should be instantiated with
        // this constructor, so it can register the
        // field_vector Vector.
        //
        public deleteFieldWatcher (Vector v) {
            field_vector = v;
        }

        // Invoke removeField(), and then validate
        // the FieldPanel, resize it, and resize
        // the parent container.
        //
        public void actionPerformed ( ActionEvent e ) {
            removeField(field_vector);

            validate();
            setSize(getPreferredSize());
            MsqlTables p = (MsqlTables) getParent();
            if (p != null) {
                p.pack();
            }
        }
    }
    }
}

}
```

YesNoAlert.java

This class implements a rather quick and dirty alert box. The user is prompted with a message, and may choose Yes or No in response. When the user presses one of the buttons, the `Dialog` disappears, since `setVisible()` is called with a value of `false`. This keeps the object around long enough for the program that instantiated the object to check the `getState()` method and see what button the user pressed. A YesNoAlert object is shown in Figure 5.6.

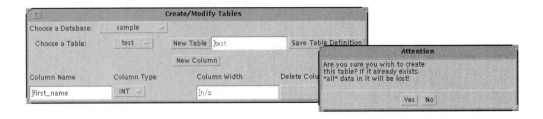

FIGURE 5.6 The `YesNoAlert` class is used within MsqlTables when a user response (Yes or No) is required.

```java
import java.awt.*;
import java.awt.event.*;

/**
 *
 * An Alert box with Yes/No buttons.
 *
 */
class YesNoAlert extends Dialog {

    public static int NO  = 0;
    public static int YES = 1;
    int state = NO;

    /**
     *
     * Constructs a new YesNoAlert.
     *
     * @param f parent Frame
     * @param message the message string
     *
     */
    public YesNoAlert(Frame f, String message) {

        // Call the superclass constructor - make the title
        // "Attention", and make the alert modal.
        //
        super(f, "Attention", true);

        // Use a BorderLayout.
        //
        setLayout(new BorderLayout());

        // Here, we're (ab)using? a TextArea for the message.
        //
        TextArea text =
          new TextArea(message, 4, 45,
                       TextArea.SCROLLBARS_NONE);
        text.setEditable(false);
        add("Center", text);

        // Create a panel to hold the Yes/No buttons.
        //
        Panel button_panel = new Panel();
        button_panel.setLayout(new FlowLayout());

        // Add a "yes" button, and instantiate a setState
        // object as an ActionListener, so it will handle
        // a button-press event.
        //
        Button yes = new Button("Yes");
        button_panel.add( yes );
```

```
        yes.addActionListener(
            new setState(YesNoAlert.YES) );

        // Add a "no" button, and instantiate a setState
        // object as an ActionListener, so it will handle
        // a button-press event.
        //
        Button no = new Button("No");
        button_panel.add( no );
        no.addActionListener(
            new setState(YesNoAlert.NO) );

        // Add the button_panel, and pack the alert.
        //
        add("South", button_panel);

        pack();
    }

/**
 *
 * getState - Return the state of the alert (yes or no
 * pressed).
 *
 */
public int getState() {
    return state;
}

/**
 *
 * setState - set the state of the alert in response to
 * a user pressing Yes or No.
 *
 */
class setState implements ActionListener {

    int state_value;

    /**
     *
     * Construct a new setState object with a fixed
     * state value. If the user presses the button,
     * the state_value gets set to the corresponding
     * value.
     *
     */
    public setState(int i) {
        state_value = i;
    }

    /**
```

```
         *
         * actionPerformed - set the state and make the
         * alert disappear.
         *
         */
        public void actionPerformed ( ActionEvent e ) {
            state = state_value;
            setVisible(false);
        }

    }

}
```

Alert.java

This class implements an even simpler alert than the YesNoAlert class. The user is given a
message, and is given a single button to press, labeled "OK." An instance of this class is shown
in Figure 5.7.

```
import java.awt.*;
import java.awt.event.*;

/**
 *
 * An Alert box with an OK button.
 *
 */
class Alert extends Dialog {

    /**
     *
     * Constructs a new Alert.
     *
     * @param f parent Frame
```

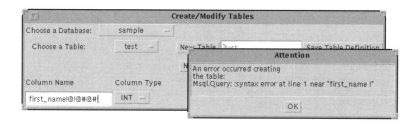

**FIGURE 5.7 The Alert class is used to inform the user when a condition
has occurred that needs attention. Here, the user has typed an invalid column name, which has caused the error shown in the Alert.**

```
     * @param message the message string
     *
     */
    public Alert(Frame f, String message) {

        // Call the superclass constructor - make the title
        // "Attention", and make the alert modal.
        //
        super(f, "Attention", true);

        // Use a BorderLayout.
        //
        setLayout(new BorderLayout());

        // Here, we're (ab)using? a TextArea for the message.
        //
        TextArea text =
          new TextArea(message, 4, 45,
                          TextArea.SCROLLBARS_NONE);
        text.setEditable(false);
        add("Center", text);

        // Create a panel to hold the button.
        //
        Panel button_panel = new Panel();
        button_panel.setLayout(new FlowLayout());

        // Add an OK button, and instantiate a setState
        // object as an ActionListener, so it will handle
        // a button press event.
        //
        Button ok = new Button("OK");
        button_panel.add( ok );
        ok.addActionListener( new okAction() );

        // Add the button_panel, and pack the alert.
        //
        add("South", button_panel);
        pack();
    }

    // Handle a button press by making the Alert go away.
    //
    class okAction implements ActionListener {
        public void actionPerformed ( ActionEvent e ) {
            setVisible(false);
        }
    }
}
```

Wrapped and Sealed with Masking Tape

MsqlJava is a great choice for Java development, and is especially good for applet development. It is well known that JDBC applet development is tricky under "older" (pre-JDK 1.1) Java-enabled browsers such as Netscape Navigator 2 and 3, as well as Microsoft's Internet Explorer 3.0. The JDBC classes are part of the `java.*` package, and browsers that support a pre-JDK 1.1 API cannot use JDBC directly because of this. While JDK 1.1 includes the JDBC driver manager in its locally installed classes, prior JDKs do not. As a result, pre-JDK 1.1 browsers have to load these classes over the network or have them installed locally by hand. It is a security violation to load classes into a local package such as `java.*`. As a result, programmers who want to use JDBC applets with older browsers need to modify the JDBC classes to use a different package name; this change has to be made to the driver as well.

This difficulty, coupled with other minor troubles, makes it very clumsy to use JDBC applets in pre-JDK 1.1 browsers. As a result, MsqlJava, which does not rely on JDBC, and which loads into a nonprivileged package (`msql.*`), is immune to these difficulties. The fact that MsqlJava does not rely on the JDBC classes offers another benefit: It is naturally somewhat leaner, since it is only loading classes from the `msql.*` package. None of this is meant to put down JDBC as a solution. Depending upon your concerns, you may have two choices when doing Java database development: go with a JDBC driver such as mSQL-JDBC, or use a custom API such as MsqlJava. Going with JDBC will give you database independence. Database independence means that you and/or your programmers don't need to learn a new API for each database. Further, applications can be easily migrated to a different database platform as needed. However, using a custom API such as MsqlJava may give you access to more database-specific features, since JDBC generalizes the interface across all database products. The choice is ultimately up to you; you must determine which API suits your needs best. In the next chapter, we'll explore the use of JDBC in building a generic database management system.

RDBMS: A Generic Query and Data Entry Tool with mSQL-JDBC

If the mission of a relational database management system is to not only store data, but to represent the relationships between that data, then it stands to reason that discoveries about those relationships can be used to build applications that rely less on the developer's explicitly defining those relationships within the application code, and more on the representation of those relationships within the database. This is quite easy with a high-end database product such as SQL Server, where those relationships are easily accessible. In fact, data servers such as SQL Server store the information about these relationships in tables, so that the information can be easily discovered at run time using SQL SELECT statements, or by invoking a *stored procedure*. A stored procedure is compiled code that resides on the server, and is written in the dialect of SQL that the database server speaks. In the case of SQL Server, it's written in a dialect known as Transact-SQL, which offers a very rich set of functionality that exceeds that of lightweight data engines such as Mini SQL.

Some time ago, one of us was engaged to work on a database system for a local Internet development firm. They entered the market at a time when database-enabled Web sites were starting to get hot, and they had been contracted to develop such a site for the first time. They chose excellent tools, including Mini SQL for the database and PHP/FI for developing dynamic Web documents. As we started to work on the project, we realized we'd need some sort of framework for developing data-entry interfaces, so we set about writing something called SimpleSQL. This system used a special definition file to define the tables within the database; in addition to table definitions, the file format offered a means of declaring the relationships between tables. All of this information, which is commonly referred to as *metadata*, is stored in tables that are created by a utility program. The utility program uses the information contained within the definition file to create the tables.

When the PHP/FI front end was asked to generate a data entry form for a given table, it would not only know what columns were in the table, what the size of each column was, and descriptive labels to use for the columns, but it would also understand when information from a related table was necessary. If a customer record required a popup menu for city names, it would be automatically generated from the related table.

SimpleSQL has had many offspring. The first was `Msql::RDBMS`, a version of SimpleSQL that uses MsqlPerl and the `CGI` Perl module to produce CGI query forms. When we started work on this book, we knew it was time to port it to Java and JDBC. It's far from the most exemplary work of JDBC coding. For one, JDBC itself defines methods for accessing the sort of metadata we need to generate the data entry screens. Since the mSQL-JDBC driver does not support this sort of metadata, it was necessary to rely on the same sort of add-on metadata tables that SimpleSQL and `Msql::RDBMS` use.

The Java version of RDBMS presents some issues that did not affect the prior versions. For one, both SimpleSQL and `Msql::RDBMS` used system table names (`systables`, `syscolumns`, `syskeys`, etc.) that conflicted with those used in SQL Server. This wasn't a problem with SimpleSQL and `Msql::RDBMS`, since it would only be used with Mini SQL. However, a version that uses JDBC is likely to be used with other data sources, so the table names have been changed to `RDBMSsystables`, `RDBMSsyscolumns`, and `RDBMSsyskeys`. Additionally, Simple SQL and Msql::RDBMS use mSQL-specific means of obtaining sequence values (i.e., `SELECT _seq FROM table_name`). Some JDBC data sources don't support this sort of thing at all, but under data servers such as Oracle and Sybase, this functionality is implemented differently. In order to maintain portability between database servers, the SQL statement that is used to fetch a new key is embedded in the `RDBMSsystables` table; this will make it easier going forward to offer versions for other database servers.

Programming with JDBC

Starting with release 1.1 of the Java Development Kit (JDK), the JDBC classes have been bundled with Java. The JDBC classes basically consist of a set of *interfaces* (these are similar to abstract classes, except for the fact that all of an interface's methods are abstract) that reside in the `java.sql` package. The JDBC interfaces are useless on their own; in order to make use of them, you will need a JDBC driver. A JDBC driver is simply a set of classes that implement all of the methods present in the JDBC interfaces.

Since each driver exposes only those methods defined in the JDBC interfaces, every driver looks exactly the same from the Java programmer's standpoint. In fact, the Java programmer will never need to deal directly with the JDBC driver's classes, except to register the driver with the JDBC driver manager. So, while the mSQL-JDBC driver is known as `COM.imaginary.sql.msql.MsqlDriver`, you only need to tell the `java.sql.DriverManager` about it and then invoke the `DriverManager`'s `getConnection()` method to obtain a connection to the database. From that point on, the objects you will deal with are instances of classes that are defined as part of the JDBC driver, and are implementations of classes such as `java.sql.Connection`, `java.sql.Statement`, and `java.sql.ResultSet`. However, since they implement methods from the interfaces, you will not need to refer to the `MsqlConnection` object as an `MsqlConnection`. Before you are given the connection by the `DriverManager`, it is cast to a `Connection`. This makes it very easy to change your programs to use a different driver; the only code that needs to change is the code that registers the driver and the invocation of the `getConnection()` method, which uses a special URL to specify which type of database server and which physical server to connect to.

About the Creator of mSQL-JDBC

George Reese, the author of mSQL-JDBC, the first JDBC driver ever written, is involved with travel both real and virtual. His favorite hobby is traveling, and he has visited Canada, China, Mexico, England, France, Germany, Sweden, Switzerland, Austria, Greece, Russia, and Yugoslavia. The experiences on these travels led to the creation of an Internet Travel Guide, available at:

    www.imaginary.com/~borg/TravelGuide/

When he's not working or traveling, George is often working on muds in one way or another. A mud is a multi-user virtual environment, and George not only maintains two muds, but he has also written developer's libraries for LPC, a programming language with which people can craft LPMuds. LPMuds can be developed without a great deal of programming knowledge, and are suitable for novice and expert alike. George's LPMud page can be found at:

    www.imaginary.com/~borg/LPMud/

There can be no doubt that George's eclectic experiences (a Philosophy major in college, he was heavily involved with college radio and TV) provided the kind of creative ferment that help produce software such as mSQL-JDBC and George's mud libraries. For the full story, George's on-line account of himself can be found at:

    www.imaginary.com/~borg

TIP Since work on the driver progresses continuously, you should check George's Web site (www.imaginary.com/~borg/Java) for the latest release. Each release of the driver will include complete installation instructions as well as example programs to verify the installation. Once you have installed mSQL-JDBC according to the instructions, you can begin working with the examples in this chapter.

Connecting to a Database with the mSQL-JDBC Driver

Once the mSQL-JDBC driver is installed correctly, you can begin using it within your Java applications. Before your application can do anything at all with JDBC, you must import the `java.sql.*` package. Then, within the body of the class, you must use the `Class.forName()` method to locate and load each JDBC driver you wish to use. You must supply the full name of the class for each driver. In this chapter, we'll be working solely with the mSQL-JDBC driver, so our `Class.forName()` invocation will be as follows:

```
Class.forName("com.imaginary.sql.msql.MsqlDriver");
```

The call to `Class.forName()` causes Java to locate and load the class, in case it hasn't already been loaded. Although we're not taking any output from the call to `forName()`, it performs another important function. Every JDBC driver includes a static initializer that is invoked automatically when the class is loaded. This causes the driver to register itself with the JDBC driver manager (`java.sql.DriverManager`), so the driver can be located by the driver manager at a later time. When you ask the driver manager for a driver, you pass it a special URL. This URL always starts with `jdbc:`, followed by the remainder of the URL, which is specific to the driver. The driver manager then invokes a method in each loaded driver that connects to the database if it's capable of reading the URL. The driver manager will use the first driver that is capable of connecting to the data source. If it fails to find one, an `SQLException` is thrown. The way the driver manager interacts with drivers allows you to write programs that load multiple JDBC drivers; these programs can be configured at run time to connect to a particular database by changing the URL. The URL that the mSQL-JDBC driver uses is of the form:

```
jdbc:msql://DATABASE_HOST:PORT/DATABASE_NAME
```

where the DATABASE_HOST is the name of the computer running the Mini SQL server, the PORT is the TCP Socket as reported by the `msqladmin` utility, and DATABASE_NAME is the name of the database that contains the tables with which you want to work. An example program, `connect.java`, is shown next; it makes a connection to an mSQL database. To compile it, you should type `javac connect.java`. To run it, you must type `java connect URL` where URL is the information needed to connect to your database, so you might type:

```
java connect jdbc:msql://localhost:1114/msql_sourcebook
```

You can also supply a userid and/or password after the URL, if you are using a data source that requires it. Generally, Mini SQL does not require a userid or password. Here's the source code to `connect.java`:

```
/**
 *
 * connect.java - make a connection to a database using JDBC.
```

```
     *
     */

import java.sql.*;

public class connect {

    public static void main( String argv[] ) {

        // The user should have passed in at least a URL,
        // and optionally, a user id and password.
        //
        if (argv.length < 1) {
            System.out.println(
                "Usage:\n" +
                "java connect URL [UID PWD]");
            System.exit(0);
        }

        String url, uid, pwd;

        // Get the URL.
        //
        url = argv[0];

        // If there's a user id, get it from argv[].
        //
        if (argv.length > 1) {
            uid = argv[1];
        } else {
            uid = "";
        }

        // If there's a password, get it from argv[].
        //
        if (argv.length > 2) {
            pwd = argv[2];
        } else {
            pwd = "";
        }

        // Now, we'll try to register the mSQL-JDBC driver;
        // if this fails, it will throw a
        // ClassNotFoundException.
        //
        try {

            // Register the mSQL-JDBC Driver.
            //
```

```
        Class.forName(
            "com.imaginary.sql.msql.MsqlDriver");

    } catch (ClassNotFoundException e) {

        e.printStackTrace();
        System.exit(0);

    }

    // If the driver class was loaded okay, we can now
    // move on and try to make a connection to the
    // database server. This could throw an SQLException
    // if it fails.
    //
    try {

        // Get a java.sql.Connection from the Driver
        // Manager.
        //
        Connection conn =
            DriverManager.getConnection(url, uid, pwd);

    } catch (SQLException e) {

        e.printStackTrace();
        System.exit(0);

    }

  }

}
```

Issuing a Query with the mSQL-JDBC Driver

In order to demonstrate how to issue a query and process its results in mSQL-JDBC, it will be necessary to introduce two more objects here: `Statement` and `ResultSet`. In the last example, we created a `Connection` object by invoking the driver manager's `getConnection()` method. Using the `Connection` object, you can create a `Statement` object, which can be used to execute SQL queries. The `Statement` object offers two methods of prime interest: `executeUpdate()` and `executeQuery()`. The `executeUpdate()` method is used to send queries that aren't expected to produce results, such as `DROP TABLE`, `CREATE TABLE`, `UPDATE`, `INSERT`, and `DELETE`. The `executeQuery()` method is generally used for `SELECT` statements, and it returns a `ResultSet` object.

The `ResultSet` object offers a method to iterate over each row; it's called `next()`. There is no `previous()` method, unfortunately. JDBC only allows you to traverse the result set in one direction. If you need to scroll backwards, you will need to roll your own buffering scheme. In practice, as will be seen with the RDBMS application, the `next()` method is sufficient for most applications.

Every time you invoke the `next()` method, the next row in the result set is fetched, and you can retrieve column values from that row by using any one of several methods, such as `getInt()` and `getString()`. These methods will try to return the data in the format you request (`String`, `int`, `Date`, etc.), irrespective of the underlying data type. However, you should use caution when making these sorts of implicit conversions, as it does not make sense to perform conversions between wildly different types of data. Each of the "get" methods are available in two flavors. In one flavor, you pass in the column name you wish to retrieve; the other (my favorite) requires you to use an index that corresponds to the column's position in the row. If your `SELECT` statement was "`SELECT name, id FROM customer`" and you wanted the id for the current row, you could use either `getInt("id")` or `getInt(2)`.

Notice that unlike arrays, the columns in a result set are numbered beginning with 1. The JDBC spec recommends that you only fetch columns in the same order in which they appear in the `SELECT` statement. For this reason, and since fetching by column name requires the driver to match the column name to its position, which involves extra overhead, we recommend using the column position wherever possible. Table 6.1 lists all "get" methods, with explanations (`colIndex` refers to the column index, and `colName` refers to the column name).

Table 6.1 The Variety of "Get" Methods that May Be Issued Against a ResultSet Object

Method	Return Type(or Class)	Explanation
getAsciiStream(int colIndex) getAsciiStream(String colName)	java.io.InputStream	Returns the column value as an ASCII stream
getBigDecimal(int colIndex, int scale) getBigDecimal(String colName, int scale)	java.lang.BigDecimal	Returns the column value as a BigDecimal with the specified scale
getBinaryStream(int colIndex) getBinaryStream(String colName)	java.io.InputStream	Returns the column value as a binary stream
getBoolean(int colIndex) getBoolean(String colName)	boolean	Returns the column value as boolean

Continues

Table 6.1 The Variety of "Get" Methods that May Be Issued Against a ResultSet Object (*Continued*)

Method	Return Type(or Class)	Explanation
getByte(int colIndex) getByte(String colName)	byte	Returns the column value as a byte
getBytes(int colIndex) getBytes(String colName)	byte[]	Returns the column value as a byte array
getDate(int colIndex) getDate(String colName)	java.sql.Date	Returns the column value as a Date object
getDouble(int colIndex) getDouble(String colName)	double	Returns the column value as a double
getFloat(int colIndex) getFloat(String colName)	float	Returns the column value as a float
getInt(int colIndex) getInt(String colName)	int	Returns the column value as an int
getLong(int colIndex) getLong(String colName)	long	Returns the column value as a long
getObject(int colIndex) getObject(String colName)	java.lang.Object	Returns the column value as an Object
getShort(int colIndex) getShort(String colName)	short	Returns the column value as a short
getString(int colIndex) getString(String colName)	java.lang.String	Returns the column value as a String object
getTime(int colIndex) getTime(String colName)	java.sql.Time	Returns the column value as a Time object
getTimestamp(int colIndex) getTimestamp(String colName)	java.sql.Timestamp	Returns the column value as a Timestamp object
getUnicodeStream(int colIndex) getUnicodeStream(String colName)	java.io.InputStream	Returns the column value as a stream of Unicode characters

The following example program, query.java, uses the Connection object to get a Statement. Then it issues a DROP TABLE statement for a table that may or may not exist, and creates the table. The DROP TABLE is there so you can run this example many times without running into problems, since this program will create the table and add data to it each time you execute it. After it creates the table, it will issue some SQL `INSERT` statements, and then finally, it will query the data and display the output all nicely formatted in a `Frame`. Figure 6.1 shows this program in action.

```java
/**
 *
 * query.java - make a connection to a database and issue
 * several updates and one query using JDBC. Display the
 * query results in a Frame.
 *
 */

import java.sql.*;
import java.awt.*;
import java.awt.event.*;

public class query {

    // Unlike the last example, we need to treat this class
    // as a proper class. In the last example, we did
    // everything within the main() method, but here, we
    // need to use an inner class. Everyone is happier if we
    // instantiate the query object and handle all of the
    // database and GUI stuff in the object.
    //
    public static void main( String argv[] ) {
        query q = new query(argv);
    }

    public query(String argv[]) {

        // The user should have passed in at least a URL,
        // and optionally, a user id and password.
        //
        if (argv.length < 1) {
            System.out.println(
                "Usage:\n" +
                "java query URL [UID PWD]");
            System.exit(0);
        }

        String url, uid, pwd;

        // Get the URL.
        //
        url = argv[0];

        // If there's a user id, get it from argv[].
        //
        if (argv.length > 1) {
```

```
    uid = argv[1];
} else {
    uid = "";
}

// If there's a password, get it from argv[].
//
if (argv.length > 2) {
    pwd = argv[2];
} else {
    pwd = "";
}

// Now, we'll try to register the mSQL-JDBC driver;
// if this fails, it will throw a
// ClassNotFoundException.
//
try {

    // Register the mSQL-JDBC Driver.
    //
    Class.forName(
        "com.imaginary.sql.msql.MsqlDriver");

} catch (ClassNotFoundException e) {

    e.printStackTrace();
    System.exit(0);

}

// If the driver class was loaded okay, we can now
// move on and try to make a connection to the
// database server. This could throw an SQLException
// if it fails.
//
try {

    // Get a java.sql.Connection from the Driver
    // Manager.
    //
    Connection conn =
        DriverManager.getConnection(url, uid, pwd);

    // Get a Statement object. We'll use this for
    // all subsequent updates and queries.
    //
    Statement stmt = conn.createStatement();

    // Try to drop the test table. If it doesn't
    // exist, we'll get an exception, so we are
```

```java
// explicitly ignoring any SQLException that is
// thrown here.
//
try {
    stmt.executeUpdate("DROP TABLE characters");
} catch (SQLException e) {
    // ignore the exception
}

// Now, use executeUpdate() to create the table,
// give it a unique index, and then send several
// inserts to add some data to it.
//
stmt.executeUpdate("CREATE TABLE characters " +
                   "(name CHAR(15), id INT)");
stmt.executeUpdate("CREATE UNIQUE INDEX ix_id "+
                   "ON characters (id)");

stmt.executeUpdate("INSERT INTO characters " +
                   "(name, id) " +
                   "VALUES ('Hagbard', 1)");
stmt.executeUpdate("INSERT INTO characters " +
                   "(name, id) " +
                   "VALUES ('Roger', 2)");
stmt.executeUpdate("INSERT INTO characters " +
                   "(name, id) " +
                   "VALUES ('Eric', 3)");
stmt.executeUpdate("INSERT INTO characters " +
                   "(name, id) " +
                   "VALUES ('Brian', 4)");
stmt.executeUpdate("INSERT INTO characters " +
                   "(name, id) " +
                   "VALUES ('Oscar', 5)");
stmt.executeUpdate("INSERT INTO characters " +
                   "(name, id) " +
                   "VALUES ('Bob', 6)");
stmt.executeUpdate("INSERT INTO characters " +
                   "(name, id) " +
                   "VALUES ('Sebastian', 7)");
stmt.executeUpdate("INSERT INTO characters " +
                   "(name, id) " +
                   "VALUES ('Shamrock', 8)");

// Now that we've added some data to the table,
// let's issue a query that will retrieve all
// the names and ids. Instead of displaying the
// output to System.out, we'll display a Frame,
// and add the data to it using a GridLayout.
//
Frame f = new Frame("Characters");
```

```
GridLayout g = new GridLayout(1, 2);
f.setLayout(g);

// Let's create two column headings, one for
// name, the other for id. We'll give them a
// nice big font, as well.
//
Label l_name = new Label("Name");
l_name.setFont( new Font("Helvetica",
                           Font.BOLD, 14));
f.add(l_name);

Label l_id = new Label("Id");
l_id.setFont( new Font("Helvetica",
                         Font.BOLD, 14));
f.add(l_id);

// Issue the SELECT statement, which will return
// a result set.
//
ResultSet rs = stmt.executeQuery(
    "SELECT name, id FROM characters");

// Add a grid row with the name and id for each
// row in the result set.
//
while (rs.next()) {

    // Add a new row to the GridLayout.
    //
    g.setRows( g.getRows() + 1);

    // Get the name value as a String.
    //
    String name = rs.getString(1);

    // Create a Label using the value, and add
    // it to the Frame.
    //
    Label n = new Label(name);
    f.add(n);

    // Get the id value as a String.
    //
    String id = rs.getString(2);

    // Create a Label using the value, and add
    // it to the Frame.
    //
    Label i = new Label(id);
    f.add(i);
```

```
            }

            // Attach a listener that will be used to intercept
            // events to close the Frame.
            //
            f.addWindowListener(new WinEventHandler() );

            f.pack();
            f.show();

        } catch (SQLException e) {

            e.printStackTrace();
            System.exit(0);

        }

    }

    // This will take care of handling the event that is
    // generated when the user closes the Frame.
    //
    class WinEventHandler extends WindowAdapter {
        public void windowClosing(WindowEvent e) {
            System.exit(0);
        }
    }

}
```

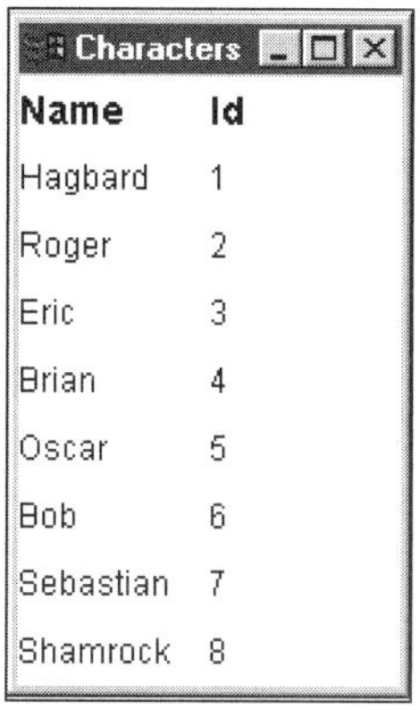

Name	Id
Hagbard	1
Roger	2
Eric	3
Brian	4
Oscar	5
Bob	6
Sebastian	7
Shamrock	8

Characters

FIGURE 6.1 The results of the query performed in query.java are displayed here in a Frame.

Running RDBMS

In this chapter, we won't be digging too deeply into the inner workings of RDBMS. Since a more in-depth study is provided in Appendix B, we're going to present an overview of how to use RDBMS. Unfortunately, this puts you in the role of a "mere user" for a little while. But don't worry, after you look at the superficial workings of this application, you can get under the hood of RDBMS by reading the annotated source code in Appendix B.

The RDBMS application, in accordance with JavaSoft's recommended package-naming convention, resides in a package that reflects the domain name with which the author is affiliated (as220.org), and the application name (rdbms). As a result, the package name is ORG.as220.rdbms, and the RDBMS classes can be imported into your applications with:

```
import ORG.as220.rdbms.*;
```

You can also explicitly refer to one of the classes with the full package name, as will be seen shortly. The RDBMS application won't run on just any mSQL database table. mSQL does not provide any representation of the relationships between tables, so it is necessary for the RDBMS system to supply that functionality. The RDBMSmSQLInit class will parse a schema definition table, and will generate the tables specified therein. As it generates the tables, it also creates and adds records to the system metadata tables, RDBMSsystables, RDBMSsyscolumns, and RDBMSsyskeys.

> **TIP** In order to run this example, you should make sure that your current directory is the /eg/ch06 directory, which you should copy from the CD-ROM onto a local drive. Instructions for installing the examples that are included on the CD-ROM can be found in Appendix E.

If you examine a directory listing of the /eg/ch06 directory, you'll notice that there are a few files there, and a directory named ORG. This is the top of the ORG.as220.rdbms package, and in order to use these examples you will need to do one of two things: either include the complete path to ch06 in your CLASSPATH (e.g., something similar to C:\EG\CH06 or /home/username/eg/ch06), or include the current directory (.) in your CLASSPATH. If you choose to include "." in your CLASSPATH, you will have to ensure that your current working directory is the /eg/ch06 directory, or Java will not be able to find the classes.

Schema Definition Files

The /eg/ch06 directory also contains a file named schema.def. This is the file that is used to create the tables within a given database. The utility class, ORG.as220.rdbms .RDBMSmSQLInit, parses the data contained in this file, and generates the tables. The entries in the schema.def table are of two forms. The first entry is a table header; it includes the word "table," followed by the name of the table and a descriptive name for the table, such as

```
table:publication:Publications
```

Immediately following the table lines should be one or more column definitions. The `ORG.as220.rdbms.RDBMSmSQLInit` class continues adding columns to the last table defined, until it encounters a new table definition. Column definitions include the column name, the column data type, and the column width (if applicable—it's not necessary for data types such as `int`). It also includes any additional arguments to the column definition, such as `NOT NULL`, followed by the description of the column, the type of key (if any), and a 0 or 1 to indicate whether the column should be displayed as a search term when RDBMS builds an interactive query screen. Here are a couple of sample column definitions for a publications table:

```
pub_name:char:30:not null:Publication Name:LABEL:1
pub_id:int::not null:Unique Id:PRIMARY:0
```

When you run the `ORG.as220.rdbms.RDBMSmSQLInit` utility, it not only creates the tables listed in the definition file, but also the system tables that hold information about the tables you create. These tables are consulted by the RDBMS system at run time, and are used to build generic data entry screens that are "aware" of the relationships between the tables. Tables 6.2 to 6.4 explain each of the system tables.

Table 6.2 The `RDBMSsystables` Table Definition

Column	Type	Length	Purpose
tbl_name	char	32	This is the name of the table.
tbl_description	char	128	This is a descriptive name for the table.
tbl_getnextkey	char	128	This is a complete SQL statement that can be sent to the server to get a new unique key for the table. mSQL uses something of the form `SELECT _seq FROM table_name`. Keeping this sort of information in the table makes it easy to support other database servers in addition to mSQL.

Table 6.3 The `RDBMSsyscolumns` Table Definition

Column	Type	Length	Purpose
col_name	char	32	This is the name of the column.
col_label	char	128	This is a descriptive name for the column.

Continues

Table 6.3 The `RDBMSsyscolumns` Table Definition (*Continued*)

Column	Type	Length	Purpose
col_type	char	4	The mSQL data type for this column.
col_len	int	n/a	For CHAR and TEXT data types, this will be the length of the column. For other types, it will be blank or 0.
tbl_name	char	32	The table to which this column belongs.
col_query	int	n/a	If this is set to 1, then the column will appear on automatically generated query forms.
col_disp	int	n/a	This is reserved for future use, and will control whether the column should appear on automatically generated output, such as a report.

Table 6.4 The `RDBMSsyskeys` Table Definition

Column	Type	Length	Purpose
col_name	char	32	This is the name of the column.
tbl_name	char	32	The table to which this column belongs.
key_type	char	15	This can be any one of PRIMARY, FOREIGN, or LABEL. If it is PRIMARY, then it indicates that this column is the primary key for the specified table. If it is FOREIGN, then it indicates that the column is a reference to another table's primary key. When the RDBMS system resolves this, it looks for a table that has this column as its primary key. If the key_type is set to LABEL, then the column is used as a descriptive name in picklists and other situations that require user interaction.

The /eg/ch06 directory contains a sample schema definition file, called schema.def. The contents of this file are shown next. The tables that are defined for this example have been designed for a fictional subscription management system. It allows you to track information such as recipient name and address, publications, shippers, and subscriptions.

```
#
# schema.def
#
# Start a table definition with:
#
# table:table_name:table_description
#
```

```
# where:
#
# table_name         is the name of the table
# table description is the description of the table
#
# define each column with:
# name:type:width:args:desc:key_type:int1
#
# where:
#
# name         is the name of the column
# type         is a valid mSQL data type
# width        is the width of the column, if applicable
# args         additional args to the column
#              definition, like 'not null'
# desc         is a short description of the table
# key_type     type of key: PRIMARY, LABEL, FOREIGN
# int1         non-zero to prompt for this column in queries
#


# This sample schema is designed to support a subscription
# system, and will represent the relationships between
# recipients, publications, and other related elements.
#


# the publication table
table:publication:Publications
pub_name:char:30:not null:Publication:LABEL:1
pub_id:int::not null:Unique Id:PRIMARY:0

# the shipper table
table:shipper:Shippers
shp_name:char:30:not null:Shipper:LABEL:1
shp_id:int::not null:Unique Id:PRIMARY:0

# the Recipient table
#
table:recipient:Recipients
#
rec_id:int::not null:Unique Id:PRIMARY:0
rec_name:char:36:not null:Recipient:LABEL:1
rec_address1:char:36::Address Line One::0
rec_address2:char:36::Address Line Two::0
rec_city:char:32::City::1
rec_state:char:2::State::1
rec_zip:char:11::Zip Code::1
rec_ctry:char:20::Country::1
rec_phone:char:14::Phone::0
rec_fax:char:14::Fax::0
rec_email:char:64::E-mail Address::0

# the subscription table
table:subscription:Subscription
```

```
sub_id:int::not null:Unique Id:PRIMARY:0
rec_id:int::not null:Recipient:FOREIGN:1
shp_id:int::not null:Shipper:FOREIGN:1
pub_id:int::not null:Publication:FOREIGN:1
sub_copies:int::not null:Number of Copies::1
```

Initializing the Tables

The RDBMSmSQLInit class will parse this file, and create the corresponding tables in the database, including system metadata tables. Before you run this program, make sure at least one of two cases is true: your CLASSPATH includes a " . " in it, which corresponds to your current working directory, or your CLASSPATH includes the full path to the /eg/ch06 directory. Before you can run the file through RDBMSmSQLInit, you should create a database called rdbms using the msqladmin tool, and ensure that you have read/write access to it in the msql.acl file.

In order to run the schema.def file through the RDBMSmSQLInit class, you should change your current working directory to /eg/ch06, which contains the schema.def file, and say something like:

```
java ORG.as220.rdbms.RDBMSmSQLInit URL FILENAME
```

where URL is equal to the mSQL-JDBC URL for your data source, such as:

```
jdbc:msql://localhost:1114/rdbms
```

And where FILENAME is the name of the schema file, such as:

```
schema.def
```

The following example shows an example session with RDBMSmSQLInit. Notice that the long line has been wrapped with the \ character, and bash-2.00$ is the shell prompt, similar to the MS-DOS/Win32 C:\> prompt. You should type the whole thing as one line, but don't type the \ character or hit enter between the lines, unless you are using a Unix shell that understands it, such as /bin/sh or /usr/local/bin/bash.

```
bash-2.00$ java ORG.as220.rdbms.RDBMSmSQLInit \
           jdbc:msql://localhost:1114/rdbms schema.def
Defining table: publication
Defining table: shipper
Defining table: recipient
Defining table: subscription
bash-2.00$
```

After you've generated the tables, they will be completely devoid of data, so you can either enter your own sample data by hand, or you can use the handy load_data.sql file to put some of our sample data in. The load_data.sql file is suitable for feeding into the msql monitor utility, and you can process it with the command:

```
msql rdbms < load_data.sql
```

The contents of the load_data.sql file are shown next, but the file is included on the CD-ROM, in the /eg/ch06 directory. Notice that in the following code, the SEQUENCE is dropped and recreated from each table. This is done to ensure that the sequence is in sync with the id values that actually reside in the tables.

```
# load_data.sql
#
# This will populate the chapter 6 example tables with
# enough data to get you started.
#

# The publication table.
#
DELETE FROM publication\g

INSERT INTO publication
            (pub_name, pub_id)
    VALUES ('Ask Dr. Cthulu', 1)\g

INSERT INTO publication
            (pub_name, pub_id)
    VALUES ('The Realist', 2)\g

INSERT INTO publication
            (pub_name, pub_id)
    VALUES ('Militia Wear Weekly', 3)\g

INSERT INTO publication
            (pub_name, pub_id)
    VALUES ('Collectible Troll Review', 4)\g

INSERT INTO publication
            (pub_name, pub_id)
    VALUES ('New Totemic Advisor', 6)\g

DROP SEQUENCE FROM publication\g

CREATE SEQUENCE ON publication STEP 1 VALUE 7\g


# The shipper table
#
DELETE FROM shipper\g

INSERT INTO shipper
            (shp_name, shp_id)
    VALUES ('DHL', 1)\g

INSERT INTO shipper
            (shp_name, shp_id)
    VALUES ('Federal Express', 2)\g

INSERT INTO shipper
            (shp_name, shp_id)
```

```
       VALUES ('UPS', 3)\g

INSERT INTO shipper
           (shp_name, shp_id)
     VALUES ('US Postal Service', 4)\g

INSERT INTO shipper
           (shp_name, shp_id)
     VALUES ('Airborne Express', 5)\g


DROP SEQUENCE FROM shipper\g

CREATE SEQUENCE ON shipper STEP 1 VALUE 6\g

# The Recipient table
#
DELETE FROM recipient\g

INSERT INTO recipient
           (rec_id, rec_name, rec_address1, rec_address2,
            rec_city, rec_state, rec_zip, rec_ctry,
            rec_phone, rec_fax, rec_email)
     VALUES (2, 'Brian Jepson', '50 Hudson Street', '',
            'Providence', 'RI', '02909', 'USA', '', '',
            'bjepson@ids.net')\g

INSERT INTO recipient
           (rec_id, rec_name, rec_address1, rec_address2,
            rec_city, rec_state, rec_zip, rec_ctry,
            rec_phone, rec_fax, rec_email)
     VALUES (3, 'Dr. Cthulu', 'Under the Bridge', '',
            'Quonochautaug', 'RI', '02813', 'USA',
            '(401) 555-1111', '(401) 555-1112',
            'cthulu@cthulathon.gov')\g

INSERT INTO recipient
           (rec_id, rec_name, rec_address1, rec_address2,
            rec_city, rec_state, rec_zip, rec_ctry,
            rec_phone, rec_fax, rec_email)
     VALUES (4, 'Glen Runciter', '100 Armstrong Blvd.', '',
            'Milhousville', '', '', 'Luna',
            '+0094 555-1234', '+0094 555-1235',
            'glen@runciter.com.luna')\g

DROP SEQUENCE FROM recipient\g

CREATE SEQUENCE ON recipient STEP 1 VALUE 4\g

# The subscription table
#
DELETE FROM subscription\g
```

```
INSERT INTO subscription
          (sub_id, rec_id, shp_id, pub_id, sub_copies)
     VALUES (1,2,4,1,5)\g

INSERT INTO subscription
          (sub_id, rec_id, shp_id, pub_id, sub_copies)
     VALUES (2,3,1,6,1)\g

DROP SEQUENCE FROM subscription\g

CREATE SEQUENCE ON subscription STEP 1 VALUE 3\g
```

Running the System

Once you've added some data to the tables, you can begin working with the system. You'll be able to add, delete, and search within the system. In order to start the system, you should ensure that your CLASSPATH is set as explained in the previous section. From within the /eg/ch06 directory, you should issue the following command:

```
java ORG.as220.rdbms.RDBMS URL DB
```

where URL is the same JDBC URL you used for the RDBMSmSQLInit example, and DB is the name of the database. In this example, you should use rdbms as the database name. If your mSQL server is on the localhost, and it is using the root port (1114), you can say:

```
java ORG.as220.rdbms.RDBMS \
     jdbc:msql://localhost:1114/rdbms rdbms
```

(The long line has been separated with a \ and broken up, as in the previous example. If your shell doesn't understand this, remove the \ and type it as one line.)

The first screen that you will see in the system is rather modest, and is shown in Figure 6.2. There's a little bit of text to explain what's going on, a Choice object, and two Button objects. Using the system is quite simple. If you want to add a new row to a table, choose the table's name and click the Add button. To search for a row in the table, click on the Query button.

Figure 6.3 shows the screen that appears when you click the Add button for the Recipients table. You can click the Save button to save the record you're working on, and the New Record button will bring up a blank form. The Delete button will delete the current record, and you can

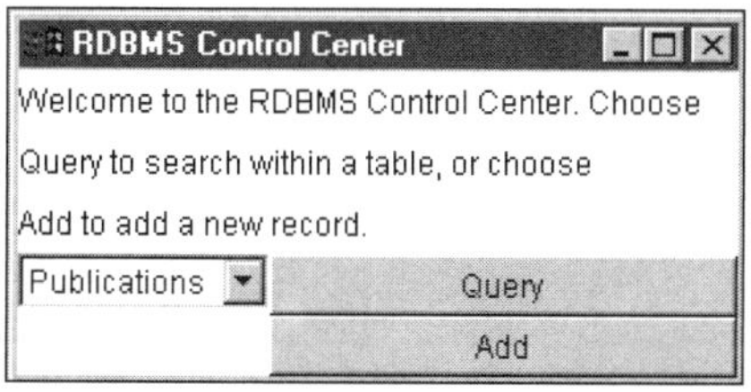

FIGURE 6.2 The main RDBMS screen.

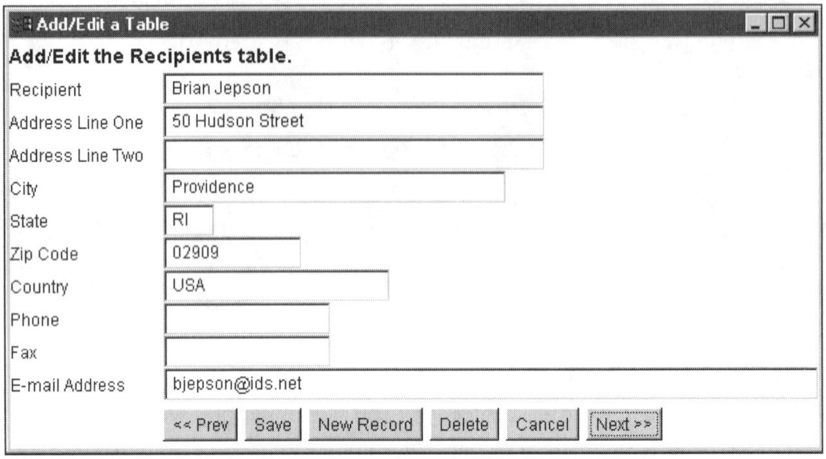

FIGURE 6.3 Adding or editing a recipient.

use the Next and Previous buttons to skip through the table. The Cancel button will dismiss the screen, and any status messages will appear in the console (Win32) or shell window (Unix) in which you started the program.

The RDBMS system, while quite generic, offers fairly sophisticated querying capabilities. If you choose a table, and then click on the Query button, a query window appears. The query window for the subscriptions table is shown in Figure 6.4. Only columns that were marked as "queryable" in the schema.def file show up as query terms.

In Figure 6.4, the recipient, shipper, and publication terms are left blank, and the only search term is "Number of Copies." When you click on the Query button, a list of subscriptions will appear for all recipients receiving more than one copy of the publication. This is shown in Figure 6.5. If you click on one of the results, and then click on the Edit button, the Add/Edit screen will bring the selected record up so you can view or edit it.

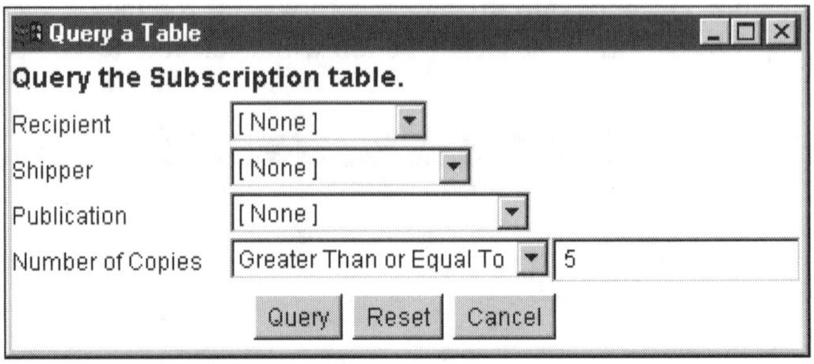

FIGURE 6.4 Querying the subscription table.

FIGURE 6.5 The Query Results screen.

Conclusion

The RDBMS, SimpleSQL, and the `Msql::RDBMS` packages represent an attempt at building an extensible and simple development framework for Internet and Intranet database development. These packages will evolve towards a point where they are fully in sync, and can be used with Mini SQL, as well as other database management systems, such as SQL Server. They will continue to be offered under the GNU General Public License, which means they can be freely redistributed for no charge. As time goes on, expect to see a Perl version that uses the DBI rather than MsqlPerl; this will ensure that it remains compatible with Mini SQL while still offering compatibility with other database packages. At some point, the schema definition file will be replaced by a user interface that allows the tables to be created and modified, hopefully in a fashion that preserves any existing data within the affected table.

From Zero to Sixty in Perl

It's probably quite difficult to find a Web developer who hasn't heard of Perl, since it has emerged as one of the most popular languages for developing CGI scripts. CGI stands for *Common Gateway Interface*; it is a standardized interface for developing executable Web content that runs on the Web server rather than on the Web browser. Java and JavaScript are two examples of Web content that runs within the browser; CGI scripts execute on the server, and typically process data that come from an HTML data entry form. The results of a CGI script are some form of content the browser understands, usually an HTML document, but sometimes a graphics file such as a GIF or JPEG.

About Perl

Perl wasn't designed as a CGI scripting language, but was called into being by its creator, Larry Wall, to produce reports. Hence its name, "Practical Extraction and Reporting Language." It borrows a lot of ideas from text-processing programs such as *awk* and *sed*, but also resembles C and the Bourne Shell. You don't need to master Perl to do a lot of stuff with it; the Bible of Perl, *Programming Perl*, sports a 34-page first chapter that gives you enough information to Improve Your Life with Perl. We think it says something about the practicality of a language (and the quality of the book) if you can get that far in 34 pages.

The core Perl distribution is available in source form for many platforms, including Unix, Windows NT, OS/2, and Amiga. Ports are available for other platforms. Perl is distributed under two public licenses (GPL and the Artistic License), which allow Perl to be freely redistributed, but does not impose similar restrictions upon products developed with Perl.

One of the wonderful features of Perl is that it is easily extended using native Perl modules as well as C extensions. C extensions can be accessed through Perl modules, so anything you add to your installation either looks like a library module or an extension to Perl itself.

While Perl imposes no restriction upon code you write with Perl, the generosity of Perl's authors has become quite infectious. This, coupled with the fact that Perl is quite extensible, has led to a plethora of useful modules that can be obtained from the *Comprehensive Perl Archive Network* (CPAN), a global collection of cooperating FTP archive sites. The Perl community provides very high-quality documentation and support; besides the manpages, there are several FAQs (Frequently Asked Questions) available as well as smaller documents, called FMTEYEWTKAs (Far More Than Everything You've Ever Wanted To Know About . . .).

TIP All of the FAQs and related documents can be found on the perl.com site, which is available at:

```
http://www.perl.com
```

This site also includes Tom Christiansen's CPAN Multiplexer; if you supply a URL similar to the following (note that the last slash is significant), you will be automatically redirected to a nearby CPAN site:

```
www.perl.com/CPAN/
```

You can also include any standard CPAN subdirectory, and the multiplexer will not only redirect you to the site, but place you in the appropriate directory. Here's a URL that will take you to a CPAN directory containing all of the CPAN modules, organized by module name:

```
www.perl.com/CPAN/modules/by-module
```

As of version 5.004, Perl ships with a CPAN module, which allows you to peruse, select, and install a module from CPAN, without all that tedious mucking about in FTP.

Once you've read all the documentation, it doesn't end there. The `comp.lang.perl.misc`, `comp.lang.perl.modules`, and `comp.lang.perl.tk` newsgroups are excellent sources of information, especially if you've done your homework first. So much information is already available in the various FAQs, which cover everything from basic Perl techniques to solving CGI problems, that your posts are likely to get little attention if the answer is in the FAQ. This, as they say, is a FAQ of life. However, if you're posting a well-formed query that raises a question that isn't dealt with elsewhere, you will get a courteous and informative response, often quite quickly. Perl's culture grew out of a spirit of sharing and enjoying; nowhere does this shine through more than in the newsgroups. A Perl programmer never stands quite so tall as when he stoops to help a newbie . . .

Scope and Purpose of this Section

The following chapters will demonstrate several ways you can use Mini SQL from Perl. There are three modules of interest here, and each will be covered in its own chapter. The first is the MsqlPerl module, which provides an API that closely resembles the C API for mSQL. The second is the DBI::mSQL module, which is the mSQL implementation of the Perl DBI. The DBI is a database-independence module for Perl, similar to ODBC. Finally, the Win32::ODBC module will be covered, which allows the use of ODBC data sources from Perl for Win32 (Windows NT, Windows 95). Win32::ODBC can be used with the mSQL ODBC driver to access mSQL data from Perl on Win32 operating systems.

History Lesson (Let the Stories Tell Themselves)

MsqlPerl represents the present state of database access in Perl. Back in the old days, in the age of Perl version 4.something-or-another, a database-enabled version of Perl often involved building a new binary, statically linked to the database code. With the advent of Perl 5.00x, database connectivity could be added to Perl using dynamically loaded modules, such as MsqlPerl.

When a new binary was required for every database product, you could end up with a collection of perls, such as sybperl, oraperl, isqlperl, and so forth. Using Perl 5's dynamic loading, you can use one Perl binary, but choose the database module you want to work with. In theory, you should be able to load multiple database modules and connect to more than one database product at a time. However, this is not good enough; each database product has its own peculiar API, which means you have to learn something new each time you work with a different database product. Something new is changing all that, called DBI. DBI is a database-independence module for Perl, which lets you work with various database products using the same API. Regardless of the database, you invoke the same method to send a query, to fetch a row, or to obtain metadata information from the database.

The DBI consists of two parts: a driver, which is the DBI module itself; and a database driver, usually DBD::something, such as DBD::mSQL. The DBD provides all of the glue to connect the driver manager to the database. The DBI is the future of database connectivity in Perl; it provides a common, consistent interface, which is easy to use and expressive.

Programming Perl

This chapter can hardly suffice as a comprehensive tutorial or reference for the language. Instead, it will focus in on many of the components of Perl that are used in the examples in the following chapters. If you see a Perl in your future, it is wise to avail yourself of the copious online documentation and a good book, such as *Programming Perl* by Larry Wall, Tom Christiansen, and Randal L. Schwartz. It's the definitive book that covers all of the details of the language, and provides a comprehensive reference as well.

Installing Perl

The Perl core distribution can be obtained during a visit to http://www.perl.com. You should follow the links to the "Perl Language Home Page," and then follow the links to "Software." The core distribution includes source code that should build on any modern Unix, as well as Windows NT/95, OS/2, and the Amiga. Ports are available (also from this page) for DOS-based systems, the Macintosh, and other operating systems. Each distribution of Perl will include installation instructions, usually in a file conveniently called README.

Running Perl

There are many ways to run your Perl programs. Before we take a look at the various means, let's look at a really basic Perl program, the always reliable, somewhat ubiquitous, "hello, world" example.

```
print "hello, world\n";
```

This is a complete Perl program that displays the text `"hello, world"`, followed by a newline (the funny character `\n`). The double quotes are used to enclose the string expression, and the semicolon character, `;`, is used to explain to Perl that the statement is completed. The semicolon is used to separate statements in Perl, as it is in the C programming language.

When you're ready to run a Perl program, or Perl script, as they are often called, you need to feed it to your Perl interpreter. This can be done in several ways. For very simple programs, such as the "hello, world" example, you can start the Perl interpreter up and type your program in. At this point, we are going to assume that you have installed Perl on your machine, and have followed the installation instructions. If you've done so, the Perl interpreter should be installed and in your path. On almost any operating system, you can invoke Perl from your shell (or command prompt, under a Windows-esque operating system) by typing:

```
perl
```

Once you have done this, you can begin typing Perl commands to the interpreter. When you are finished, you should type the keystrokes needed to indicate the end of input (under Unix, this is Ctrl+D, and under Windows NT/95, it's Ctrl+Z). If you type in the Perl program shown earlier, it might look something like this under Unix (commands you type are shown in **bold**):

```
bash$ perl
print "hello, world\n";
^D
hello, world
bash$
```

Of course, this isn't the only way to run a small program with Perl. You can also start Perl with the `-e` switch, which allows you to supply a small program within single quotes (this may be handled differently under Windows NT and 95, which don't come with a shell, just a command processor that doesn't seem to handle single quotes too well).

```
perl -e 'print "hello, world\n";'
```

Under Windows NT/95, you might try

```
perl -e "print qq[hello, world\n];"
```

By far, the easiest way to deal with running your Perl programs is to save them in a file of some sort. You can create this file with your favorite editor, and name it anything you want. Under an operating system (Unix and its variants) that supports the "shebang" syntax for running scripts, you can include a shebang (#!), which should precede the path to the perl interpreter at the top of the program, followed by a newline and then the program itself.

```
#!/usr/bin/perl
print "hello, world\n";
```

The #! syntax is special magic that instructs your shell to use the specified interpreter to run the script. You will need to follow one more step to get this working; under Unix and similar operating systems, you must make the script executable (and readable, since the interpreter needs to read it as well) with the chmod command (assuming you saved it as hello.pl).

```
chmod +rx hello.pl
```

Then, assuming that the script is in your current directory, you can invoke it from the shell with something like:

```
./hello.pl
```

You can also supply a script name to Perl, as in:

```
perl hello.pl
```

The Win32 version of Perl includes a program called pl2bat, that will convert a Perl script into a batch file which invokes the perl interpreter. In any case, you should consult both your operating system's documentation and the documentation that accompanied the version of Perl you obtained for more information. You can also use the -c switch to have the interpreter compile, but not execute, the Perl script. This can be useful for finding syntax errors in your scripts. Another help is the -w switch; -w displays many useful warnings that can keep you from making silly mistakes.

Manpages and Their Friends

When you install Perl on your system, many manpages are installed that can be read with the man command. Under Win32, these are supplied as HTML files. The following section makes reference to manpages that are relevant to the topics being discussed, and these manpages should be perused for further study.

Variables in Perl

Relevant manpages: perldata, perlop.

Unlike many other languages, Perl doesn't put a lot of arbitrary constraints on how you use variables. You don't need to worry about declaring them, or even what their data type is; Perl will always evaluate them in the appropriate context. A string value can become a numeric value, and vice versa, depending on how you use it. Scalar variables are prefixed with the $ symbol. Perl uses prefixes such as $ to distinguish between various kinds of variables. It's probably easier to think of scalar variables as singular variables, as opposed to the other two kinds, which are plural, and are both arrays of sorts.

```
$real_rate = 1000;
print "You're getting paid $real_rate.\n";
$rate = "100";
$fantasy_rate = $rate * 100;
print "You'd like to get paid $fantasy_rate.\n";
```

In the example just shown, you may also notice that we're evaluating variables within quoted strings. This is a feature of Perl known as *variable substitution*, and it only occurs within certain types of quotes. Within such quotes, which includes double quotes, escape sequences such as \n (newline) are also expanded. This sort of expansion does not occur within single quotes.

Besides scalar (singular) data, Perl also supports plural kinds of data. The most simple of the two, and the one which may seem the most familiar, is the *array*. An array is a list of scalar values, which can be referenced by an index value, numbering from zero to the last element in the array (the number of elements in the array minus 1). Since an individual array element is singular, you must prefix it with a $ symbol. However, the array itself is prefixed with the @ symbol. Array indexes (subscripts) are supplied as numeric values between brackets. Here's some Perl code that defines some elements of the array @colors:

```
$colors[0] = 'red';
$colors[1] = 'green';
$colors[2] = 'blue';
```

Perl allows you to construct a list, which can be a comma-separated series of values within parentheses. This can be used to assign directly to an array.

```
@colors = ('red', 'green', 'blue');
```

Another type of array is the *hash*. Unlike regular arrays, which are subscripted by a numeric index, hashes are subscripted by a string value. As regular arrays are prefixed with the @ symbol, a hash is prefixed with the % symbol. Also, the indexes, or keys to the hash, are delimited with braces { } rather than the brackets [ ] used for arrays.

```
$salary{'Brian'} = 1000;
$salary{'Elmer'} = 900;
$salary{'Garth'} = 1200;
```

Like a regular array, you can fill a hash with data using a list. However, since each element of the hash includes a key and a value, it can get a little ugly.

```
%salary = ('Brian', 1000, 'Elmer', 900, 'Garth', 1200);
```

Fortunately, Perl provides an alternative to the comma, which can be used to make this a little more readable.

```
%salary = ('Brian' => 1000,
           'Elmer' => 900,
           'Garth' => 1200);
```

Those => symbols are synonyms for commas. In fact, you could say:

```
%salary =
    ('Brian' => 1000 => 'Elmer' => 900 => 'Garth' => 1200);
```

but that would be even less readable than just with the commas, wouldn't it?

Playing with Variables

Relevant manpages: perldata, perlop.

Once you've got your data into variables, it can be a lot of fun to play around with them. Perl provides many arithmetic operators that resemble those found in C and similar languages. Note that in the following examples, the values to be printed are followed by a comma and a quoted newline. The print operator will accept a list of values and concatenate them, placing no space between them.

```
$shoe_size = 9;

print $shoe_size + 1, "\n";    # print shoe_size + 1
print $shoe_size - 1, "\n";    # print shoe_size - 1
print ++$shoe_size, "\n";      # increment by one, then print
print $shoe_size++, "\n";      # print, then increment by one

$iq = $shoe_size * 2;    # set IQ to double the shoe size
$height = $iq / 4;       # set height to 1/4 IQ
```

You can have your own sort of fun with arrays; as seen earlier, you can pull out specific elements of an array, as in:

```
@colors = ('red', 'green', 'blue', 'orange');
print "$colors[0]\n";                    # prints 'red'
```

But if you simply say:

```
print @colors;
```

you'll get all of the elements concatenated together, as in:

```
redgreenblueorange
```

If you force the array to be interpreted as a scalar value, either by assigning it to a scalar or by using the scalar() function, you get the number of elements in the array.

```
$i = @colors;                    # gets 4
print "$i\n";
print scalar(@colors), "\n";     # also 4
```

Similarly, if you refer to $#colors, you get the index of the last element of the array.

```
print "$#colors\n"; # gets 3 (array is numbered 0-3)
```

You can also grab a slice of the array, as in:

```
print @colors[0,2], "\n";            # 0th and 2nd element
print @colors[0..2], "\n";           # 0-2nd element
print @colors[0..$#colors], "\n";    # 0-last element
```

It can be a lot nicer to separate the elements of the array with something like a newline. The `join()` function will, as its name implies, join all the elements of a list. Its first argument is the delimiter you wish to use, followed by the list. The `join()` function only puts the delimiter between elements, so there is no trailing delimiter (this is why we have so many occurrences of \n, including one before "All My Colors").

```
print "\nAll My Colors:\n";
print join("\n", @colors);      # separated by linefeeds

print "\nAll My Colors:<p>\n";
print join("<p>\n", @colors);   # separated by html paragraphs
                                # and \n, for you webheads
```

Hashes, like arrays, can be treated like lists. If you instruct the `print` operator to print out a hash, you'll get all of the key/value pairs printed out, side by side.

```
%salary = ('Brian' => 1000,
           'Elmer' => 900,
           'Garth' => 1200);
print %salary;
```

which would display:

```
Brian1000Elmer900Garth1200
```

You can use the `join()` function with this, as well.

```
print join("\n", %salary);
```

If you'd like to see all the indexes (or keys) of a hash, you can use the `keys` operator to retrieve them as a list.

```
print "\nEmployees:\n";
print join("\n", keys %salary);
```

You can also fetch a slice of the hash, but you must prefix it with the @ symbol. Note that you still use the braces { } to delimit the list of keys.

```
print "\nSalaries for Two Employees:\n";
print join("\n", @salary{'Brian', 'Garth'});
```

If you'd like to see all the salaries, you can use the `keys` operator, and perhaps grab all the hash values with a slice.

```
print "\nSalaries for All Employees:\n";
print join("\n", @salary{ keys %salary });
```

Flow of Control

Relevant manpages: perlsyn.

Perl provides many flow-of-control statements that may appear familiar to users of other languages. One example is the `while` statement, which causes a block to be executed as long as a specified condition remains true. A block in Perl is generally delimited with curly braces { }, and can contain zero or more lines of code. Here's a simple one that loops while a variable is less than 10:

```
$i = 0;                         # initialize the value
while ($i < 10) {               # loop while it's less than 10
    print "It's now: $i\n";     # print it out
    $i++;                       # increment it
}
```

If you never perform the increment, the condition will never evaluate to True, and the loop will continue until you kill the program.

The `while` statement is often used in conjunction with the `<>` operator. The `<>` operator is used to read data, one line at a time, from a filehandle. Perl provides a filehandle called STDIN, by default. STDIN is the input stream to the program; it can either be piped in from another process or file (if the user has redirected the input), or it can simply be typed in by the user. Appropriately, STDOUT is the filehandle that is used to send output to the user, or to a process or file in cases where the user has redirected the output. STDERR is the filehandle for error output; it is unbuffered, and will be displayed to the user, if he or she is using a terminal, a shell running in an xterm, or a command window on Win32. If the Perl script is run by an application, such as a Web server, the application will receive and handle the output.

In the following example, notice the use of `chomp` to remove the trailing newline, and `split()`, which turns the string value that you typed into a list. The `split()` function can be used to split a string based on a delimiter, but here it splits on nothing, which causes it to split between each character.

```
print "\nPlease type something.\n";
print "Type ^D (Unix) or ^Z (Win32) when finished.\n";
while (<STDIN>) {
    chomp;                           # remove final \n from $_
    print reverse split(//, $_);     # print $_ backwards
    print "\n";
}
```

You may be asking yourself what that `$_` variable is for. Well, that's one of the magical things about Perl. It's the default input variable, and it also is the default pattern-matching space (more on this later). There are lots of operators and functions that use `$_` by default, and the `<>` operator is one of them. When you say:

```
while (<STDIN>) {
    ...
}
```

you're really saying:

```
while ($_ = <STDIN>) {
    ...
}
```

In the example just shown, chomp operates on the $_ variable, and the output of split() is handled by reverse, which spits out a list in reverse order before it is printed.

Perl supports other flow-of-control statements, such as the for statement, which will look familiar to C programmers.

```
for ($i = 0; $i < 100; $i++) {
    print "$i\n";
}
```

This example executes the code within the block for as long as the test condition (the center one) remains True. The first argument to for is executed once at the beginning, and the last argument is executed each time the test expression evaluates to True. The example just shown prints the numbers 0 through 99. Perl also supplies various conditional statements, such as the if construct. Note that the = operator is not used to test the condition, since this would always result in an assignment. The == operator should be used to compare.

```
if ($i == 100) {
    print "The value is equal to 100.\n";
}
```

You can also use the else or the elsif (no e in the middle!) in conjunction with if to specify alternative conditions.

```
if ($i == 100) {
    print "The value is equal to 100.\n";
} elsif ($i < 100) {
    print "The value is less than 100.\n";
} elsif ($i > 100) {
    print "The value is greater than 100.\n";
} else {
    print "I don't know what to tell you, bub...\n";
}
```

One of if's friends is unless, which does the opposite of if. As you've seen, if only executes the block that follows in cases where its test condition is True. The unless statement, on the other hand, only executes the block when the test condition is False.

```
unless ($i == 100) {
    print "The value is not equal to 100.\n";
}
```

The last control structure that will be covered here is foreach—it is used to process list data, and the inner block is executed for each element in the list. It can be used to process arrays, as in:

```
@colors = ('red', 'green', 'blue', 'orange');
foreach (@colors) {
    print $_, "\n";
}
```

By default, each element of the array is stored in `$_`, unless you specify a variable name after the `foreach` and before the list.

```
foreach $color (@colors) {
    print $color, "\n";
}
```

The `foreach` statement can be very handy when used in conjunction with a hash and the `keys` operator. In the following example, `foreach` iterates over each key in the `%salary` hash. This yields each person's name, and enables us to refer to the salary using that name as the key.

```
%salary = ('Brian' => 1000,
           'Elmer' => 900,
           'Garth' => 1200);
foreach $index (keys %salary) {
    print "$index\'s salary is $salary{$index}.\n";
}
```

Pattern Matching and Substitution

Relevant manpages: perlre, perlop.

We've made mention of the fact that `$_`, in addition to being the default variable for certain operators, is also the default pattern matching space. What does this mean? Well, one of Perl's strengths lies in its extensive support for regular expressions; regular expressions are a venerable part of Unix that allow you to specify complicated patterns that can be matched within a text file, user input, or any other sort of data.

Simple Matching

If you've used wildcards in Unix, DOS, or SQL, you've gotten a very small taste of the sort of task that regular expressions deal with.

```
/* SQL Example: matches Foxborough or Foxboro */
SELECT *
   FROM address
   WHERE city LIKE 'Foxbor%'
/* SQL Example: matches any character at the _, and
   any number of characters at the %. This would match
   Brooklyn or Brookline
*/
SELECT *
   FROM address
   WHERE city LIKE 'Brookl_n%'

REM DOS example - all files ending in .pl
```

```
REM
C:\WINDOWS> DIR *.pl
REM DOS example - would match foo.pl or foo.pm
REM
C:\WINDOWS> DIR foo.p?

# Unix shell example - all files ending in .pl
#
bash$ ls -l *.pl
# Unix shell example - would match foo.pl or foo.pm
#
bash$ ls -l foo.p?
```

These examples are quite simple; in SQL, the symbol that matches any number of characters is the %, while in Unix or DOS, it's the *. Similarly, in SQL, the symbol for one single character is _, while in Unix or DOS, it's ?. Pattern matching is the sort of thing that regular expressions are designed to deal with. However, regular expressions are much more powerful than the simple wildcard matching shown in the preceding example.

The `while` statement, which was shown earlier, can be used to read in a file or other form of input. The pattern matching and substitution operators can help you manipulate that input in interesting and useful ways. Here's an example that uses the pattern matching operator (m/ /). It returns True only if the specified pattern (in this case, the word "hello") is found within $_.

```
print "\nPlease type something.\n";
print "Type ^D (Unix) or ^Z (Win32) when finished.\n";
while (<STDIN>) {
    if (m/hello/) {
        print "Well, hello to you, too!\n";
    }
}
```

The m part of the matching operator is not compulsory. However, if you use it, you can choose your own delimiters for the match, if you don't like the / /. This can be nearly any character, provided it appears after the m and again at the end of the pattern. You can also use paired delimiters, like [], {}, or (). The following examples are equivalent to the previous one:

```
print "\nPlease type something.\n";
print "Type ^D (Unix) or ^Z (Win32) when finished.\n";
while (<STDIN>) {
    if (/hello/) {    # no m
        print "Well, hello to you, too!\n";
    }
}

print "\nPlease type something.\n";
print "Type ^D (Unix) or ^Z (Win32) when finished.\n";
while (<STDIN>) {
    if (m!hello!) {    # alternative delimiter
        print "Well, hello to you, too!\n";
    }
```

```
    }

print "\nPlease type something.\n";
print "Type ^D (Unix) or ^Z (Win32) when finished.\n";
while (<STDIN>) {
    if (m[hello]) {    # paired delimiters
        print "Well, hello to you, too!\n";
    }
}
```

A commonly used portion of Perl's pattern matching is the . metacharacter, which is used to match any character. You can quantify the metacharacter by including a + (match one or more of anything) or a * (match zero or more of anything). There are other quantifiers; see the `perlre` manpage for more details. A special feature of Perl's pattern-matching capabilities is *backreferences*; you can enclose part of the pattern match in parentheses, and refer to the values matched within each set of parentheses with $1, $2, $3, and so on. Here's a way of grabbing anything the user types, even if it's not "hello." Note how it uses the . metacharacter, quantified by the * quantifier. It grabs *everything* the user types.

```
print "\nBackreference example:\n";
print "\nPlease type something.\n";
print "Type ^D (Unix) or ^Z (Win32) when finished.\n";
while (<STDIN>) {
    if (m[(.*)]) {    # paired delimiters
        print "Well, $1 to you, too!\n";
    }
}
```

Greedy versus Non-Greedy Matching

These previous examples show very rudimentary pattern matching; if "hello" is found anywhere within $_, the match will return True. It's helpful to think of a match as "gobbling" something up. In basic pattern matching, once you have matched a pattern, it is exhausted, and the pattern match begins searching from the remainder of the string. By default, Perl's pattern matches are said to be "greedy," in that they'll gobble up everything they can before moving on. If you wanted to match all of the text between <b></b> tags in an HTML document, it might be tempting to write something like the example shown next. Note that in this example, the pattern match is performed on a variable using the pattern binding operator =~, which allows you to perform a pattern match on any given variable, rather than defaulting to $_. That's not the only thing we're doing differently here. By supplying a list context using join, the match returns each matched value as a list; the g modifier ensures that we return more than one match. Finally, notice that the / in the </b> needs to be escaped as <\/b>, since the / would normally terminate the expression.

```
$text = qq[<b>This</b> is some <b>text</b>.];
print join("\n", $text =~ /<b>(.*)<\/b>/g);
```

But, instead of getting the words "This" and "text" returned, we get "This</b> is some <b>text." This happens because the .* is greedy, and matches everything up to the final </b>.

You can add another modifier to the match, `?`, which causes it to match the minimum number of times, and so we get the expected results from this version:

```
$text = qq[<b>This</b> is some <b>text</b>.];
print join("\n", $text =~ /<b>(.*?)<\/b>/g);
```

Substitution

A close relative of the pattern-matching operator is the substitution operator, which lets you substitute anything you matched with another value. There are two parts to the substitution: the pattern to match, and the value to substitute. Here's an example that will substitute hello with goodbye:

```
$text = qq[You say hello.];
$text =~ s/hello/goodbye/;
print qq[$text\n];
```

You can also use the backreferences (`$1`, `$2`, `$3`, and so on) in the right-hand side of the substitution. This example will find anything within `<b>` and `</b>`, and replace it with `<strong></strong>`:

```
$text = qq[<b>This</b> is some <b>text</b>.];
$text =~ s/<b>(.*?)<\/b>/<strong>$1<\/strong>/g;
print "$text\n";
```

But Wait . . . There's More

This section has really only been meant to give you a basic introduction to pattern matching and regular expressions; this is one area of Perl that provides powerful functionality. If you wish to explore the power of regular expressions further, we suggest that you check out the `perlre` manpage, or *Programming Perl*, by Larry Wall, Tom Christiansen, and Randal L. Schwartz.

References

Relevant manpages: perlref, perldsc, perllol.

Perl provides support for managing complex data structures through *references*. A reference allows you to use a simple scalar variable (or array or hash element) that acts as a reference to another value, be it a scalar variable, an array, or a hash. This can be useful in many circumstances. Let's look at a Perl subroutine that returns a hash, which is really just a list. Note the use of the `@_` variable, which is a special variable used to refer to the arguments to the subroutine as an array. This example also introduces the `my` operator, which will declare a variable to be local only within the specified block:

```
#!/usr/local/bin/perl
#

%favorite_color = ( 'Brian' => 'Blue',
                    'Elvis' => 'Puce',
                    'Oscar' => 'Orange' );
%new_hash = capitalize(%favorite_color);
```

```
foreach (keys %new_hash) {
    print "$_\'s favorite color is $new_hash{$_}.\n";
}

sub capitalize {
    my %hash = @_;
    my $key;
    foreach $key (keys %hash) {
        $hash{$key} = qq[\U$hash{$key}];
    }
    return %hash;
}
```

This is all fine and good, but what if we want to return two hashes? Maybe one hash could be capitalized and the other could be lowercased.

```
#!/usr/local/bin/perl
#

%favorite_color = ( 'Brian' => 'Blue',
                    'Elvis' => 'Puce',
                    'Oscar' => 'Orange' );
(%lchash, %uchash) = change_case(%favorite_color);

print "Lowercase:\n";
foreach (keys %lchash) {
    print "$_\'s favorite color is $lchash{$_}.\n";
}
print "Uppercase:\n";
foreach (keys %uchash) {
    print "$_\'s favorite color is $uchash{$_}.\n";
}

sub change_case {
    my %hash = @_;
    my $key;
    my (%uc, %lc);
    foreach $key (keys %hash) {
        $uc{$key} = qq[\U$hash{$key}];
        $lc{$key} = qq[\L$hash{$key}];
    }
    return (%lc,%uc);
}
```

Well, this doesn't work, as you can see by the output.

```
Lowercase:
Oscar's favorite color is ORANGE.
Elvis's favorite color is PUCE.
Brian's favorite color is BLUE.
Uppercase:
```

What's happened is that the first hash in the list, %lchash, gobbles up all of the return values, and %uchash doesn't get any. What's worse, since both hashes have the same keys, the lowercase values get overwritten by the uppercase values. This problem can be solved by simply returning two scalars that contain references to %uc and %lc, and then *dereference* them back into hashes after getting them from the subroutine. When you create a reference by prefixing a variable or array name with \, the variable or array is preserved as long as there is a variable that holds the reference. Even if the referenced array or variable goes out of scope, it can still be retrieved by using a variable that refers to it. The process of retrieving this value is called *dereferencing*, and is done by prefixing the scalar variable with the appropriate symbol. If it's a scalar that's being dereferenced, it would be a $, so you get two $, as in:

```
$var = 555;
$ref = \$var;
print "ref=$$ref\n";
```

If you modify the reference, it changes the referenced variable. This is very different from assigning the value of the referenced variable to another variable, which is, in effect, copying the variable.

```
$var = 555;
$ref = \$var;
$copy = $var;
$$ref = 111;
print "var=$var, copy=$copy\n";
```

Just as you can use the $ to dereference a scalar, you can use @ and % to dereference an array or a hash. Here's the final revision of the favorite color example, which returns two hashes by using references:

```
#!/usr/local/bin/perl
#

%favorite_color = ( 'Brian' => 'Blue',
                    'Elvis' => 'Puce',
                    'Oscar' => 'Orange' );
($lcref, $ucref) = change_case(%favorite_color);

%lchash = %$lcref;
%uchash = %$ucref;

print "Lowercase:\n";
foreach (keys %lchash) {
    print "$_\'s favorite color is $lchash{$_}.\n";
}
print "Uppercase:\n";
foreach (keys %uchash) {
    print "$_\'s favorite color is $uchash{$_}.\n";
}

sub change_case {
```

```
    my %hash = @_;
    my $key;
    my (%uc, %lc);
    foreach $key (keys %hash) {
        $uc{$key} = qq[\U$hash{$key}];
        $lc{$key} = qq[\L$hash{$key}];
    }
    return (\%lc,\%uc);
}
```

Packages

Relevant manpages: perlsub, perlmod.

Perl provides a means of organizing data and subroutines into *packages*, to keep distinct, but identically named items from stomping on each other. The package mechanism is a critical part of Perl's object orientation, as will be seen shortly. A package can be declared within your Perl program with the `package` statement; any subroutine within that method can be invoked as `package_name::subroutine`, and any variable, array, or hash that is declared as a package variable using `local()` can be referred to as `$package_name::variable`, `@package_name::array`, or `%package_name::hash`, respectively.

A `local()` declaration can be used to declare a variable, hash, or array to be local within a package. This allows other packages to access the variable using the `$package_name::variable` notation. If it is scoped with a `my()` declaration, it is inaccessible outside of that package, unless one of the packages' subroutines returns a reference to it.

This following example shows two packages, named `one` and `two`. The package named `one` includes a package-scoped variable called `$var`, which is initialized to 200. It includes a subroutine called `higher()`, which simply multiplies the `$var` that belongs to that package (package `one`) by 100.

The second package, `two`, is a little more involved. It, too, includes its own variable named `$var`, which is initialized to 100. One of the first things that happens in this package is that it displays the value of `$one::var`, and then invokes `one`'s `higher()` subroutine. This multiplies `$one::var` by 100, but does not affect `$two::var`. To prove this, `two`'s `higher()` subroutine is invoked, which does something a little different from `one`'s. This version of the subroutine makes a *copy* of the package variable named `$var` into a variable of the same name that is scoped within the subroutine using `my()`. Next, this variable is multiplied by 100, and it is returned to the caller, without affecting the original `$var`. This gets stored in `$high`, and both `$var` and `$high` are displayed side by side.

```
#!/usr/local/bin/perl

package one;

local $var = 200; # package variable

# increase the value of $var; this operates
```

```
# on the package variable $var
#
sub higher {
    $var = $var * 100;
}

package two;

local $var  = 100; # package variable

# print out $one::var, increase it, and then print it again
#
print "before: one::var=", ${one::var}, "\n";
one::higher();
print "after:  one::var=", ${one::var}, "\n";

# work on $two::var - note how it is
# unaffected  by the operations on $one::var
#
$high = higher();
print "two::var=$var, two::high=$high\n";

sub higher {
    my $var = $two::var; # copy the package variable
    $var = $var * 100;   # increase it
    return $var;         # return the copy
}
```

Perl Objects

Relevant manpages: perlmod, perlobj, perlbot, perltoot.

So far, we've only covered just enough of Perl to make you think it's a procedural language. In fact, Perl offers object-oriented features by using a combination of references, packages, and a little magic. An object in Perl is simply a reference with this little magic thrown in. It's a reference that belongs to a package, and it happens to know what package it belongs to. The great thing about this is that it can find its own data and subroutines, which we now have to call *properties* and *methods*, since we're in Object-Oriented territory.

Since packages can share common data, it's important that all of the object's data (properties) be stored within the object itself. For this reason, the object is usually a reference to an unnamed (anonymous) hash that gets created each time you need a new object. This act is called *construction* or *instantiation*. The hash is created with syntax similar to

```
my $self = {};
```

This constructs a reference to an anonymous hash; the { } denotes a reference to an empty hash that has no name, so the scalar variable $self is the sole reference to an empty hash. Finally, the bless operator is used on the $self variable, which promotes it to a full-fledged object. The details of this are best left to the manpages, since it is a fairly complex aspect of Perl.

However, when you use an object, which we'll be doing in the next chapter, you don't need to know so much about the internals of Perl objects; while Perl's objects are a little complex when you get "under the hood," they are very simple to use in everyday practice. If you are going to do any serious development with Perl, it would be useful to learn this aspect of the language. Here's an example of Perl objects in action:

```perl
#!/usr/local/bin/perl

package Test;

sub new {

    # create the reference to the anonymous hash
    my($self) = {};

    bless $self;      # bless it

    # dereference the hash, create an element keyed by the
    # string 'value'. This is commonly written as:
    #     $self->{value} = 1;
    # an alternative syntax for dereferencing a hash, but
    # one you haven't seen yet.
    #
    $$self{value} = 1;

    return $self;     # return it

}

sub increment {

    # a method call on an object always passes the object
    # in first
    #
    my $self = shift;

    ($self->{value})++;   # increment it

}

sub print {
    my $self = shift;
    print "The value is: ", $self->{value}, ".\n";
}

package main; # the default package

$x = new Test;
$y = new Test;

# increment $x's value twice
#
```

```
$x->increment;
$x->increment;

# but only increment $y's value once
#
$y->increment;

# now, let's see them
#
$x->print;
$y->print;
```

The Final Word

Perl is a powerful and rich language that can be used to build complex applications that are both fast and elegant. We've only offered up enough information for you to understand the examples in the following chapters on Mini SQL and Perl; for more information, you should consult the extensive documentation that ships with Perl, or *Programming Perl*, by Larry Wall, Tom Christiansen, and Randal L. Schwartz. The various manpages for Perl are quite extensive, and make the language quite clear. Some distributions of Perl for Windows NT or Windows 95 include these pages as HTML documents, since Win32 does not support Unix manual pages.

Perl CGI Programming with MsqlPerl

In order to best show the use of the MsqlPerl API, we'll develop a nifty application. The customer is a department of a fictitious educational institution, The University of Drivel's Office of the Registrar. It's actually one component of an application that will be completed in the next chapter; we'll be developing the University of Drivel's Registration Management System, which allows users to input the names of students, lecturers, course descriptions, and course schedules. This is just the back end, and the front end, which will be developed in the next chapter, will allow students to register for the courses.

This chapter will also introduce another useful package for Perl development, the `CGI.pm` module, which offers many useful features for developing a CGI-based user interface. This application will be entirely Web based, using HTML forms as the user interface. It's helpful if the reader of this chapter has some familiarity with the principles of CGI scripting, as well as some familiarity with object-oriented programming. The `perltoot` manpage, which is included with the core Perl distribution, includes some basic information on object-oriented development, as well as a comprehensive tutorial on object-oriented programming in Perl. You can read this manpage with either of the following commands: `man perltoot` or `perldoc perltoot`.

The Msql Module

The `Msql` module is a Perl module written by Andreas Koenig (koenig@franz.ww.tu-berlin.de). This module provides an object-oriented interface to Mini SQL, and includes methods for querying the database, retrieving information about the database, and handling errors.

About the Author of the Msql Module

Andreas Koenig, the creator of the MsqlPerl interface, is no stranger to the world of collaborative free software. Andreas has long been a contributor to the Perl community, and has been involved with numerous useful Perl modules: He is one of the authors of the crucial MakeMaker module, and he is the creator and maintainer of the CPAN module, which allows Perl users to interactively query, download, and build Perl modules.

Andreas credits the desire to write and give away free software to a number of factors. Not neglecting the ethical aspects of sharing information, he points out that sharing software offers a practical gain to users of a particular tool. Few Perl modules are written without a good reason, and are usually written by the author because he or she needs the module, not because the author thinks it will be popular. Andreas also points out that the Net offers "better testing and debugging than you usually have in commercial products," but reminds us of the lure of "free fun with all the fellow hackers." It is a shame that in this day and age, we have to remind the audience that hacker is a term that has been shamelessly abused by the media to sell more papers and magazines. In Andreas' sense, hacker refers to someone who enjoys programming, is quite good at it, and is interested, perhaps obsessed, with exploring every nook and cranny of their programming environment. This is in contrast to the media's usage of the term to denote one who breaks into computer systems—the correct term for this is cracker.

Like many great programmers, most of Andreas' programming knowledge came from self-tutoring and individual exploration. Andreas is one of the 200 or so "Perl 5 Porters," the group of developers who work on Perl, maintaining whatever happens to be the current release, and releasing new versions as often as every six months.

Availability

You can obtain the `Msql` module from CPAN; the following URL will take you to the directory containing the latest release:

```
www.perl.com/CPAN/modules/by-module/Msql
```

Once you have downloaded and extracted the module, you should follow the installation instructions contained in the README file. If you are using Perl 5.004 or greater, the CPAN module will be installed on your site by default. If you are using the CPAN module, you can enter the CPAN shell with the command:

```
perl -MCPAN -e shell
```

You will need a connection to the Internet in order to use this, as it downloads modules from remote sites. The first time you start the shell, you will be asked a number of configuration questions. After that, you can install a module with the command `install <module name>`. You can install the Msql module with the command `install Msql`.

The `Msql` module is really composed of two classes: `Msql` and `Msql::Statement`. The only time you deal with `Msql::Statement` is when it's sent to you as a query result, and you never invoke its constructor directly. To import the `Msql` module, you must issue a:

```
use Msql;
```

The CGI Module

Lincoln D. Stein's (lstein@genome.wi.mit.edu) `CGI.pm` module is quite possibly one of the most useful modules available for Perl. Regardless of the database back end, be it GNU DBM, Sybase, or Mini SQL, we've always used `CGI.pm` to develop our Web user interfaces and deal with input from the users. Like the `Msql` module, `CGI.pm` can be obtained from CPAN, and you can use the following URL:

```
www.perl.com/CPAN/modules/by-module/CGI
```

Versions 5.004 and greater of Perl include the `CGI` module by default.

Laying a Foundation

This chapter's application is going to be made up of several scripts with a lot of common characteristics, so it might be a good idea to come up with some sort of foundation to build on. Since Perl is object-oriented, it makes sense to build a `Framework` object that can be subclassed each time we write a new script. It would be nice if this object would take care of the database connection, some of the CGI stuff, and error handling.

In order to make this happen, we'll have to use one of the fundamental features of object-oriented programming. This feature is *inheritance*, which allows you to define classes or modules that are derived from one another. Using this, we can define all the properties and methods of a `Framework` module, and then cook up a script that allows you to edit a lecturer's information. If the `Framework` module contains all sorts of nifty methods for dealing with CGI programming and database access, the lecturer information script could inherit all of those nifty methods, and add a few of its own as well.

Running the Examples

The examples for the chapter are designed to be run under a Web server. Under most environments, this is a matter of installing the `Framework` and `Courses` modules, telling your Web server how to execute the `.cgi` scripts, and calling up the scripts from your browser. You will also need to initialize the database by feeding the `tables.sql` script into the `msql` monitor program, which will set up the tables and some sample data.

Installing the Example Modules

The `Framework` and `Courses` modules must be installed under your Perl distribution. In order to make these work, it's best that you run Perl 5.004 or later. Perl's MakeMaker facility takes care of automating the installation. If the release of Perl that you are using supports MakeMaker, then it's quite easy to install most extensions, such as the `Framework` module, the `Courses` module, and most modules you get from CPAN. You simply need to enter the directory containing the module, and run the following commands:

```
perl Makefile.PL
```

```
make
make install
```

This needs to be performed for both the MsqlSourceBook-Course and Msql-Framework directories under the /eg/ch08 directories included with the example code. See the README files in the /eg/ch08/Msql-Framework and /eg/ch08/MsqlSourceBook-Courses directories for more information.

Installing the Scripts

The /eg/ch08 directory contains several files that end in .cgi. These should be installed in a cgi-bin directory on your Web server. You may need to modify each script at the bottom to pass a hostname to the new() method, unless your mSQL server is running on the same machine as your Web server. Unless you pass in a hostname to this method, it assumes that you want to connect to localhost. For example, if your mSQL host was msqlhost.mydomain.com, you would need to change the line in the view_schedule.cgi file:

```
my $f = new view_schedule;
```

to:

```
my $f = new view_schedule("msqlhost.mydomain.com");
```

This change must be performed for each .cgi file.

Also, you must ensure that scripts are marked as executable; this can be done using the chmod command:

```
chmod uog+x *.cgi
```

The #! syntax at the top of each script ensures that under Unix, the script is handled by the appropriate interpreter; in this case, /usr/local/bin/perl. If Perl 5.004 is installed in a different location (such as /usr/bin/perl), you may need to modify this. If you wish to run these scripts in a document directory, you will need to consult your Web server's documentation for information on how to configure the server so that files with the .cgi extension are treated as executables, rather than as documents. Under the Apache server, this is a matter of adding the line:

```
AddType application/x-httpd-cgi .cgi
```

to your Web server's srm.conf file. Other Web servers may offer a similar configuration option; you should consult the documentation supplied with your Web server.

Setting Up the Sample Data

Before you feed the contents of tables.sql into the msql monitor program, you should make sure that there is a database called msql_sourcebook in the system. As the Mini SQL admin user (typically root), you should issue a:

```
msqladmin create msql_sourcebook
```

Once you have done this, you may feed the contents of tables.sql into the `msql` monitor by saying:

```
msql msql_sourcebook < tables.sql
```

Here's the contents of tables.sql:

```
#
# mSQL Dump   (requires mSQL 2.0 Beta 5 or newer)
#
# Host: localhost    Database: msql_sourcebook
#--------------------------


#
# Table structure for table 'lecturer'
#
DROP TABLE lecturer \g

CREATE TABLE lecturer (
   first_name CHAR(25),
   last_name CHAR(25),
   id INT
) \g

CREATE UNIQUE INDEX ix_id
   ON lecturer (id) \g

CREATE SEQUENCE ON lecturer STEP 1 VALUE 9 \g

#
# Dumping data for table 'lecturer'
#

INSERT INTO lecturer (first_name, last_name, id)
   VALUES ('Brian','Jepson',1)\g
INSERT INTO lecturer (first_name, last_name, id)
   VALUES ('Oscar','LeCat',2)\g
INSERT INTO lecturer (first_name, last_name, id)
   VALUES ('Hagbard','Celine',3)\g
INSERT INTO lecturer (first_name, last_name, id)
   VALUES ('Bob','Shairp',4)\g
INSERT INTO lecturer (first_name, last_name, id)
   VALUES ('Sebastian','Tombs',5)\g
INSERT INTO lecturer (first_name, last_name, id)
   VALUES ('Roger','Conway',6)\g
INSERT INTO lecturer (first_name, last_name, id)
   VALUES ('Eric','Hearble',7)\g
INSERT INTO lecturer (first_name, last_name, id)
   VALUES ('Shamrock','Womlbs',8)\g

#
```

```
# Table structure for table 'student'
#
DROP TABLE student \g

CREATE TABLE student (
  first_name CHAR(25),
  last_name CHAR(25),
  ssn CHAR(9),
  id INT
) \g

CREATE UNIQUE INDEX ix_id
  ON student (id) \g

CREATE SEQUENCE ON student STEP 1 VALUE 1 \g

#
# Dumping data for table 'student'
#


#
# Table structure for table 'course'
#
DROP TABLE course \g

CREATE TABLE course (
  course_name CHAR(25),
  course_code CHAR(6),
  credits INT,
  id INT,
  course_desc TEXT(256)
) \g

CREATE UNIQUE  INDEX ix_id
  ON course (id) \g

CREATE SEQUENCE ON course STEP 1 VALUE 9 \g

#
# Dumping data for table 'course'
#

INSERT INTO course
  (course_name, course_code, credits, id, course_desc)
  VALUES ('Basic Programming','CS100',3,1,'')\g
INSERT INTO course
  (course_name, course_code, credits, id, course_desc)
  VALUES ('Patterns in Programming','CS300',4,2,'')\g
INSERT INTO course
  (course_name, course_code, credits, id, course_desc)
  VALUES ('Near-Quasi Symbolic Logic','E101',3,3,'In this course, we\'ll
```

```
 practically start covering the subject matter.')\g
INSERT INTO course
  (course_name, course_code, credits, id, course_desc)
  VALUES ('Half-Dreaded Linguistics','E301',3,4,'')\g
INSERT INTO course
  (course_name, course_code, credits, id, course_desc)
  VALUES ('Computational Phrenology','CS309',3,5,'')\g
INSERT INTO course
  (course_name, course_code, credits, id, course_desc)
  VALUES ('Literature of the Beats','ENG444',4,6,'')\g
INSERT INTO course
  (course_name, course_code, credits, id, course_desc)
  VALUES ('Revolutionary Suicide','ENG201',2,8,'')\g

#
# Table structure for table 'schedule'
#
DROP TABLE schedule \g

CREATE TABLE schedule (
  course_id INT,
  lecturer_id INT,
  semester CHAR(1),
  dow_string CHAR(5),
  start_time CHAR(8),
  id INT
) \g

CREATE UNIQUE  INDEX ix_id
  ON schedule (id) \g

CREATE SEQUENCE ON schedule STEP 1 VALUE 12 \g

#
# Dumping data for table 'schedule'
#

INSERT INTO schedule
  (course_id, lecturer_id, semester, dow_string, start_time, id)
  VALUES (1,1,'S','135','8:00 AM',8)\g
INSERT INTO schedule
  (course_id, lecturer_id, semester, dow_string, start_time, id)
  VALUES (2,2,'S','135','12:00 PM',2)\g
INSERT INTO schedule
  (course_id, lecturer_id, semester, dow_string, start_time, id)
  VALUES (5,2,'S','24','8:00 AM',7)\g
INSERT INTO schedule
  (course_id, lecturer_id, semester, dow_string, start_time, id)
  VALUES (4,1,'S','135','4:00 PM',9)\g
INSERT INTO schedule
  (course_id, lecturer_id, semester, dow_string, start_time, id)
  VALUES (8,5,'S','24','1:00 PM',10)\g
```

```
INSERT INTO schedule
  (course_id, lecturer_id, semester, dow_string, start_time, id)
  VALUES (4,5,'S','24','9:15 AM',11)\g
```

Running the Scripts

Once you have the modules installed, and have configured your Web server to run the scripts, either by putting them in a `cgi-bin` directory or by marking `.cgi` files as executable scripts, you can try running them. Perhaps the best entry point is the `view_schedule` script; if you've installed the `*.cgi` scripts under your Web server's `cgi-bin` directory, you can visit this page in your browser by opening the following URL, substituting the Web server hostname for `localhost`:

    http://localhost/cgi-bin/view_schedule.cgi

If it's been installed under a user's document directory, and the Web server knows that `.cgi` is an executable extension, you might try something like the following, substituting the Web server hostname for `localhost`:

    http://localhost/~bjepson/eg/ch08/view_schedule.cgi

Figure 8.1 shows this page in action. Each page includes instructions for use, and the bottom of each page features links that you can use to further explore the system.

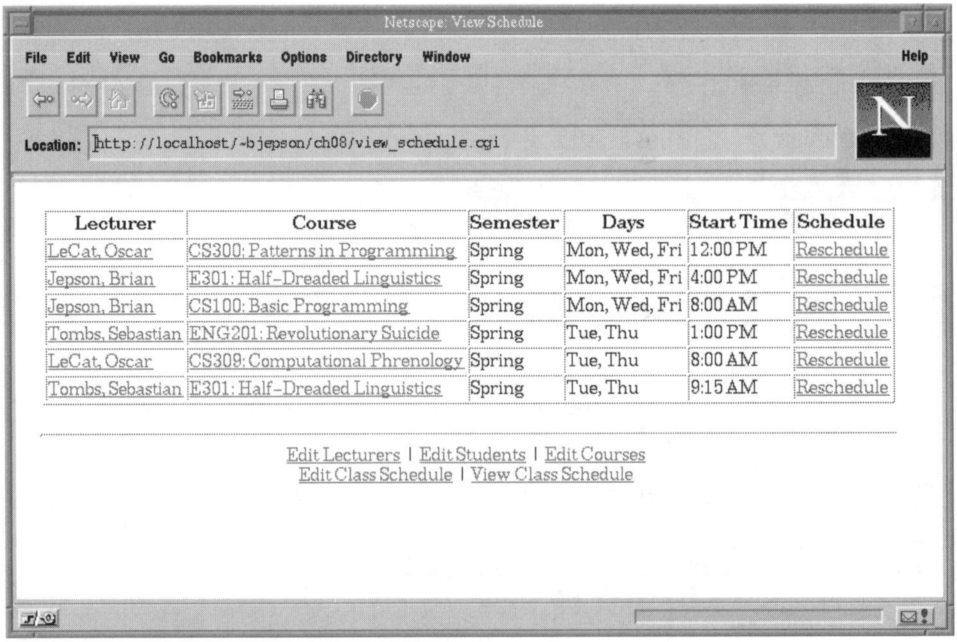

FIGURE 8.1 The View Schedule page.

Where to Get Help for Using CGI Scripts on Your Web Server

Getting the CGI bit of this right can be a little complicated. For one, there are a great many Web servers available, and each of them deals with CGI scripts in a different way. Fortunately, there are many places where you can find more information. The best place to learn about dealing with Perl CGI programming issues is the Perl CGI Programming FAQ, available from:

    www.perl.org/CPAN/doc/FAQs/cgi/perl-cgi-faq.html

The Perl for Win32 FAQ is located at either of these locations:

    www.endcontsw.com/people/evangelo/Perl_for_Win32_FAQ.html

    www.perl.org/CPAN/doc/FAQs/win32/Perl_for_Win32_FAQ.html

You may also want to see the disturbingly named "Idiot's Guide to Solving Perl CGI Problems," which is located at:

    www.perl.com/perl/faq/cgi/idiots-guide.html

All of these FAQs, and more, can be found at the following page:

    www.perl.com/perl/faq/index.html

TIP Of course, if none of this helps, you can always send us an e-mail at `bjepson@ids.net`.

Connecting to the mSQL Server

Unlike many other Perl modules, the constructor for the Msql object is the `connect()` method. Most modules use `new()` as their constructor, but Perl does not enforce this, and it makes sense within the context of a database connection to use `connect()` as the name for the constructor. This method returns a "database handle," and can be called in one of three ways. The first is with no arguments, which assumes that the `localhost` is the database server.

```
my $dbh = Msql->connect;
```

The second form that the connect method takes is one that accepts the name of the database server as an argument, as in this example, which would connect to the database server at `dbserver.as220.org`:

```
my $dbh = Msql->connect('dbserver.as220.org');
```

Although you can use the `selectdb()` method to choose a database to use on your server, you can include the name of a database as the second argument to `connect()`. The following example connects to an mSQL server at `dbhost.bjepson.com`, and selects the `msql_sourcebook` database:

```
my $dbh = Msql->connect('dbhost.bjepson.com',
                        'msql_sourcebook');
```

It's a good idea to make sure the connection really happened. If the connection fails, you get an undefined value rather than an object that represents a database handle. So, the following example would cause your program to crash and burn if it couldn't connect to the database. In real life, though, you'll probably use more sophisticated error checking.

```
my $dbh = Msql->connect() ||
    die "Could not connect to mSQL server.";
```

If you didn't use the host/database form of the `connect()` method, you can explicitly set the database with the `selectdb()` method. This method is invoked through the `Msql` object, which represents the database handle.

```
$dbh->selectdb('msql_sourcebook');
```

Issuing Queries

The `Msql` object provides a method known as `query()`, which is used to send queries to the database. This method returns an `Msql::Statement` object, which has methods for reading in the query results. Here's an example that issues a simple `SELECT` statement:

```
my $sth = $dbh->query(qq[SELECT first_name, last_name
                        FROM lecturer]);
```

The `Msql::Statement` object, also known as a *statement handle,* can be used to retrieve rows until all of the results are exhausted. The `fetchhash()` method retrieves a row as a hash, which is convenient, since each column in the row is a hash element, keyed by the column name. The `fetchhash()` method returns True until there are no more results to fetch. Here's an example:

```
my $sth = $dbh->query(qq[SELECT first_name, last_name
                        FROM lecturer]);
my %hash;
while (%hash = $sth->fetchhash) {
    print "$hash{first_name} $hash{last_name}\n"
}
```

The method `fetchrow()` retrieves one row as a list, with each list element corresponding to one of the columns in the query. This method should be slightly faster than the `fetch-hash()` method, and is the only method that can be used when you are selecting from multiple tables that have duplicate column names.

```
my $sth = $dbh->query(qq[SELECT first_name, last_name
                        FROM lecturer]);
my @result;
while (@result = $sth->fetchrow) {
    print "$result[0] $result[1]\n"
}
```

You can also use the `query()` method to send updates and inserts, but you won't be looking for any results with `fetchrow()` or `fetchhash()`.

Statement Handle Metadata

The statement handle is capable of providing you with interesting metadata; you can discover the number of rows in the result set as well as the number of fields in each row. You can also find out the name of each column, the table names that correspond to each column, the data type and size of each column, and also whether the column is nullable. Here's a little example that tells you everything you want to know about your results. Notice that the question of whether a column is nullable is actually "is this column not nullable," so we reverse the answer with !, which changes a 0 to 1 and a 1 to 0.

```
# issue a query with more than one table
#
my $sth = $dbh->query(
                qq[SELECT schedule.start_time,
                          course.course_name,
                          course.id
                  FROM course, schedule
                  WHERE schedule.course_id = course.id]);

print qq[The query returned ]. $sth->numrows .qq[ rows.\n];

my @columns  = $sth->name;    # the names of each column
my @tables   = $sth->table;   # the table corresponding to
                              # each column
my @types    = $sth->type;    # the types of each column
my @lengths  = $sth->length;  # the lengths of each column

my @nullable = $sth->isnotnull;  # non-nullable columns

# use printf to provide structure formatting for
# the output - precise spacing for each column
#
printf "%14s%10s%6s%8s%6s\n",
       "Column", "Table", "Type", "Length", "Null";
foreach (@columns) {

    printf "%14s%10s%6s%8s%6s\n",
        pop @columns,
        pop @tables,
        pop @types,
        pop @lengths,
        !(pop @nullable)

}
```

The Msql Perl module provides other methods for interacting with the mSQL server; documentation is embedded within the module itself, and if the package has been installed using MakeMaker, you should be able to read the documentation by saying:

```
man Msql
```

or:

```
perldoc Msql
```

Working with the `Msql::Framework` Module

When we designed this module, it was difficult to decide which package to put it in; is it a CGI module with Msql extensions, or an Msql module with CGI extensions? Since the book is about Mini SQL, we decided to put it in the `Msql` package, and name it `Msql::Framework`. Here's the source code for the `Msql::Framework` module. It's all bundled up into one package, aptly named `Msql::Framework`. It includes a constructor named `new()`, which uses the "fancy" double-bless technique of constructing an object. For a complete rundown on this technique, and a comprehensive overview of using objects with Perl, see the `perltoot` manpage, or visit:

> www.perl.com/perl/everything_to_know/perltoot.html

Here's the complete source to `Msql::Framework`:

```
package Msql::Framework;

=head1 NAME

Msql::Framework - a very basic CGI application object.

=head1 DESCRIPTION

The Framework object takes care of some of the rudimentary
aspects of developing a CGI application with hooks to
Mini SQL.

=head1 SYNOPSIS

  package my_package;

  use Msql::Framework;
  @ISA = ("Msql::Framework");
```

TIP The `@ISA` array in Perl is used to implement inheritence. When a program says `@ISA = ("SomeModuleName")`, all of the methods and properties of the `SomeModuleName` are inherited by the current module. In the `SYNOPSIS` section later in the chapter, the example program inherits from `Msql::Framework`. That's how `Msql::Framework` is used. If you want to use it in a program, you should subclass it and extend it, as later examples will show.

```
[...] add your methods here; you should
      have an "init" method
[...]

#####################
package main;
my $f = new my_package;

# OR...
#
# my $f = new my_package("msql_hostname.foobar.com");

$f->init;
$f->display_page;


=head1 METHODS

=cut

# the Msql and CGI packages, which are used by this module.
#
use Msql;
use CGI;

#### Method: new()
=pod

=over 4

=item new()

This is the constructor for the Framework object. It will
take an optional parameter for the host name of the mSQL
server, or it will assume that the hostname is localhost.

=back

=cut
####
sub new {

    # standard Perl object construction.
    # (see the perltoot manpage)
    #
    my $proto = shift;
    my $class = ref($proto) || $proto;
    my $self = {};
    bless ($self, $class);

    # take an optional host name as a parameter, or simply
    # default to localhost.
```

```
    #
    my $hostname = shift || "localhost";

    # try to connect to the host.
    #
    $self->{dbh} = Msql->connect($hostname) ||
        die "Couldn't connect to server";

    # process any error within the error trapping routine.
    #
    $self->error($self->{dbh}->errmsg);

    # construct a new CGI object
    #
    $self->{query} = new CGI;

    # give this object a default title. This should be
    # modified by anything that subclasses the framework.
    #
    $self->{title} = "NO TITLE";

    # initialize the buffer; this is where all the HTML
    # goes.
    #
    $self->{buffer} = "";

    # initialize the tag; this is printed at the bottom
    # of each document.
    #
    $self->{tag} = "";

    # return the object to whoever called this constructor.
    #
    return $self;

}

#### Method: init()
=pod

=over 4

=item init()
```

This method is empty, for now; is is suggested that the
implementations of this module supply an init method,
and that the invocation of the implementation follow
the method outlined in the SYNOPSIS section of this
documentation.

Although this method is empty, it is possible that it
may do something in the future, so any subclasses *should*

explicitly invoke the superclass method with:

```
$self->SUPER::init;
```

=back

=cut
####
sub init {

}

Method: display_page()
=pod

=over 4

=item display_page()

The display_page method empties out the HTML buffer, and includes a header and title before it does so; you shouldn't put anything but the document body into the HTML buffer. See the printbuff() method for a means of adding to the HTML buffer.

This method will also display a "tag line" at the bottom of each page, which you can set with set_tag(). If you override this method, either ensure that you duplicate its functionality (bad) or invoke it at the end of your method (better).

This method will also display errors at the top of the form by calling the errors() method.

=back

=cut
####
sub display_page {

```
    my $self = shift;

    # Print out the HTTP header and the start of the HTML
    # The title can be set with set_title().
    #
    print $self->{query}->header;
    print $self->{query}->start_html(
        -BGCOLOR=> "#FFFFFF",
        -title => $self->{title});

    # display any errors.
    #
```

```
    $self->errors;

    # add the contents of the tag to the buffer.
    #
    $self->printbuff($self->{tag});

    # empty the html buffer.
    #
    print $self->{buffer};

    # end the html.
    #
    print $self->{query}->end_html;

}

#### Method: error()
=pod

=over 4

=item error()

The error handling method will handle errors in two ways.
The first is to pass it no values whatsoever; it will
check the Mini SQL connection for errors, and register
any error that is found with the list of errors for this
form. The second way to use this is to pass in a
user-defined error, which will be registered in the list
of errors, but this will not check the Mini SQL connection
for errors. This is a good method to invoke after any SQL
call; it returns true if there was an error, and all
errors will get displayed when you invoke display_page().

=back

=cut
####
sub error {

    my $self = shift;

    # if the user passed in an error, use that
    # message, or look for one in the mSQL connection.
    #
    my $error = shift || $self->{dbh}->errmsg;

    # if there was an error, add it to the list of errors,
    # and return 1.
    #
    if ($error) {
        push @{$self->{errors}}, $error;
```

```
            return 1;
        }
}


#### Method: errors()
=pod

=over 4

=item errors()

This method displays all of the errors in the list of
errors. Each error is displayed in a threatening red
color. This is normally called by display_page(), but
if you want to annoy your users, you should call it as
often as possible.

=back

=cut
####
sub errors {

    my $self = shift;
    my @errors = @{$self->{errors}};

    # iterate over the list of errors, and display them
    # in a big red font.
    #
    foreach (@errors) {
        print qq[<font size="+2" color="red">];
        print;
        print qq[</font><p>];
    }

}

#### Method: printbuff()
=pod

=over 4

=item printbuff()

Adds some text to the HTML buffer.

=back

=cut
####
sub printbuff {
```

```
    my $self = shift;
    my $data = shift;
    $self->{buffer} .= $data;

}

#### Method: set_tag()
=pod

=over 4

=item set_tag()

Sets an optional tag line that is displayed at the
bottom of each form.

=back

=cut
####
sub set_tag {

    my $self = shift;
    $self->{tag} = shift;

}

#### Method: set_title()
=pod

=over 4

=item set_title()

Sets the HTML title for this document.

=back

=cut
####
sub set_title {

    my $self = shift;
    $self->{title} = shift;

}

=head1 AUTHOR

Brian Jepson - bjepson@ids.net
```

```
=head1 SEE ALSO

Msql.pm, CGI.pm

=cut

1;
```

Working with the `MsqlSourceBook` `::Courses` Application

The Courses application needs to have one consistent item throughout the system: some HTML at the bottom of each form, which displays a series of navigational links. In order to accomplish this, we'll create a class called `MsqlSourceBook::Courses` that inherits all of `Msql::Framework`'s methods and properties. This is called *subclassing*, and `MsqlSourceBook::Courses` is said to *inherit* from `Msql::Framework`. The only thing we'll add is a method called `init()`, which will take care of adding the links with the `set_tag()` method.

```
package MsqlSourceBook::Courses;

=head1 NAME

MsqlSourceBook::Courses - a subclass of Framework with
common features for the Course application

=head1 DESCRIPTION

This module subclasses the Framework module and adds any
reusable components within the Course application.

=cut

use Msql::Framework;
@ISA = ("Msql::Framework");

#### Method: init()
=pod

=over 4

=item init()
```

This method simply adds a tag to the script, by invoking the set_tag() method; this tag is displayed at the bottom of each page, and adds consistent navigation to each page in the Courses application.

When you create your own init() method, be sure to invoke this one explicitly with:

```
$self->SUPER::init;
```

```
=back

=cut
####
sub init {

    my $self = shift;

    my $tag = <<EOF;
<p>
<center>
<hr>
<a href="edit_lecturer.cgi">Edit Lecturers</a> |
<a href="edit_student.cgi">Edit Students</a> |
<a href="edit_course.cgi">Edit Courses</a><br>
<a href="edit_schedule.cgi">Edit Class Schedule</a> |
<a href="view_schedule.cgi">View Class Schedule</a><br>
EOF

    $self->set_tag($tag);

    # invoke the superclass method
    #
    $self->SUPER::init;

}

1;
```

Working with the MsqlSourceBook::Courses view_schedule.cgi Package

The MsqlSourceBook::Courses package will form the basis of all of our remaining scripts; each of them will inherit its properties and methods from MsqlSourceBook ::Courses. One thing we need to be aware of is that each script will have its own init() method. If we add our own init() method, we will override the init() method we just defined! How do we get around that? Well, as far as our scripts are concerned, `MsqlSourceBook::Courses` is the parent class, or superclass. Perl provides a means of invoking a superclass method explicitly; this should be included in the overridden method.

```
$self->SUPER::init;
```

You can see this at work in the next script that will be included here, view_schedule.cgi. This is one of the scripts in the Courses application; it displays the current schedule of lecturers, classes, and meeting times. Here's the source code to view_schedule.cgi:

```
#!/usr/local/bin/perl

package view_schedule;

=head1 NAME

view_schedule - provides a synopsis of all the scheduled
courses, with links to appropriate forms.

=head1 DESCRIPTION

This package is embedded in a perl script which instantiates
a view_schedule object and calls its init() method.

=head1 SYNOPSIS

  http://localhost/cgi-bin/view_schedule.cgi

=head1 METHODS

=cut

use MsqlSourceBook::Courses;
@ISA = ("MsqlSourceBook::Courses");
use strict 'vars';

#### Method: init()
=pod

=over 4

=item init()

This method takes care of selecting the database and calling
the view_schedule() method to display the synopsis of class
schedules.

=back

=cut
####
```

```perl
sub init {

    my $self = shift;

    # use the msql_sourcebook database.
    #
    $self->{dbh}->selectdb("msql_sourcebook");

    # create an array of "day-of-week" id values,
    # and a hash which maps these to three-letter
    # day names.
    #
    @{$self->{dow_array}} = (0..6);
    %{$self->{dow_hash}} = (0 => 'Sun', 1 => 'Mon',
                            2 => 'Tue', 3 => 'Wed',
                            4 => 'Thu', 5 => 'Fri',
                            6 => 'Sat');

    # display the schedule.
    #
    $self->view_schedule;

    # make sure you call the superclass method.
    #
    $self->SUPER::init;

}

#### Method: view_schedule()
=pod

=over 4

=item view_schedule()

Display a synopsis of class schedules.

=back

=cut
####
sub view_schedule {

    my $self = shift;

    # set the title of the page.
    #
    $self->set_title("View Schedule");

    # a lookup hash to map the semester codes from the
    # schedule table to their full names.
    #
```

```perl
my %semester = ('S' => 'Spring', 'F' => 'Fall');

# a SELECT statement to fetch all of the schedule
# information.
#
my $sql = qq[select lecturer.first_name,
                    lecturer.last_name,
                    lecturer.id,
                    course.course_code,
                    course.course_name,
                    course.id,
                    schedule.start_time,
                    schedule.semester,
                    schedule.dow_string,
                    schedule.id
             FROM lecturer, course, schedule
             WHERE lecturer.id = schedule.lecturer_id
             AND   course.id   = schedule.course_id
             ORDER BY schedule.semester,
                      schedule.dow_string,
                      schedule.start_time];

# execute the query, and check for errors. If we get
# an error, display the page and exit the script.
#
my $sth = $self->{dbh}->query($sql);
unless (defined $sth) {
    $self->error( $self->{dbh}->errmsg );
    $self->display_page;
    exit;
}

# print the schedule as a centered table, with some
# nice headers.
#
$self->printbuff( qq[<center>] );
$self->printbuff( qq[<table border>] );
$self->printbuff( qq[<th>Lecturer</th><th>Course</th>
                     <th>Semester</th> <th>Days</th>
                     <th>Start Time</th>
                     <th>Schedule</th>] );

# process each row, and display each scheduled class.
#
my $i;
my $rowcount = $sth->numrows;
for ($i = 0; $i < $rowcount; $i++) {

    # don't use the fetchhash method, since we have some
    # duplicate column names; use the fetchrow method
    # instead, and pull the data into named scalars.
    #
```

```perl
my ($lec_first_name, $lec_last_name,
    $lec_id, $course_code, $course_name,
    $course_id, $start_time, $semester,
    $dow_string, $id) = $sth->fetchrow;

# make some names that are suitable for display.
#
my $lecturer = qq[$lec_last_name, $lec_first_name];
my $course   = qq[$course_code: $course_name];

# if the start time is blank, make it five
# non-breaking spaces.
#
$start_time  = $start_time || (" " x 5);

# convert the day-of-week string into human-readable
# form, using comma-separated three-letter names.
#
my @dow;

# the dow_string is a string consisting of
# day-of-week numbers between 0 and 6. This next
# construct will loop over each character using
# foreach; it splits the string on the empty space
# between characters, and sorts the resulting list.
#
foreach (sort split(//, $dow_string)) {

    # look up each day-of-week number in the
    # dow_hash, which yields the three-letter
    # day name.
    #
    my $dow_shortname = $self->{dow_hash}->{$_};

    # add the day name to the @dow array.
    #
    push @dow, $dow_shortname;

}

# create a string that is the comma-delimited
# list of days. If it's blank, use five non-
# breaking spaces.
#
my $dow = join(", ", @dow) || (" " x 5);

# build a table row with the information.
#
$self->printbuff(qq[<tr>]);

# show the name of the lecturer, but also make it
# a URL that takes the user to the "edit lecturer"
```

```perl
        # form.
        #
        $self->printbuff(
          qq[<td><a href="edit_lecturer.cgi?id=$lec_id">
             $lecturer</a></td>]);

        # show the name of the course, but also make it
        # a URL that lets the user edit the course.
        #
        $self->printbuff(
          qq[<td><a href="edit_course.cgi?id=$course_id">
             $course</a></td>]);

        # display the semester full name, the days of the
        # week, and the start time, each in a separate
        # <td> element.
        #
        $self->printbuff(qq[<td>$semester{$semester}</td>]);
        $self->printbuff(qq[<td>$dow</td>]);
        $self->printbuff(qq[<td>$start_time</td>]);

        # this URL will call edit_schedule.cgi with the id
        # of this scheduled entry, and with the submit
        # variable set to BY_SCHEDULE, which will bring
        # this entry up for editing.
        #
        my $schedule_url = qq[edit_schedule.cgi?] .
                               qq[schedule_id=$id] .
                               qq[&submit=BY_SCHEDULE];
        $self->printbuff( qq[<td align=center>
                        <a href="$schedule_url">
                              Reschedule</a></td>] );

        # end the row
        #
        $self->printbuff(qq[</tr>]);
    }

    # end the table, and turn centering off.
    #
    $self->printbuff( qq[</table>] );
    $self->printbuff( qq[</center>] );

}


#
# Instantiate a new view_schedule object. Then, call
# its init() method, and finally, its display_page()
# method. If your mSQL server is not on the same machine
# you're running the script on, make sure you pass
# that hostname as a parameter to new().
#
```

```
package main;
my $f = new view_schedule;
$f->init;
$f->display_page;
```

Moving On

There are four remaining scripts, three of which are not annotated here in the book. The edit_schedule.cgi script is annotated in Appendix C. The other three are edit_student.cgi, edit_course.cgi, and edit_lecturer.cgi. The remainder of the Courses application is contained within these scripts. They are included with the example code in the /eg/ch08 directory, and are fully documented. The courses application is nearly complete; it allows users to add, edit, and remove courses from the schedule. The next chapter will show the other half of this application, which allows students to sign up for courses. However, it will be built using the Msql DBI module, rather than MsqlPerl.

Perl CGI Programming with DBI and DBD::mSQL

The Perl DBI is an exciting innovation in the world of Perl development. With the advent of Perl 5, developers gained the ability to load extensions into their Perl interpreter at run time. Prior versions of Perl offered the ability to extend Perl, but at the cost of having to link extensions in at compile time, increasing the size of the Perl executable. Along with dynamic modules, Perl 5 offers object-oriented features, which are tightly integrated with the extension model.

Database extensions number among the most popular modules that have been developed for Perl. Many of these extensions are developed to more or less emulate the C API (Application Program Interface) for the target database engine. Therefore, if you're going to be using the Sybase Perl module, it helps to have access to reference material concerning Client-Library (CT-lib) programming in C. Fortunately, both the C and Perl APIs for mSQL are quite simple, mirroring the simplicity of the mSQL engine itself.

The diversity of APIs presents a problem. The sheer number of different database engines (Informix, Sybase, Oracle, and mSQL, to name a few) gives rise to complicated circumstances, in that someone who wants to develop Perl applications with a given database must become skilled in that database's API. The developer who wants to work with Informix must become an expert in Perl-Informix programming, someone who wants to develop applications that interface with Sybase must become a Perl-Sybase expert, and so on. Good luck to those who must develop an application that talks to many different data engines! Within many organizations, it is not uncommon to find numerous systems (especially legacy systems) that were developed before the organization standardized on one database package. Of course, if the organization never standardized on one, you'll most certainly encounter applications written for disparate database engines. In any case, developing applications, data feeds, or replication servers that work with several different database engines can be quite difficult if you must grapple with a different database development API for each engine.

Here's where the DBI comes in; the DBI is the Perl 5 Database Interface. Designed and implemented by Tim Bunce (along with a host of co-conspirators), the Perl 5 DBI provides a certain level of database independence for your Perl 5 modules and scripts. The methods used for connecting to and interacting with the database server are the same, regardless of what data server you are using. The DBI module serves the same purpose as ODBC's driver manager. It is responsible for loading a database driver, or DBD. From that point on, it directs any database interaction to the appropriate driver for execution.

In order to use the DBI, you will need to install the DBI module. For each type of database engine you wish to use, you will need to install the corresponding database driver, or DBD module, such as `DBD::mSQL`. The mSQL driver was originally written by Alligator Descartes (descarte@hermetica.com).

DBI Architecture

The DBI achieves its database independence by providing a common API for all database servers (the term *server* is used interchangeably with the term *engine*; both terms refer to a specific type of database server, such as Sybase SQL Server, or the Mini SQL server). The DBI module is responsible for delegating method invocations to a given driver. The beauty of this is that you only need to tell the DBI module what driver you want to use (Sybase, Oracle, mSQL, etc.), and the DBI module then "knows" which driver will handle database interactions. Your application will ask the DBI module for a connection to the database, and the DBI module will make use of the correct driver.

Each driver provides an implementation of certain DBI methods, and these are implemented (behind the scenes, of course) using a programming API that is specific to that database. For example, the DBI mSQL driver is written using the mSQL C API. However, the drive exposes the methods that are defined in the DBI specification, so the developer need not be concerned with the specifics of the mSQL C API. While the developer is using the DBI module to issue standard methods such as `execute()`, the developer does not need to know that the DBI module is using the mSQL driver, which is secretly invoking mSQL library functions like `msqlQuery()`.

Database Independence—
The Rosy Picture

The DBI API allows the developer to ignore many of the differences between database engines. Among other things, the present incarnation of the DBI allows the developer to make a connection to a database, issue queries and updates, and fetch results. For database engines that support the grouping of multiple SQL statements into transactions that can be committed or rolled back, the DBI offers methods that support such features. The DBI also offers a method for quoting string values, which takes care of escaping the single- or double-quote character, depending upon the needs of the underlying data engine.

What does the DBI's database independence offer the developer? The most obvious benefit is *portability*. An application that makes use of the vendor API of a database engine such as Sybase cannot easily be ported to another database engine such as Oracle. DBI can ease this transition and, in many cases, such a port can be undertaken with little change to the application. Since a good portion of that application is concerned with the sort of functionality offered by the DBI (connecting, querying, etc.), the amount of changes that must be made to the application become smaller than if you had used the vendor's API.

Another benefit is a reduced learning curve. Rather than learn a different API for each database package, the developer learns one API— that of the DBI. This can be a significant advantage, as anyone who has worked with more than one database API can attest.

Given the inventory of the DBI's features, it is easy to see how the DBI can come in handy from a database development perspective. Most of the database-specific features that are commonly used by developers have been incorporated into the DBI. The ultimate goal of any database independence API (DBI, ODBC, JDBC) is to provide 100-percent portability. In practice, this is not always possible, but using one of these APIs in your applications will reduce your workload in many circumstances. For one, the amount of time that must be spent on a port is reduced, and components that you develop can easily be reused across applications.

Database Dependence— The Myth of Upsizing

One of the promises of database independence is that you can develop your application with a lightweight SQL engine, and then easily upsize to something like Sybase or Oracle. To a large extent, this is possible, and is great when going from a prototype to development phase. However, the features offered by high-end database packages are so different from those offered by a lightweight engine such as Mini SQL, that in some cases, to upsize without reengineering your application would be a mistake.

High-end database servers can allow you to specify a number of permissions on tables. In a high-volume environment, where many users are connecting from many machines, and where users must insert, update, and delete records, stored procedures are often used to restrict access to the tables in the database. Stored procedures are compiled procedures written in the database server's SQL dialect. They are stored in the database and execute on the server. Since stored procedures typically execute with the permissions of their creator, the developer can set the database up in such a way so that end users do not have permissions to change or even update the tables. In these circumstances, they are only given permission to execute stored procedures, so the security threat is minimized. The rule of thumb is that if the user can connect to your dataserver from a desktop application, they can probably connect from an interactive query tool like isql, which would give them more liberal access to the database than an application would.

Also, stored procedures are often used to encapsulate very complex database operations, and to enforce business rules. Since the SQL dialect used by Mini SQL is much leaner than that of Oracle, Sybase, or Informix, complex operations within mSQL often involve a mixture of client code and SQL calls. In the case of high-end database servers, the program will simply invoke a stored procedure and retrieve a result set. The stored procedures will act as a "black box" to the client program. This provides a lot of independence from your front end; the same business rules are enforced whether you connect from Perl, Powerbuilder, or Java. One developer's boon is the bane of another—if you wish to upsize from a lightweight engine like mSQL, you will miss out on these sorts of features if you attempt to upsize without leveraging the high-end features. These features are also necessary to maximize the performance of high-end servers; if you do not use stored procedures, you may not see performance improvements on the order that you expected, and will have been better off sticking with mSQL!

Using DBD::mSQL

Before delving too deeply into the use of the mSQL driver, it's important to supply a disclaimer. While DBI is mostly about database independence, it's also about "getting the job done." For this reason, the mSQL driver does things a little differently than other drivers. For example, there are a few metadata functions that are private to the mSQL driver. At the time of this writing, the DBI is still an evolving spec, and the differences in the mSQL driver reflect the fact that people are using it to get work done. It is expected that, over time, the mSQL features that have been implemented in a non-portable way will be modified to follow the DBI spec more closely. Part of the problem is that this extra functionality is not included in the current DBI specification. As both the DBI specification and the mSQL driver evolve, things will fall into place.

In order to avoid overwhelming the reader, we have elected to cover only the details of the DBI that apply to mSQL. As a result, features such as transactions will not be covered here, and readers may find that they are learning techniques that are not fully portable to other drivers. In order to remedy this, we *highly* suggest that you read both the DBI manpage and the DBI FAQ for more information. If you've installed the DBI, you can read these with the commands perldoc DBI and perldoc DBI::FAQ, respectively. Also, the upcoming book on the DBI by Alligator Descartes will be an indispensable reference and learning tool. If you end up being hooked on the DBI, as we are, you will find all of these sources useful. Alligator's book will be published by O'Reilly and Associates.

About the Creator of DBD::mSQL

> THE king sits in Dunfermline town
> Drinking the blude-red wine;
> 'O whare will I get a skeely skipper
> To sail this new ship o' mine?'
> —first stanza of Sir Patrick Spens (Author Unknown, from the Oxford Book of
> English Verse at www.bartleby.com/101/index.html)

The pages at www.arcana.co.uk/ showcase the eclectic work and interests of Alligator Descartes, the "heid bummer" (boss) of Arcane Technologies, Ltd., located in Dunfermline, Scotland. Alligator is no doubt a skeely programmer, having mastered numerous database systems, programming languages, and computing environments. Alligator's Web site includes the DBI pages as well as several pages devoted to Java, VRML, and 3D graphics programming.

In addition to *Technologia*, as Alligator names the computing-related pages, these Web pages include a fascinating *Archaeologia* section that showcases megalithic structures and pictish symbol stones. Not only are the images of the sites and stones reproduced on the pages along with descriptions, but information such as location and accessibility are included, as well. True to Alligator's programming heritage, the *Archaeologia* pages are software-generated, and the image files and raw data files are available from the site. The Archaeologia pages are rounded out by the inclusion of two articles authored by Alligator.

Along with the captivating Archaeologia pages, the pages at http://www.arcana.co.uk/ include some of Alligator's original art, and a selection of role-playing scenarios, one of which is a scenario designed for the Call of Cthulhu, a roleplaying system based on the work of Providence, Rhode Island's most famous native, H.P. Lovecraft.

Obtaining the DBI and DBD::mSQL

Like all other Perl modules, the DBI and DBD::mSQL modules are available on CPAN, the Comprehensive Perl Archive Network. If you are using a recent version of Perl, you can use the CPAN shell to install this. You can start the CPAN shell with the following command:

```
perl -MCPAN -e shell
```

Once the shell has started, you can issue the following command to install the DBI module:

```
cpan> install DBI
```

You can use the following command to install the DBD::mSQL module:

```
cpan> install DBD::mSQL
```

Please watch the installation process closely. You may be asked questions during this process, and informative messages may alert you to any problems encountered by the CPAN shell. If for any reason you find that the installation failed some of its tests, you may be able to install it successfully with the command force install module, where module is either DBI or DBD::mSQL.

You may also download these modules from CPAN and build them according to the instructions included. The DBI module can be obtained from the following URL:

```
www.perl.com/CPAN/modules/by-module/DBI
```

You should look for and download the most recent version of the DBI module, as several versions are included in this directory. You should then extract the archive and follow the instructions in the file called README. The instructions should work for any platform that is supported under the core distribution of Perl. After you have installed the DBI, you should then download the mSQL driver, by locating the most recent version of the Msql-modules package in the following directory:

```
www.perl.com/CPAN/modules/by-module/DBD
```

You should install the DBD::mSQL driver according to the instructions included with it. After you have installed both the DBI and DBD::mSQL module, you will be able to begin working with it.

Connecting to a Database

The DBI module provides a method called connect(), which returns a database handle that can be used to issue queries, obtain information about the database, and otherwise interact with the database server. The database handle is your gateway into the database. The connect() method expects a data source string, which contains all of the information needed to connect to the database. The data source string is a colon-delimited string, and must include two things at the beginning: the word "dbi, " and the name of the driver, without the DBD:: portion of the module name. In the case of DBD::mSQL, this would be dbi:mSQL.

The remainder of the string is driver dependent, and should contain whatever information is required by the driver to connect. In the case of DBD::mSQL, this should include a database name, hostname, and port number. A valid data source string for the msql_sourcebook database, installed on the local server, would be dbi:mSQL:msql_sourcebook:local-host:1114. In cases where the local server is running the mSQL daemon on a default port, the "localhost" and "1114" portions of the data source may be blank.

Here's an example that uses the DBI->connect() method to connect to the mSQL daemon running on the local host; it selects the msql_sourcebook database, which was used in the examples in the last chapter. If you wish to use a different database on the server, you may change the database name. You may also change the hostname or port number, if your mSQL daemon is running on a different host or on a nonstandard port. This example is included with the example code as dbi_connect.pl, in the /eg/ch09 directory.

```perl
#!/usr/local/bin/perl

use DBI;

# The mSQL datasource string consists of the DBI identifier,
# the name of the driver (mSQL), the database name, and the
# hostname. These should all be separated by a colon.
#
my $datasource = "dbi:mSQL:msql_sourcebook:localhost:1114";

# Attempt to connect to the datasource. If this connection
# fails, then report the error.
#
my $dbh = DBI->connect($datasource) ||
    die "Could not connect:$DBI::errstr";

# Report the success.
#
print "Connected ok.\n";

# Disconnect from the server.
#
$dbh->disconnect;
```

Issuing a Query and Processing Results

The connect() method shown in the preceding example returns a database handle, which is an object that offers useful methods for dealing with the database. One of these methods is the prepare() method. The prepare() method is used to prepare an SQL statement for execution, and it returns a statement handle. This statement handle ($sth in the next example) offers an execute() method, which, as its name implies, executes the statement. If this method does not return a True value, it means that an error occurred while executing the statement. In this case, you can discover the error string by invoking the $sth->errstr method.

After you've executed the statement, you can use one of the statement handle's fetch() methods to retrieve the rows that the SQL statement returned. There are several fetch() methods, and each of them is explained in Table 9.1.

Table 9.1 All of the Fetch-Like Methods that the Statement Handle Offers

Method	Explanation
$ref = $sth->fetchrow_arrayref()	This should be the fastest way to fetch rows from a statement handle. Each time this method is invoked, it returns a scalar value that is a reference to an array. The method returns a reference until there are no more rows to be fetched, after which it returns an undefined value (undef).
	If you assign the output of the method to the variable $ref, you can refer to the array with @$ref. The array contains all of the values in each row, in the order in which they appeared in the SELECT statement. NULL columns are returned as undef.
$ref = $sth->fetch()	This is an alias for fetchrow_arrayref().
@arr = $sth->fetchrow_array()	This method will return a list of column values until there are no more rows to fetch. At that point, it returns an empty list. NULL columns are included in the list as undef.
$ref = $sth->fetchrow_hashref()	This is probably the slowest way to fetch rows from the statement handle. Like fetchrow_arrayref(), this returns a reference for each row, and returns undef when there are no more rows to fetch. Instead of a reference to an array of column values, this method returns a reference to a hash. That hash contains values for each column, keyed by the column name. The names of the columns can be obtained by examining

Continues

Table 9.1 All of the Fetch-Like Methods that the Statement Handle Offers (*Continued*)

Method	Explanation
	the $sth->{NAME} property. The fetchrow _hashref() method allows you to obtain to a column's value as $ref->{column_name}.
$bigref = $sth->fetchall_arrayref()	This method is a lot like fetchrow_arrayref(), except that it returns a reference to an array holding all of the rows in the table. Each element of that array is also a reference of the same sort returned by fetchrow_arrayref().

When you have finished fetching rows from the statement handle, you should tell the handle you are finished by invoking the finish() method. This ensures that any resources used by the statement are freed. Here's an example, dbi_query.pl, that summarizes many of the methods discussed in this section:

```perl
#!/usr/local/bin/perl

use DBI;

# Attempt to connect to the server. If this connection
# fails, then report the error.
#
my $datasource = "dbi:mSQL:msql_sourcebook:localhost:1114";
my $dbh = DBI->connect($datasource) ||
    die "Could not connect:$DBI::errstr";

# Create a SELECT statement to get the names of all the
# lecturers.
#
my $sql = "SELECT first_name, last_name " .
        "FROM lecturer";

# Invoke the database handle's prepare() method to get a
# statement handle.
#
my $sth = $dbh->prepare($sql);

# Execute the statement - if it returns a non-zero value,
# then it failed, and the program exits.
#
unless ($sth->execute) {
    die "Statement failed: " . $sth->errstr;
}

# Fetch each row as a reference to a hash of the values,
# keyed by the column name. This is not the most efficient
# means of fetching, but it is quite convenient.
#
```

```
my $hash_ref;
while ($hash_ref = $sth->fetchrow_hashref) {

    my $first_name = $hash_ref->{first_name};
    my $last_name  = $hash_ref->{last_name};
    print qq[$first_name $last_name\n];

}
$sth->finish;

# Disconnect from the server.
#
$dbh->disconnect;
```

Issuing Updates

When you want to send an SQL statement that updates the database, it can be a little easier than sending a query that expects results. The sort of SQL statements that fall into this category include UPDATE, INSERT, and DELETE. Since you do not expect them to return any results, you do not need a statement handle. You can execute these sort of statements directly from the database handle using the do() method. The do() method returns the number of rows affected, if that value can be determined.

One method that can come in handy, especially when sending an update, is the $dbh->quote method. This will prepare a string for the target database driver—in the case of mSQL, it will escape any single quotes as \', and will wrap the string in single quotes. The following example, dbi_query2.pl, shows the use of the quote() and do() methods for an INSERT and DELETE statement:

```
#!/usr/local/bin/perl

use DBI;

# Attempt to connect to the server. If this connection
# fails, then report the error.
#
my $datasource = "dbi:mSQL:msql_sourcebook:localhost:1114";
my $dbh = DBI->connect($datasource) ||
    die "Could not connect:$DBI::errstr";

# Insert a new lecturer. Note the use of the quote() method
# to prepare the string for insertion.
#
my $first_name = $dbh->quote( qq[Trombone] );
my $last_name  = $dbh->quote( qq[O'Trimslacks] );
my $id         = get_next_id($dbh, 'lecturer');

my $insert_sql = qq[INSERT INTO lecturer ] .
                 qq[(id, first_name, last_name) ] .
                 qq[VALUES($id, $first_name, $last_name)];
```

```perl
# Since statements like insert, update, or delete do not
# produce a result set, we don't need to get a statement
# handle, so we can execute this statement with the do()
# method.
#
unless ($dbh->do($insert_sql)) {
    die "Insert failed: " . $DBI::errstr;
}

# Prepare and execute a SELECT statement to get the names
# of all the lecturers.
#
my $sql = "SELECT first_name, last_name " .
            "FROM lecturer ";
my $sth = $dbh->prepare($sql);
unless ($sth->execute) {
    die "Statement failed: " . $sth->errstr;
}

# Fetch each row as an array.
#
my $row;
while ($row = $sth->fetch) {
    print qq[$$row[0] $$row[1]\n];
}
$sth->finish;

# Clean up the record we added.
#
my $delete_sql = qq[DELETE FROM lecturer ] .
                    qq[WHERE last_name = $last_name];

unless ($dbh->do($delete_sql)) {
    die "Delete failed: " . $DBI::errstr;
}

# Disconnect from the server.
#
$dbh->disconnect;

sub get_next_id {

    my $dbh = shift;
    my $tbl_name = shift;

    # This SQL statement will retrieve a new id value for
    # the given table.
    #
    my $sql = "SELECT _seq FROM $tbl_name";

    # Prepare the statement.
    #
```

```
my $sth = $dbh->prepare($sql);

# Execute the statement - if it returns a non-zero value,
# then it failed.
#
unless ($sth->execute) {
    die "Statement failed: " . $sth->errstr;
}

# There should only be one row and one column.
#
my $row = $sth->fetch;
my $id = $$row[0];

$sth->finish;

return $id;

}
```

mSQL-Specific Features of DBD::Msql

While the purpose of the DBI is to provide database independence, there are some features of the mSQL driver that violate this principle. Most of these private methods are designed to provide metadata; since the present DBI spec does not encompass this, they are implemented as private methods via the $dbh->func() method. As the DBI metadata strategy evolves, you can expect to see these implemented using methods in the specification, which will ensure that they will be implemented in a portable fashion.

mSQL-Specific Metadata

The private functions for retrieving metadata are issued using func() method calls. You can retrieve a list of all tables in the current database by invoking the _ListTables function. This method is made available through the database handle, and returns a list of tables.

```
my @tables = $dbh->func('_ListTables');
```

Given a table name, you can use the _ListFields private method to get the attributes of a given column (aka field). This method is a little more intricate than the _ListTables method. Instead of an array of values, it returns a reference to a hash.

```
$ref = $dbh->func('table_name', '_ListFields');
```

The hash can be dereferenced to obtain an array containing the attributes of each column, as shown in Table 9.2. Note that the index of the elements in the NAME array corresponds to the index of the elements of each array returned, so you can use the same index (as shown in the following example) to get the corresponding type, length, or other attribute of a given column.

Table 9.2 The Attributes of a Table's Columns, as Reported by the `_Listfields` `Private` Method

Expression	Description
`@{ $ref->{NAME} }`	An array containing the name of each column in the table.
`@{ $ref->{TYPE} }`	An array that contains the type of each column in the table.
`@{ $ref->{LENGTH} }`	This array contains the length of each column.
`@{ $ref->{IS_NOT_NULL} }`	For each column, an element of this array contains a 1 if the column is not NULL.
`$ref->{NUMFIELDS}`	This is the number of columns in the table.

The following example, `dbi_meta.pl`, shows how these private methods can be used to retrieve metadata from the database:

```perl
#!/usr/local/bin/perl

use DBI;

# Attempt to connect to the server.
#
my $datasource = "dbi:mSQL:msql_sourcebook:localhost:1114";
my $dbh = DBI->connect($datasource) ||
    die "Could not connect:$DBI::errstr";

# Get a list of all tables.
#
my @tables = $dbh->func('_ListTables');

# For each table, get the attributes for each of that
# table's columns.
#
my $tbl_name;
foreach $tbl_name (@tables) {

    print " TABLE: $tbl_name\n";

    # Get the column attributes for this table.
    #
    $ref = $dbh->func($tbl_name, '_ListFields');

    # Each column attribute is stored as an array reference
    # within the hash reference returned by the method call.
    #
    my @col_names  = @{ $ref->{NAME} };
    my @col_types  = @{ $ref->{TYPE} };
```

```
    my @col_length = @{ $ref->{LENGTH} };

    my $i;
    for ($i = 0; $i < $ref->{NUMFIELDS}; $i++) {
        print " Column: $col_names[i]\n";
        print "   Type:   $col_types[$i]\n";
        print "   Length: $col_length[$i]\n";
    }

}

# Disconnect from the server.
#
$dbh->disconnect;
```

MsqlSourceBook::MsqlFramework—
A Simple Framework for CGI Applications

The remaining examples in this chapter will build on the MsqlSourceBook::
MsqlFramework module, which is a simple framework for application development using
DBD::mSQL and the CGI module. It borrows a lot of ideas from the framework shown in the
previous chapter, but offers a number of new features. This module is included in the ch09
directory underneath the eg directory on the CD-ROM. If you can instruct your Web server to
treat the ch09 directory as a directory that contains executable scripts, and also instruct the
server to treat the .cgi file extension as an executable script, you can run this example. If you
are running on a non-Unix platform, you will most likely have to take an extra step, and let your
Web server know that .cgi should be executed by the Perl interpreter. The previous chapter
includes more instructions on how to configure this for your Web server.

The MsqlSourceBook directory under the /eg/ch09 directory contains the source
code to that module. You should cd to this directory, and view the README file contained there.
This includes instructions on installing the module. Under most circumstances, you can install it
with the following commands:

```
perl Makefile.PL
make
make install
```

Before examining the framework's source code, we will examine the source code to a small
sample application that uses the framework. It and the source code to the framework are in the
MsqlSourceBook subdirectory of the ch09 directory. The sample application is called
test.cgi. There is also a file in that directory called test.sql; you should feed it into the
msql monitor program using the msql_sourcebook database, as in:

```
msql msql_sourcebook < test.sql
```

The `test.sql` script creates a table called `author`, and adds one row to it. The contents of `test.sql` are shown here:

```
#
#
# This SQL file should be fed into the mSQL monitor program.
#

DROP TABLE author
\g

CREATE TABLE author
    (au_lname CHAR(35),
     au_fname CHAR(35),
     au_id    INT)
\g

INSERT INTO author
    VALUES('Burroughs', 'William', 1)
\g

CREATE SEQUENCE ON author STEP 1 VALUE 10
\g
```

The `test.cgi` Sample Application

The `test.cgi` sample program allows you to add and edit authors in the author table. If you've installed the `ch09` directory such that it can be accessed under a given user's account (we're using the name, `bjepson`, as an example), you should be able to load the first example with something similar to this URL:

> `http://localhost/~bjepson/ch09/MsqlSourceBook/test.cgi`

You should be able to set this up by copying the `ch09` directory to your personal space on your Web server. You can also configure the directory as an executable script directory, and open up the appropriate URL using your Web browser. Your Web server should allow you to call this directory anything you want. If, for some reason, you can't get the example running on your Web site, you can get access to a working, online example by pointing your browser at:

> `http://users.ids.net/~bjepson/msql/eg/ch09/MsqlSourceBook/test.cgi`

Figure 9.1 shows the main page of the `test.cgi` application. You can select the name of an existing author and click the Edit button, or press the New button, which will let you add a new author. Figure 9.2 shows the page that lets you add or edit an author.

The `MsqlSourceBook::MsqlFramework` offers a number of features to simplify application development. Like the framework shown in the previous chapter, it provides buffered output; the entire HTML page can be built in a temporary buffer, and when it's complete, it is displayed to the user. This works quite well in conjunction with the error handling, since the error messages can be accumulated and displayed before the page is shown. If the page

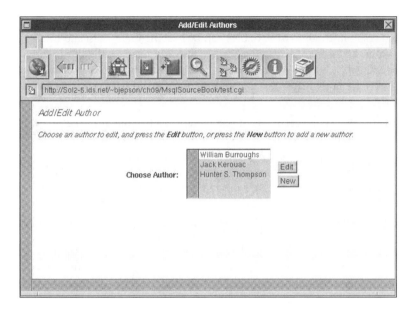

FIGURE 9.1 The main page of the sample application.

were displayed as it was built, error messages would have to be interspersed among HTML, providing an unpleasant appearance.

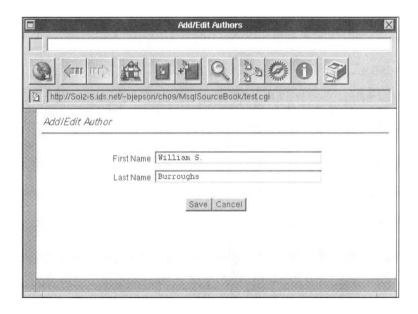

FIGURE 9.2 The Add/Edit Authors page.

One of the most advanced features of this framework is the ability to bind CGI parameters to a table and column. Binding of variables can be used in simple cases to transparently propagate values from the form to the database. Once they are bound in this fashion, you can let the users edit or add data, and you need only call an `update_table()` method to automatically send an UPDATE or an INSERT. You can also use the `fetch_data()` method to load the values into the CGI parameters.

In the case of the Authors table, CGI parameters can be bound for the `au_id`, `au_lname` and `au_fname` columns. This binding is simply an association between the CGI parameter and the column. The association is "remembered" from one instance of the script to another. Along with this association, the framework remembers which column is to be used as a key for updates and inserts. This is used when the framework builds the `WHERE au_id = somevalue` clause of an UPDATE statement, and is also used when the framework needs to retrieve a new id value for an INSERT statement. It's also used by the `fetch_data()` method, as it uses the key value when it fetches a row. It's up to you to set the id value; it can be very convenient to construct a picklist that lets the user choose a record to edit, and you use the CGI parameter for the picklist that corresponds to the row id within that table. When you submit that form, the key value will already be set for the fetch and any subsequent updates. The `test.cgi` example, which will be examined shortly, uses this technique.

When you want to fetch the data from the record, you must set the CGI parameter that corresponds to the record id. In subsequent invocations of your script, you can call `fetch_data()` to get the values from the database and automatically set the CGI parameters appropriately. This will make sure the right values are shown in the form when it's loaded by the Web browser. Similarly, you can invoke `update_table()` when the user has submitted the form. If the record id is blank, `update_table()` assumes that the user is adding a new record, and gets a new sequence id appropriately. If there is a value for the record id, `update_table()` uses the SQL UPDATE statement to update the corresponding row.

The `test.cgi` Source Code

The following listing contains all of the source code to the `test.cgi` application. Since the framework does a lot of work, it's easy to pack a lot of functionality into a small space. At the very top of this package, the framework module is used, and then the `@ISA` array is used to inherit the framework's properties and methods.

```
#!/usr/local/bin/perl

package sample;

use MsqlSourceBook::MsqlFramework;
@ISA = qw(MsqlSourceBook::MsqlFramework);
```

The `init()` method works as little more than a master routine that invokes all of the other methods. After setting the title, this method invokes the `db_init()` and `gui_init()` methods, and then goes on to invoke its superclass constructor.

```
#
# Initialize this script and invoke the methods needed to
# display the document.
#
sub init {

    my $self = shift;

    # Set a title.
    #
    $self->set_title("Add/Edit Authors");

    $self->db_init;
    $self->gui_init;

    $self->SUPER::init;

}
```

The db_init() method binds each of the parameters (au_id, au_lname, and au_fname) to columns in the database. As is so often the case, the parameters have the same name as the columns.

```
#
# Perform database-specific initialization. This will take
# care of binding parameters to the table columns.
#
sub db_init {

    my $self = shift;
    my $query = $self->{query};

    # Bind all the parameters to columns in the table.
    #
    $self->bind_param('au_id',    'author', 'au_id');
    $self->bind_param('au_lname', 'author', 'au_lname');
    $self->bind_param('au_fname', 'author', 'au_fname');

    # Set the key to au_id
    #
    $self->set_key('author', 'au_id');

}
```

The gui_init() method takes care of several cases. The default case is the last one in the method, but it is the first thing the users see when starting this script. This script can display any of two user interfaces: a chooser page (Figure 9.1) or an Add/Edit page (Figure 9.2). The reason that the chooser appears first is that the Add/Edit page is only displayed if the user pressed Add or Edit. However, after a user presses Cancel or Save (the two buttons on the Add/Edit page), the user is returned to the chooser form. If this script doesn't check for (and deal with) the possibility that the user pressed Save before the script displays the form, the chooser list may get obsolete data. Since the chooser list is made up of the names of the authors, and the Add/Edit form lets them change those names, the list must be built after any changes are committed, and after any new records are added. The gui_init() method makes use of the edit_author_form() method, which follows immediately after.

```perl
#
# Perform graphical user interface initialization.
# Basically, this displays the whole form.
#
sub gui_init {

    my $self = shift;
    my $query = $self->{query};

    # Start an HTML form.
    #
    $self->printbuff( $query->startform );

    # Get the value of the submit variable.
    #
    my $submit = $query->param('submit');

    # Print out a header.
    #
    $self->printbuff( qq[<font size="+1"><i>
                         Add/Edit Author</i></font><hr>] );

    # The user might have chosen edit or new from the main
    # selection screen. The main selection screen is *only*
    # displayed when the user didn't press New or Edit.

    # Did they choose edit? If so, fetch the data and invoke
    # the method that displays a data entry form.
    #
    if ($submit =~ /^EDIT$/i) {
        $query->param('au_id',
            $query->param('choose_au_id') );
        $self->fetch_data("author");
        $self->edit_author_form;
    }

    # Did they choose new? If so, zero out the author id,
    # fetch the data (this will populate the row with
    # blanks), and invoke the method that displays the form.
    #
    if ($submit =~ /^NEW$/i) {
        $query->delete('au_id');
        $self->fetch_data("author");
        $self->edit_author_form;
    }
```

```perl
# This and the preceding options are mutually exclusive,
# so if they didn't select Edit or New, they might have
# chosen save.
#
if ($query->param('submit') =~ /SAVE/i) {
    $self->update_table('author');
}

# If the user did not choose Edit or New, then we must
# display a form that lets them choose an author. We'll
# do this if they selected save, however. Since the
# Cancel option is not handled specially, it will also
# result in dropping through to this option.
#
if ($submit !~ /^EDIT$/i & $submit !~ /^NEW$/i) {

    # Create a picklist for authors using a framework
    # method designed for this purpose. Since we're
    # using the id value that was set as a key (and
    # bound to a CGI parameter of the same name, au_id),
    # the value of this parameter will be set by the
    # user's selection. If the user hits the Edit
    # button, then the au_id value will be set when we
    # invoke fetch_data().
    #
    my $sl = $self->db_scroll_list(
        table     => 'author',
        row_id    => 'au_id',
        order_by  => 'au_lname, au_fname',
        row_label => 'au_fname au_lname',
        cgi_parm  => 'choose_au_id' );

    # Create an Edit and a New button.
    #
    my $btn_edit = $query->submit( -name  => 'submit',
                                   -value => 'Edit' );
    my $btn_new  = $query->submit( -name  => 'submit',
                                   -value => 'New' );


    # Display a prompt that instructs the user.
    #
    $self->printbuff( qq[<i>Choose an author to edit,
                        and press the
                        <strong>Edit</strong> button,
                        or press the
                        <strong>New</strong> button to
                        add a new author.</i>] );

    # Now, display all of the visual components.
    #
```

```
        $self->printbuff('<center>');
        $self->printbuff(
            qq[<table>
                <tr>
                <td><strong>Choose Author:</strong></td>
                <td>$sl</td>
                <td align="left">$btn_edit<br>
                                 $btn_new</td>
                </tr>
                </table>]);
        $self->printbuff('</center>');
    }

    # Before each call to endform(), you must invoke the
    # hidden_fields() method, which displays some hidden
    # fields that are required by the Framework.
    #
    $self->hidden_fields;
    $self->printbuff( $query->endform );

}


#
# This method displays a data entry form for adding or
# editing authors.
#
sub edit_author_form {

    my $self = shift;
    my $query = $self->{query};

    # Create two textfields - one for the last name, one for
    # the first name.
    #
    my $tf_fname = $query->textfield( -name    => 'au_fname',
                                      -size    => 35,
                                      -maxlen => 35);
    my $tf_lname = $query->textfield( -name    => 'au_lname',
                                      -size    => 35,
                                      -maxlen => 35);

    # Display the fields in a nicely formatted table.
    #
    $self->printbuff('<center>');
    $self->printbuff(
        qq[<table>
            <tr>
            <td align="right">First Name</td>
            <td align="left" >$tf_fname</td>
            </tr>
            <tr>
            <td align="right">Last Name</td>
```

```
            <td align="left" >$tf_lname</td>
            </tr>
            </table>]);

   # Display a hidden field for the au_id field, since we
   # don't want the user modifying the key value.
   #
   $self->printbuff( $query->hidden( 'au_id' ) );

   # Display two submit buttons; one for Save and one for
   # Cancel.
   #
   $self->printbuff( $query->submit( -name => 'submit',
                                     -value => 'Save') );
   $self->printbuff( $query->submit( -name => 'submit',
                                     -value => 'Cancel') );
   $self->printbuff('</center>');
}
```

Finally, within the `main` package, the script instantiates a new object of the type (`sample`) defined in this module. It calls the `init()` method, and then it invokes the `display_page()` method, which is defined in the sample's superclass, `MsqlSourceBook::MsqlFramework`.

```
package main;
use DBI;
my $dbh = DBI->connect("dbi:mSQL:msql_sourcebook:localhost");
$frm = new sample($dbh);
$frm->init;
$frm->display_page;
$dbh->disconnect;
```

The `register.cgi` Student Registration Application

The previous chapter introduced an application that allowed you to manage classes, lecturers, students, and scheduled courses. One of the scripts in that collection of applications is the `edit_student.cgi` script, which you can access from the set of navigation links from any example in that chapter. Figure 9.3 shows the Add/Edit student page in action; you should add a few students using it before you proceed any further. After you have done that, you should run the `registration.sql` script through the msql monitor program. This sets up the registration table, which is a cross-reference between the schedule (scheduled courses) and student tables. Here are the contents of `registration.sql`, which is included in the `/eg/ch09` directory:

```
#
# Definition for the student registration table.
#
```

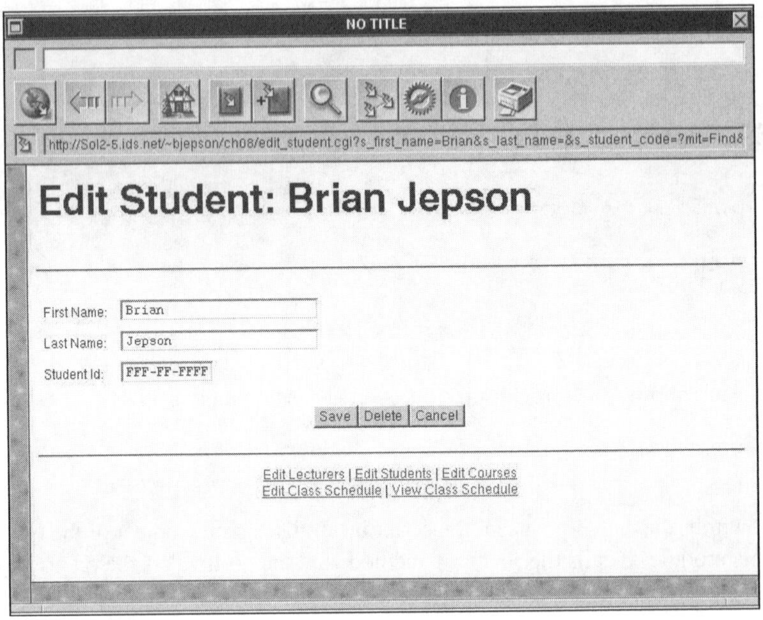

FIGURE 9.3 The Add/Edit Students page.

```
CREATE TABLE registration
     (student_id   INT,
      schedule_id INT)
\g
```

Once you have added some students to the database, you can use the `register.cgi` application to assume one of the student's identity. Figure 9.4 shows the login screen for that program. You can reach this page by starting the `register.cgi` application from your browser. Depending upon how you have configured your browser for the examples shown earlier in this chapter, you should be able to open the `register.cgi` example with a URL like:

```
http://sol2-5.ids.net/~bjepson/ch09/register.cgi
```

However, if you cannot bring the example up under your Web server, you can see a live example at work on:

```
http://users.ids.net/~bjepson/msql/eg/ch09/register.cgi
```

In order to log in to the `register.cgi` application, you must supply the first and last name of the student, as well as a password. The password is the student id. Figure 9.5 shows the registration page. At the top of the page is a list of available courses. These can be filtered using the Filter Options at the bottom of the page. Once you have chosen the desired filter, you can press the Set Filter button to apply it. Only the scheduled courses that meet the criteria will be displayed.

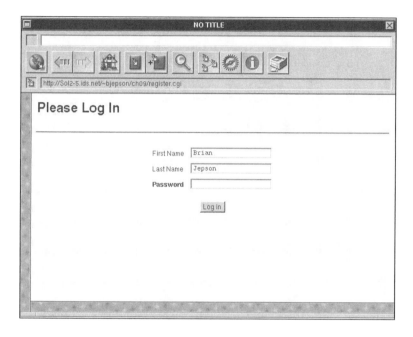

FIGURE 9.4 The login form.

If you wish to register for one or more courses, simply select the checkbox next to the courses you wish to register for, and press the Register Selected Courses button. If you are already registered for a class, you may drop it by selecting the checkbox next to the courses you wish to drop, and you should then press the Drop Selected Courses button.

The `register.cgi` Source Code

The register object is a Perl module that encapsulates the behavior needed to allow students to register for classes. It includes primitive authentication; students must supply their first and last name as a user id, and their student id is used as a password. Using the form that this script displays, the user (student) can add or drop courses, and apply a filter to the list of available courses.

```
#!/usr/local/bin/perl

package register;
use MsqlSourceBook::MsqlFramework;
@ISA = qw(MsqlSourceBook::MsqlFramework);
use strict 'vars';
```

The `init()` method takes care of some basic initialization for this module. It calls the `login()` method, and if it succeeds, it invokes the `db_init()` and `gui_init()` methods. After this, the superclass `init()` method is invoked.

```
sub init {
```

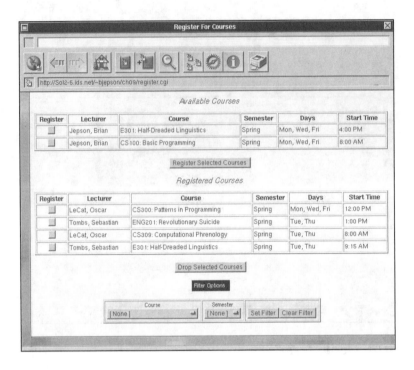

FIGURE 9.5 The registration page.

```
my $self = shift;

# create an array of "day-of-week" id values,
# and a hash which maps these to three-letter
# day names.
#
@{$self->{dow_array}} = (0..6);
%{$self->{dow_hash}} = (0 => 'Sun', 1 => 'Mon',
                        2 => 'Tue', 3 => 'Wed',
                        4 => 'Thu', 5 => 'Fri',
                        6 => 'Sat');

# Invoke the login method. If it returns a true value,
# then call db_init() and gui_init(). Since the login()
# method displays a form if the user needs to log in, we
# don't need to worry about what happens if the login()
# method returns a non-true value.
#
if ($self->login (
        table          => 'student',
        username_col   => ['first_name', 'last_name'],
        username_label => ['First Name', 'Last Name'],
        uid_col        => 'id',
```

```
                pwd_col          => 'student_code') )
    {

        $self->db_init;
        $self->gui_init;
    }

    $self->SUPER::init;

}
```

The gui_init() method takes care of displaying the data entry form. In the case of this module, it displays two tables: one for the list of classes that the student may register for, and one for the classes to which the student is currently registered. For this, it uses the show_unregistered() and show_registered() methods. After that, it displays a set of controls that allow the user to filter the list of available courses.

```
sub gui_init {

    my $self  = shift;
    my $query = $self->{query};
    my $dbh   = $self->{dbh};

    # Set the title of the page.
    #
    $self->set_title("Register For Courses");

    # Display the user interface
    #
    $self->printbuff( $query->startform );

    $self->printbuff( qq[<center>] );

    $self->show_unregistered;
    $self->show_registered;

    # Display some filtering options. First, a popup for
    # courses.
    #
    $self->printbuff( qq[<p>] );
    $self->printbuff( qq[<table bgcolor="#000000">] );
    $self->printbuff( qq[<tr><td>] );
    $self->printbuff(
        qq[<font color="#FFFFFF" size="-1">
            Filter Options</font>] );
    $self->printbuff( qq[</td></tr></table>] );

    $self->printbuff( qq[<table border bgcolor="#DDDDDD">] );
    $self->printbuff( qq[<tr align="center" valign="bottom">] );
    my $sl =
      $self->db_scroll_list( table    => 'course',
```

```
                        size       => 1,
                        row_id     => 'id',
                        order_by   => 'course_name',
                        row_label  => 'course_name',
                        none_option => 'true',
                        cgi_parm   => 'course_id' );
$self->printbuff(qq[<td><font size="-1">Course</font>
                 <br>$sl</td>]);

# Picklist for Semesters.
#
my @sem = (0, 'S', 'F');
my %sem = ('0' => '[ None ]',
           'S' => 'Spring',
           'F' => 'Fall');
my $pm = $query->popup_menu( -name    => 'semester',
                             -values => \@sem,
                             -labels => \%sem );
$self->printbuff(qq[<td><font size="-1">Semester</font>
                 <br>$pm</td>]);

# Display a Set Filter button and a Clear Filter button.
#
$self->printbuff( qq[<td>] );
$self->printbuff(
    $query->submit( -name => 'submit',
                    -value =>'Set Filter' ) );
$self->printbuff(
    $query->submit( -name => 'submit',
                    -value =>'Clear Filter' ) );
$self->printbuff( qq[</td></tr></table>] );
$self->printbuff( qq[</center>] );

$self->printbuff( $query->hidden('id') );
$self->hidden_fields;
$self->printbuff( $query->endform );

}
```

Although the framework supports the binding of CGI parameters to columns, this module does not make use of that feature (the bindings are usually initialized in the db_init() method). However, this method performs an important function. It checks the value of the Submit button (this is set to whatever action the user chose), and performs one of two actions. If the user pressed the Register Selected Courses button, then this method will insert a row into the registration table for each selected course. If the user presses the Drop Selected Courses button, then for each selected course, the corresponding rows are deleted from the registration table.

The rows in the registration table are a cross-reference between the schedule (list of available courses) and the student table. The student id is gleaned by retrieving the _uid CGI parameter. That value is set by the login() method, and corresponds to the record id in the student table. This demonstrates one of the advantages of the login() method; any table can be used for user authentication, and the user's identity can be obtained from the _uid parameter.

```perl
sub db_init {

    my $self  = shift;
    my $query = $self->{query};
    my $dbh   = $self->{dbh};

    my $action = $query->param('submit');
    my $uid    = $query->param('_uid');

    # If the user pressed the Register Selected Courses
    # button, then we need to issue an INSERT for each of
    # the selected courses. The available CGI parameter
    # holds each of these.
    #
    if ($query->param('submit') =~ /REGISTER/i) {

        my @selected = $query->param('available');
        foreach (@selected) {
            my $sql = qq[INSERT INTO registration
                                (schedule_id, student_id)
                                VALUES($_, $uid)];
            my $sth = $dbh->prepare($sql);
            unless ($sth->execute) {
                $self->error;
                return;
            }
        }
    }

    # If the user pressed the Drop Selected Courses button,
    # then, for each course that is selected from the list
    # of registered courses, we need to issue a DELETE
    # statement for the row in the registration table.
    #
    if ($query->param('submit') =~ /DROP/i) {
        my @selected = $query->param('registered');
        foreach (@selected) {
            my $sql = qq[DELETE FROM registration
                                WHERE schedule_id = $_
                                AND   student_id  = $uid];
            my $sth = $dbh->prepare($sql);
            unless ($sth->execute) {
                $self->error;
                return;
            }
        }
    }

}
```

The `display_table()` method is a generalized method that is used by both the `show_registered()` and `show_unregistered()` methods. Since the tables for the list of registered and unregistered are basically the same, this method comes in quite handy. Using the same method to build the table in both cases eliminates an incident of redundant code.

```perl
sub display_table {

    my $self           = shift;
    my $row            = shift;
    my $checkbox_name  = shift;
    my $all_checked    = shift;

    my $query = $self->{query};

    # A lookup hash to map the semester codes from the
    # schedule table to their full names.
    #
    my %semester = ('S' => 'Spring', 'F' => 'Fall');

    # Print the schedule as a centered table, with some
    # nice headers.
    #
    $self->printbuff( qq[<center>] );
    $self->printbuff( qq[<table border width="100%">] );
    $self->printbuff( qq[<th>Register</th><th>Lecturer</th>
                <th>Course</th><th>Semester</th>
                <th>Days</th><th>Start Time</th>]);

    # Process each row, and display each scheduled class.
    #
    my $i;
    foreach ( @{$row} ) {
        my @row = @{ $_ };

        my ($lec_first_name, $lec_last_name,
            $lec_id, $course_code, $course_name,
            $course_id, $course_credits, $start_time,
            $semester, $dow_string, $id) = @row;

        # make some names that are suitable for display.
        #
        my $lecturer = qq[$lec_last_name, $lec_first_name];
        my $course   = qq[$course_code: $course_name];

        # if the start time is blank, make it five
        # non-breaking spaces.
        #
        $start_time  = $start_time || (" " x 5);

        # convert the day-of-week string into human-readable
        # form, using comma-separated three-letter names.
        #
```

```perl
    my @dow;

    # the dow_string is a string consisting of
    # day-of-week numbers between 0 and 6. This next
    # construct will loop over each character using
    # foreach; it splits the string on the empty space
    # between characters, and sorts the resulting list.
    #
    foreach (sort split(//, $dow_string)) {

        # look up each day-of-week number in the
        # dow_hash, which yields the three-letter
        # day name.
        #
        my $dow_shortname = $self->{dow_hash}->{$_};

        # add the day name to the @dow array.
        #
        push @dow, $dow_shortname;

    }

    # create a string that is the comma-delimited
    # list of days. If it's blank, use five non-
    # breaking spaces.
    #
    my $dow = join(", ", @dow) || (" " x 5);

    # build a table row with the information.
    #
    $self->printbuff(qq[<tr>]);

    # display a checkbox to register for this class.
    #
    my $checked;
    if ($all_checked) {
        $checked = 'checked';
    }
    $self->printbuff( qq[<td align="center">] );
    $self->printbuff( qq[<input type="checkbox"
                                name="$checkbox_name"
                                value=$id $checked>]);
    $self->printbuff( qq[</td>] );

    # Show the name of the lecturer.
    #
    $self->printbuff( qq[<td>$lecturer</td>] );

    # Show the name of the course.
    #
    $self->printbuff( qq[<td>$course</td>] );
```

```
        # display the semester full name, the days of the
        # week, and the start time, each in a separate
        # <td> element.
        #
        $self->printbuff(qq[<td>$semester{$semester}</td>]);
        $self->printbuff(qq[<td>$dow</td>]);
        $self->printbuff(qq[<td>$start_time</td>]);

        # end the row
        #
        $self->printbuff(qq[</tr>]);
    }

    # end the table, and turn centering off.
    #
    $self->printbuff( qq[</table>] );
    $self->printbuff( qq[</center>] );

}
```

The show_unregistered() method displays all of the classes that are not currently
registered by the student who is logged in. Since mSQL does not provide the ability to perform
a subquery or outer join, we must make two passes against the database to determine which rows
meet this criteria. The first pass gets a list of all courses that are available. For each result in this
first pass, we check to see if the current student is registered for the course. If not, that course is
added to the list of unregistered courses, and is ultimately shown in the table displayed by the
display_table() method.

```
sub show_unregistered {

    my $self  = shift;
    my $query = $self->{query};
    my $dbh   = $self->{dbh};

    # a SELECT statement to fetch all of the schedule
    # information.
    #
    my $filter = $query->param('submit');
    my $extra_where_clause;

    # If the user pressed the Set Filter button, then we
    # need to apply a filter.
    #
    if ($filter =~ /^SET FILTER$/i) {
        my $semester  = $query->param('semester');
        my $course_id = $query->param('course_id');
        if ($semester) {
            $extra_where_clause .=
                qq[ AND schedule.semester = '$semester' ];
        }
        if ($course_id) {
```

```
            $extra_where_clause .=
                qq[ AND schedule.course_id = $course_id ];
        }
    }

    # Build the SELECT statement, and add in the filter
    # ($extra_where_clause). If the filter is blank, it will
    # have no effect.
    #
    my $uid = $query->param('_uid');
    my $sql = qq[select lecturer.first_name,
                        lecturer.last_name,
                        lecturer.id,
                        course.course_code,
                        course.course_name,
                        course.id,
                        course.credits,
                        schedule.start_time,
                        schedule.semester,
                        schedule.dow_string,
                        schedule.id
                 FROM lecturer, course, schedule
                 WHERE lecturer.id = schedule.lecturer_id
                 AND   course.id   = schedule.course_id
                 $extra_where_clause
                 ORDER BY schedule.semester,
                          schedule.dow_string,
                          schedule.start_time];

    # execute the query, and check for errors. If we get
    # an error, display the page and exit the script.
    #
    my $sth = $dbh->prepare($sql);
    unless ($sth->execute) {
        $self->error;
        return;
    }

    # eliminate any rows that are already registered by the
    # student.
    #
    my (@row, @registered_rows, @unregistered_rows);
    while (@row = $sth->fetchrow()) {

        # Get the id of the current row
        #
        my $id = $row[$#row];

        # Build the select statement.
        #
        my $sql = qq[SELECT *
                     FROM registration
```

```
                              WHERE student_id = $uid
                              AND   schedule_id = $id];

       my $sth_2 = $dbh->prepare($sql);
       unless ($sth_2->execute) {
           $self->error;
           return;
       }

       # If the current row in the first select has a match
       # in the list of classes registered by the student,
       # do not add it to the list of courses that are
       # unregistered.
       #
       my @tmp_row = @row;
       unless ($sth_2->fetchrow) {
           push @unregistered_rows, \@tmp_row;
       }
   }

   $self->printbuff( qq[<p><font size="+1"><i>
                        Available Courses</i></font>] );
   $self->display_table(\@unregistered_rows, 'available');
   $self->printbuff(
     $query->submit(-name  => 'submit',
                    -value =>'Register Selected Courses'));
}
```

The `show_registered()` method is similar to the previous method, except for the fact that it only needs to make one pass against the data. Since the logic of the SELECT statement (all courses registered by this student) can be easily expressed using a single SQL statement, there is no need to query the database more than once.

```
sub show_registered {

    my $self  = shift;
    my $query = $self->{query};
    my $dbh   = $self->{dbh};

    # a SELECT statement to fetch all of the schedule
    # information.
    #
    my $uid = $query->param('_uid');
    my $sql = qq[select lecturer.first_name,
                        lecturer.last_name,
                        lecturer.id,
                        course.course_code,
                        course.course_name,
                        course.id,
                        course.credits,
                        schedule.start_time,
```

```
                        schedule.semester,
                        schedule.dow_string,
                        schedule.id
                FROM lecturer, course, schedule,
                        registration
                WHERE lecturer.id = schedule.lecturer_id
                AND   course.id   = schedule.course_id
                AND   registration.schedule_id = schedule.id
                AND   registration.student_id  = $uid
                ORDER BY schedule.semester,
                            schedule.dow_string,
                            schedule.start_time];

    # execute the query, and check for errors. If we get
    # an error, display the page and exit the script.
    #
    my $sth = $dbh->prepare($sql);
    unless ($sth->execute) {
        $self->error;
        return;
    }

    # eliminate any rows that are already registered by the
    # student.
    #
    my (@row, @registered_rows);
    while (@row = $sth->fetchrow()) {
        my @tmp_row = @row;
        push @registered_rows, \@tmp_row;
    }

    $self->printbuff( qq[<p><font size="+1"><i>
                            Registered Courses</i></font>] );
    $self->display_table(\@registered_rows, 'registered');
    $self->printbuff(
      $query->submit(-name  => 'submit',
                        -value =>'Drop Selected Courses'));
}
```

Like the previous example, the connection to the database is managed in the `main` package. Also, the instantiation of the object defined in this module is handled here.

```
package main;
use DBI;
my $dbh = DBI->connect("dbi:mSQL:msql_sourcebook:localhost");
my $frm = new register($dbh);
$frm->init;
$frm->display_page;
$dbh->disconnect;

1;
```

Wholesome Food Caught without Net or Trap

DBI is "where it's at" as far as Perl database development is concerned. Although the MsqlPerl API will continue to evolve, and will have a life of its own, it's likely that this life will be little more than an emulation layer. That is to say, the `Msql` module that you use will likely be implemented on top of the `DBD::mSQL` driver, so you'll be using the DBI anyway, whether you like it or not. Of course, both the MsqlPerl module and the DBI mSQL driver are very useful in their own right; it is up to you to decide which module works best for you. Thanks to the private functions included in `DBD::mSQL`, it's possible to write Perl applications with all the functionality of applications written using MsqlPerl. Since the DBI is the future of Perl database development, and since the same developer is maintaining both MsqlPerl and `DBD::mSQL`, it is certainly worth your while to become familiar with both packages. As the DBI evolves, `DBD::mSQL` will evolve with it, and what was once an amorphous future will coalesce into the here and now.

mSQL Development
with PHP/FI

10

Although Mini SQL can be combined with powerful programming languages such as C, Java, and Perl, there are many applications where a more lightweight development tool can be useful. Rasmus Lerdorf's (rasmus@lerdorf.on.ca) PHP/FI (Personal Home Page/Form Interpreter) package is such a tool. The original version of PHP/FI was a CGI wrapper written in Perl. It was built by the author to provide a simple way of tracking accesses to his online résumé. He found that the Web server on which his résumé resided had difficulty forking processes due to the constant load on it (no doubt caused by accesses to his résumé :-). In order to reduce the size of the program, Rasmus rewrote the CGI wrapper using C, and through the magic of creeping featurism, this humble CGI wrapper has become PHP/FI.

PHP/FI occupies a niche similar to one of Perl's in that both are popular tools for developing database-enabled Web pages. However, when Perl is used with CGI, it is commonly used to generate HTML documents from scratch. PHP/FI, on the other hand, is much more like Sybase's web.sql or Netscape's Livewire, in that it is embedded within HTML documents. Unlike embedded JavaScript, which is executed on the browser, embedded PHP/FI is executed on the server, and the output of it is used to create the final HTML document that is sent to the user's browser.

This chapter assumes that you are running a modern flavor of Unix, have a Web server installed on your machine, and are capable of administering the Web server. PHP works like a charm with the Apache Web server, which is the most popular Web server software on the Internet. It is supported on both Unix and Win32, and is completely free. If you are not running Apache, you can still use PHP, but your Web server must support the ability to execute CGI scripts. Although PHP/FI is typically distributed as Unix source code, there are experimental versions of PHP/FI available for Win32, and these include support for Mini SQL. At the time of this writing, these versions are unsupported.

Obtaining and Installing PHP/FI

The PHP/FI homepage is located at `http://php.iquest.net/`. This page offers a wealth of information regarding PHP/FI. That page includes a link marked "File Archive," from which you may download PHP/FI. You should be able to build and install the core distribution of PHP/FI on most Unix platforms. Experimental versions are available for Windows NT and Windows 95—versions are available that include support Mini SQL 1.0.16 and Mini SQL 2.0. As the Windows NT version of the Apache server evolves, a version of PHP/FI may emerge for Windows NT that includes mSQL support, and hopefully won't be considered an experimental work.

Why You Want to Use Apache

If you are using PHP/FI on a Unix platform, and you have some control over the choice of Web servers to use, you should strongly consider using the Apache Web server (`www.apache.org`). Beyond the fact that it is the most popular Web server on the Internet, PHP/FI integrates extremely well with Apache. Under Apache, you may choose to build PHP/FI as an Apache module, which allows you to avoid the overhead of using CGI. Also, PHP/FI can be associated with a document extension (usually `.phtml`), so every document ending with that extension will automatically be fed into the PHP/FI module before it is sent to the user's Web browser. Further, the use of PHP/FI can be restricted by directory when it is built as an Apache module. This can be extremely convenient when you want to offer PHP/FI to a limited number of developers.

Installing PHP/FI

After you've downloaded the source code, you should extract it and examine the README file. The README file includes complete instructions on compiling and installing PHP/FI for your machine. Before you build it, you'll need to determine whether you will build it as an Apache module, or if you will choose to run it as a CGI executable. If you choose to install it as a CGI executable, the executable `php.cgi` will be created, and this can be installed in your cgi-bin directory. If you have configured your Web server to recognize the file extension `.cgi` as an executable CGI type, then you can install `php.cgi` in any location you feel is convenient.

If you are using the Apache PHP module, you will need to copy the examples for this chapter to a directory that your Web server recognizes as a document directory. If you are using PHP as a CGI script, your PHP document names must be appended to the URL of the `php.cgi` executable, such as `http://myhost.com/cgi-bin/php.cgi/webdocs/sample.phtml`. There are a number of security issues regarding PHP if it is used as a CGI executable rather than as an Apache module. See the *Security Issues* section of the PHP/FI documentation, which is included in the docs/doc.html file under the top-level PHP distribution directory.

When you configure and install PHP/FI according to the instructions in the README file, please be sure to include support for Mini SQL, and point it to the correct installation location of Mini SQL (usually the /usr/local/Hughes directory). You will also be asked if you want to use Mini SQL for access logging. This feature is not necessary to run the examples in this chapter, but you may wish to use it anyway.

After you have installed PHP/FI, you should verify that it operates correctly before attempting to run any of the examples in this chapter.

If You Have Problems

If you have trouble installing PHP/FI and cannot run the examples, please consult the README file included with the source code. The PHP homepage at http://php.iquest.net/ includes a link to the FAQ and to the PHP/FI mailing list archives, either of which may provide answers to your problem. This archive is searchable, and is a good point to start at before posting a question to the mailing list. Information on subscribing to the mailing list can be found in the README file.

Running the Examples

If you have installed PHP/FI as an Apache module according to the instructions in the README file that accompanies the PHP/FI distribution, then you will be able to create documents that have the `.phtml` extension, and they will automatically be processed by PHP/FI when you load them in a Web browser. If you install the CGI version of PHP/FI, then you will need to supply the pathname for each document to the `php.cgi` executable, as in

```
www.yourhost.com/cgi-bin/php.cgi/~username/document.html
```

(This example assumes that `php.cgi` was installed in your server's cgi-bin directory.)

In order to run the examples in the /eg/ch10 directory, you can copy the *.phtml files to a Web document directory or set up the /eg/ch10 directory as a document directory under your Web server. Once you have done this, you can access them directly by typing the URL for the document in your Web browser.

Using PHP/FI

PHP/FI commands are embedded into HTML documents using the <? > markup tag. The commands are executed by PHP/FI and the resulting HTML document is sent to the user. None of the source code is visible to the user, since all of the PHP/FI code is interpreted before the browser gets its hands on the document. The following code listing (/eg/ch10/helloworld.phtml) shows a simple PHP/FI program that simply says "Hello, World." Figure 10.1 shows the output of this program.

```
<HTML>
<HEAD>
<TITLE>A Sample Page</TITLE>
</HEAD>

<BODY BGCOLOR="#FFFFFF">

<?

    /* This is a comment. */
```

```
     /* Display a greeting */
     echo "Hello, World<p>";


>

</BODY>
</HTML>
```

A Simple Form Example

Like Perl, PHP is not a strongly typed language, since you don't need to explicitly declare the type of a variable before you use it. Unlike Perl, PHP/FI is not very sensitive to context, and cannot always determine whether a value should be treated as a string, integer, or double value. The `SetType()` function allows you to explicitly state this, even after a variable has been initialized. The following example makes use of this feature as the user is asked to enter a number into an HTML form. This form does not contain an explicit target, so the same `.phtml` file is loaded when the user presses the Submit button. At first, a string comparison is made on the value of `$number` to ensure that the user actually typed something. If the value of `$number` is not an empty string, it is treated as a number, as the program counts from the value of `$number−10` to the value of `$number + 10`. Figure 10.2 shows the output of this document, which is included on the CD-ROM as the file /eg/ch10/formexample.phtml.

```
<HTML>
<HEAD>
<TITLE>Form Example</TITLE>
</HEAD>

<BODY>
<H1>Form Example</H1>
```

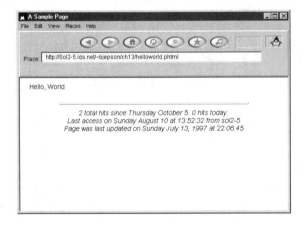

Figure 10.1 The output of the helloworld.phtml document.

```
<FORM>
Please enter a number:
<INPUT TYPE="text" NAME="number">
<INPUT TYPE="submit" VALUE="Submit">
</FORM>

<?

    if ($number != "") {

        /* Make sure to treat the number variable as an integer
         * and not as a string. Otherwise, the + and - operators
         * will not do the Right Thing.
         */
        SetType($number, "integer");

        /* Count from ten values before the value of $number to
         * ten values after.
         */
        $low  = $number - 10;
        $high = $number + 10;
        $i = $low;
        while ($i <= $high) {

            /* If the current value is the number the user
             * typed, print it in a strong typeface. Otherwise,
             * just print it in a normal typeface.
             */
            if ($i == $number) {
                echo "<STRONG>$i</STRONG>";
            } else {
                echo "$i";
            }

            /* Display something to separate each number */
            echo "..";

            /* increment the counter */
            $i++;

        }
    }
>
</BODY>
</HTML>
```

Using PHP/FI with Mini SQL

When you build PHP/FI, you are given the opportunity to configure it for one or more database engines, include Mini SQL. If you have enabled Mini SQL support in PHP/FI, you will have

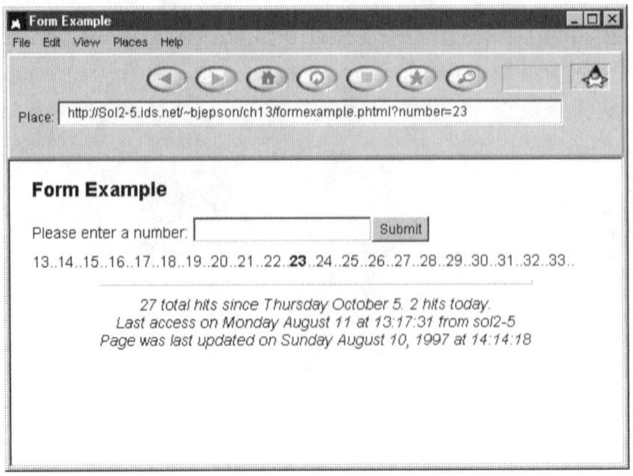

FIGURE 10.2 The formexample.phtml document counts from 13 to 33.

access to a number of functions that relate to Mini SQL. The following section lists the Mini SQL commands available in PHP/FI. You may substitute string literals for variables shown in this section.

Functions for Connecting and Querying   The following functions allow you to connect to and query the Mini SQL server from PHP/FI.

> **msql_connect($hostname)**   Connects to the mSQL server on the host specified by $hostname. This should usually be "localhost," unless you are running Mini SQL on a different host.
>
> **msql_Close()**   Closes the current Mini SQL connection.
>
> **$result = msql($database, $query)**   Sends the SQL statement contained in $query to the Mini SQL server that you are currently connected to. The name of the database you wish to use for the query should be contained in the $database value. If you have not connected to a Mini SQL server with msql_connect(), PHP/FI will attempt to connect to the server on the localhost the first time you use this function. Once you have a result set, you can use the msql_NumRows($result) function to determine the number of rows returned, and you can also use the msql_Result($result, $i, $field) function to fetch a value from a specific row.
>
> **msql_NumRows($result)**   Returns the number of rows that the result set $result contains.
>
> **msql_Result($result, $i, $field)**   Returns the value of the field specified by $field, from the result set $result, at the row specified by $i.
>
> **msql_NumFields($result)**   Returns the number of columns (aka fields) in the result set $result.
>
> **msql_FreeResult($result)**   Destroys a result set and frees any memory it is using.

Functions for Manipulating Databases   The following functions allow you to create, drop, or list databases.

msql_CreateDB($database)   Creates a database with the name specified as $database.

msql_DropDB($database)   Drops the database with the name specified as $database.

$result = msql_ListDBs()   Returns a special result set that can be used to retrieve a list of databases using the msql_dbName() function. You can use msql_NumRows($result) to find out how many database names have been retrieved.

msql_dbName($result, $i)   Returns the database name from the result set at the row specified by $i. The result set $result should have been obtained from the msql_ListDBs() method.

Functions for Working with Tables   The following functions allow you to obtain information about tables.

$result = msql_ListTables($database)   Returns a special result set that can be used to retrieve a list of all tables contained within the database $database using the msql_TableName() function. You can use msql_NumRows($result) to find out how many table names have been retrieved.

msql_TableName($result, $i)   Returns the table name from the result set at the row specified by $i. The result set $result should have been obtained from the msql_ListTables() method.

Functions for Working with Columns   The following functions allow you to obtain information about columns.

$result = msql_ListFields($db, $tbl)   Returns a special result set that consists of information about all fields contained within the table $tbl. The table must be contained within the database $db. You can use the msql_FieldFlags(), msql_FieldLen(), msql_FieldName(), and msql_FieldType() functions to learn more about the given field. You can also use msql_NumRows($result) to find out how many fields have been retrieved.

msql_FieldName($result, $i)   Returns the field name from the field result set at the row specified by $i.

msql_FieldLen($result, $i)   Returns the field length from the field result set at the row specified by $i.

msql_FieldType($result, $i)   Returns the field's data type from the result set at the row specified by $i.

msql_FieldFlags($result, $i)   Returns flags that contain information about the field from the result set at the row specified by $i. This will be set to NOT NULL if the field is not capable of accepting nulls.

A PHP/FI Document Using Mini SQL   The following code listing, included on the CD-ROM as /eg/ch10/msqlexample.phtml, shows how to connect to the Mini SQL database server, and how to retrieve a list of tables from the server. Figure 10.3 shows the output generated by this document.

```
<HTML>
<HEAD>
<TITLE>mSQL Example</TITLE>
</HEAD>

<BODY BGCOLOR="#FFFFFF">

<H1>mSQL Example</H1>
<HR>

<CENTER>
<TABLE BORDER>
<TH>Database Name</TH>
<?

    /*
     * Connect to the database.
     */
    msql_Connect("localhost");

    /*
     * Get a List of Databases.
     */
    $result = msql_ListDBs();
```

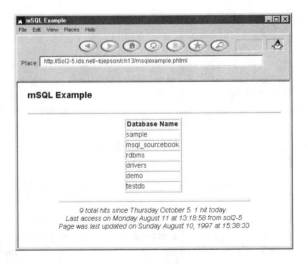

FIGURE 10.3 Displaying a list of database names.

```
    $i = 0;
    while ($i < msql_NumRows($result)) {

        /*
         * Fetch the database name.
         */
        $name = msql_dbName($result, $i);
        echo "<TR><TD>$name</TD></TR>\n";

        $i++;
    }

>

</TABLE>
</CENTER>

</BODY>
</HTML>
```

Issuing Queries and Retrieving Results

The /eg/ch10 directory contains a file that will create and populate two databases: `artist` and `album`. This SQL dump is contained in the file called examples.sql, and if fed to the `msql` monitor program, will create the two tables and insert a modest amount of data. This data includes the names of a few popular musicians and the names of some of their record albums. The tables and rows created by the file, /eg/ch10/examples.sql, can be installed in the `msql_sourcebook` database with a command similar to the following:

```
msql msql_sourcebook < examples.sql
```

You may receive some errors the first time that you execute the SQL statements in that file, since it issues a DROP TABLE statement for each of the two tables, whether they exist or not. You may safely ignore these errors. The contents of `examples.sql` are shown here:

```
#
# Create a sample database for the Chapter 10 PHP/FI
# Examples.
#
# You should run this through the msql monitor program, with
# something like:
#
# msql msql_sourcebook < examples.sql
#
#

# Drop the artist table.
#
DROP TABLE artist \g
```

```
# Create the artist table.
#
CREATE TABLE artist
    (name char(45), id int) \g

# Add some data to the table.
#
INSERT INTO artist
    VALUES('Husker Du', 1)
\g

INSERT INTO artist
    VALUES('Rolling Stones', 2)
\g

INSERT INTO artist
    VALUES('Jimi Hendrix Experience, The', 3)
\g

INSERT INTO artist
    VALUES('Beatles, The', 4)
\g

INSERT INTO artist
    VALUES('Minutemen', 5)
\g

INSERT INTO artist
    VALUES('Bob Dylan', 6)
\g

# Create a sequence on the artist table.
#
CREATE SEQUENCE ON artist STEP 1 VALUE 6\g

# Drop the album table.
#
DROP TABLE album\g

# Create the album table.
#
CREATE TABLE album
    (name char(35), artist_id int, id int)\g

# Add some data to the album table
#
INSERT INTO album
    VALUES('Revolver', 4, 1)
\g

INSERT INTO album
    VALUES('Warehouse: Songs and Stories', 1, 2)
\g
```

```
INSERT INTO album
    VALUES('Exile on Main Street', 2, 3)
\g

INSERT INTO album
    VALUES('Electric Ladyland', 3, 4)
\g

INSERT INTO album
    VALUES('Double Nickels on the Dime', 5, 5)
\g

INSERT INTO album
    VALUES('Highway 61 Revisited', 6, 6)
\g

INSERT INTO album
    VALUES('Let It Be', 4, 7)
\g

INSERT INTO album
    VALUES('Beggars Banquet', 2, 8)
\g

INSERT INTO album
    VALUES('Are You Experienced', 3, 9)
\g

INSERT INTO album
    VALUES('Beatles For Sale', 4, 10)
\g

# Create a sequence for the album table.
#
CREATE SEQUENCE ON album STEP 1 VALUE 11\g
```

The following example program, /eg/ch10/listartists.phtml, performs a simple SQL query to fetch all the names of the artists. It then displays them one by one, separating them with a line break (<br>). Figure 10.4 shows the output of this document.

```
<HTML>
<HEAD>
<TITLE>Listing of Artists</TITLE>
</HEAD>

<BODY BGCOLOR="#FFFFFF">

<H1>List of Artists</H1>
<HR>

<?

    msql_Connect("localhost");
```

```
/*
 * Issue a query and get a result set.
 */
$result = msql("msql_sourcebook",
               "select name from artist order by name");
$i = 0;
while ($i < msql_NumRows($result)) {

    /*
     * Fetch the name from the result set. The second
     * parameter is the row number within the result
     * set, and the last parameter is the name of the
     * column to retrieve.
     */
    $name = msql_Result($result, $i, "name");

    /*
     * Display the name of the artist.
     */
    echo "$name<br>";

    /*
     * Make sure you increment the row index!
     */
    $i++;

}
>
</BODY>
</HTML>
```

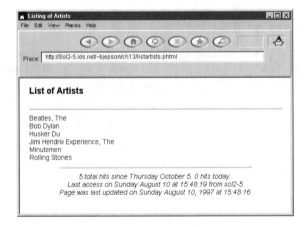

Figure 10.4 The listartists.phtml document shows all of the artists from the artist table.

The following example, /eg/ch10/showalbums.phtml, is somewhat interactive. It also shows how PHP/FI commands can be interspersed among HTML markup, rather than being placed within the code as one monolithic block, as in previous examples. The first block of PHP/FI code makes the connection to the Mini SQL database. This is immediately followed by an HTML form. Since the form has no target specified, the same document (showalbums.phtml) is loaded when the form is submitted, and it can then process any user input. After the form starts, a SELECT (the HTML equivalent of a popup menu) control is added to the form, and the PHP/FI code in between the <SELECT> and </SELECT> takes care of adding options to that list. Since this form will invoke itself when it is submitted, the code that generates the options checks the value of the option the user last selected. If it is the same as the one that it is processing within the loop, it puts the "SELECTED" attribute in the option. This causes it to be the default selection the next time the form is loaded, adding a small degree of persistence between invocations.

```
<HTML>
<HEAD>
<TITLE>Show Albums by Artist</TITLE>
</HEAD>

<BODY BGCOLOR="#FFFFFF">

<?
    /* Connect to the database.  */
    msql_Connect("localhost");
>

<H1>Show Albums by Artist</H1>
<HR>

<I>Please choose an artist name and then click on the
<strong>Show</strong> button to show the albums in your
collection by that artist.</I>

<FORM>
<SELECT NAME="artist_id">
<?
    /*
     * Query the database to get a list of all artists and
     * their ids.
     */
    $sql = "select name, id from artist order by name";
    $result = msql("msql_sourcebook", $sql);

    $i = 0;
    while ($i < msql_NumRows($result)) {

        /*
         * Fetch the name and id.
         */
        $name = msql_Result($result, $i, "name");
        $id   = msql_Result($result, $i, "id");
```

```
    /*
     * If the id of the current row is the same as the
     * selected artist_id, then make sure that the
     * option is selected.
     */
    if ($id == $artist_id) {
        echo "<OPTION SELECTED VALUE=$id>$name\n";
    } else {
        echo "<OPTION VALUE=$id>$name\n";
    }

    $i++;
}


>
</SELECT>
<INPUT TYPE="submit" NAME="submit" VALUE="Show">
```

The next block of PHP/FI code checks to see if the user pressed the Submit button. If so, then it gets the value of the artist ID, which corresponds to the value that is currently selected on the popup menu. Then, it uses the msql() function to get a list of all albums for that artist, and displays them in a comma-delimited list. Figure 10.5 shows the results of selecting one of the artists.

```
<?

    /*
     * If the user pressed "Show", display the albums that
     * the selected artist has.
     */
    if ($submit == "Show") {

        $sql = "select name, id from album " +
               "where artist_id = $artist_id";
        $result = msql("msql_sourcebook", $sql);

        if (msql_NumRows($result) > 0) {

            /*
             * Fetch and display each album.
             */
            echo "<p>";
            echo "<font color=\"blue\"><b>Albums: </b>";
            $i = 0;
            while ($i < msql_NumRows($result)) {
                $name = msql_Result($result, $i, "name");
                echo $name;
                $i++;
                if ($i < msql_NumRows($result)) {
                    echo ", ";
                }
            }
        }
```

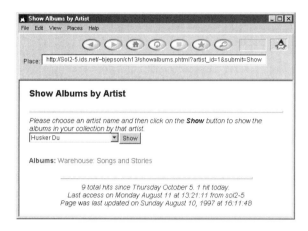

FIGURE 10.5 The results of an artist query from showalbums.phtml.

```
            echo "</font><p>";
        }
    }
>

</FORM>

</BODY>
</HTML>
```

PHP'ing It All Back Home

These fairly simple examples give you a small taste of the kind of tasks to which PHP/FI can be applied. It is possible to build sophisticated database-enabled applications that make use of PHP/FI. The PHP/FI homepage at `http://php.iquest.net/` includes a link titled "Gallery." The gallery contains links to demonstration sites that make use of PHP/FI, and shows the versatility of this simple and powerful package. PHP/FI, while offering constructs and features found in more complex languages, manages to provide a simple way of developing dynamic Web pages. Not only are hooks available for popular database engines such as Mini SQL, Sybase, PostgreSQL, and Oracle, but PHP/FI can also be integrated with GD, a popular dynamic image generation program. PHP/FI is a great solution for Web page development, and is extremely practical where a large number of users need the ability to develop dynamic Web pages. Since it is simple and does not tax the Web server excessively, it is a good dynamic content solution on sites where server resources are thinly spread among many developers.

Mini SQL and the Apache Web Server

M ini SQL has enjoyed immense popularity in its role as an SQL server for World Wide Web applications. It should come as no surprise that there are some fancy things you can do above and beyond the CGI applications showcased in much of this book. Mini SQL can be used to store authentication information for the Apache Web server, and Perl scripts that you develop with Mini SQL can be developed to leverage the Apache *module API*, greatly improving the performance of your scripts. Apache modules are server plug-ins that run with increased speed, since they bypass the slower CGI interface in favor of a faster server API.

Using Mini-SQL to Authenticate Remote Users

Apache is a freely redistributable Web server based on the NCSA HTTPD Web server. Although Apache bears some resemblance to the NCSA server, it has grown considerably, and offers a wide variety of configuration options, making it a perfect fit for almost any environment. Apache is consistently ranked as the most popular Web server by the Netcraft survey at http://www .netcraft.com/survey/.

It is quite easy to configure the Apache Web server to use Mini SQL for authentication of remote users, but it involves a number of steps. The `Apache::ModAuthMsql` module and the examples in this chapter were inspired by Dirk van Gulik's (Dirk.vanGulik@jrc.it) Apache-mSQL demo kit, available from http://me-www.jrc.it/~dirkx/apache-msql-demo.tar.gz.

Installing Apache with `mod_auth_msql`

The latest Apache source code may be obtained from http://www.apache.org. Apache versions 1.2 and earlier can be compiled on most Unix platforms. Apache 1.3 introduces support for Windows NT, but as of this writing, that product has not come out of beta, so it is not known whether it will include support for Mini SQL.

The Apache source code is available as a tar file compressed with GNU zip or the compress utility. When you download it, please try to use a mirror site. After you download it, you should choose a directory to extract the source in. To simplify things, you may want to extract it into the directory where you wish to install Apache and its related files. If you extract the distribution into /usr/local (you will probably need to be root to do this), you will end up with a top-level directory called apache_1.2.3 (or whatever version you choose to install). You may wish to rename this to apache or create a symbolic link from it to the apache directory.

After you `cd` to the directory of your choice (/usr/local is suggested), you can extract the source code with a command similar to one of the following (you will need to supply the full pathname to the file):

Using `gzip` and Unix `tar`:

```
gzip -d -c apache_1.2.3.tar.gz | tar xvf -
```

Using `gzip` and GNU `tar`:

```
tar xvfz apache_1.2.3.tar.gz
```

Using `zcat` and Unix `tar`:

```
zcat apache_1.2.3.tar.Z | tar xvf -
```

Any of these commands will create the top-level apache_1.2.3 directory. The actual directory name will vary depending upon the version of Apache that you downloaded. Since we'll be building the distribution in the same directory in which it's installed, we'll need to rename or link the directory name to apache. You can rename it with:

```
mv apache_1.2.3 apache
```

or you can create a symbolic link with:

```
ln -s apache_1.2.3 apache
```

Once you have done either of these things, you can `cd` into the apache directory. Before reading any more in this book, please read the README file carefully. Since new versions of Apache come out quite often, you may find some variation between the instructions in this chapter and those included in the README file. The README file is the authoritative word on this matter. The README file should direct you to `cd` to the src directory, where you will find a file called INSTALL. You should read this file as well.

In order to add support for Mini SQL authorization, you will need to edit the Configuration file. Before you do this, you will need to copy the Configuration.tmpl file to Configuration. After you have copied Configuration.tmpl to Configuration, locate the following line in the Configuration file:

```
# Module msql_auth_module     mod_auth_msql.o
```

You should uncomment this line by removing the leading #. This line should now read:

```
Module msql_auth_module     mod_auth_msql.o
```

Next, you need to add a directive to the `EXTRA_INCLUDES` line. This line supplies a list of directories in which the compiler should look for include (`*.h`) files. In this case, we'll add the include directory of the Mini SQL distribution. I'm assuming that you installed Mini SQL in `/usr/local/Hughes`, so if you installed it someplace different, you will need to change this line accordingly. Locate the line in the Configuration file that starts with `EXTRA_INCLUDES=`. Normally, this line will be blank after the equals sign, but if it is not, simply add a space after what is already there when you add the path to the include directory. This should leave your `EXTRA_INCLUDES` line looking something like:

```
EXTRA_INCLUDES=-I/usr/local/Hughes/include
```

Similarly, you will need to add a line to the `EXTRA_LIBS`, which are switches that are needed by the linker. In this case, we'll tell it where to find the Mini SQL libraries (the `-L` switch), and the name of the library (the `-l` switch). You should change the line to read:

```
EXTRA_LIBS=-lmsql -L/usr/local/Hughes/lib
```

If there was already one or more flags on this line, please add these switches after what was already there, but include a space before the switches you add.

This is the extent of the modifications that you must make to the Configuration file. You can now generate the `Makefile` for Apache by running the `Configure` program.

```
./Configure
```

Once this is done, you can type `make` to build the Apache Web server. When this finishes, you will be returned to the shell prompt, and your current working directory will still be the src directory. The httpd binary should be sitting in this directory, ready for you to use or abuse as you see fit.

Before you install it, you should consider two things. First, if you are already running another version of Apache, then you should stop the currently running Apache process. This can be accomplished with a command like:

```
kill 'cat /usr/local/apache/logs/httpd.pid'
```

The exact location of the pid (process id) file will vary according to your installation of Apache. You will probably need to issue this command as the super-user (`root`), which brings us to the second thing: You will need to be `root` to install the Web server. Installing it should be a simple matter of copying it to a publicly accessible directory, such as /usr/local/bin. Once you have done this, you will need to modify the configuration files contained in the /usr/local/apache/conf directory (you may have chosen another directory when you extracted the distribution). Basic instructions on setting these up is included in the README file in the top-level apache directory. You will first need to copy each of the *-dist files to the appropriate *.conf file, as in:

```
cp access.conf-dist access.conf
cp httpd.conf-dist httpd.conf
cp srm.conf-dist srm.conf
```

You will then need to edit the httpd.conf file and change the `ServerRoot` directive to point to the top-level apache directory, as in:

`ServerRoot /usr/local/apache`

You should also check and set the user/group setting in the httpd.conf file, since the default may not be appropriate for your operating system.

Next, you will need to edit the srm.conf file and change the `DocumentRoot` directive to point to the location of the htdocs (this is your server's document root) directory, as in:

`DocumentRoot /usr/local/apache/htdocs`

Once you have made these changes, you should be able to start the server with:

`/usr/local/bin/httpd -f /usr/local/apache/conf/httpd.conf`

After issuing this command, if you do not see any errors, examine the end of the file /usr/local/apache/logs/error_log (correct this for the directory you chose for the apache directory). You should see the line:

`Server configured -- resuming normal operations`

If you cannot get the server to start properly, or if a strange error appears in the log, you should carefully consult the documentation included in the README and INSTALL files, or visit the `www.apache.org` site for links to documentation, the FAQ, and other information.

Installing `Apache::ModAuthMsql`

The accompanying CD includes some samples in the /eg/ch11 directory, as well as a Perl module that facilitates working with `mod_auth_msql`, `Apache::ModAuthMsql`. To install the file, you will need to extract the Apache-ModAuthMsql.tar.gz file into a temporary directory with the following command (substituting the correct path to the file):

Unix tar:

`gzip -d -c /cdrom/eg/ch11/Apache-ModAuthMsql.tar.gz | tar xvf -`

GNU tar:

`tar xvfz /cdrom/eg/ch11/Apache-ModAuthMsql.tar.gz`

After you extract the file, it will create the directory called Apache-ModAuthMsql. You can enter this directory and type `perl Makefile.PL`. This program will ask you a number of questions, as shown in the next listing. This program will attempt to determine the username of the Mini SQL Admin user, which is often `root`. If it needs to create the database, it will prompt you for that user's password and run the `msqladmin` program to create the database. *If you are uncomfortable giving your password to a strange program*, you should use `msqladmin` to create the database before running `perl Makefile.PL`, and you will not be prompted for the password, since this program won't need to create the database. The defaults for each option are shown in brackets, and commands you type are shown in bold text. At each prompt, you may type something or accept the default by pressing [Return] or [Enter].

```
bash-2.00$ perl Makefile.PL
What is the name of the database to use for authentication? [db_mod_auth]:
Using db_mod_auth.

Where is your mSQL installation? [/usr/local/Hughes]:
Using /usr/local/Hughes.

Database db_mod_auth does not exist. I will create it for you.

I will now use the su command to become the user
root and create the database. You will need
to know that user's password.

**BEFORE YOU ANSWER THE FOLLOWING QUESTION,
**PLEASE BE SURE YOU HAVE READ THE SOURCE
**CODE TO Makefile.PL SO YOU KNOW WHO YOU
**ARE GIVING A PASSWORD TO!!!
Password: ********
Database "db_mod_auth" created.

What is the name of the table to store users in? [auth_user]:
Using auth_user.

What is the name of the table to store groups in? [auth_group]:
Using auth_group.

The database has been configured.
Writing Makefile for Apache::ModAuthMsql
```

After you have run `perl Makefile.PL`, you should run the `make ; make install` commands. This will build and install the module under your Perl installation's site-specific library directory. You will probably need to be `root` to perform the `make install` step, unless your sysadmin has given you write permissions to the local Perl installation.

The configuration subroutine within `Makefile.PL` does a number of steps behind the scenes. First of all, it creates a Mini SQL database to hold the authentication tables, if that database does not already exist. Next, the subroutine creates two tables, `auth_user` and `auth_group` (or table names that you have supplied), which have the following definitions:

```
CREATE TABLE auth_user
    (user_name CHAR(32),
     password  CHAR(32))

CREATE TABLE auth_group
    (user_name CHAR(32),
     grp_name  CHAR(32))
```

The `auth_user` table simply consists of user names paired with passwords, and the group table consists of user names paired with the name of the group to which the user belongs. Notice that the `auth_group` table is not fully normalized. That is to say, the group name is repeated for each user that belongs to a group. As a result, it may be easy to misspell the name of a group when adding a user to the group, so you should keep this issue in mind. If there was a separate table for a group and a separate table for the user-group cross-reference, the possibility of errors could be eliminated, as the group name would only appear once, and users and groups could be cross-referenced using unique identifiers. See Chapter 2 for more information on fully normalized tables.

Creating Users and Groups with `Apache::ModAuthMsql`

Enough carping about the way the database for `mod_auth_msql` is designed; after all, you're here to learn, not to listen to us rant! The simplicity of the database design mirrors the simplicity of the authentication mechanism. Each row in the `auth_user table` corresponds to a given user, and includes the username and an encrypted password. Each row in the `auth_group` table corresponds not to a given user, but to a user's membership in a group. A user that appears in the `auth_group` table must also appear in the `auth_user` table. The `Apache::ModAuthMsql` module includes several methods that are exported by default. These can be used to add, modify, or delete users from the database.

The following examples are "one-liners" that manipulate the `mod_auth` database. The `-MApache::ModAuthMsql` switch is the equivalent of having `use Apache::ModAuthMsql` within your script, and the `-e` switch lets you supply a small chunk of Perl code that should be executed. The methods shown next make use of internal features of the module, and don't require the usual instantiation of the object, so they can be quite simple to use from the shell.

To add a user to the database that was created when you ran Perl `Makefile.PL`, you can use the `auth_add_user()` method.

```
perl -MApache::ModAuthMsql -e \
      'auth_add_user("username","password")'
```

To update a user's password, you can use the `auth_update_user()` method.

```
perl -MApache::ModAuthMsql -e \
      'auth_update_user("username","newpassword")'
```

To add a user to a group, you can use the `auth_add_to_group()` method.

```
perl -MApache::ModAuthMsql -e \
      'auth_add_to_group("username", "group_name")'
```

To remove a user from a group, you can use the `auth_drop_from_group()` method.

```
perl -MApache::ModAuthMsql -e \
      'auth_drop_from_group("username", "group_name")'
```

To completely remove a user, including all group memberships, you can use the `auth_drop_user()` method.

```
perl -MApache::ModAuthMsql -e \
      'auth_drop_user("username")'
```

You can also write a Perl script that constructs a new instance of `Apache::ModAuth Msql`, and use any of the package methods. The /eg/ch11 directory contains a file called create_ sample_users.pl, which uses this technique to create some users and add them to different groups.

```perl
#!/usr/local/bin/perl

use Apache::ModAuthMsql;

$m = new Apache::ModAuthMsql;

# Create some new users.
#
$m->add_user("neal",  "cod1");
$m->add_user("jack",  "sa1");
$m->add_user("allen", "carl0");

# Set up a couple of groups.
#
$m->add_to_group("neal", "drivers");
$m->add_to_group("neal", "riders");
$m->add_to_group("jack", "riders");
```

At this time, you should execute the create_sample_users.pl script, since it will create the users that are needed in the next examples.

Using `mod_auth_msql` to Control Permissions

After you have created users and groups, you can then restrict access to certain users or groups within a given directory. In whichever directory you want to protect, you should create the file .htaccess. This file makes reference to the tables and columns in the database, and causes the Web server to look up the authentication information when a remote user attempts to access the directory. At this point, you should choose a document directory to test the examples in. The /eg/ch11 directory contains a tar file called webdirs.tar. You should `cd` to a document directory, such as a public document directory or your personal ~/public_html or ~/www directory. Then, you should extract the tar file, substituting the path to /eg/ch11 as appropriate.

```
tar xvf /cdrom/eg/ch11/webdirs.tar
```

Once you have extracted this tar file into a document directory, you should open the directory in a Web browser. If you extracted it into the document root, you should use the URL:

```
http://localhost:80/webdirs
```

If you extracted it into your document directory, you should use a URL similar to the following:

```
http://localhost:80/~username/webdirs
```

You should substitute the hostname and port number as necessary, depending upon the configuration of your Web server. Once you open the directory, you will be presented with a listing of the subdirectories, as shown in Figure 11.1. Within each of these subdirectories is an .htaccess file, which determines who can and who can't access the document in that directory.

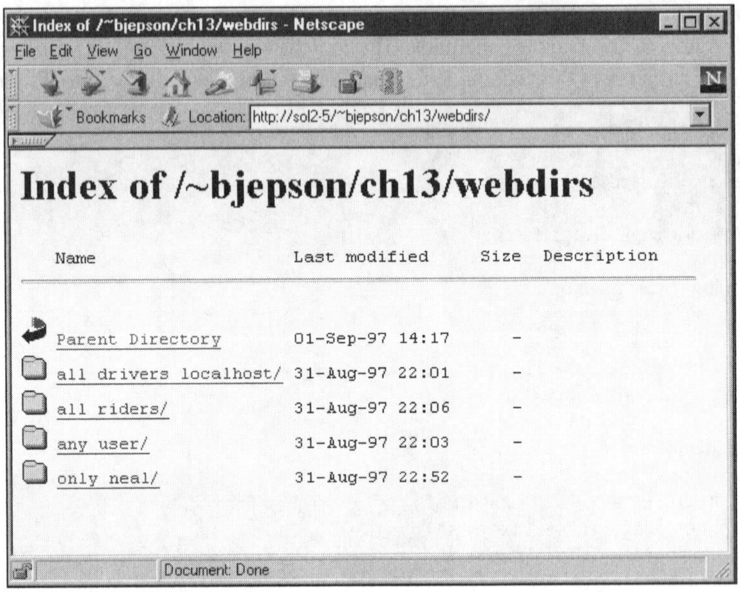

FIGURE 11.1 The subdirectories included in webdirs.tar.

The any_user directory is perhaps the simplest. If you try to enter that directory from your Web browser, you will be prompted for a user id and password. You can supply any user id or password that was created in the create_sample_users.pl file. The contents of the .htaccess file that resides in the any_user directory are shown here:

```
AuthName valid user
AuthType Basic
Auth_MSQLdatabase          db_mod_auth
Auth_MSQLpwd_table         auth_user
Auth_MSQLgrp_table         auth_group
Auth_MSQLuid_field         user_name
Auth_MSQLgrp_field         grp_name
Auth_MSQLpwd_field         password

allow from all
require valid-user
```

The first directive in the .htaccess file is the name of the authentication. This is the prompt that the remote user sees, as shown in Figure 11.2. The AuthType directive is always set to "Basic," as it is the only type that is currently implemented. After these two directives, the information about the Mini SQL database appears. The first is the name of the database, the Auth_MSQLdatabase directive. This is followed by Auth_MSQLpwd_table, which is the name of the user/password table. After this, the name of the group table appears, under the `Auth_MSQLgrp_table` directive. Next, the names of the columns for username, group name, and password appear, under the directives `Auth_MSQLuid_field`, `Auth_MSQLgrp_field`, and `Auth_MSQLpwd_field`, respectively.

The `allow from all` line directs the server to allow users from any hostname. This is followed by the `require valid-user` line, which will only allow users who are in the database to access the directory, if they supply a valid password.

The following .htaccess file is from the all_drivers_localhost directory, and it will allow any member of the `drivers` group to access the directory from a machine named `localhost` or `Sol2-5`:

```
AuthName member of the drivers group
AuthType Basic
Auth_MSQLdatabase              db_mod_auth
Auth_MSQLpwd_table             auth_user
Auth_MSQLgrp_table             auth_group
Auth_MSQLuid_field             user_name
Auth_MSQLgrp_field             grp_name
Auth_MSQLpwd_field             password

allow from localhost, sol2-5
require group drivers
```

The following .htaccess file is from the all_riders subdirectory. This file will only allow members of the `riders` group, regardless of the host they log in from.

```
AuthName member of the riders group
AuthType Basic
Auth_MSQLdatabase              db_mod_auth
Auth_MSQLpwd_table             auth_user
Auth_MSQLgrp_table             auth_group
Auth_MSQLuid_field             user_name
Auth_MSQLgrp_field             grp_name
Auth_MSQLpwd_field             password
```

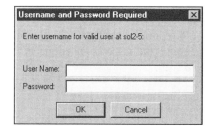

FIGURE 11.2 Authentication prompt as seen by remote users.

```
allow from all
require group riders
```

Finally, this .htaccess file, which is from the only_neal subdirectory, will only allow the user `neal` to access the directory.

```
AuthName one valid user
AuthType Basic
Auth_MSQLdatabase          db_mod_auth
Auth_MSQLpwd_table         auth_user
Auth_MSQLgrp_table         auth_group
Auth_MSQLuid_field         user_name
Auth_MSQLgrp_field         grp_name
Auth_MSQLpwd_field         password

allow from all
require user neal
```

The previous examples are a small sample of the sorts of things that can be done with Apache's authentication. An excellent tutorial on the user authentication scheme used in NCSA httpd, upon which Apache is based, can be found at:

```
http://hoohoo.ncsa.uiuc.edu/docs/tutorials/user.html
```

Further documentation on Apache modules, including `mod_auth` and `mod_auth_msql`, can be found at:

```
www.apache.org/docs/mod/
```

Faster Web Pages with MsqlPerl

If you've built a system using Mini SQL, CGI, and Perl, you're no stranger to the experience of waiting for your pages to load. Why is this? Well, if truth be told, CGI itself is a fairly slow way to serve up Web pages. After the `httpd` process receives a request from a remote client, it's got to execute a program of some sort. When that program is Perl, and you're running some sort of CGI script that uses both the `CGI.pm` and `Msql.pm` modules, you've got a lot of overhead. For, not only does Perl have to parse and compile your script, but it has to parse and compile both of those modules. Further, it's well known that establishing a database connection is time consuming in and of itself, even with a lightweight engine like Mini SQL.

Wouldn't it be nice if there was something that could get rid of the need to repeatedly start Perl, parse your script, and make the database connection. "Yeah, right," you say, "when St. Anthony's pig sprouts wings and flies."

Well, you're just going to have to trust us on this one. There is an object, the most wonderful object in the world, called `mod_perl`. This little module hooks directly into the Apache Web server and binds a Perl interpreter in with each `httpd` process. Why is this useful? The Web server handles requests by dispatching each remote request to a separate `httpd` process. On startup, the Web server can be configured to start extra processes so there is little wait when the requests start coming in. The great thing about these processes is that they are long lived. After the `httpd` process serves up a Web page, it goes back and waits for another request to come in. The neat thing about having the Perl interpreter embedded in the process is that the Perl interpreter doesn't terminate either, so it doesn't need to compile a script or module each time, and best of all, you can reuse objects from instance to instance. So, if your script creates a database connection in just the right way, it doesn't need to create it again the next time the script is run! The `mod_perl` kit provides this feature to Perl developers. When you write scripts that use this interface, `mod_perl` supplies a CGI-like API, so you can continue programming using your trusty CGI development techniques.

Obtaining and Installing `mod_perl`

The `mod_perl` kit, which includes modules that live in the `Apache::` package, can be downloaded and installed from CPAN (the Comprehensive Perl Archive Network) in two ways. If you are using the most recent version of Perl, you can use the CPAN shell. The CPAN shell is started with the following command:

```
perl -MCPAN -e shell
```

Within the shell, you can use the `install` command to locate the latest version of a module or bundle of modules, download it to a temporary working location, and install it for you. In most Perl installations, you will need to be the `root` user to install modules, unless you have special permission to write to the Perl installation directories. The first time you run the CPAN module, it asks you a number of questions about your machine and configures the CPAN module. For a complete explanation of how the CPAN module works, issue the following command:

```
perldoc CPAN
```

Once you have started the CPAN shell and have set it up for its first use, you can issue the following command at the `cpan>` prompt to install the Apache modules:

```
cpan> install Apache
```

> **TIP** If you are using an older version of Perl 5, you may not have all of the CGI modules needed to use the goodies included in the `mod_perl` kit. You will also have lots of bugs that have been fixed in recent releases of Perl. If upgrading is not an option, you should obtain the `CGI.pm` distribution, available at `www.perl.com/CPAN/modules/by-module/CGI/`. This will include the `CGI::Apache` and `CGI::Switch` module, which is required by the `Apache` module. You should consult the `README` file supplied with both the `mod_perl` and `CGI.pm` distribution to identify other modules that may need to be installed.

Although the name of the archive that contains the Apache modules is called mod_perl, you can also refer to it as Apache—CPAN is smart enough to find the right module.

After the CPAN module locates and downloads the module, you will enter an interactive configuration session that looks something like the following listing. Be sure to give it the correct path to your Apache src directory, or this process will fail.

If you cannot use the CPAN module, then you will need to download the module from www.perl.com/CPAN/modules/by-module/Apache. After you extract the file, you should follow the instructions in the README document to determine how to install the module. Using the CPAN module is a much better alternative, if it is available.

Regardless of whether you use the CPAN module to install mod_perl, or you download and install it by hand, the installation process will look similar to the following:

```
CPAN.pm: Going to build DOUGM/mod_perl-1.00.tar.gz


ReadLine support enabled
Enter 'q' to stop search
Please tell me where I can find your apache src []
 /usr/homes/bjepson/build/apache_1.2.3/src
Configure mod_perl with /usr/homes/bjepson/build/apache_1.2.3/src ? [y] y
Shall I build httpd in /usr/homes/bjepson/build/apache_1.2.1/src for you?
 [y] y
Appending mod_perl to src/Configuration
Using config file: /usr/homes/bjepson/.cpan/build/mod_perl-
1.00/src/Configuration
Using Makefile template file: Makefile.tmpl
 + configured for Solaris 2 platform
 + setting C compiler to gcc
 + setting C compiler optimization-level to -O2
EXTRA_CFLAGS: -DSOLARIS2
PerlHandler..............enabled
PerlChildInitHandler.....disabled (need 1.3a1 or higher)
PerlChildExitHandler.....disabled (need 1.3a2-dev or higher)
PerlTransHandler........disabled (enable with PERL_TRANS=1)
PerlAuthenHandler........disabled (enable with PERL_AUTHEN=1)
PerlAuthzHandler........disabled (enable with PERL_AUTHZ=1)
PerlAccessHandler........disabled (enable with PERL_ACCESS=1)
PerlTypeHandler.........disabled (enable with PERL_TYPE=1)
PerlFixupHandler........disabled (enable with PERL_FIXUP=1)
PerlLogHandler..........disabled (enable with PERL_LOG=1)
PerlHeaderParserHandler..disabled (enable with PERL_HEADER_PARSER=1)
PerlInitHandler.........disabled (enable with PERL_INIT=1)
PerlCleanupHandler.......disabled (enable with PERL_CLEANUP=1)
PerlStackedHandlers......disabled (enable with PERL_STACKED_HANDLERS=1)
PerlMethodHandlers.......disabled (enable with PERL_METHOD_HANDLERS=1)
PerlSections............disabled (enable with PERL_SECTIONS=1)
PerlSSI.................disabled (enable with PERL_SSI=1)
Will run tests as User: 'bjepson' Group: 'staff'
Checking for LWP::UserAgent...ok
Checking CGI.pm VERSION.......ok
```

```
Checking if your kit is complete...
Looks good
Writing Makefile for Apache
Writing Makefile for Apache::Constants
Writing Makefile for mod_perl
[The compilation process begins here...]
```

Once the compilation process is finished, you will find a new `httpd` binary in the Apache src directory. If the Apache `httpd` server is currently running on your machine, you should shut it down before installing the new binary. It's probably a good idea to back up your existing binary, and you can copy the new binary you've created over your copy of `httpd`. We keep ours in /usr/local/bin/httpd, so after we finished building the Apache module, we left the CPAN shell and did the following:

```
# cd /usr/homes/bjepson/build/apache_1.2.3/src
# /etc/init.d/httpd stop
# mv /usr/local/bin/httpd /usr/local/bin/httpd.orig
# cp httpd /usr/local/bin/httpd
# /etc/init.d/httpd start
```

The /etc/init.d/httpd script is a simple script that starts and stops the `httpd` server, and can be used by the System V init to start and stop the server when the system enters a certain run level. This is supported by Unix variants such as Solaris and some distributions of Linux (including RedHat). A full description of the System V init process is outside the scope of this chapter, but you can use the same script from the command line to start and stop the server at your leisure. Here is the /etc/init.d/httpd file we use to start and stop the server. If you are not using System V init, you can adapt this for your system's startup method.

```
#!/bin/sh
#
# Apache httpd start/stop script.
#

APACHE_BIN=/usr/local/bin/httpd
APACHE_LIB=/usr/local/apache

mode=$1

set 'id'
if [ $1 != "uid=0(root)" ]; then
 echo "$0: You must be root to use this script"
 exit 1
fi

case "$mode" in
'start')
 # Start httpd
 $APACHE_BIN -f $APACHE_LIB/conf/httpd.conf
            ;;

'stop')
```

```
# Stop httpd
 kill `cat $APACHE_LIB/logs/httpd.pid`
                 ;;

*)      # usage
 echo "usage: $0 start|stop"
 exit 1
 ;;

esac
```

We keep our configuration files in /usr/local/apache/conf, but it is up to you to decide where these files will go when you build and install your version of Apache. In order to make use of mod_perl, at least one of these files must be modified. After installing the new Apache binary, you should definitely peruse the online documentation for mod_perl, using the command perldoc mod_perl.

Configuring a mod_perl **Executable Directory**

There are two ways you can make use of mod_perl for developing Web scripts. The first is to create a directory that will contain mod_perl scripts. In order to do this, the directory you want to serve scripts out of should exist, and you should add the following lines to your server's http.conf file:

```
 Alias /perl/   /real/path/to/perl-scripts/

<Location /perl>
SetHandler   perl-script
PerlHandler Apache::Registry
Options ExecCGI
</Location>
```

For each directory you configure in this fashion, you'll need a different Alias, and you'll also need to set up a <Location dirname></Location> block for the directory.

Associating an Extension with mod_perl

You can also associate a file extension with mod_perl. Using this feature, mod_perl scripts can reside in any directory, including user directories. With this in mind, you should be cautious about using this feature. If you don't want every user on your system to be able to develop Perl scripts, it might be better to go with creating one or more directories to hold the scripts as detailed in the previous paragraphs. To set up an association between .pl files and mod_perl, you can add the following to your httpd.conf file:

```
<Files *.pl>
SetHandler perl-script
PerlHandler Apache::Registry
Options ExecCGI
</Files>
```

Msql-Perl and mod_perl

After you have made the desired change to your httpd.conf file, you should stop and restart the Apache server. Developing scripts with mod_perl is very simple. Instead of using the CGI module, you must use a module called CGI::Switch, which ends up using the CGI::Apache module "under the hood." After this, you can develop scripts almost exactly the way you have with the CGI module. The biggest difference is that you must use the print() method of the CGI::Apache object that CGI::Switch returned to you. If you wish to keep the database handle persistent between invocations, you should use a global variable for it, as shown in the following script. This script is located in /eg/ch11/mod_perl_example.pl. The global variable is "kept around" between each invocation of the script, and allows you to make the database connection only the first time the script is executed, eliminating the need to connect to the database each time the script is invoked.

```perl
#!/usr/local/bin/perl
#
# mod_perl_example.pl
#
# A sample script showing how to use MsqlPerl with mod_perl.
#


# The CGI::Switch module ensures that we use the CGI::Apache
# "under the hood" - do a 'perldoc CGI::Switch' for more
# information.
#
use CGI::Switch;

# Use the Msql module.
#
use Msql;

# We use the 'strict' pragma to ensure that the programmer
# avoids unsafe constructs. This requires that all variables
# (except those listed in 'use vars' below) be scoped with
# the my() operator, does not permit symbolic references,
# and will generate a compile-time error if certain bareword
# identifiers are used. For more information, you can try
# both 'perldoc strict' and 'perldoc vars'
#
use strict;
use vars qw($X $X_COUNT $X_TIME);

# Instantiate a new CGI object.
#
my $query = new CGI::Switch;

# Print a Content-type header.
#
$query->print( $query->header );

# Start the HTML document and display a header with the
```

```perl
# title.
#
$query->print(
    $query->start_html(-title => 'mod_perl Example') );
$query->print( '<h1>mod_perl Example</h1>' );

# $X is a global variable that holds the database handle. It
# doesn't go away between invocations of the script. The ||=
# ensures that the Msql->Connect method is not invoked if
# the database handle already exists.
#
unless ( $X ||= Msql->Connect ) {
    $query->print( qq[Could not connect to the database: ] .
                   qq[$Msql::db_errstr] );
} else {

    # $X_COUNT is another variable that does not go away
    # between invocations. It keeps track of the number
    # of times the database handle $X has been used.
    #
    $X_COUNT++;

    # $X_TIME keeps track of when the database handle
    # was instantiated. Like the $X variable, the ||=
    # assignment operator does not make the assignment if
    # the variable has a value, so the time does not get
    # overwritten between invocations.
    #
    $X_TIME ||= scalar( localtime(time) );

    # Get the current time.
    #
    my $time = localtime( time );

    # Tell the user about the database handle.
    #
    $query->print( qq[The DBH id is $X.<br>] );
    $query->print( qq[It has been used $X_COUNT times.<br>] );
    $query->print( qq[The DBH was instantiated at $X_TIME.<br>] );
    $query->print( qq[It is now $time.<br>] );

}


# End the HTML.
#
$query->print( $query->end_html );
```

Since the Apache Web server keeps multiple `httpd` processes running at one time, each process will have its own instance of this script in memory. If you would like to see the power of this programming technique, you will need to reload the page at least *n* number of times, where *n* is the number of `httpd` process as defined by the `StartServers` directive in httpd.conf. If you have a fairly busy Web server, the number of processes may peak according

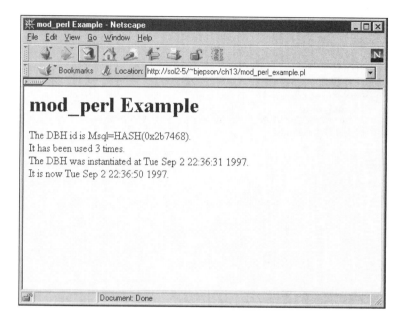

FIGURE 11.3 mod_perl in action. Notice that the counter shows that this httpd process has been used three times.

to the `MinSpareServers` and `MaxSpareServers` directives in httpd.conf. Figure 11.3 shows the results of visiting the script after I had reloaded the page 20 times. This relentless reloading only needs to occur when you first start the httpd server, and will happen on its own after *n* number of users have visited the site. The first *n* visitors will pay the startup penalty, but subsequent visits will be significantly faster.

mod_perl and DBI

The `Apache::DBI` module is an Apache module written in Perl that allows you to use the Perl DBI no differently than you would use it in a CGI script. In the previous `MsqlPerl` example, you saw that the script was responsible for maintaining persistent connections. The `Apache::DBI` module not only handles this behind the scenes, but allows you to use the DBI module directly, so your existing scripts can work with the standard DBI or the `Apache::DBI` module.

The `Apache::DBI` module can be installed using the CPAN tool as outlined earlier in this chapter. You can issue the command `install Apache::DBI` to install it. Alternatively, you can download it from www.perl.com/CPAN/modules/by-module/Apache and install it by hand. After you have installed it, you will need to add the line:

```
PerlModule    Apache::DBI
```

to your `httpd.conf`. This *must* appear before any other Apache modules. Once you have done this, you should stop and restart the Web server. The following script, included in

/eg/ch11/mod_perl_DBI_example.pl, illustrates the way in which the `Apache::DBI` module is used:

```perl
#!/usr/local/bin/perl
#
# mod_perl_example.pl
#
# A sample script showing how to use MsqlPerl with mod_perl
# and the Apache DBI module.
#

use CGI::Switch;

# Use the DBI module.
#
use DBI;

use strict;
use vars qw($X_COUNT $X_TIME);

# Instantiate a new CGI object.
#
my $query = new CGI::Switch;

# Print a Content-type header.
#
$query->print( $query->header );

# Start the HTML document and display a header with the
# title.
#
$query->print(
    $query->start_html(-title => 'mod_perl DBI Example') );
$query->print( '<h1>mod_perl DBI Example</h1>' );

# Attempt to connect to the database. If this connection
# fails, then report the error.
#
my $datasource = "dbi:mSQL:msql_sourcebook:localhost:1114";
my $dbh;
unless ($dbh = DBI->connect($datasource)) {
    $query->print( qq[Could not connect to the database: ] .
                   qq[$DBI::errstr] );
} else {

    $X_COUNT++;
    $X_TIME ||= scalar( localtime(time) );

    # Get the current time.
    #
    my $time = localtime( time );

    # Tell the user about the database handle.
```

```
     #
     $query->print( qq[The DBH id is $dbh.<br>] );
     $query->print( qq[It has been used $X_COUNT times.<br>] );
     $query->print( qq[The DBH was instantiated at $X_TIME.<br>] );
     $query->print( qq[It is now $time.<br>] );

}

# End the HTML.
#
$query->print( $query->end_html );
```

The Quick and the Dead: If Speed Kills, I've Been Dead for Years (Or How I Learned to Stop Waiting and Love `mod_perl`)

One thing that users want is speed. That's why they keep buying faster computers, faster cars, and even faster ways of becoming inebriated. The consequences of the latter became all too familiar to me when I was at the local package store, looking for a six-pack of decent microbrew to serve to some guests who were visiting. What do I find staring me in the face when I open the cooler, but a new brand of malt liquor, disconcertingly named Phat Boy? What got me about this product was, not only does it get the customer "there" quicker, like many other malt liquors, but it contains ginseng. I'm not sure why the ginseng is there—maybe it aids in the absorption of alcohol, maybe it eases the hangover. I'm afraid to find out.

However, the need to get places quicker is not always a bad thing, as some feel it is with malt liquor. In the case of a Web server, it's natural to want to serve pages faster, since the Web has earned itself nicknames like "the World Wide Wait." When you are developing Web-based systems that need to make database connections, the wait increases. The `mod_perl` kit is an excellent way of addressing both the sluggishness of CGI scripts and the overhead of making a database connection. If you have the option of using Apache and `mod_perl`, you'll be spinning your disk in vain if you don't do it!

Mini SQL Internals

The fundamental design criteria for a database engine such as Mini SQL (mSQL) is that it must be able to store and retrieve data with the highest level of performance possible on the host platform. For "basic" data storage schemes such as DBM or the Berkeley DB library, the problem is straightforward and ample algorithms have been designed to provide solutions. Adding a "flexible" query language, such as SQL, to the data access methodology provides a level of complexity that impacts every aspect of the engine's operation.

The complexities are imposed upon such a database system in three main ways: data management performance, system overheads during data management operations, and efficiency of data storage. This chapter outlines these problems and covers the solutions chosen during the implementation of the second-generation Mini SQL database engine.

A Tale of Two Engines

The original implementation of Mini SQL was designed to provide rapid access to small data sets using a subset of the ANSI SQL standard. The requirements that Mini SQL 1.x was designed to fill were minimal: provide high performance for simple operations on basic platforms. The requirements were based on the needs of a network management system in which vast quantities of simple data rows were gathered, stored, and retrieved.

To provide better functionality to the growing mSQL user base, mSQL 1.x was extended to provide capabilities beyond the original requirements specification. Among these capabilities were multiuser support, relational joins, sorting, and table aliasing. The original design goal was to perform at least 100 simple operations per second on data sets of up to 5000 rows. These limits are perfectly valid for a network management/monitoring system but do not lend themselves to large-scale data applications. Within the product life of mSQL 1.x, users were reporting performance problems when building databases with up to 1 million data rows! The capabilities added to Mini SQL effectively allowed it to be applied to problems that were beyond the scope of its functionality and performance capacity.

At the time of the 1.0.10 release of mSQL the code-base was branched and the development of mSQL 2.0 was started. The revised design goals were to provide over 500 indexed operations per second using 100,000-row tables on average PC hardware (e.g., Pentium-class hardware).

The performance of mSQL 1.x was directly proportional to the amount of data being handled. A query would take twice as long if it was issued against a 20,000-row table compared to a 10,000-row table. The limiting factor was the simplistic "single key" indexing mechanism provided by the engine. The design of the 2.0 engine had to produce a nonlinear performance curve in which the query execution time was related more closely to the amount of data being returned by a query, and not by the amount of data stored in the database. To achieve this, a more sophisticated indexing scheme was designed as the mainstay of the 2.0 engine.

The goal of providing high performance on "small" platforms impacts not only the CPU resources available to the engine but also the memory. More traditional performance concerns, such as disk I/O bandwidth, do not factor greatly in modern-day hardware as even "basic" PC hardware offers bus architectures and drive controllers capable of providing serious throughput. Memory consumption remained the primary concern after the limited CPU resource. The end design sought to conserve system resource utilization in four ways. First, sophisticated data selection schemes ensured that the minimum possible processor time was required per query. Second, the new design made efficient use of small amounts of "real" memory. Minimization of the number of kernel traps (system call invocations required to complete any given task) offered a third optimization. Finally, the new design offered vigorous caching of "expensive" resources (such as open file descriptors).

Indexing, Or the Art of Being Lazy

The main downfall of handling large data sets stems from the fact that the software has to do a lot of work in answering the query. It is obvious that the number of computations required to complete a query will have a profound impact on the query execution speed. If a sequential search of 10,000 rows of data produces 10 results, all 10,000 rows must be matched against the query conditions before the 10 results are returned. If the number of rows compared is reduced, then the execution time is reduced. There is no greater single performance benefit than that gained by comprehensive indexing of the data.

The mSQL 1.x engine provided a simple "primary key" based indexing scheme that enforced major restrictions on the use of the index. First, there could only be one index per table. Second, the index could be comprised of only a single table field. Finally, the value of the index had to be unique across the entire data table. Naturally, there are situations where a single-field, unique index is of great benefit, such as in the case of a username lookup using the userid as the index, but such situations are certainly the minority of possible indexing applications. To continue with the username example, it would also be handy to be able to fetch a user based on not just the username, but possibly the name of shell used (`bash`, `tcsh`, `sh`, `csh`, etc.). Naturally, the username is unique but the shell wouldn't be. In this situation, we could gain performance benefits from defining three indices: two unique (username, username+shell) and one nonunique (shell). Obviously, such a design would not be possible in mSQL 1.x.

The 2.0 engine allows for much more sophisticated use of indices. First, there can be multiple indices defined per table (currently five). Second, each index may be comprised of up to 10 table fields (such as a person's first name and last name). Finally, an index may be defined as either unique or nonunique. Once the indices have been defined, any data inserted into the table forces creation of index entries for each index defined for that table. The underlying indexing scheme is currently based upon AVL trees. The decision to implement an AVL tree-based scheme rather than a B-Tree scheme was due to the simplicity of the AVL algorithm. The 2.0 engine provides a framework for supporting multiple indexing schemes, although the AVL scheme is the only one available at the time of writing.

Once the indices have been defined and created, the engine can use them when performing data lookups. By isolating parts of the query condition, the engine can extract the literal conditional values and construct index lookup keys in real time. Each index defined for the specified table is checked in turn against the conditions provided in the query. If the conditions provided could be used on more than one index, an index is selected based either on the length of the index (i.e., the number of fields used to construct the index) or the unique/nonunique status. Naturally, a unique index will result in at most a single table row being checked, so it is chosen if possible.

After that, the longest index will be used based on the assumption that the more fields used to create the index will reduce the number of entries with the same index value. Index lookups on single queries, such as the query shown next, do not pose a great problem as the index lookup value is provided with the query.

```
Select uname from passwd where uid = 1003
```

Consider, however, a query such as:

```
Select staff.name, dept.dept_name from staff, dept
where staff.dept_id = dept.dept_id
```

If `dept_id` is defined as an index on the `dept` table, we can easily use the `dept_id` value from each row in the `staff` table to perform an index lookup to determine the department name. The problem is that we only know the value of the `dept_id` field during the execution of the query and that the value changes with every new row from the `staff` table. Using optimum data access methods during a table join as just shown poses an interesting problem.

Query Optimization— If You've Got It, Flaunt It

Query optimization takes many forms. In high-end RDBMSs such as Oracle, queries are evaluated and sometimes rewritten by the engine in real time based on complex heuristics. mSQL does not perform such optimization. The main concern of the mSQL optimizes is the determination of which data access methods will produce the best possible performance. The indexing in 2.0 produces very rapid data access but only if the engine can decide on a way to use the indices during data lookups.

The previous section described the simple problem of determining which index to use if there are multiple possible indices for a simple query. It then touched on the complexity of handling index-based lookups in multitable queries. The complexities don't stop with just calculating the index value for the lookup. There's an entire Pandora's box of problems to be considered.

The basic logic behind a multitable join is very simple:

```
For each row in table A
    For each row in table B
        Merge the row from Table A with the row from Table B
        Apply the condition from the query
        If the condition matches
            Store the merged row in a temporary result table
```

Obviously, the preceding simplistic algorithm will result in a sequential pass through every row in Table A. It also produces a sequential pass through every row in Table B for each row in Table A. If Table A contains 10,000 rows and Table B contains 10,000 rows there will be 10,000 * 10,000 file access, row merges, and condition evaluations. That sounds fair until you realize that it will take over 100 million of each operation to execute the query! Obviously, the name of the game is to reduce either the number of lookups required to handle the "inner table" (Table B in this example) or to reduce the number of rows in the "outer table" (Table A) that force the execution of the inner loop.

For the following discussion we will use the following query as an example. Our discussion will be based on the staff table being the outer table and the dept table being the inner table.

```
Select staff.first_name, staff.last_name, dept.dept_name
    From staff, dept
    Where staff.dept_id = dept.dept_id
    And staff.last_name = 'Hughes'
```

Inner Loop Reduction

If the inner table contained only 10 rows rather than 10,000 rows the preceding query would require only 100,000 operations rather than 100,000,000 operations. Similarly, if we could use an index to limit the number of rows checked in the inner loop we would achieve the same result. By evaluating the condition we can determine that the value of dept_id in the staff table will be the key in determining which rows from the dept table we need. This case is obvious— we need an index on the dept table built from the dept_id field. If such an index exists then the engine will use it. If it doesn't, the engine will look at the indices defined for the staff table and, if possible, reverse the inner and outer tables to ensure that the inner loop uses an index lookup rather than a sequential search. Performing a table swap such as this requires the conditional clause to be rewritten. If, for example, the query condition included

```
Where staff.dept_id > dept.dept_id
```

the condition would naturally need to be rewritten to

```
Where dept.dept_id < staff.dept_id
```

Outer Loop Reduction

In rare situations, the outer loop can be reduced in a similar manner by employing an index lookup for the outer table as well as the inner table. In the example query, if the `staff` table was defined with an index constructed from the `last_name` field, we could perform a much more efficient search:

```
For each row in "staff" with a last_name index value of "Hughes"
    For each row in "dept" with a dept_id index value being that
    of the current staff row's dept_id value
        merge the rows
        evaluate the remainder of the condition
        store the merged row if the condition matches
```

If there was only one "Hughes" in the `staff` table and the `dept_id` field of the `dept` table was unique, the query would result in only two lookups (one for the `staff` row and one for the `dept` row). Naturally, this is the ultimate situation and will certainly outperform the sequential search method requiring 100,000,000 row lookups.

Partial Match Reduction

Another technique utilized by the mSQL engine is a practice we call *partial match reduction*. The aim of partial match reduction is to achieve results similar to the outer loop reduction outlined previously when no outer table index is available. If a literal condition is provided for the outer table (such as `staff.last_id = 'Hughes'` in our example), the optimizer will note that partial matching is possible and ensure the tables are ordered to take advantage of it. The partial matching algorithm is used to reduce the number of times the inner loop is executed. The algorithm is illustrated as

```
For each row in staff
    If staff.last_name = 'Hughes'
        Perform the inner loop
```

That is, we apply a subset of the conditional clause to the values in the outer table's row before we continue into the inner loop. In our original example (using sequential searching for both the outer and inner loops), partial matching shows a dramatic performance benefit. If there were five rows in `staff` with `last_name = 'Hughes'`, the query would require 5 * 10,000 operations rather than performing the 10,000 * 10,000 operations. The inner loop (i.e., a sequential search of 10,000 rows) is only executed for the five rows from the outer table that could provide a match for the total condition. If the `last_name` field from the current `staff` table row does not contain `'Hughes'` then it is not possible for the result of a merger of any merged row from the `dept` table with this row to satisfy the complete condition. In such a case, there is no point performing the extra work, so the entire inner loop is skipped and the next row from the outer table is fetched.

Candidate Row Abstraction—
The Smoke and the Mirrors

By reading the previous section it becomes apparent that a lot of logic is involved in the selection of each individual row from a data table. In the case of a join, the logic must be applied in different ways to the inner and outer table operations. This results in a single logical area in which design errors or implementation bugs could easily be found. Also, the addition of new indexing schemes, new algorithms, or simply better handling of the table accessing is spread through large sections of the main logic code. To overcome these problems, mSQL hides the entire operation of row selection from the main code of the engine by using an abstraction called the *candidate row abstraction*.

The concept of the abstraction is to allow the main logic of the engine to request the next row that is a potential candidate for the query being executed. Details such as the access method used to determine the next row to be read (e.g., index equality, index range, sequential search, etc.) are not of concern to the main logic of the engine: they are mere operational issues. All such information and complexity is hidden within the abstraction.

Prior to accessing a data table, the main logic code calls the `createCandidate()` function and passes it the entire query condition and details about the data table being accessed. This function evaluates the conditions, checks for indices, rewrites conditions as required, and returns a candidate structure in which the resulting information is held. From that time on, the main logic code simply calls `getCandidate()` passing the candidate structure and is returned the internal row ID of the next table row that should be accessed. The row ID may have been held in an index or it may be just the next row in a sequential search. The main logic code is not concerned with how the row was selected, and is merely interested in the fact that it's the next row that may result in a match of the conditional expression included in the SQL query.

Data Access—To Map or Not to Map

The engine has been designed around extensive use of memory-mapped files (`mmap()` on Unix platforms). The rationale for this design was twofold. First, all file access is via pointers rather than system calls, producing a reduction in kernel traps that is a significant gain. Second, implementation of a user-process-level buffering scheme would only replicate the actions of the kernel's VM subsystem. It is assumed that the kernel's ability to manage page faults is more efficient than a user-level buffer cache.

Following these assumptions has brought about mixed results. For small databases or servers with only a few databases, using memory-mapped files for all major I/O operations has provided very high levels of performance. It has been reported, however, that when the amount of data managed by the mSQL engine increases beyond the size of the machine's physical memory, the impact of the excessive page faulting degrades system performance for all services provided by that machine, not only mSQL. In situations where an entire machine is dedicated to providing mSQL-based database services, this downfall is not a problem. In the more normal case, where mSQL coexists with a Web server for example, the results are not as pleasing.

Although this problem is rare at present, the entire 2.0 server development project was the result of applications pushing the 1.x server beyond its performance boundaries. Design work is under way to provide a solution to this problem to ensure that the 2.0 engine will be capable of handling data sets as large as the application requires.

The approach being taken is to provide optional access to an internal buffer cache implemented over the usual read-and-write system calls. The amount of memory allocated to the buffer cache will be configurable at run time. Utilization of the buffer cache (in preference to `mmap()`-based access) will also be configured on a per-database basis at run time. Such an implementation will allow the administrator to keep smaller data sets that are required very frequently in mapped regions, while larger data sets or those that are accessed infrequently are accessed via the buffer cache. Such a scheme is also a benefit for portability as some platforms still do not provide memory-mapped file implementations.

The Table Cache—Make Recycling a Way of Life

Many of the internal setup operations of the mSQL server are "expensive" in terms of system resource utilization and execution speed. Operations such as the loading of a table definition, opening files, mapping files into the server's VM address space, and allocating internal buffers require time and effort. If the engine is to allow rapid data access, the overhead becomes a major bottleneck.

To overcome this problem, the mSQL engine maintains an internal table cache. This cache does not hold data being read from or written to the tables. Its sole purpose is as a place in which expensive resources are held until they are no longer needed.

The cache is implemented as an LRU (Least Recently Used) cache with a size large enough to hold the resources of roughly 8 to 10 tables (depends on the platform on which the server is running and the configuration). When a query is received, a function is called that loads the table definition, sets up the file descriptors, maps any file regions required, and returns a structure containing all the relevant information. Embedded in this routine is the table cache management. The structure returned is actually a pointer to a table cache entry. When the routine is called, the cache is scanned for an existing instance of the required table. If it is not found in the cache, the oldest entry (i.e., the entry that was last accessed the longest time ago) is removed and replaced by the information for the newly loaded table. A pointer to this entry is then returned to the caller.

The table cache entry contains the following information:

- Open file descriptors for the data file, the overflow buffer file, and the index files
- Memory-mapped regions for the data file, the overflow buffers, and the index files
- The table definition
- A list of index definitions
- A single, `malloc()`'ed buffer large enough to hold an entire table row
- `malloc()`'ed buffers large enough to hold the index key for each defined index

Conclusion

The mSQL 2.0 engine has been designed with a systems programmer's mind set. That is, every aspect of the interaction between the software and the underlying operating system has been considered. By keeping the underlying operations of the operating system in mind it has been possible to greatly increase the performance of the engine by limiting the use of "expensive" functions. By applying common sense to the problems of data access, the amount of work required to complete any single query has been dramatically reduced.

Although mSQL does not provide all the high-end functionality of more sophisticated RDBMS products, on a straight performance comparison it will certainly please most testers. Performance tests on low-end hardware (such as a Pentium 133 PC, 48 MB RAM, FreeBSD) show results greater than 850 indexed operations per second on 100,000-row tables. The results on more capable machines, such as Sun Ultra SPARCs and DEC Alphas, are very impressive.

The results that have been achieved by the 2.0 engine prove that regardless of the design methodology used to engineer a software application, a good understanding of the interaction between the software and the operating system will always allow you to write high-performance applications.

Annotated Source Code to RDBMS Java

The RDBMS system is composed of several classes that work together to provide the system's functionality. The classes are divided up to handle such things as presenting the Query and Add/Edit forms, retrieving metadata from the database, and creating custom controls. Table B.1 lists each of the classes, along with a short description of the class.

Table B.1 The Classes That Comprise the RDBMS System

Class	Purpose
RDBMS	The main class, which presents the first user interface. From here, other classes are loaded in response to user actions, such as clicking on the Add or Query buttons.
RDBMSAddEdit	This class is responsible for displaying the Add/Edit form.
RDBMSCharChoice	This is a subclass of `java.awt.Choice` that produces a Choice component with comparison options for character datatypes, such as case-sensitive search, case-*insensitive* search, equality, and inequality.
RDBMSChoice	This is a subclass of `java.awt.Choice` that produces a Choice component based on a table's primary key and label key.
RDBMSException	This is a special exception thrown by certain parts of RDBMS.
RDBMSmSQLInit	The class that is responsible for parsing a schema definition file. It also creates entities within the database.

Continues

Table B.1 The Classes That Comprise the RDBMS System (*Continued*)

Class	Purpose
RDBMSNumChoice	A subclass of `java.awt.Choice` that produces a Choice component with comparison options for numeric data types (INT, REAL).
RDBMSQuery	This class is responsible for displaying the Query form.
RDBMSQueryResult	The class that handles displaying the results of a query.
RDBMSTable	A representation of a given table. This class includes a lot of metadata about the table.
RDBMSTableColumn	This is a representation of a given column, and offers metadata that pertains to the column.

ORG.as220.rdbms.RDBMS

This class produces the first screen (the RDBMS Control Center) that the user sees. It provides a very simple interface: a `Choice` object with table names, and Query and Add `Button` objects. Since the `Choice` object lists the descriptive names of the tables, rather than the names of the tables as mSQL knows them, you can't just get the text of the selected item and use it in an SQL statement. mSQL doesn't know that "Subscriptions" means the subscription table, even though they are very close. We need some way of correlating the descriptive name to the table's real name. While it would be possible to issue a query against `RDBMSsystables` to get this information, it's quicker and easier to put each table name in a `Vector` each time an item is added to the `Choice` object. That way, it's only a matter of finding the selected index of the `Choice` object, and looking up the corresponding element from the `Vector`. Here's the source code to RDBMS, included on the CD-ROM as /eg/ch06/ORG/as220/rdbms/RDBMS.java:

```
/*
 *
 * RDBMS.java
 * Copyright (C) 1997 Brian Jepson (bjepson@ids.net)
 *
 * This program is free software; you can redistribute it
 * and/or modify it under the terms of the GNU General
 * Public License as published by the Free Software
 * Foundation; either version 2 of the License, or (at
 * your option) any later version.
 *
 * This program is distributed in the hope that it will be
 * useful, but WITHOUT ANY WARRANTY; without even the
 * implied warranty of MERCHANTABILITY or FITNESS FOR A
 * PARTICULAR PURPOSE.  See the GNU General Public License
 * for more details.
 *
 * You should have received a copy of the GNU General Public
```

```
 * License along with this program; if not, write to the
 * Free Software Foundation, Inc., 59 Temple Place - Suite
 * 330, Boston, MA 02111-1307, USA
 *
 */

package ORG.as220.rdbms;
import java.awt.*;
import java.awt.event.*;
import java.util.*;
import java.sql.*;

/**
 *
 * This is the master driver for the RDBMS system. For
 * each table in the database, it displays an Add button
 * and a Query button.
 *
 */
public class RDBMS extends Frame {
```

Before the constructor or any of the other methods, several objects are declared, and some are defined. The first are the names of the system tables (RDBMSsystables, RDBMSsyscolumns, RDBMSsyskeys). These Strings are static, which means that they can be referenced directly in any class that either 1) is in the same package as RDBMS, or 2) is a class that includes the import ORG.as220.rdbms.* statement.

The constructor, which will appear shortly, includes a java.sql.Connection object as one of its required parameters. Since the Connection is so critical to the proper working of this class, it will get assigned a permanent home as the dbconn field (a Java class' field, not a database field—fields in a Java class are sometimes called *properties*) of the RDBMS object. Similarly, the database name is stored in dbname. After this, the layout manager and the layout constraints objects are declared, as well as the Choice object and table lookup Vector mentioned earlier.

```
    // System-wide constants. These are used in many other
    // classes within this system.
    //
    static String systables  = "RDBMSsystables";
    static String syscolumns = "RDBMSsyscolumns";
    static String syskeys    = "RDBMSsyskeys";

    Connection dbconn;   // The JDBC connection to mSQL.
    String dbname;       // The name of the database.

    GridBagLayout gb;         // The layout manager.
    GridBagConstraints gbc;   // Constraints for the above.

    Choice tbl_choice;   // A Choice object for the tables.
    Vector tbl_index;    // A lookup Vector for table names.
```

This class has only one constructor. It needs to be passed a Connection object as well as a String containing the database name. Within the constructor, the RDBMS object (which is a subclass of java.awt.Frame) is given a layout manager. Three labels are added, which include instructive text. Next, the Choice object is created. For each table, an item is added to the Choice object with the descriptive name of the table as its prompt. At the same time, the table's real name is added to the Vector. Query and Add buttons are added, and listeners are attached to them so that the appropriate action can be performed when the user clicks on the button. Finally, a WindowListener is attached to the RDBMS object, so it can close down properly when the user closes the window.

```java
/**
 * Construct a new RDBMS object.
 *
 * @param conn A JDBC Connection
 * @param db The database name to work in.
 */
public RDBMS(Connection conn, String db) {

    super("RDBMS Control Center");

    // Set the system-wide Connection object.
    //
    dbconn = conn;

    // We're using GridbagLayout to manage the user
    // interface. Of course, we need to bring his
    // friend along, a GridBagConstraints.
    //
    gb  = new GridBagLayout();
    gbc = new GridBagConstraints();
    setLayout(gb);

    // Set some sane defaults for the
    // GridBagConstraints.
    //
    gbc.fill    = GridBagConstraints.BOTH;
    gbc.gridwidth = GridBagConstraints.REMAINDER;
    gbc.gridx = 0; gbc.gridy = 0;

    // Display some simple prompts to get the user
    // started. There are probably easier ways to
    // display a multi-line Label, but this is the best
    // my slow mind can do...
    //
    Label p;
    p = new Label(
        "Welcome to the RDBMS Control Center. Choose");
    gb.setConstraints(p, gbc);
    p.setBackground(Color.white);
    add(p);
    gbc.gridy++;
```

```
p = new Label(
    "Query to search within a table, or choose Add");
gb.setConstraints(p, gbc);
p.setBackground(Color.white);
add(p);
gbc.gridy++;

p = new Label(
    "to add a new record.");
gb.setConstraints(p, gbc);
p.setBackground(Color.white);
add(p);
gbc.gridy++;

// Next, create a Choice object that allows the user
// to choose a table. As each choice is added to the
// object, we'll make sure to create an association
// between that choice (the table long name) and the
// table name, using a Vector that is indexed by the
// selectedIndex() value that would correspond to
// the table.
//
tbl_choice = new Choice();
tbl_index  = new Vector();

try {

    // For some reason, Msql-JDBC doesn't support
    // this method, and requires the URL to specify
    // the database name. This will do nothing under
    // mSQL-JDBC, but it is included here for
    // compatibility with other drivers.
    //
    conn.setCatalog(db);

    // Get a Statement object from the connection.
    //
    Statement stmt = dbconn.createStatement();

    // Issue a query to get the names of all the
    // tables.
    //
    ResultSet rs = stmt.executeQuery(
        "SELECT tbl_name, tbl_description" +
        " FROM " + RDBMS.systables +
        " ORDER BY tbl_description");

    // Continue fetching rows until there are no
    // more available.
    //
    while (rs.next()) {
```

```
    String tbl_name = rs.getString(1);
    String tbl_desc = rs.getString(2);

    // Add the table name to the tbl_index
    // Vector, and the table description to the
    // Choice object. This will ensure that the
    // Choice and Vector elements are numbered
    // the same, so we can use the Choice
    // object's getSelectedIndex() method to
    // find the index of the corresponding item
    // in the Vector.
    //
    tbl_index.addElement(tbl_name);
    tbl_choice.add(tbl_desc);
}

// Add the Choice object.
//
gbc.gridwidth = 1;
gb.setConstraints(tbl_choice, gbc);
add(tbl_choice);

// Move one column over and add the query
// button.
//
Button q = new Button("Query");
gbc.gridx++;
gb.setConstraints(q, gbc);
add(q);

// This action listener will take care of
// creating a Query form for the selected table
// when someone clicks onthe query button.
//
q.addActionListener(new queryButtonWatcher());

// This blank label in the lower left corner
// balances things out kind of neatly.
//
gbc.gridx = 0;
gbc.gridy++;
Label blank = new Label("");
gb.setConstraints(blank, gbc);
add(blank);

// Advance one column before adding the next
// Button.
//
gbc.gridx++;
Button a = new Button("Add");
gb.setConstraints(a, gbc);
add(a);
```

```
            // This action listener will take care of
            // creating an Add/Edit form for the table when
            // someone clicks on the Add button.
            //
            a.addActionListener(new addButtonWatcher());

        } catch (SQLException e) {
            e.printStackTrace();
            System.exit(0);
        }

        // Attach a listener that will be used to intercept
        // calls to close the Frame; otherwise they won't be
        // able to quit this program using a window close
        // control.
        //
        addWindowListener(new WinEventHandler() );

        // Pack and show the Frame.
        //
        pack();
        show();
    }
```

The next thing in this class is an inner class, the event handler for any window actions that affect the RDBMS object. The only one that is of interest is the windowClosing event, which is simply used to effect an exit from the Java interpreter, completely shutting down the RDBMS system. Following this, two ActionListeners are defined. The queryButtonWatcher's actionPerformed() method is invoked when the user clicks the Query button. The basic purpose of this is to display a query form for the selected table. In order to keep the screen from getting too cluttered, there's only one query form displayed at a time for a given table. If the query form is already on screen, it's simply brought to the front. If the RDBMSQuery object is null (this means it has never been assigned) or if its disposed property is set to true, a new object is instantiated. The same sort of behavior is shown in the addButtonWatcher object, except it deals with RDBMSAddEdit objects.

```
// This is the event handler that deals with cases
// where a user closes the window.
//
class WinEventHandler extends WindowAdapter {
    public void windowClosing(WindowEvent e) {
        System.exit(0);
    }
}

/**
 *
 * A listener for query buttons.
 *
```

```
    */
class queryButtonWatcher implements ActionListener {

    // We'll keep the RDBMSQuery object around in
    // between calls to this object's actionPerformed()
    // method. That way, we don't keep instantiating the
    // RDBMSQuery objects, and can just bring it to the
    // front if we already have one. Each time we create
    // a new one, it will get added to this HashTable,
    // and will be keyed by the table name.
    //
    Hashtable queries = new Hashtable();

    // When the user clicks the button, check to see if
    // the RDBMSQuery object is null, or if it was
    // disposed of (disposed flag will be true). If so,
    // create a new one. Otherwise, bring the old one to
    // the front.
    //
    public void actionPerformed( ActionEvent e ) {

        // Find out what the selected index of the
        // tbl_choice object is.
        //
        int i = tbl_choice.getSelectedIndex();

        // Get the table name from the tbl_index Vector.
        //
        String tbl_name = (String) tbl_index.elementAt(i);

        // If there's no RDBMSQuery object that
        // corresponds to this table in the queries
        // Hashtable, then make a new RDBMSQuery.
        // Otherwise, just bring the old one to the
        // front.
        //
        RDBMSQuery query =
            (RDBMSQuery) queries.get(tbl_name);

        if (query == null || query.disposed) {
            query = new RDBMSQuery(dbconn, tbl_name);
            queries.put(tbl_name, query);
        } else {
            query.toFront();
        }

    }
}

/**
 *
 * A listener for add buttons.
 *
```

```
    */
    class addButtonWatcher implements ActionListener {

        // We'll keep the RDBMSAddEdit object around in
        // between calls to this object's actionPerformed()
        // method. Each time we create a new one, it will
        // get added to this HashTable, and will be keyed
        // by the table name.
        //
        Hashtable adds = new Hashtable();

        // When the user clicks the button, check to see if
        // the RDBMSAddEdit object is null, or if it was
        // disposed of. If so, create a new one. Otherwise,
        // bring the old one to the front.
        //
        public void actionPerformed( ActionEvent e ) {

            // Find out what the selected index of the
            // tbl_choice object is.
            //
            int i = tbl_choice.getSelectedIndex();

            // Get the table name from the tbl_index Vector.
            //
            String tbl_name = (String) tbl_index.elementAt(i);

            // If there's no RDBMSQuery object that
            // corresponds to this table in the queries
            // Hashtable, then make a new RDBMSQuery.
            // Otherwise, just bring the old one to the
            // front.
            //
            RDBMSAddEdit add =
                (RDBMSAddEdit) adds.get(tbl_name);
            if (add == null || add.disposed) {
                add = new RDBMSAddEdit(dbconn, tbl_name);
                adds.put(tbl_name, add);
            } else {
                add.toFront();
            }

        }
    }
```

Finally, a static `main()` method is included. This will accept the URL and database name on the command line, and will instantiate a new RDBMS object. It is also responsible for creating a JDBC `Connection` object, and includes some error checking on the data that was supplied on the command line.

```
    /**
     * Static method that is automatically invoked when this
     * class is executed on the command line.
```

```
 */
public static void main(String argv[]) {

    // The URL comes in from argv[0], so
    // display a usage message if the user
    // didn't specify a URL.
    //
    if (argv.length < 2) {
        System.err.println("Usage:");
        System.err.println("");
        System.err.println("java runRDBMS URL dbname");
        System.exit(1);
    }

    try {

        // Register the mSQL driver with the Driver
        // Manager.
        //
        Class.forName("COM.imaginary.sql.msql.MsqlDriver");

    } catch (ClassNotFoundException e) {

        e.printStackTrace();
        System.exit(0);
    }

    // Get the URL and database name from the arguments
    // on the command line.
    //
    String url = argv[0];
    String db  = argv[1];

    // the user might have passed in a user name or
    // password, so try to read those in, as well.
    //
    String user, pwd;
    if (argv.length > 2) {
        user = argv[2];
    } else {
        user = "";
    }
    if (argv.length > 3) {
        pwd = argv[3];
    } else {
        pwd = "";
    }

    try {

        // make a connection to the specified URL
        //
        Connection con =
```

```
            DriverManager.getConnection(url, user, pwd);

            // Create a new RDBMS object.
            //
            RDBMS r = new RDBMS(con, db);

        } catch( Exception e ) {
            System.out.println(e.getMessage());
            e.printStackTrace();
        }
    }
}
```

ORG.as220.rdbms.RDBMSTable

The strength of the RDBMS system is its reliance on system-wide metadata. The `RDBMSTable` class plays a big part of that scheme. It is a simple class that needs only a JDBC `Connection` object and the name of a table to do its work. It performs all initialization automatically, and the object can be queried using one of many get-style methods. This allows for runtime discovery of such things as the table's descriptive name, primary key, and other information.

```
/*
 *
 * RDBMSTable.java
 * Copyright (C) 1997 Brian Jepson (bjepson@ids.net)
 *
 * This program is free software; you can redistribute it
 * and/or modify it under the terms of the GNU General
 * Public License as published by the Free Software
 * Foundation; either version 2 of the License, or (at
 * your option) any later version.
 *
 * This program is distributed in the hope that it will be
 * useful, but WITHOUT ANY WARRANTY; without even the
 * implied warranty of MERCHANTABILITY or FITNESS FOR A
 * PARTICULAR PURPOSE.  See the GNU General Public License
 * for more details.
 *
 * You should have received a copy of the GNU General Public
 * License along with this program; if not, write to the
 * Free Software Foundation, Inc., 59 Temple Place - Suite
 * 330, Boston, MA 02111-1307, USA
 *
 */

package ORG.as220.rdbms;
import java.util.*;
import java.sql.*;

/**
 *
```

```
 * RDBMSTable provides a metadata object that contains
 * a lot of information about a given table, such as
 * information regarding foreign keys, primary keys, and
 * other useful stuff. I'm intentionally *not* using the
 * JDBC methods for gathering this data, since I want this
 * stuff to work with mini-SQL. At the present time, the
 * JDBC driver for mini-SQL doesn't support a database
 * metadata object. However, this class definition could
 * be easily rewritten to use a DatabaseMetaData object.
 *
 * Right now, it relies on the system tables that are
 * created using the RDBMS*Init class, and this should
 * work for any JDBC data source.
 *
 */
public class RDBMSTable {
```

There are several objects that need to be available to all methods of the class. This includes very fundamental things such as the name of the table, the descriptive name of the table, the primary key column, and the label column (a column that is descriptive of each row). Also, a String object called getnextkey is needed. This contains the exact SQL statement that needs to be issued in order to fetch a new primary key. In the case of Mini SQL, this will always make use of the SELECT _seq FROM table SQL statement, but it could be the name of a stored procedure, if a database engine such as Sybase or Oracle were used. This SQL statement is originally inserted into the RDBMSsystables table back when the RDBMSmSQLInit class was run.

In addition to these String objects, two Vectors are also used. The first, columns, contains references to each of the RDBMSTableColumn objects that correspond to the actual columns in the table. The second Vector, dep_tables, contains the name of each table that depends on this table. A dependent table is one that has a foreign key reference to this table. When a row is inserted, deleted, or updated in the table, this is used by other classes to send a message to any RDBMSChoice objects that refer to this table. The message simply tells the object to reload the data from the table, so it always refers to the most current data. Finally, since the JDBC Connection object is so darn useful, the dbconn object is used to ensure that it is available to all methods of the class.

```
    private String name;        // table name
    private String title;       // descriptive table name
    private String getnextkey;  // SQL to get a new key
    private String primary_key; // the primary key column
    private String label_column; // the descriptive column

    Vector columns = new Vector(); // column metadata

    // A Vector of tables that depend on this table.
    //
    Vector dep_tables = new Vector();

    Connection dbconn;                  // the database connection
```

For the most part, the only methods that other classes will invoke (aside from the constructor) are the following get-style methods. The exception to this is the `fetchLabel()` method, which is the last method in this class, and is explained in detail later in the appendix. With the exception of `getColumns()` and `getDepends()`, each of these methods returns a `String` object. `getColumns()` returns an array of `RDBMSTableColumn` objects, and `getDepends()` returns an array of `String` objects.

```java
/**
 * getName - returns the name of the table.
 */
public String getName() { return name; }

/**
 * getTitle - returns the descriptive name of the table.
 */
public String getTitle() { return title; }

/**
 * getGetNextKey - returns an SQL statement you can use
 * to fetch a new sequential key.
 */
public String getGetNextKey() { return getnextkey; }

/**
 * getPrimaryKey - returns the table's primary key.
 */
public String getPrimaryKey() { return primary_key; }

/**
 * getLabelColumn - returns the table's label column.
 */
public String getLabelColumn() { return label_column; }

/**
 *
 * getColumns - Return an array of this table's columns.
 *
 */
public RDBMSTableColumn[] getColumns() {

    RDBMSTableColumn[] cols =
        new RDBMSTableColumn[columns.size()];

    columns.copyInto((Object[]) cols);

    return cols;

}

/**
 *
 * getDepends - Return an array of tables that depend on
```

```
     * this one.
     *
     */
    public String[] getDepends() {

        String[] tbls =
            new String[dep_tables.size()];

        dep_tables.copyInto((Object[]) tbls);

        return tbls;

    }
```

The constructor, shown next, takes care of transferring the table name and Connection to objects that are available throughout the class. After this, it invokes a series of methods that take care of populating the other objects that were declared at the top of the class.

```
    /**
     * Constructs a new RDBMSTable object.
     *
     * @param con the JDBC Connection object
     * @param table_name the name of the table
     */
    public RDBMSTable (Connection con, String table_name) {

        // Make sure that the Connection and table name are
        // referenced in class-wide objects.
        //
        name    = table_name;
        dbconn = con;

        try {

            // Invoke all of the methods that gather
            // metadata.
            //
            getTableInfo();
            getKeyInfo();
            getColumnInfo();
            getDependencies();

        } catch (RDBMSException e) {

            e.printStackTrace();
            System.exit(0);

        }

    }
```

The `getDependencies()` method consults the `RDBMSsyskeys` table to find all tables that have a foreign key reference into this table. These tables, if any, are added to the `dep_tables Vector`, and can be retrieved with the `getDepends()` method.

```
/**
 * getDependencies - gather a list of tables that
 * depend on this table. This will be all tables that
 * have a foreign key reference into this table.
 */
private void getDependencies() {

    // This SQL SELECT will find the names of all tables
    // that depend on this table.
    //
    String sql =
        "SELECT tbl_name " +
        " FROM " + RDBMS.syskeys +
        " WHERE key_type ='FOREIGN'" +
        " AND    col_name = '" + getPrimaryKey() + "'";

    try {

        // Get a Statement object from the connection.
        //
        Statement stmt = dbconn.createStatement();

        // Execute the query, and get a result set
        //
        ResultSet rs = stmt.executeQuery(sql);

        // Add each table name to the dep_tables Vector.
        //
        while (rs.next()) {
            dep_tables.addElement(rs.getString(1));
        }
        stmt.close();

    } catch (SQLException e) {

        e.printStackTrace();
        System.exit(0);

    }

}
```

The `getTableInfo` method simply queries the `RDBMSsystables` table to get a descriptive title for the table and the SQL code that is used to fetch a new primary key value for the table. This information is stored in the `title` and `getnextkey String` objects, respectively.

```
/**
 * getTableInfo - retrieve information about this table,
```

```java
 * such as its descriptive name and the SQL string
 * needed to retrieve another unique identifier.
 */
private void getTableInfo() throws RDBMSException {

    // Here is the SQL statement that will retrieve
    // the table description and information on getting
    // a new key from the systables metadata table.
    //
    String sql = "SELECT tbl_description, " +
                 "         tbl_getnextkey " +
                 "    FROM " + RDBMS.systables +
                 "   WHERE tbl_name = '" + name + "'";

    try {

        // Get a Statement object from the connection.
        //
        Statement stmt = dbconn.createStatement();

        // Execute the query, and get a result set
        //
        ResultSet rs = stmt.executeQuery(sql);

        // Get the descriptive name from the first column of
        // the first row.
        //
        if (!rs.next()) {

            // If the table definition was not found,
            // then throw an exception.
            //
            throw new RDBMSException(
                "Could not locate " + RDBMS.systables +
                " entry for table " + name + ".");

        }

        title     = rs.getString(1);
        getnextkey = rs.getString(2);

        stmt.close();

    } catch (SQLException e) {

        e.printStackTrace();
        System.exit(0);

    }

}
```

The RDBMSsyskeys table is consulted in this method, getKeyInfo(). The two keys of interest are the *label key* (a descriptive column that uniquely describes each row) and the *primary key* (an integer column that uniquely *identifies* each row). While the primary key and label key both uniquely identify a row, the label key is ideal for displaying to users. The distinction here is between uniquely describing (explaining to humans) and uniquely qualifying (explaining to the computer). The label key is usually the name of whatever is being described by the table. For example, a table of publication recipients would have a unique id, which is used by the system to internally identify a recipient, but the recipient name would be used by users, and would be the label key.

```java
/**
 * getKeyInfo - retrieve the label (descriptive) and
 * primary key for this table.
 */
private void getKeyInfo() throws RDBMSException {

    // Here is the SQL statement that will retrieve
    // the primary key and label key information from
    // the metadata table.
    //
    String sql = "SELECT col_name, key_type " +
                 "   FROM " + RDBMS.syskeys +
                 "   WHERE tbl_name = '" + name + "'";
    try {

        // Get a Statement object from the connection.
        //
        Statement stmt = dbconn.createStatement();

        // Execute the query, and get a result set
        //
        ResultSet rs = stmt.executeQuery(sql);

        // This flag will indicate whether or not the
        // primary key was located. If it wasn't, then
        // we have to throw an exception.
        //
        boolean found_primary_key  = false;

        // Get the descriptive name from the first column of
        // the first row.
        //
        while(rs.next()) {

            String col_name = rs.getString(1);
            String key_type = rs.getString(2);

            // If it's a primary key, register the column
            // as such.
            //
```

```
                if (key_type.equals("PRIMARY")) {
                    primary_key = col_name;
                    found_primary_key = true;
                }

                // If it's a label column, register the column
                // as such.
                //
                if (key_type.equals("LABEL")) {
                    label_column = col_name;
                }
            }

            stmt.close();

            // If the primary key was not found, then throw
            // an exception.
            //
            if (!found_primary_key) {
                throw new RDBMSException(
                    "Could not locate primary key for " +
                    "table " + name + ".");
            }


        } catch (SQLException e) {

            e.printStackTrace();
            System.exit(0);

        }

    }
```

The `getColumnInfo()` method uses the `RDBMSsyscolumns` table to get a list of columns that this table contains. Then it instantiates an `RDBMSTableColumn` object for that column, and constructs a reference to it within the `columns Vector`.

```
/**
    * getColumnInfo - retrieve column information for this
    * table.
    */
    private void getColumnInfo() throws RDBMSException {

        // Here is the SQL statement that will retrieve
        // the column info from the syscolumns table.
        //
        String sql = "SELECT col_name " +
                     "  FROM " + RDBMS.syscolumns +
                     "  WHERE tbl_name = '" + name + "'";
        try {
```

```
        // Get a Statement object from the connection.
        //
        Statement stmt = dbconn.createStatement();

        // Execute the query, and get a result set
        //
        ResultSet rs = stmt.executeQuery(sql);

        // Add each column's name to the column_names
        // vector. We can't call the constructor for
        // RDBMSTableColumn here, since it needs to work
        // with multiple statements off of the same
        // connection. This should work with most
        // drivers, but why tempt fate?
        //
        Vector column_names = new Vector();
        while (rs.next()) {
            column_names.addElement(rs.getString(1));
        }
        stmt.close();

        // Add a new column object for each column in
        // the table to the columns Vector.
        //
        for (int i = 0; i < column_names.size(); i++) {
            String col_name =
                (String) column_names.elementAt(i);

            RDBMSTableColumn col_object =
                new RDBMSTableColumn(dbconn,
                                    name, col_name);

            columns.addElement(col_object);
        }

    } catch (SQLException e) {

        e.printStackTrace();
        System.exit(0);

    }

}
```

The `fetchLabel()` method is used by other classes that need to get a label value for a given row. This method requires a primary key value, and uses that value to find the row and get the label. Since all tables are not guaranteed to have a label column, it is necessary to use this method to get a suitable value. The label column is used for displaying a descriptive name for a given row, so if the row is merely a cross-reference table, the only descriptive name that can be produced is a list of all of the cross-referenced values! For example, the `subscription` table is a cross-reference of Recipients, Publications, and Shippers. For rows within that table, the label key would be a concatenation of the label values from each table. The `fetchLabel()` method needs to "drill-down" into each table to get that value. Since it invokes the `fetchLabel()` method of each of those tables, it's entirely possible to drill-down through multiple levels of cross-references. Of course, for tables that have a label key, that value is simply fetched and returned.

```
/**
 *
 * fetchLabel - given a primary key, this method will
 * return either the label value, if one exists, or it
 * will concatenate all of the labels from related
 * tables to produce a meaningful key.
 *
 * This method is here to support tables that don't have
 * an explicit label (descriptive) column. In
 * particular, this includes tables that are primarily
 * cross-reference tables.
 *
 * @param pkey_val the primary key for the record you
 * wish to fetch
 */
public String fetchLabel(int pkey_val) {

        // Get the primary key and label column.
        //
        String key   = getPrimaryKey();
        String label = getLabelColumn();

        String result = "";

        // Handle any SQLExceptions.
        //
        try {

                // Get a Statement object from the connection.
                //
                Statement stmt = dbconn.createStatement();

                // If the label column is not null, then it's only a
                // matter of fetching the label column from the
                // table for the key value that was supplied.
                //
                if (label != null) {

                        // Fetch the row.
                        //
                        String sql = "SELECT " + label +
                                  " FROM " + name +
                                  " WHERE " +key + "=" +pkey_val;

                        // Execute the query, and get a result set
                        //
```

```java
        ResultSet rs = stmt.executeQuery(sql);

        // We are only expecting one row.
        //
        if (rs.next()) {
            result = rs.getString(1);
        }

} else {

    // If the label column was null, then we
    // need to identify any columns that are
    // foreign key columns, and fetch them from
    // the row in the table. Then, we need to
    // fetch a label value for each of them.
    // We'll actually identify them by table
    // name, and create a new RDBMSTable for
    // that table, and use this method to get
    // its label.

    // Get the column metadata
    //
    RDBMSTableColumn[] cols = getColumns();

    // We'll go through the list of columns
    // here. Each time we find one that is a
    // foreign key reference, we'll fetch the
    // value from table, and then drill down to
    // the related table to help build a label
    // String.
    //
    StringBuffer label_value=new StringBuffer();
    int total_columns_found = 0;
    for (int i=0; i < cols.length; i++) {

        // If this column is a foreign key, then
        // fetch its value.
        //
        if (cols[i].isForeignKey()) {

            // Fetch the row.
            //
            String sql =
                "SELECT " + cols[i].getName() +
                " FROM " + name +
                " WHERE " + key + "=" + pkey_val;

            // Execute the query, and get a result
            // set.
            //
            ResultSet rs = stmt.executeQuery(sql);
```

```
// Since this query fetched based on
// a primary key, it only should
// produce one row.
//
if (!rs.next()) {
    throw new SQLException(
        "Could not locate a row in "+
        name + " that matched the "+
        "primary key value " +
        pkey_val);
}

// This is the foreign key value
// from this table that refers to
// the primary key in the related
// table.
//
int foreign_key = rs.getInt(1);

// Get the table name in which this
// column resides.
//
String table_name =
    cols[i].getForeignTable();

// Construct a new RDBMSTable
// object.
//
RDBMSTable t =
    new RDBMSTable(dbconn,
                   table_name);

// Get the label value from that
// table using the foreign key value
// that was fetched from this table.
//
String label_val =
    t.fetchLabel(foreign_key);

// If there's anything in the
// label_value StringBuffer, then
// add a comma before adding the
// next value. This makes things
// look nice and pretty.
//
if (total_columns_found > 0) {
    label_value.append(", ");
}
total_columns_found++;

// Add the descriptive label and the
// value of the foreign label. This
```

```
                         // way, we get stuff like:
                         //
                         // "Shipper: DHL, Recipient: Elvis"
                         //
                         String label_desc = cols[i].getLabel();
                         label_value.append(
                             label_desc + ": " + label_val);
                    }
                }

                // Convert the label_value into a String and
                // use the result String to refer to it.
                //
                result = label_value.toString();
            }

        } catch (SQLException e) {
            e.printStackTrace();
            System.exit(0);
        }

        return result;

    }

}
```

ORG.as220.rdbms.RDBMSTableColumn

One of the classes that is used by RDBMSTable is RDBMSTableColumn. An object of this class provides a convenient representation of a column, and supplies relevant metadata. This includes the name of the table to which the column belongs, the column's name, its descriptive name, data type, and other useful information. If the column happens to be a foreign key that refers to another table, that fact is represented by a boolean value, and the foreign table name is made available as well.

```
/*
 *
 * RDBMSTableColumn.java
 * Copyright (C) 1997 Brian Jepson (bjepson@ids.net)
 *
 * This program is free software; you can redistribute it
 * and/or modify it under the terms of the GNU General
 * Public License as published by the Free Software
 * Foundation; either version 2 of the License, or (at
 * your option) any later version.
 *
 * This program is distributed in the hope that it will be
 * useful, but WITHOUT ANY WARRANTY; without even the
 * implied warranty of MERCHANTABILITY or FITNESS FOR A
```

```
 * PARTICULAR PURPOSE.   See the GNU General Public License
 * for more details.
 *
 * You should have received a copy of the GNU General Public
 * License along with this program; if not, write to the
 * Free Software Foundation, Inc., 59 Temple Place - Suite
 * 330, Boston, MA 02111-1307, USA
 *
 */

package ORG.as220.rdbms;
import java.sql.*;

/**
 *
 * RDBMSTableColumn is a class definition that represents
 * column metadata.
 *
 */
public class RDBMSTableColumn {
```

This class is much simpler than the RDBMSTable class. Like that class, it also encapsulates of lot of information about its subject. Each detail about the column is declared as an object or variable that will be initialized later on. As in other classes, a Connection object named dbconn is declared here, so it will be available to all methods within the class. In the present incarnation of this class, the Connection is only used during instantiation, and does not need to survive after that, since the methods that are invoked during the life span of the object simply retrieve the values that are declared below. However, it's not unthinkable that future enhancements could include other methods that need to query the database, so it is useful and convenient to keep the Connection object around.

```
    String name;            // the name of the column
    String label;           // descriptive column name
    String type;            // data type
    int length;             // length
    String table;           // table name
    boolean queryable;      // show column on query forms?
    boolean visible;        // show column on display forms?
    boolean fkey;           // is this column a foreign key?
    String foreign_table;   // name of related table

    Connection dbconn; // database connection
```

The constructor fetches most of the information needed to populate the variables and objects that were declared at the top of this class. Before it finishes, it invokes the getForeignInfo() method, which retrieves information about any table that is referred to by this column.

```
    /**
     * Construct a new RDBMSTableColumn object.
     *
     * @param conn the JDBC Connection object
```

```java
 * @param table_name the name of the table
 * @param column_name the name of the column
 */
public RDBMSTableColumn(Connection conn,
                        String table_name,
                        String column_name)
        throws RDBMSException {

    dbconn = conn;

    try {

        // This SQL statement will fetch all of the
        // column metadata for the specified column.
        //
        String sql =
            "SELECT col_label, col_type, col_len, " +
            "          col_query, col_disp " +
            "    FROM " + RDBMS.syscolumns +
            "    WHERE tbl_name = '" + table_name + "' " +
            "    AND   col_name = '" + column_name + "'";

        // Get a Statement object from the connection.
        //
        Statement stmt = dbconn.createStatement();

        // Execute the query, and get a result set
        //
        ResultSet rs = stmt.executeQuery(sql);

        if (!rs.next()) {
            throw new RDBMSException(
              "Could not locate record in " +
              RDBMS.syscolumns  + "for " + table_name +
              "." + column_name + ".");
        }

        // Transfer all of the column metadata values
        // to class-wide objects.
        //
        name      = column_name;
        table     = table_name;

        label     = rs.getString(1);
        type      = rs.getString(2);
        length    = rs.getInt(3);

        // These two are boolean values, and the logical
        // truth-value of this comparison will yield the
        // correct boolean value. In other words, if the
        // value is 1, it is true. Any other value
        // indicates that it should be treated as false.
```

```
            //
            queryable = (rs.getInt(4) == 1);
            visible   = (rs.getInt(5) == 1);

            stmt.close();

    } catch (SQLException e) {
        e.printStackTrace();
        System.exit(0);
    }

    getForeignInfo();

}
```

The `getForeignInfo()` method is used to determine whether this column is a reference to the primary key of another table. If it is, the table name is very useful to have around. From the table, it is possible to instantiate an `RDBMSTable` object. If this column is a foreign key, and you fetch a value for this column from a row, you can get its descriptive name from the `fetchLabel()` method of an `RDBMSTable` object. You must create that object using the table name that is stored in the `RDBMSTableColumn` object. For example, if you are fetching rows from the table of subscriptions, you can look up the `RDBMSTableColumn` object that corresponds to the recipient ID column. From that, you can get the name of the recipient table, create a new `RDBMSTable` object for it, and pass the value of recipient ID column in the subscription table to the `fetchLabel()` method. This sort of thing is done behind the scenes in the RDBMS system, and makes it easy for RDBMS to construct a user interface based on metadata.

```
/**
 *
 * getForeignInfo - Find out if the column is a foreign
 * key reference into another table. If it is, set the
 * fkey flag and store the name of the related table.
 *
 */
private void getForeignInfo() {

    try {

            // In order to do this sort of query in one
            // SELECT, it is necessary to join RDBMSsyskeys
            // to itself. The first table alias, 'a', is the
            // row in RDBMSsyskeys that corresponds to the
            // column represented by the object. The second
            // alias, 'b', is the row from RDBMSsyskeys that
            // represents the corresponding primary key in
            // the referenced table.
            //
            String sql =
                "SELECT b.tbl_name " +
```

```
                    " FROM " + RDBMS.syskeys + " a," +
                            RDBMS.syskeys + " b " +
                    "WHERE a.tbl_name = '" + table + "' " +
                    "  AND a.col_name = '" + name + "'" +
                    "  AND a.key_type = 'FOREIGN' " +
                    "  AND b.col_name = a.col_name " +
                    "  AND b.key_type = 'PRIMARY'";

            // Get a Statement object from the connection.
            //
            Statement stmt = dbconn.createStatement();

            // Execute the query, and get a result set
            //
            ResultSet rs = stmt.executeQuery(sql);

            // If any results were found, then it means that
            // there is an instance of this column in
            // RDBMSsyskeys, and that it is a foreign key
            // reference. This should produce but one row,
            // which will have the name of the table that is
            // referenced by this key.
            //
            if (rs.next()) {
                fkey = true;
                foreign_table = rs.getString(1);
            }
            stmt.close();

        } catch (SQLException e) {
            e.printStackTrace();
            System.exit(0);
        }
    }
}
```

The remaining methods in this class include a series of get-style methods that return the information stored in the objects and variables declared at the top of this class.

```
/**
 * getName - Returns the name of this column.
 */
public String getName() { return name; }

/**
 * getLabel - Returns the descriptive name of this
 * column.
 */
public String getLabel() { return label; }

/**
 * getType - Returns the type of this column.
 */
```

```
    public String getType() { return type; }

    /**
     * getLength - Returns the length of this column.
     */
    public int getLength() { return length; }

    /**
     * getTable - Returns the table name.
     */
    public String getTable() { return table; }

    /**
     * isQueryable - Returns true if we want this column to
     * show up in a query form.
     */
    public boolean isQueryable() { return queryable; }

    /*
     * isVisible - Returns true if we want this column to
     * show up in a display screen or report.
     */
    public boolean isVisible() { return visible; }

    /*
     * isForeignKey - Returns true if this column is a
     * foreign key reference to another table.
     */
    public boolean isForeignKey() { return fkey; }

    /*
     * getForeignTable() - Returns the name of the table
     * that this column references.
     */
    public String getForeignTable() { return foreign_table; }

}
```

ORG.as220.rdbms.RDBMSChoice

The RDBMSChoice object is a simple extension of the AWT Choice object. The constructor accepts a JDBC Connection object and table name as arguments, and returns a Choice object that has an item for each row in the table. It also includes a "none" choice. The values for each item are the "label" or descriptive column from the table. This class wouldn't be very useful if it didn't let you find the corresponding primary key value for the selected item. For this, RDBMSChoice offers a method called getSelectedKey().

```
/*
 *
 * RDBMSChoice.java
 * Copyright (C) 1997 Brian Jepson (bjepson@ids.net)
```

```
 *
 * This program is free software; you can redistribute it
 * and/or modify it under the terms of the GNU General
 * Public License as published by the Free Software
 * Foundation; either version 2 of the License, or (at
 * your option) any later version.
 *
 * This program is distributed in the hope that it will be
 * useful, but WITHOUT ANY WARRANTY; without even the
 * implied warranty of MERCHANTABILITY or FITNESS FOR A
 * PARTICULAR PURPOSE.  See the GNU General Public License
 * for more details.
 *
 * You should have received a copy of the GNU General Public
 * License along with this program; if not, write to the
 * Free Software Foundation, Inc., 59 Temple Place - Suite
 * 330, Boston, MA 02111-1307, USA
 *
 */

package ORG.as220.rdbms;
import java.sql.*;
import java.awt.*;
import java.util.*;

/**
 *
 * RDBMSChoice is a simple AWT choice object that not only
 * tracks the String that was selected, but can correlate it
 * to an id value, so a table's label and id keys can be
 * matched upon selection.
 *
 */
public class RDBMSChoice extends Choice {
```

We mentioned earlier that when a table is updated, either by an insert, delete, or update, it's somewhat polite to notify any RDBMSChoice objects of this. For this reason, each time a new RDBMSChoice object is instantiated, it is added to a Hashtable that is keyed by the table name. In order to allow for the likely possibility that there may be more than one RDBMSChoice object in existence, each element in the Hashtable is actually a Vector of all the RDBMSChoice objects that correspond to the given table. The Hashtable (table_hash) and the method that registers each object (registerChoice()) are both declared static. This is important, because if the Hashtable were not declared static, there would be a different Hashtable for each instance of RDBMSChoice, and we would have only one RDBMSChoice object in each Hashtable.

```
    // Keep track of all objects that have been
    // instantiated, keyed by table name.
    //
    static Hashtable table_hash = new Hashtable();
```

```
/**
 * registerChoice() - this is called by the constructor.
 */
static void registerChoice(String t, RDBMSChoice c) {

    // The table_hash Hashtable should contain Vectors
    // with all of the RDBMSChoice objects that correspond
    // to a given table. If it doesn't have a Vector for
    // this table, we should create one.
    //
    Vector v;
    if (!table_hash.containsKey(t)) {

        // Create the new Vector.
        //
        v = new Vector();

        // Add the Vector to the Hashtable.
        //
        table_hash.put(t, v);

    } else {

        // Get the Vector from the Hashtable.
        //
        v = (Vector) table_hash.get(t);
    }

    // Add the RDBMSChoice object to the Vector.
    //
    v.addElement(c);
}
```

The reQuery() method is another static method. For a given table name, it checks to see if there is a Vector within the table_hash that holds a reference to one or more RDBMSChoice objects. If there is such a Vector, this methods iterates over each RDBMSChoice object, and invokes its addAllOptions() method. This causes the RDBMSChoice object to be filled with the most recent data. The reQuery() method must be declared static, since it will be invoked by any object that modifies a table. It's likely that this object will not be the same object that contains the chooser; for example, an instance of the RDBMSAddEdit object that's called into existence for the recipient table will need to notify all RDBMSChoice objects that depend upon the recipient table. A query or add/edit form based on the subscription table would have a chooser for the recipient table. However, the form that is based on the recipient table is not going to have any reference to RDBMSChoice objects in other forms, so it needs to rely on the RDBMSChoice class' static method reQuery() and static Hashtable table_hash to keep track of them.

```
/**
 *
 * reQuery - cause each RDBMSChoice to read the latest
```

```
 * data from the table.
 *
 */
public static void reQuery(String tbl) {

    // Only requery the table if there's an RDBMSChoice
    // object that relies on this table.
    //
    if (table_hash.containsKey(tbl)) {

        // Get the Vector from the Hashtable.
        //
        Vector v = (Vector) table_hash.get(tbl);


        // Call the addAllOptions() method on each
        // RDBMSChoice object in the Vector.
        //
        for (int i = 0; i < v.size(); i++) {
            RDBMSChoice c = (RDBMSChoice) v.elementAt(i);
            c.addAllOptions();
        }
    }
}
```

Traveling on down the source code for this class, we find some objects that are instance fields of the class. For each instance of an RDBMSChoice, there will be a database connection, a Vector of primary keys that correspond to each choice item, a table metadata object, and a String that holds the name of the table. Following these declarations, the constructor appears, which retrieves the table metadata object, invokes the addAllOptions() method, and registers this object using registerChoice().

```
Connection dbconn; // the database connection
Vector keys;       // keys associated with each choice
RDBMSTable table;  // table metadata object
String table_name; // name of the table.

public RDBMSChoice(Connection conn, String tbl) {

    dbconn = conn;
    table_name = tbl;

    // Get an RDBMSTable object with metadata about this
    // table.
    //
    table  = new RDBMSTable(dbconn, table_name);

    // Add the options to this Choice object.
    //
    addAllOptions();
```

```
        // Register this object.
        //
        registerChoice(table_name, this);

    }
```

The first time through in this class, the addAllOptions() method is invoked. This is the same method that is invoked by reQuery(), so there are some motions that this method goes through that don't make complete sense within initialization, but they do not have any side effects that adversely affect the initialization. The first thing it does is save the currently selected key by invoking getSelectedKey(). This is only meaningful if the method was invoked in reQuery(), and has no effect on initialization. From the standpoint of reQuery(), it's essential to save the key of the current option, especially if the number of options have been changed, or if the label text of the selected option has changed. Since the primary key of a row is immutable, this represents an optimistic attempt to leave the RDBMSChoice in the same state in which it was found. The only thing that would stand in the way of this would be the deletion of the row that corresponds to the selected item.

After saving the selected key value in an int variable, the removeAll() method is invoked, which removes all items from the object. Then, the table metadata object is used to discover the name of the primary and label key. After this, an SQL SELECT statement is issued to retrieve all the label/primary key values from the table. Then the result set is processed, and each label (descriptive) column is added to the RDBMSChoice object. As this occurs, each primary key is added to the keys Vector. Since there is a one-to-one correspondence between elements added to the RDBMSChoice object and the keys Vector, the selected index of the RDBMSChoice object can be used to fetch the corresponding key from the keys Vector. It's worth nothing that a "none" option is always added, with a key value of zero. Finally, the selectKey method is invoked with the selected key value that was saved earlier.

```
/**
 *
 * Delete all of the options from the table, and then
 * (re)create them from the data in the table.
 *
 */
public void addAllOptions() {

    // If there's a selected option, remember it.
    //
    int curr = getSelectedKey();

    // Remove all of the current options, if any exist.
    //
    removeAll();

    // Get the primary key and label column.
    //
    String key   = table.getPrimaryKey();
    String label = table.getLabelColumn();
```

```java
// This SQL SELECT will get all of the labels and
// keys from the database.
//
String sql = "SELECT " + label + ", " +
                          key +    " "  +
                " FROM " + table_name +
                " ORDER BY " + label;
try {

    // Get a Statement object from the connection.
    //
    Statement stmt = dbconn.createStatement();

    // Execute the query, and get a result set
    //
    ResultSet rs = stmt.executeQuery(sql);

    // Initialize the Vector of keys.
    //
    keys = new Vector();

    // Add a None option, so the user doesn't have
    // to specify a value.
    //
    add("[ None ]");
    keys.addElement(new Integer(0));

    // Add each label to this (Choice) object,
    // and each key value to the keys Vector.
    //
    while (rs.next()) {

        add(rs.getString(1));
        keys.addElement(
            new Integer(rs.getInt(2)) );

    }
    stmt.close();

} catch (SQLException e) {

    e.printStackTrace();
    System.exit(0);

}

// Try to reselect the previously selected item.
//
if (curr != -1) {
    selectKey(curr);
}
```

```
    }
```

This method uses the fact that there is a one-to-one correspondence between elements in the keys Vector and in the RDBMSChoice object itself to find the key that corresponds to the selected item. The selected key value is returned as an integer. The following method, selectKey(), will attempt to set the current item in the RDBMSChoice object to the one that corresponds to the key value supplied. If it can't find a match, it does not complain, and leaves the state of the RDBMSChoice object as it was.

```java
/**
 *
 * getSelectedKey - returns the key value corresponding
 * to the label that is the currently selected item.
 *
 */
public int getSelectedKey() {

    // If there are no items in the chooser, then return
    // -1; the None option returns 0.
    //
    if (getItemCount() == 0) {
        return -1;
    }

    // Get the current index.
    //
    int selected_index = getSelectedIndex();

    // Get the corresponding Integer from the keys
    // Vector.
    //
    Integer selected_key =
        (Integer) keys.elementAt(selected_index);

    // Return that Integer's intValue();
    //
    return selected_key.intValue();

}

/**
 *
 * selectKey - selects an element, given an integer
 * value for its primary key.
 *
 */
public void selectKey(int key_val) {

    for (int i = 0; i < keys.size(); i++) {

        // Get the corresponding Integer from the keys
        // Vector.
```

```
            //
            Integer key = (Integer) keys.elementAt(i);

            // If the key value of that Vector is equal to
            // the ket_val that was passed in, then select
            // the corresponding option.
            //
            if (key.intValue() == key_val) {
                select(i);
            }
        }
    }

}
```

ORG.as220.rdbms.RDBMSCharChoice

This class provides a simple Choice object that provides a list of comparison operators that are applicable to CHAR data types. The comparisons are provided in human-readable form, such as "Find Similar." The getExpression() method will conveniently accept a String value, and return a comparison consisting of the right-hand side of the appropriate expression, including the comparison operator. If a user had selected "Find Similar," and the String value was "JEPSON, " it would return LIKE '%JEPSON%'.

```
/*
 *
 * RDBMSCharChoice.java
 * Copyright (C) 1997 Brian Jepson (bjepson@ids.net)
 *
 * This program is free software; you can redistribute it
 * and/or modify it under the terms of the GNU General
 * Public License as published by the Free Software
 * Foundation; either version 2 of the License, or (at
 * your option) any later version.
 *
 * This program is distributed in the hope that it will be
 * useful, but WITHOUT ANY WARRANTY; without even the
 * implied warranty of MERCHANTABILITY or FITNESS FOR A
 * PARTICULAR PURPOSE.  See the GNU General Public License
 * for more details.
 *
 * You should have received a copy of the GNU General Public
 * License along with this program; if not, write to the
 * Free Software Foundation, Inc., 59 Temple Place - Suite
 * 330, Boston, MA 02111-1307, USA
 *
 */

package ORG.as220.rdbms;
import java.awt.*;
import java.util.*;
```

```
/**
 *
 * RDBMSCharChoice is a simple AWT choice object that supplies
 * some comparison options for SQL char datatypes. The
 * getExpression() method will return something that you can
 * use in an SQL statement.
 *
 */
public class RDBMSCharChoice extends Choice {

    // Descriptive names of the CHAR comparison options.
    //
    String[] comp_char_opt =
        { "Find Similar (Case-Insensitive)",
          "Find Similar",
          "Equal To",
          "Not Equal To" };

    // The CHAR comparison options as they will be used in
    // SQL SELECT statements.
    String[] comp_char_ops =
        { "CLIKE", "LIKE", "=", "<>" };

    /**
     * Construct a new RDBMSCharChoice object, and add each
     * comparison operator's descriptive name to the list.
     */
    public RDBMSCharChoice() {

        int j;
        int limit = comp_char_opt.length;
        for (j = 0; j < limit; j++) {
            add(comp_char_opt[j]);
        }

    }

    /**
     *
     * getExpression() - returns the mSQL expression to
     * include in a WHERE clause, given the current choice
     * and a String value.
     *
     */
    public String getExpression(String value) {

        // Get the current index.
        //
        int selected_index = getSelectedIndex();

        // Get the corresponding operator from
        // comp_char_ops.
```

```
        //
        String op = comp_char_ops[selected_index];

        String sqlval;

        if (op.equals("CLIKE") || op.equals("LIKE")) {
            sqlval = " " + op + " '%" + value + "%'";
        } else {
            sqlval = " " + op + " '" + value + "'";
        }

        return sqlval;

    }

}
```

ORG.as220.rdbms.RDBMSNumChoice

RDBMSNumChoice provides similar features to those of RDBMSCharChoice. However, the options are specific to numeric (REAL, INT) data types, and include such things as =, <>, and >=, among others.

```
/*
 *
 *  RDBMSNumChoice.java
 *  Copyright (C) 1997 Brian Jepson (bjepson@ids.net)
 *
 *  This program is free software; you can redistribute it
 *  and/or modify it under the terms of the GNU General
 *  Public License as published by the Free Software
 *  Foundation; either version 2 of the License, or (at
 *  your option) any later version.
 *
 *  This program is distributed in the hope that it will be
 *  useful, but WITHOUT ANY WARRANTY; without even the
 *  implied warranty of MERCHANTABILITY or FITNESS FOR A
 *  PARTICULAR PURPOSE.  See the GNU General Public License
 *  for more details.
 *
 *  You should have received a copy of the GNU General Public
 *  License along with this program; if not, write to the
 *  Free Software Foundation, Inc., 59 Temple Place - Suite
 *  330, Boston, MA 02111-1307, USA
 *
 */

package ORG.as220.rdbms;
import java.awt.*;
import java.util.*;
```

```
/**
 *
 * RDBMSNumChoice is a simple AWT choice object that supplies
 * some comparison options for SQL real or int datatypes.
 * The getExpression() method will return something that
 * you can use in an SQL statement.
 *
 */
public class RDBMSNumChoice extends Choice {

    // INT, REAL comparison options in human-readable form.
    //
    String[] comp_num_opt = { "Equal To",
                              "Greater Than",
                              "Less Than",
                              "Less Than or Equal To",
                              "Greater Than or Equal To",
                              "Not Equal To" };

    // INT, REAL comparison options as mSQL likes to see
    // them.
    //
    String[] comp_num_ops =
        { "=", ">", "<", "<=", ">=", "<>" };

    /**
     * Construct a new RDBMSNumChoice object and add all of
     * the Choice elements to it.
     */
    public RDBMSNumChoice() {

        int j;
        int limit = comp_num_opt.length;
        for (j = 0; j < limit; j++) {
            add(comp_num_opt[j]);
        }

    }

    /**
     *
     * getExpression() - returns the mSQL expression to
     * include in a WHERE clause, given the current choice
     * and a String value (yes, String).
     *
     */
    public String getExpression(String value) {

        // Get the current index.
        //
        int selected_index = getSelectedIndex();

        // Get the corresponding operator from
        // comp_num_ops.
```

```
        //
        String op = comp_num_ops[selected_index];

        String sqlval = " " + op + " " + value;

        return sqlval;

    }

}
```

ORG.as220.rdbms.RDBMSException

This is a very simple subclass of SQLException that is used for custom exceptions thrown by portions of the RDBMS system.

```
/*
 *
 * RDBMSTable.java
 * Copyright (C) 1997 Brian Jepson (bjepson@ids.net)
 *
 * This program is free software; you can redistribute it
 * and/or modify it under the terms of the GNU General
 * Public License as published by the Free Software
 * Foundation; either version 2 of the License, or (at
 * your option) any later version.
 *
 * This program is distributed in the hope that it will be
 * useful, but WITHOUT ANY WARRANTY; without even the
 * implied warranty of MERCHANTABILITY or FITNESS FOR A
 * PARTICULAR PURPOSE.  See the GNU General Public License
 * for more details.
 *
 * You should have received a copy of the GNU General Public
 * License along with this program; if not, write to the
 * Free Software Foundation, Inc., 59 Temple Place - Suite
 * 330, Boston, MA 02111-1307, USA
 *
 */

package ORG.as220.rdbms;

import java.sql.SQLException;

/**
 * Special exception class for the rdbms kit. Based on the
 * MsqlException class definition from George Reese'
 * mSQL-JDBC driver.
 */

public class RDBMSException extends SQLException {

    public RDBMSException(String data) {
```

```
        super(data);
    }

    public RDBMSException(Exception e) {
        super(e.getMessage());
    }
}
```

ORG.as220.rdbms.RDBMSAddEdit

This class is the largest among all the classes used in the RDBMS system. It not only provides a data entry form that lets the user add or edit data in a given table, but it allows the user to skip records in the database, and make changes at any point along the way. Also, it is responsible for constructing and executing the SQL necessary to save the record. This process is heavily dependent upon the metadata in the system tables.

```
/*
 *
 * RDBMSAddEdit.java
 * Copyright (C) 1997 Brian Jepson (bjepson@ids.net)
 *
 * This program is free software; you can redistribute it
 * and/or modify it under the terms of the GNU General
 * Public License as published by the Free Software
 * Foundation; either version 2 of the License, or (at
 * your option) any later version.
 *
 * This program is distributed in the hope that it will be
 * useful, but WITHOUT ANY WARRANTY; without even the
 * implied warranty of MERCHANTABILITY or FITNESS FOR A
 * PARTICULAR PURPOSE.  See the GNU General Public License
 * for more details.
 *
 * You should have received a copy of the GNU General Public
 * License along with this program; if not, write to the
 * Free Software Foundation, Inc., 59 Temple Place - Suite
 * 330, Boston, MA 02111-1307, USA
 *
 */

package ORG.as220.rdbms;
import java.awt.*;
import java.awt.event.*;
import java.util.*;
import java.sql.*;

/**
 *
 * RDBMSAddEdit will generate a user interface to add or
 * edit a given table. The user interface is defined using
 * the metadata gleaned from the RDBMSTable object.
```

```
    *
    */
public class RDBMSAddEdit extends Frame {
```

A given instance of this class always corresponds to one table. For this reason, one of the most important fields of this class is the RDBMSTable object. This object provides all of the metadata that concerns the table. Naturally, there is a JDBC Connection object that is available to all methods of the class. The fearsome GridBagLayout and GridBagConstraints are also declared here, as they are used to manage the layout of the Frame—RDBMSAddEdit is derived from the java.awt.Frame class.

Some of the other fields of this class include a primary key value and a Vector that holds references to all of the visual components for a given column. The primary key corresponds to whatever row is being displayed at a given time. If the primary key value (int pkey) is zero, then it is assumed that the user is editing a new row.

Since this class' interface is built at run time, it is not possible to know all of the components ahead of time, and they must be tracked in the column_criteria Vector. This is essential, for when the row is saved, the state and contents of the components (TextField and Choice objects) must be discovered.

A field is also supplied, called disposed, which is a boolean value. If the form has been disposed of, it may not have been automatically collected by Java's garbage collection. In this case, objects that have constructed an RDBMSAddEdit object can check the state of this flag to see if it is still available. Finally, the TextField that is used for the label, or descriptive column, is tracked in a separate field as a convenience. It is also tracked in the column_criteria Vector.

```
    RDBMSTable table;    // the table we are querying
    Connection dbconn;   // the database connection

    // We will use a GridBagLayout to manage this Frame.
    // This also requires the use of a GridBagConstraints
    // object.
    //
    GridBagLayout gb;
    GridBagConstraints gbc;

    // This is primary key for the currently displayed
    // record. If it's blank, it means the user is editing
    // a new record.
    //
    int pkey = 0;

    // A vector to hold each set of Components that
    // correspond to a given column. This includes the
    // Choice object that contains the comparison operator,
    // as well as a TextField that contains search terms
    // entered by the user.
    //
    Vector column_criteria;
```

```
// This is set if we disposed of this window with the
// cancel button or using a window control to close it.
//
boolean disposed = false;

// The textfield that corresponds to the table's "label
// column," which is a descriptive column for a given
// record.
//
TextField label_textfield;
```

There are three constructors for this class. The first simply accepts a `Connection` object and a table name. It uses a default window title to invoke the second form of the constructor, which accepts a `Connection` object, table name, and window title. The third form of the constructor accepts a `Connection` object, table name, and row id. It is used by other objects, such as `RDBMSQueryResults`, to construct an `RDBMSAddEdit` object, and to immediately bring up a specific row for editing.

The second form of the constructor is used by both of the other methods. It simply sets the window title, gets an `RDBMSTable` object, and invokes the `GUI_init()` method. After this, it packs and shows the `RDBMSAddEdit` object.

```
/**
 * Constructs a new instance of this class with a
 * default Window title.
 *
 */
public RDBMSAddEdit(Connection conn, String table_name) {
    this(conn, table_name, "Add/Edit a Table");
}

/**
 * Constructs a new instance of this class with a
 * default Window title.
 */
public RDBMSAddEdit(Connection conn, String table_name,
                    String window_title) {

    super(window_title);

    dbconn = conn;
    table = new RDBMSTable(dbconn, table_name);

    GUI_init();

    pack();
    show();

}

public RDBMSAddEdit(Connection conn,
                    String table_name,
```

```
                              int rowid) {

        this(conn, table_name);
        loadData(rowid);

    }

    public RDBMSAddEdit(Connection conn,
                        String table_name,
                        String window_title,
                        int rowid) {

        this(conn, table_name, window_title);
        loadData(rowid);

    }
```

The `GUI_init()` method is responsible for displaying all of the user interface components common to every table. This includes nothing more than a label that displays the name of the table, as well as a series of buttons that allow the user to navigate through the database, save records, create new records, and exit the form. `GUI_init()` makes a call to `GUI_add_column_widgets()`, which takes care of all of the table-specific stuff.

```
    /**
     *
     * GUI_init - prepares and displays the user interface.
     *
     */
    private void GUI_init() {

        // Using a GridbagLayout to manage the user
        // interface. Of course, we need to bring his
        // friend along, a GridBagConstraints.
        //
        gb  = new GridBagLayout();
        gbc = new GridBagConstraints();

        // Set the layout manager.
        //
        setLayout(gb);

        // Make sure horizontal and vertical fill is off
        // for the objects we create and add to the
        // interface.
        //
        gbc.fill = GridBagConstraints.NONE;

        // Add a label for the name of the table.
        //
        Label tbl_label = new Label(
            "Add/Edit the " + table.getTitle() + " table.");
```

```
tbl_label.setFont( new Font("Helvetica",
                                Font.BOLD, 14) );

gbc.anchor = GridBagConstraints.NORTHWEST;
gbc.gridx = 0; gbc.gridy = 0;
gbc.gridwidth = GridBagConstraints.REMAINDER;
gb.setConstraints(tbl_label, gbc);
add(tbl_label);

// From here on in, we'll set every component to
// appear in the upper left corner of its cell.
//
gbc.anchor = GridBagConstraints.NORTHWEST;

GUI_add_column_widgets();

// Add a panel to contain the buttons.
//
gbc.gridx = 0; gbc.gridy++;
gbc.gridwidth = GridBagConstraints.REMAINDER;
gbc.anchor = GridBagConstraints.CENTER;
Panel p = new Panel();
gb.setConstraints(p, gbc);
add(p);

Button prev_button = new Button("<< Prev");
p.add(prev_button);
prev_button.addActionListener(
    new prevButtonWatcher());

Button save_button = new Button("Save");
p.add(save_button);
save_button.addActionListener(
    new saveButtonWatcher());

Button new_button = new Button("New Record");
p.add(new_button);
new_button.addActionListener(
    new newButtonWatcher());

Button del_button = new Button("Delete");
p.add(del_button);
del_button.addActionListener(
    new deleteButtonWatcher());

Button cancel_button = new Button("Cancel");
p.add(cancel_button);
cancel_button.addActionListener(
    new cancelButtonWatcher());

Button next_button = new Button("Next >>");
p.add(next_button);
```

```
next_button.addActionListener(
    new nextButtonWatcher());

// Attach a listener that will be used to intercept
// calls to close this object.
//
addWindowListener(new WinEventHandler() );

}
```

If this were a normal application, the next method would just take care of adding a component or two for each column in the table. Maybe a `TextField` here, perhaps a few `Choice` objects for columns that are foreign key references into other tables.

Well, this is no ordinary application, as you no doubt know by now. Sure, this method will add those components. If it's adding a column that is simply character or numeric data, you'll get a `Label` object with the descriptive name of the column, and a `TextField` in which the user can enter the data. If it's a foreign key reference into another table, you'll still get the `Label`, but instead of a `TextField`, you'll get a `Choice` object; actually, an `RDBMSChoice` object, which "knows" from which table it is derived, and can not only tell you the text of the selected item, but the underlying primary key of that item.

But wait, that's not all. Remember, this is no ordinary application. In a conventional application, where table information is embedded in the application, rather than being drawn from the database at run time, components such as those described herein are often hardcoded into the program. Because of that, it is easy to check up on their values, because you know in advance exactly which `TextField` and `Choice` objects correspond to which column. In order to allow other methods, such as the `saveSQL()` method, to determine what the user typed into each `TextField`, or what they selected from a `Choice` object, both the `RDBMSTableColumn` object and either the `TextField` or `Choice` object must be added to a `Vector`. This `Vector` is created for each column, and then added in turn to the master `column_criteria` Vector. Other methods can iterate over each element in the `column_criteria` Vector, pull out the `Vector` (Vectors within Vectors!) that contains the `RDBMSTableColumn`/Component (`TextField` or `RDBMSChoice`) pair, and figure out what the column value was set to. The only exception to this is the primary key, which is not included on the form as a data entry field.

```
/**
 * GUI_add_column_widgets - adds widgets that allow the
 * user to enter values for each column in the table.
 */
private void GUI_add_column_widgets() {

    RDBMSTableColumn[] cols = table.getColumns();

    // Initialize the column_criteria Vector.
    //
    column_criteria = new Vector();

    for (int i = 0; i < cols.length; i++) {
```

```java
String name   = cols[i].getName();
String type   = cols[i].getType();
int length    = cols[i].getLength();

// Create a Vector to hold the column object
// and any components that correspond to the
// column. This Vector will get added to the
// column_criteria Vector.
//
Vector criteria = new Vector();

// Add this column to the criteria Vector.
//
criteria.addElement(cols[i]);

// Don't display an entry field for the Primary
// Key column.
//
if (name.equals( table.getPrimaryKey() )) {

    // add the Vector "as is" - later methods
    // know not to look for a component if it's
    // the primary key.
    //
    column_criteria.addElement(criteria);
    continue; // skip the rest, continue looping
}

// Add a new row, and display a label for
// the columns's descriptive name.
// Set the column cell (gridx) to 0, and
// increment the row cell (gridy), so we'll
// move to a new row.
//
gbc.gridx = 0; gbc.gridy++;
Label col_label =
   new Label(cols[i].getLabel());

// Set the gridwidth so this Component
// occupies one cell.
//
gbc.gridwidth = 1;

// Constrain this component, and add it to
// the Frame.
//
gb.setConstraints(col_label, gbc);
add(col_label);

// Increment the column cell index
// (gridx), but leave the row cell index
```

```java
// (gridy) alone.
//
//
gbc.gridx++;

// If this column is a foreign key
// reference, then we want a Choice object
// with all possible values.
//
if (cols[i].isForeignKey()) {

    RDBMSChoice c =
        new RDBMSChoice(dbconn,
            cols[i].getForeignTable());

    gb.setConstraints(c, gbc);
    add(c);

    // Add this Choice to the criteria Vector.
    //
    criteria.addElement(c);

} else {

    // With INT or REAL columns, we don't have
    // a length, so let's set it to something
    // arbitrary, that should be big enough (in
    // theory...)
    //
    if (type.equalsIgnoreCase("REAL") ||
        type.equalsIgnoreCase("INT")) {

        length = 15;

    }

    // Add a TextField for the column.
    //
    TextField t = new TextField(length);
    gb.setConstraints(t, gbc);
    add(t);

    // Add this TextField to the criteria
    // Vector.
    //
    criteria.addElement(t);

    // If the current field we are adding is the
    // table's 'label key,' then we'll also
    // associate it with the label_textfield
    // property. This will make it easy to look
    // up the current label value later.
```

```
            //
            if (name.equals( table.getLabelColumn() )) {
                label_textfield = t;
            }
        }

        // Add the criteria Vector to the
        // column_criteria Vector. We can look at
        // this later, and use each component to
        // build a query string.
        //
        column_criteria.addElement(criteria);

    }

}
```

The `clearForm()` method is used to prepare the form for adding a new record. It iterates over the `column_criteria Vector`, and examines the `RDBMSTableColumn` object contained within. If it determines that the column is a foreign key, then it sets the corresponding `RDBMSChoice` object to zero (None). If the column is the primary key, the `pkey` value is set to zero, and if it's free-form text or numeric data, it blanks the corresponding `TextField`.

```
/**
 *
 * clearForm - Clears the form and prepares it for a new
 * record.
 *
 */
private void clearForm() {

    // Walk over the column_criteria Vector.
    //
    for (int i = 0; i < column_criteria.size(); i++) {

        // Pull out a Vector that contains the column
        // and any Components that are related to it.
        //
        Vector criteria =
            (Vector) column_criteria.elementAt(i);

        // Get the RDBMSTableColumn from that Vector.
        //
        RDBMSTableColumn col =
            (RDBMSTableColumn) criteria.elementAt(0);
        String col_name = col.getName();

        // If it's a foreign key, we need to get the
        // RDBMSChoice object, and set it to 0.
        //
        if (col.isForeignKey()) {

            // Get the RDBMSChoice Component.
```

```
            //
            RDBMSChoice c =
                (RDBMSChoice) criteria.elementAt(1);

            // Set the RDBMSChoice Component.
            //
            c.selectKey(0);

        } else {

            // If it's the primary key, we should
            // set pkey to 0. All other columns simply
            // have their TextField set to ""
            //
            String pkey_name = table.getPrimaryKey();
            if (col_name.equals(pkey_name)) {

                pkey = 0;

            } else {

                // Get the corresponding TextField
                // Component.
                //
                TextField t =
                    (TextField) criteria.elementAt(1);

                // Set the textfield
                //
                t.setText("");
            }
        }
    }
}
```

The `loadData()` method also makes use of the `column_criteria` Vector. It builds an SQL SELECT statement using the names of the columns in the Vector. The SELECT statement only retrieves a single row, the row that is indicated by the value of `pkey`. After it issues the SELECT statement, this method iterates over the columns that are represented in the `column_criteria` Vector. Then it updates all of the on-screen components with the values found in the result set.

```
/**
 *
 * loadData - This will fetch the row that is referred
 * to by pkey.
 *
 */
public void loadData(int rowid) {

    pkey = rowid;
```

```
// It's very important that the columns in a JDBC
// result set be fetched in order. Since we're going
// to iterate over the list of columns in the order
// dictated by column_criteria, let's build a list
// of columns that matches the order of elements in
// column_criteria.
//
StringBuffer col_list  = new StringBuffer();

int i;  // generic iterator variable

// Walk through each element in column_criteria.
//
for (i = 0; i < column_criteria.size(); i++) {

    // Pull out a Vector that contains the column
    // and any Components that are related to it.
    //
    Vector criteria =
        (Vector) column_criteria.elementAt(i);

    // Get the RDBMSTableColumn from that Vector.
    //
    RDBMSTableColumn col =
        (RDBMSTableColumn) criteria.elementAt(0);

    // Now, get the column name and add it to the
    // StringBuffer.
    //
    String col_name = col.getName();

    col_list.append(col_name);

    // If we're not on the final item, then add a
    // comma between column names.
    //
    if (i < column_criteria.size() - 1) {
        col_list.append(", ");
    }

}

// Build the SQL Statement
//
String sql = "SELECT " + col_list +
             " FROM " + table.getName() +
             " WHERE " + table.getPrimaryKey() +
             " = " + pkey;

try {

    // Get a statement object from
    // the Connection.
    //
```

```java
Statement stmt = dbconn.createStatement();

// Issue the SQL.
//
ResultSet rs = stmt.executeQuery(sql);

// There is only one row we're interested in.
//
rs.next();

// Let's walk over the list of column_criteria
// Vector again.
//
for (i = 0; i < column_criteria.size(); i++) {

    // Pull out a Vector that contains the column
    // and any Components that are related to it.
    //
    Vector criteria =
        (Vector) column_criteria.elementAt(i);

    // Get the RDBMSTableColumn from that Vector.
    //
    RDBMSTableColumn col =
        (RDBMSTableColumn) criteria.elementAt(0);
    String col_name = col.getName();

    // If it's a foreign key, we need to get the
    // value for the RDBMSChoice object, and set it
    // by that key value.
    //
    if (col.isForeignKey()) {

        // Get the RDBMSChoice Component.
        //
        RDBMSChoice c =
            (RDBMSChoice) criteria.elementAt(1);

        // Get the value of the current column.
        //
        int value = rs.getInt(i + 1);

        // Set the RDBMSChoice Component.
        //
        c.selectKey(value);

    } else {

        String value = rs.getString(i + 1);

        // If it's the primary key, we should
        // do nothing. The primary key's value
        // is already known, and it is not
```

```
                     // displayed on the form.
                     //
                     String pkey_name =
                         table.getPrimaryKey();
                     if (!col_name.equals(pkey_name)) {

                         // Get the corresponding TextField
                         // Component.
                         //
                         TextField t =
                             (TextField) criteria.elementAt(1);

                         // Set the textfield
                         //
                         t.setText(value);
                     }
                 }
             }

         } catch (SQLException e) {
             e.printStackTrace();
             System.exit(0);
         }

    }
```

The `skipRecord()` method is used by the Next and Previous buttons to navigate within the table. When the user presses Next, `skipRecord()` is invoked with 1 as a parameter, and with −1 when it is called as a result of the user pressing the Previous button. This method simply issues a SELECT statement that grabs all of the rows that either have a label key less than (for previous) or greater than (for next) the current value. Then, it's only a matter of going to the first record in that result set (for next) or the last record (for previous). The reason that it goes to the last record for cases where the user has selected the previous record may not be immediately obvious. Since the result set consists of all rows whose label column is less than the current row's label, the last row in that result set will be the one that sorts alphabetically before this row. Once this method has found the record it's interested in, `loadData()` is invoked with that row's primary key.

```
/**
 *
 * skipRecord - if possible, selects the next record in
 * the table, based on label column order.
 *
 */
private void skipRecord(int direction) {

    // The direction should be 1 (forward) or -1
    // (backward). We'll set the comparison operator
    // accordingly.
    //
    String operator;
```

```java
if (direction == 1) {
    operator = " > ";
} else {
    operator = " < ";
}

String label_column = table.getLabelColumn();
String sql;

// If there is a label column for this table, it
// will be used for the ordering of the results, as
// we search for the next row.
//
if (label_column != null) {

    String text = label_textfield.getText();
    sql = "SELECT " +
            table.getPrimaryKey() +
         ", " + label_column +
         " FROM " + table.getName() +
         " WHERE " + label_column +
            operator + "'" + text + "'" +
         "ORDER BY " + label_column;

} else { // we can only order by primary key.

    sql = "SELECT " +
            table.getPrimaryKey() +
         " FROM " + table.getName() +
         " WHERE " + table.getPrimaryKey() +
            operator + pkey +
         " ORDER BY " + table.getPrimaryKey();

}

try {

    // Get a statement from the database.
    // connection.
    //
    Statement stmt = dbconn.createStatement();

    // Execute the query, and get a result
    // set.
    //
    ResultSet rs = stmt.executeQuery(sql);

    if (direction == 1) {

        // Get just the first record (if
        // it exists).
        //
```

```
                  if (rs.next()) {
                      int key = rs.getInt(1);
                      loadData(key);
                  } else {
                      System.out.println(
                          "End of file reached.");
                  }

              } else {

                  // get the last record (if it
                  // exists).
                  //
                  int key = 0;
                  while (rs.next()) {
                      key = rs.getInt(1);
                  }

                  if (key == 0) {
                      System.out.println(
                          "Beginning of file reached.");
                  } else {
                      loadData(key);
                  }

              }

              stmt.close();

          } catch (SQLException e) {
              e.printStackTrace();
              System.exit(0);
          }
      }
```

The deleteRecord() method is a little fancy. As its name implies, it will delete the current record. It also politely notifies any dependent RDBMSChoice objects by invoking the RDBMSChoice.reQuery() method. However, this method will not perform the delete if there are any records in other tables that depend on the current record. For example, if you are trying to delete a customer who has subscriptions, it will fail, and display the reason why in the console or terminal window from which you started the application.

```
/**
 *
 * deleteRecord - Delete the current record.
 *
 */
private void deleteRecord() {

    // Build the SQL Statement that will perform the
    // delete.
    //
```

```
String sql = "DELETE " +
             " FROM " + table.getName() +
             " WHERE " + table.getPrimaryKey() +
             " = " + pkey;
try {

    // Get a statement object from
    // the Connection.
    //
    Statement stmt = dbconn.createStatement();

    // Get an array of tables that depend on this
    // table.
    //
    String[] dep_tables = table.getDepends();
    for (int i = 0; i < dep_tables.length; i++) {

        String check_sql =
            "SELECT * " +
            " FROM " + dep_tables[i] +
            " WHERE " + table.getPrimaryKey() +
            " = " + pkey;

        // Issue the SQL.
        //
        ResultSet rs_check =
            stmt.executeQuery(check_sql);

        // If we find a row in the dependent table,
        // let the user know that the delete cannot
        // proceed.
        //
        if (rs_check.next()) {

            // Get a table object so we can get the
            // long name.
            //
            RDBMSTable t = new
                RDBMSTable(dbconn, dep_tables[i]);

            String tbl_title = t.getTitle();

            System.out.println(
                "The delete failed, because " +
                "there is at least one row " +
                "in the\n" + tbl_title + " table " +
                "that depends on the row you are " +
                "trying to delete.");
            return;

        }
```

```
        }

        // Issue the SQL.
        //
        stmt.executeUpdate(sql);
        clearForm();
        System.out.println("Record deleted.");

    } catch (SQLException e) {
        e.printStackTrace();
        System.exit(0);
    }

    // Make sure every choice object that depends on
    // this table is updated.
    //
    RDBMSChoice.reQuery(table.getName());

}
```

Within the `saveSQL()` method, you can see how much more mileage is possible from the `column_criteria` `Vector`. `saveSQL()` builds portions of the `UPDATE` and `INSERT` statements as it processes each column. It always builds portions for both an `UPDATE` and `INSERT` statement, since it is convenient to keep the code for those components within the same loop, and not have one loop for each case. When it determines whether or not it should issue an `UPDATE` or an `INSERT`, it constructs the appropriate statement, and sends it off to the server. Finally, it invokes the `RDBMSChoice.reQuery()` method, in case there were any `RDBMSChoice` objects around that depend on the table.

```
/**
 *
 * saveSQL - look at the components contained within
 * the column_criteria Vector and build the SQL INSERT
 * or UPDATE statement.
 *
 */
private void saveSQL() {

    // The set clause is there for an UPDATE statement,
    // while the column_list and values_list is there
    // for an INSERT statement.
    //
    StringBuffer set_clause  = new StringBuffer();
    StringBuffer column_list = new StringBuffer();
    StringBuffer values_list = new StringBuffer();

    // track the count of items added to the set_clause
    //
    int set_count = 0;

    // This flag will get set to true if this is a new
```

```java
// record, and will stay false if it isn't.
//
boolean isAdding = false;

for (int i = 0; i < column_criteria.size(); i++) {

    StringBuffer this_item = new StringBuffer();

    // Pull out a Vector that contains the column
    // and any Components that are related to it.
    //
    Vector criteria =
        (Vector) column_criteria.elementAt(i);

    // Get the RDBMSTableColumn from that Vector.
    //
    RDBMSTableColumn col =
        (RDBMSTableColumn) criteria.elementAt(0);
    String col_name = col.getName();

    // Add an item to the column list.
    //
    column_list.append(col_name);
    if (i < column_criteria.size() - 1) {
        column_list.append(", ");
    }

    String value = "";

    // If it's a foreign key, we need to get the
    // value for the comparison from the
    // RDBMSChoice object at element 1.
    //
    if (col.isForeignKey()) {

        // Get the RDBMSChoice Component.
        //
        RDBMSChoice c =
            (RDBMSChoice) criteria.elementAt(1);

        // Get the selected key (not the item, which
        // is a String) from the RDBMSChoice
        // Component.
        //
        int fkey = c.getSelectedKey();

        value = String.valueOf(fkey);

    } else {

        // If it's the primary key, we need to
        // get the value from the pkey
        // attribute - if that attribute is
```

```java
        // zero, we need a new primary key.
        //
        if (col_name.equals(table.getPrimaryKey())) {

            if (pkey == 0) {

                isAdding = true;

                try {

                    // Get a statement object from
                    // the Connection.
                    //
                    Statement stmt =
                        dbconn.createStatement();

                    // Execute a query to get the
                    // next sequence.
                    //
                    String sql =
                        table.getGetNextKey();

                    ResultSet rs =
                        stmt.executeQuery(sql);

                    // Read the new primary key
                    // value from the result set.
                    //
                    rs.next();
                    pkey = rs.getInt(1);

                    stmt.close();

                } catch (SQLException e) {
                    e.printStackTrace();
                    System.exit(0);
                }

            }

            value = String.valueOf(pkey);

        } else {

            String col_type = col.getType();

            TextField t =
                (TextField) criteria.elementAt(1);
            String text = t.getText();

            // If the column is of a character type,
            // the value needs to be within single
            // quotes.
```

```java
            //
            if (col_type.equalsIgnoreCase("CHAR")) {
                value = "'" + text + "'";
            }

            // If the column is not a character type,
            // then the value doesn't need quotes.
            //
            if (col_type.equalsIgnoreCase("REAL") ||
                col_type.equalsIgnoreCase("INT")) {
                value = text;
                if (value.equals("")) {
                    value = "0";
                }
            }
        }
    }

    // Add an item to the column list.
    //
    values_list.append(value);
    if (i < column_criteria.size() - 1) {
        values_list.append(", ");
    }

    // Don't do anything with the set_clause for the
    // primary key.
    //
    if (!col_name.equals(table.getPrimaryKey())) {

        set_clause.append(col_name + " = " + value);
        if (set_count < column_criteria.size() - 2) {
            set_clause.append(", ");
        }
        set_count++;
    }

}

// Create a StringBuffer to hold the SQL Statement.
//
StringBuffer sql = new StringBuffer();

// If we're adding, the SQL Statement should be an
// INSERT. Otherwise, it should be an UPDATE.
//
if (isAdding) {
    sql.append(
        "INSERT INTO " + table.getName() + " ");
    sql.append( "(" + column_list + ") " +
                "VALUES (" + values_list + ")");
} else {
    sql.append(
```

```
                 "UPDATE " + table.getName() + " ");
        sql.append(" SET ");
        sql.append(set_clause);
        sql.append(" WHERE " + table.getPrimaryKey() +
                   " = " + pkey);
    }

    try {

        // Get a statement object from
        // the Connection.
        //
        Statement stmt = dbconn.createStatement();

        // Issue the SQL.
        //
        stmt.executeUpdate(sql.toString());
        stmt.close();

        // Make sure every choice object that depends on
        // this table is updated.
        //
        RDBMSChoice.reQuery(table.getName());

        System.out.println(
            "The record has been saved.");

    } catch (SQLException e) {
        e.printStackTrace();
        System.exit(0);
    }

}
```

That's about it for the RDBMSAddEdit class. All that remains are some very simple event handlers. There are handlers for each button, and a handle to intercept window events. In this case, the only window event we're worried about is a close event, and that disposes of the Frame.

```
// This is the event handler that deals with cases
// where a user closes the window.
//
class WinEventHandler extends WindowAdapter {
    public void windowClosing(WindowEvent e) {
        disposed = true;
        dispose();
    }
}

/**
 *
 * A listener which gets excited when the user presses
 * the Cancel button.
 *
```

```
  */
class cancelButtonWatcher implements ActionListener {
    public void actionPerformed( ActionEvent e ) {
        disposed = true;
        dispose();
    }
}

/**
 *
 * A listener which gets excited when the user presses
 * the Save button.
 *
 */
class saveButtonWatcher implements ActionListener {
    public void actionPerformed( ActionEvent e ) {
        saveSQL();
    }
}

/**
 *
 * A listener which gets excited when the user presses
 * the "New Record" button.
 *
 */
class newButtonWatcher implements ActionListener {
    public void actionPerformed( ActionEvent e ) {
        clearForm();
    }
}

/**
 *
 * A listener which gets excited when the user presses
 * the "Delete" button.
 *
 */
class deleteButtonWatcher implements ActionListener {
    public void actionPerformed( ActionEvent e ) {
        deleteRecord();
    }
}

/**
 *
 * A listener which gets excited when the user presses
 * the "Next >>" button.
 *
 */
class nextButtonWatcher implements ActionListener {
    public void actionPerformed( ActionEvent e ) {
        skipRecord(1);
```

```
        }
    }

    /**
     *
     * A listener which gets excited when the user presses
     * the "<< Prev" button.
     *
     */
    class prevButtonWatcher implements ActionListener {
        public void actionPerformed( ActionEvent e ) {
            skipRecord(-1);
        }
    }

}
```

ORG.as220.rdbms.RDBMSQuery

RDBMSQuery provides a data-driven user interface similar to the one generated in the RDBMSAddEdit class. However, instead of a user interface that lets the user add or modify records in the tables, this class provides a "query by example" feature. Users can select search criteria for certain columns, submit the query, and can then select from a list of matching rows.

```
/*
 *
 * RDBMSQuery.java
 * Copyright (C) 1997 Brian Jepson (bjepson@ids.net)
 *
 * This program is free software; you can redistribute it
 * and/or modify it under the terms of the GNU General
 * Public License as published by the Free Software
 * Foundation; either version 2 of the License, or (at
 * your option) any later version.
 *
 * This program is distributed in the hope that it will be
 * useful, but WITHOUT ANY WARRANTY; without even the
 * implied warranty of MERCHANTABILITY or FITNESS FOR A
 * PARTICULAR PURPOSE.  See the GNU General Public License
 * for more details.
 *
 * You should have received a copy of the GNU General Public
 * License along with this program; if not, write to the
 * Free Software Foundation, Inc., 59 Temple Place - Suite
 * 330, Boston, MA 02111-1307, USA
 *
 */

package ORG.as220.rdbms;
import java.awt.*;
import java.awt.event.*;
```

```
import java.util.*;
import java.sql.*;

/**
 *
 * RDBMSQuery will generate a user interface to query a
 * given table. The user interface is defined using the
 * metadata gleaned from the RDBMSTable object.
 *
 */

public class RDBMSQuery extends Frame {
```

A lot of the fields that you see here will look very similar to the ones included in the `RDBMSAddEdit` class. Like `RDBMSAddEdit`, an instance of `RDBMSQuery` relates to one table, so an `RDBMSTable` object is used to provide table metadata. Of course, a JDBC `Connection` object is used, since it is our gateway to the database. The `RDBMSQueryResult` object is new here; it is a class that takes care of displaying results and letting the user choose a row.

The `GridBagLayout` layout manager and `GridBagConstraints` object are used to manage the layout, and a `column_criteria Vector` is used here. It performs the same function as the `Vector` of the same name in `RDBMSAddEdit`, which is keeping track of columns and the user interface components that correspond to them. Lastly, the `disposed` flag is declared, and it performs the same function as the corresponding flag in the `RDBMSAddEdit` class.

```
    RDBMSTable table;    // the table we are querying
    Connection dbconn;   // the database connection

    // An object that can display results
    //
    RDBMSQueryResult query_result;

    GridBagLayout gb;
    GridBagConstraints gbc;

    // A vector to hold each set of Components that
    // correspond to a given column.
    //
    Vector column_criteria;

    // Did we dispose of this window?
    //
    boolean disposed = false;
```

The constructor makes a call to the superclass (`java.awt.Frame`) constructor, which sets the window title. Then, it transfers the `Connection` and table name to some fields that are accessible to the whole class. Next, `GUI_init()` is invoked, and the object is packed and shown.

```
    /**
     * Constructs a new RDBMSQuery object.
```

```
    */
    public RDBMSQuery(Connection conn, String table_name) {

        super("Query a Table");

        dbconn = conn;
        table = new RDBMSTable(dbconn, table_name);

        GUI_init();

        pack();
        show();
    }
```

GUI_init() takes care of the user interface, initializing and setting the layout manager. It adds a label for the table name, so the user knows what table is being queried, and then calls GUI_add_column_widgets(). After this, Query and Cancel buttons are added, and a listener for window events is attached to this object.

```
/**
 *
 * GUI_init - prepares and displays the user interface.
 *
 */
private void GUI_init() {

    // Using a GridbagLayout to manage the user
    // interface. Of course, we need to bring his
    // friend along, a GridBagConstraints.
    //
    gb  = new GridBagLayout();
    gbc = new GridBagConstraints();

    // Set the layout manager.
    //
    setLayout(gb);

    // Make sure horizontal and vertical fill is off
    // for the objects we create and add to the
    // interface.
    //
    gbc.fill = GridBagConstraints.NONE;

    // Add a label for the name of the table.
    //
    Label tbl_label = new Label(
        "Query the " + table.getTitle() + " table.");
    tbl_label.setFont( new Font("Helvetica",
                                    Font.BOLD, 14) );

    gbc.anchor = GridBagConstraints.NORTHWEST;
    gbc.gridx = 0; gbc.gridy = 0;
```

```
gbc.gridwidth = GridBagConstraints.REMAINDER;
gb.setConstraints(tbl_label, gbc);
add(tbl_label);

// From here on in, we'll set every component to
// appear in the upper left corner of its cell.
//
gbc.anchor = GridBagConstraints.NORTHWEST;

GUI_add_column_widgets();

// Add a panel to contain a Query and Cancel button.
//
gbc.gridx = 0; gbc.gridy++;
gbc.gridwidth = GridBagConstraints.REMAINDER;
gbc.anchor = GridBagConstraints.CENTER;
Panel p = new Panel();
gb.setConstraints(p, gbc);
add(p);

Button query_button = new Button("Query");
p.add(query_button);
query_button.addActionListener(
    new queryButtonWatcher());

Button cancel_button = new Button("Cancel");
p.add(cancel_button);
cancel_button.addActionListener(
    new cancelButtonWatcher());

// Attach a listener that will be used to intercept
// calls to close the MsqlTables object.
//
addWindowListener(new WinEventHandler() );

}
```

The next method takes care of displaying components for each column that can be queried. For every column that was marked as "queryable" in the schema definition file, the `isQueryable()` method should return `true`. These columns will be displayed on the form, along with a `Choice` object and/or a `TextField` that allows the user to specify search criteria.

There are three different categories that a given column may fall under. In the case where the column is a foreign key, it's quite simple, in that only an `RDBMSChoice` object is displayed. This allows the user to choose a row from the related table, or to choose "None." For example, a user querying the subscription table could choose to constrain the search by the publication "Ask Dr. Cthulu." The other two possibilities are fairly similar to each other. In the case of a character (`CHAR` or `TEXT`) data type, an `RDBMSCharChoice` chooser is displayed to the left of a `TextField`. This allows the user to specify things like "all recipients whose names are like JEP-SON." See the documentation on the `RDBMSCharChoice` chooser for more information on this.

Like the character data types, numeric (REAL, INT) data types also use a Choice object and a TextField, but instead of an RDBMSCharChoice object, it's an RDBMSNumChoice object.

```
/**
 *
 * GUI_add_column_widgets - adds widgets that allow the
 * user to specify query criteria for each column in the
 * table.
 *
 */
private void GUI_add_column_widgets() {

    RDBMSTableColumn[] cols = table.getColumns();

    // Initialize the column_criteria Vector.
    //
    column_criteria = new Vector();

    for (int i = 0; i < cols.length; i++) {

        if (cols[i].isQueryable()) {

            // Create a Vector to hold the column object
            // and any components that correspond to the
            // column. This Vector will get added to the
            // column_criteria Vector.
            //
            Vector criteria = new Vector();

            // Add this column to the criteria Vector.
            //
            criteria.addElement(cols[i]);

            String name   = cols[i].getName();
            String type   = cols[i].getType();
            int length    = cols[i].getLength();

            // Add a new row, and display a label for
            // the columns's descriptive name.
            //

            // Set the column cell (gridx) to 0, and
            // increment the row cell (gridy), so we'll
            // move to a new row.
            //
            gbc.gridx = 0; gbc.gridy++;
            Label col_label =
                new Label(cols[i].getLabel());

            // Set the gridwidth so this Component
            // occupies one cell.
            //
```

```
gbc.gridwidth = 1;

// Constrain this component, and add it to
// the Frame.
//
gb.setConstraints(col_label, gbc);
add(col_label);

// Increment the column cell index
// (gridx), but leave the row cell index
// (gridy) alone.
//
// Remember that we are using the same
// GridBagConstraints object throughout,
// so unless we change its properties
// (such as the gridx or gridy), it uses
// whatever it used last.
//
// This set of constraints will be used by
// one of the Choice objects that can get
// created in the next section of code.
//
gbc.gridx++;

// If this column is a foreign key
// reference, then we want a Choice object
// with all possible values.
//
if (cols[i].isForeignKey()) {

    RDBMSChoice c =
        new RDBMSChoice(dbconn,
                cols[i].getForeignTable());

    gb.setConstraints(c, gbc);
    add(c);

    // Add this Choice to the criteria Vector.
    //
    criteria.addElement(c);

} else {

    // If this column is a character value,
    // let's put up a Choice Component with
    // valid comparisons.
    //
    if (type.equalsIgnoreCase("CHAR")) {

        RDBMSCharChoice c =
            new RDBMSCharChoice();
        gb.setConstraints(c, gbc);
```

```
            add(c);

            // Add this Choice to the criteria
            // Vector.
            //
            criteria.addElement(c);
        }

        // If this column is some sort of numeric
        // value, let's put up a Choice Component
        // with valid comparisons.
        //
        if (type.equalsIgnoreCase("REAL") ||
            type.equalsIgnoreCase("INT")) {

            RDBMSNumChoice c =
                new RDBMSNumChoice();
            gb.setConstraints(c, gbc);
            add(c);

            // Add this Choice to the criteria
            // Vector.
            //
            criteria.addElement(c);

            // With INT or REAL columns, we
            // don't have a length, so let's set
            // it to something arbitrary, that
            // should be big enough (in
            // theory...)
            //
            length = 15;

        }

        // Add a TextField so the user can type
        // in the arguments to the comparison.
        //
        gbc.gridx++;
        TextField t = new TextField(length);
        gb.setConstraints(t, gbc);
        add(t);

        // Add this TextField to the criteria
        // Vector.
        //
        criteria.addElement(t);

    }


    // Add the criteria Vector to the
```

```
            // column_criteria Vector. We can look at
            // this later, and use each component to
            // build a query string.
            //
            column_criteria.addElement(criteria);

        }
    }
}
```

Like the `saveSQL()` method in `RDBMSAddEdit`, the `doQuery()` method uses the `column_criteria` Vector to determine exactly what the user entered. In this method, an SQL query is built from the criteria that the user supplied. After it is executed, and if there were any results, the primary key of each selected row is added to a `Vector`. This `Vector` is then passed to the constructor of an `RDBMSQueryResults` object, which allows the user to choose from the rows that matched the query.

```
/**
 *
 * doQuery - look at the components contained within the
 * column_criteria Vector and build the SQL query
 * string.
 *
 */
private void doQuery() {

    StringBuffer where_clause = new StringBuffer();

    // A count of the number of items added.
    //
    int items_added = 0;

    for (int i = 0; i < column_criteria.size(); i++) {

        StringBuffer this_item = new StringBuffer();

        // Pull out a Vector that contains the column
        // and any Components that are related to it.
        //
        Vector criteria =
            (Vector) column_criteria.elementAt(i);

        // Get the RDBMSTableColumn from that Vector.
        //
        RDBMSTableColumn col =
            (RDBMSTableColumn) criteria.elementAt(0);

        // This flag tells us later if we added anything
        // here, so we can decide whether or not to
        // prepend an "AND" to it.
        //
```

```
boolean added_item = false;

// If it's a foreign key, we need to get the
// value for the comparison from the
// RDBMSChoice object at element 1.
//
String col_name = col.getName();
if (col.isForeignKey()) {

    // Get the RDBMSChoice Component.
    //
    RDBMSChoice c =
        (RDBMSChoice) criteria.elementAt(1);

    // Get the selected key (not the item, which
    // is a String) from the RDBMSChoice
    // Component.
    //
    int fkey = c.getSelectedKey();

    // If they selected an item from the choice,
    // this will be greater than 0.
    //
    if (fkey > 0) {
        this_item.append(col_name);
        this_item.append(" = " + fkey);
        added_item = true;
        items_added++;
    }

} else {

    String col_type = col.getType();

    // If the column is of a character type,
    // then we need to look at the state of the
    // character comparison chooser, and get the
    // value of the TextField. If the TextField
    // is blank, we won't do anything.
    //
    if (col_type.equalsIgnoreCase("CHAR")) {

        RDBMSCharChoice c = (RDBMSCharChoice)
            criteria.elementAt(1);

        TextField t =
            (TextField) criteria.elementAt(2);

        String text = t.getText();
        if (!text.equals("")) {

            this_item.append(col_name);
```

```java
                    this_item.append(
                        c.getExpression(text));
                    added_item = true;
                    items_added++;
                }

            }
            if (col_type.equalsIgnoreCase("REAL") ||
                col_type.equalsIgnoreCase("INT")) {

                RDBMSNumChoice c = (RDBMSNumChoice)
                    criteria.elementAt(1);

                TextField t =
                    (TextField) criteria.elementAt(2);

                String text = t.getText();
                if (!text.equals("")) {

                    this_item.append(col_name);
                    this_item.append(
                        c.getExpression(text));
                    added_item = true;
                    items_added++;
                }
            }

        }

        // If we added an item here, and this is the
        // first item we added, append a "WHERE"
        // followed by the criteria to the where_clause
        // StringBuffer.
        //
        if (added_item && items_added == 1) {
            where_clause.append(" WHERE " + this_item);
        }

        // If we added an item here, and this is not the
        // first item we added, append a "AND" followed
        // by the criteria to the where_clause
        // StringBuffer.
        //
        if (added_item && items_added > 1) {
            where_clause.append(" AND " + this_item);
        }

    }

    // Create a StringBuffer to hold the SQL Statement,
    // and add the top part of it.
    //
```

```java
StringBuffer sql = new StringBuffer();
sql.append(
    "SELECT " + table.getPrimaryKey() +
    " FROM " + table.getName() + " ");

// If we added any criteria (it's okay for the user
// to leave the form blank) then, we'll add a where
// clause.
//
if (items_added > 0) {
    sql.append(where_clause);
}

// Execute the query, create a Vector containing all
// the row ids, and create a new RDBMSQueryResult to
// show the result set.
//
try {

    // Get a statement from the connection.
    //
    Statement stmt = dbconn.createStatement();

    // Issue the query and get a result set.
    //
    ResultSet rs = stmt.executeQuery(sql.toString());

    // Process the result set and add it to a
    // Vector.
    //
    Vector v = new Vector();
    while (rs.next()) {

        // Get the row id.
        //
        int rowid = rs.getInt(1);
        v.addElement(new Integer(rowid));
    }

    if (v.size() > 0) {

        // Do we already have a RDBMSQueryResult
        // object instantiated? If so, dispose of it
        // before creating a new one.
        //
        if (query_result != null) {
            query_result.dispose();
            query_result = null;
        }

        String tbl_name = table.getName();
        query_result = new
```

```
                    RDBMSQueryResult(dbconn, tbl_name, v);

        } else {
            System.out.println("No results were found");
        }

    } catch (SQLException e) {
        e.printStackTrace();
        System.exit(0);
    }

}
```

The remainder of this class consists of event handlers for the object's window and each of the buttons that are displayed on the form.

```
// This is the event handler that deals with cases
// where a user closes the window.
//
class WinEventHandler extends WindowAdapter {
    public void windowClosing(WindowEvent e) {
        if (query_result != null) {
            query_result.dispose();
            query_result = null;
        }
        disposed = true;
        dispose();
    }
}

/**
 *
 * A listener which gets excited when the users presses
 * the Cancel button.
 *
 */
class cancelButtonWatcher implements ActionListener {
    public void actionPerformed( ActionEvent e ) {
        if (query_result != null) {
            query_result.dispose();
            query_result = null;
        }
        disposed = true;
        dispose();
    }
}

/**
 *
 * A listener which gets excited when the users presses
 * the Query button.
 *
```

```
    */
    class queryButtonWatcher implements ActionListener {
        public void actionPerformed( ActionEvent e ) {
            doQuery();
        }
    }

}
```

ORG.as220.rdbms.RDBMSQueryResult

This next class, RDBMSQueryResult, is a helper class for the RDBMSQuery class. Its purpose is to display the results of a query in a scrolling list object, and to allow the user to edit one of the rows in the result set. The constructor for this class requires a JDBC Connection, a table name, and a Vector containing row ids. The contents of the list are derived from the table's label column. So, while the object would be instantiated using recipient ids, its list would actually display the recipient names. Since the RDBMSTable's fetchLabel() method is used to get these names, tables without an explicit label column, such as subscription, are supported. For these tables, a label is produced by concatenating labels from the tables that are referenced by each row's foreign keys. So, for a subscription, you would see something like: "Recipient: Brian Jepson, Shipper: DHL, Publication: Ask Dr. Cthulu."

```
/*
 *
 * RDBMSQueryResult.java
 * Copyright (C) 1997 Brian Jepson (bjepson@ids.net)
 *
 * This program is free software; you can redistribute it
 * and/or modify it under the terms of the GNU General
 * Public License as published by the Free Software
 * Foundation; either version 2 of the License, or (at
 * your option) any later version.
 *
 * This program is distributed in the hope that it will be
 * useful, but WITHOUT ANY WARRANTY; without even the
 * implied warranty of MERCHANTABILITY or FITNESS FOR A
 * PARTICULAR PURPOSE.  See the GNU General Public License
 * for more details.
 *
 * You should have received a copy of the GNU General Public
 * License along with this program; if not, write to the
 * Free Software Foundation, Inc., 59 Temple Place - Suite
 * 330, Boston, MA 02111-1307, USA
 *
 */

package ORG.as220.rdbms;
import java.sql.*;
import java.awt.*;
import java.awt.event.*;
import java.util.*;
```

```
/**
 *
 * RDBMSQueryResult is a Frame that takes a table and a
 * Vector full of row ids. It will display a chooser that
 * lets the user select from the list of row ids, not by row
 * id, but by the associated descriptive (label) column.
 *
 */
public class RDBMSQueryResult extends Frame {
```

At the top of this class, declarations appear for fields that are available to all methods of the class. This includes the JDBC `Connection` object, a `Vector` that holds all the row ids, and an `RDBMSTable` object. In addition, the table name is stored as a `String`, and the `List` to display the results is declared.

```
    Connection dbconn; // the database connection
    Vector rowids;     // the rows to display
    RDBMSTable table;  // table metadata object
    String table_name; // name of the table.
    List result_list;  // the list containing results

    RDBMSAddEdit add = null; // an object to edit results

    // This is set if we disposed of this window with the
    // cancel button or using a window control to close it.
    //
    boolean disposed = false;
```

The constructor takes care of initializing the layout manager, setting up the display, and invoking `addAllRows()`, which takes care of displaying the labels in the `List`. Also, two buttons are added: one that lets the user edit the selected record, the other that lets the user cancel and remove this object from the screen.

```
    public RDBMSQueryResult(Connection conn,
                            String tbl, Vector rows) {

        super("Query Results");
        dbconn = conn;
        table_name = tbl;
        rowids = rows;

        // Get an RDBMSTable object with metadata about this
        // table.
        //
        table  = new RDBMSTable(dbconn, table_name);

        GridBagLayout gb           = new GridBagLayout();
        GridBagConstraints gbc = new GridBagConstraints();
        setLayout(gb);
        gbc.gridx = 0; gbc.gridy = 0;
```

```
// Add a label with large insets
//
Insets i = (Insets) gbc.insets.clone();
gbc.insets = new Insets(0, 150, 0, 150);
Label prompt = new Label(
    "Query Results for " + table.getTitle());
gb.setConstraints(prompt, gbc);
add(prompt);
gbc.insets = i;

// Create a list object and add it to the Frame.
//
gbc.gridy++;
gbc.anchor = GridBagConstraints.NORTH;
gbc.fill = GridBagConstraints.BOTH;
result_list = new List();

// Add the rows to the List object.
//
addAllRows();
gb.setConstraints(result_list, gbc);
add(result_list);

// Add a panel to hold two action buttons.
//
gbc.anchor = GridBagConstraints.SOUTH;
gbc.gridy++;
Panel p = new Panel();
gb.setConstraints(p, gbc);
add(p);

Button e = new Button("Edit");
p.add(e);

// This will bring up an edit form for the selected
// table.
//
e.addActionListener(new editButtonWatcher());

Button c = new Button("Cancel");
p.add(c);

// This will close the window.
//
c.addActionListener(new cancelButtonWatcher());

// Attach a listener that will be used to intercept
// calls to close this object.
//
addWindowListener(new WinEventHandler() );

pack();
```

```
        show();

    }
```

The `addAllRows()` method is quite simple. For each id in the `Vector` of row ids, it uses that id's value to invoke the `RDBMSTable` object's `fetchLabel()` method. The resulting string is added to the list. One of the nice things is, since we already have the row id values in a `Vector` (rowids), we don't need to set up a separate `Vector` to track them. The positions of the row id values in the `Vector` correspond directly to the labels in the `List`, so it's easy to figure out the row id of the selected item.

```
    /**
     * Fetch all of the rows that are in the Vector, and
     * display the corresponding label column in the list.
     */
    public void addAllRows() {

        // Get the primary key and label column.
        //
        String key   = table.getPrimaryKey();
        String label = table.getLabelColumn();

        // Process each row that is represented in the
        // Vector.
        //
        for (int i = 0; i < rowids.size(); i++) {

            // Retrieve the row id from the Vector.
            //
            int value =
                ((Integer)rowids.elementAt(i)).intValue();

            // Add the label to the List.
            //
            result_list.add(table.fetchLabel(value));

        }
    }
```

The `getSelectedKey()` method determines the id of the selected item, and returns it to the calling method. This is used by the event handler for the Edit button, as will be seen next.

```
    /**
     *
     * getSelectedKey - returns the key value corresponding
     * to the label that is the currently selected item.
     *
     */
    public int getSelectedKey() {

        // Get the current index.
        //
```

```
    int selected_index = result_list.getSelectedIndex();

    // Get the corresponding Integer from the rowids
    // Vector.
    //
    Integer selected_key =
        (Integer) rowids.elementAt(selected_index);

    // Return that Integer's intValue().
    //
    return selected_key.intValue();

}
```

The next classes are event handlers, and are basically quite simple. The WinEventHandler takes care of disposing of the object when the user closes the object using a window control, as does the cancelButtonWatcher. The editButtonWatcher is a little more involved. It gets the id of the selected item, and instantiates a new RDBMSAddEdit object based on the table for which this object is showing results. It uses a form of the constructor that takes a row id, so the RDBMSAddEdit object can bring the row up for editing right away. If there is already an RDBMSAddEdit object for this table, it invokes that object's loadData() method, and brings it to the front of the other windows.

```
// This is the event handler that deals with cases
// where a user closes the window.
//
class WinEventHandler extends WindowAdapter {
    public void windowClosing(WindowEvent e) {
        if (add != null) {
            add.dispose();
            add = null;
        }
        disposed = true;
        dispose();
    }
}

/**
 * A listener for the Cancel button.
 */
class cancelButtonWatcher implements ActionListener {

    public void actionPerformed( ActionEvent e ) {
        if (add != null) {
            add.dispose();
            add = null;
        }
        disposed = true;
        dispose();
    }
```

```
    }

    /**
     * A listener for the edit button.
     */
    class editButtonWatcher implements ActionListener {

        // When the user clicks the button, check to see if
        // the RDBMSAddEdit object is null, or if it was
        // disposed of. If so, create a new one. Otherwise,
        // bring the old one to the front, after loading the
        // requested record.
        //
        public void actionPerformed( ActionEvent e ) {

            int rownum = getSelectedKey();
            if (add == null || add.disposed) {
                add = null;

                String win_title  = table.getTitle();
                String table_name = table.getName();
                add = new RDBMSAddEdit(dbconn, table_name,
                                       win_title, rownum);
            } else {
                add.loadData(rownum);
                add.toFront();
            }

        }
    }

}
```

ORG.as220.util.Tools

This class is designed to provide any and all methods that can offer some simple generic functionality. The only method in there right now is a `split()` method, which splits a `String` on a delimiter, and returns a `Vector` of the substrings, much like the Perl function of the same name.

```
/**
 *
 * Tools.java - some tools that are used in our applications.
 *
 */

package ORG.as220.util;

import java.util.*;
import java.text.*;

public class Tools {
```

```
/**
 *
 * Splits a string on a given delimiter, and returns a
 * Vector of all the strings produced by this operation.
 *
 */
public static Vector split (String s, char delim) {

    StringCharacterIterator it =
        new StringCharacterIterator(s);

    Vector v = new Vector();

    StringBuffer curr_string = new StringBuffer();
    for (char c = it.first();
         c != StringCharacterIterator.DONE;
         c = it.next())
    {

        // If we encounter the delimiter, then we need
        // to add the current StringBuffer to the Vector
        // and start out with a new, blank StringBuffer.
        //
        if (c == delim) {
            v.addElement(curr_string.toString());
            curr_string = new StringBuffer();
        } else {
            curr_string.append(c);
        }

    }

    // Just in case there was no trailing delimiter,
    // let's add the last StringBuffer on which we were
    // working.
    //
    v.addElement(curr_string.toString());

    return v;

}

}
```

That's it for the RDBMS classes. As you can see, there is quite of bit of complexity under the hood of these classes. However, they manage to leverage the JDBC API with a little help from some metadata, and provide a set of classes that are not only useful in their own right, but will hopefully offer a practical foundation for any sort of development with JDBC and Mini SQL. Database development shouldn't be too much of a chore. If you let the data do the work for you, you can sit back and relax once in a while.

Annotated Source for the edit_schedule

This appendix showcases one of the longer sample applications from Chapter 8. It's called `edit_schedule.cgi`, and it does a couple of different things. The purpose of `edit_schedule.cgi` is to allow users to add, edit, or delete classes that have been scheduled. A scheduled class is represented by a row in the schedule table, and consists of a lecturer, course, start time, semester, and a list of days on which the class meets.

There are two ways that this form gets invoked. Assuming you installed it in your cgi-bin directory, the first way to invoke this is to simply type in a URL like:

```
http://localhost/cgi-bin/edit_schedule.cgi
```

If you installed it somewhere else, such as in a user's personal www directory, you'll need to change the URL to something different, such as:

```
http://localhost/~bjepson/edit_schedule.cgi
```

When you invoke the form in this manner, it allows you to schedule a class, as shown in Figure C.1. Selecting the class information and pressing the "Add to Schedule" button will run this script, and the `save_data()` method will handle the processing of this.

Another way in which the script can be invoked is from other scripts. Notice that there is a link called "Edit Lecturers" on the Web page. This is linked to the `edit_lecturer.cgi` script, which is not included in this printed chapter, but is available with the sample code in the /eg/ch08 directory. This script allows you to add a new lecturer, as well as search for a lecturer and then edit a lecturer. In the search screen (Figure C.2) it allows you to follow the "Lecturer Schedule" link, which also brings up the `edit_schedule.cgi` script. This sends in a parameter called `submit`, with the value of `BY_LECTURER`. This is caught in the `create_form()` method, which then brings up all of the scheduled classes for that lecturer

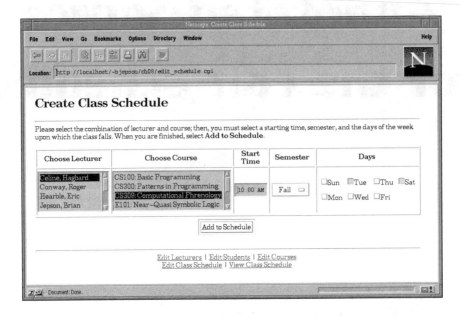

FIGURE C.1 The Create Class Schedule page.

(Figure C.3). There is similar functionality available from the "Edit Courses" and "View Class Schedule" pages. Here's the source code for edit_schedule.cgi. Note that the embedded Perl documentation has been reformatted for easier reading.

```
#!/usr/local/bin/perl

=head1 NAME

edit_schedule - package for adding, editing, and deleting
scheduled classes.

=head1 DESCRIPTION
```

This package is embedded in a Perl script that instantiates an edit_schedule object and calls its init() method. The script will display an entry form for a new class schedule entry, but can also be called to edit a schedule entry by course or by lecturer, as well as schedule id.

```
=head1 SYNOPSIS

  http://localhost/cgi-bin/edit_schedule.cgi

=head1 METHODS

=cut

package edit_schedule;
```

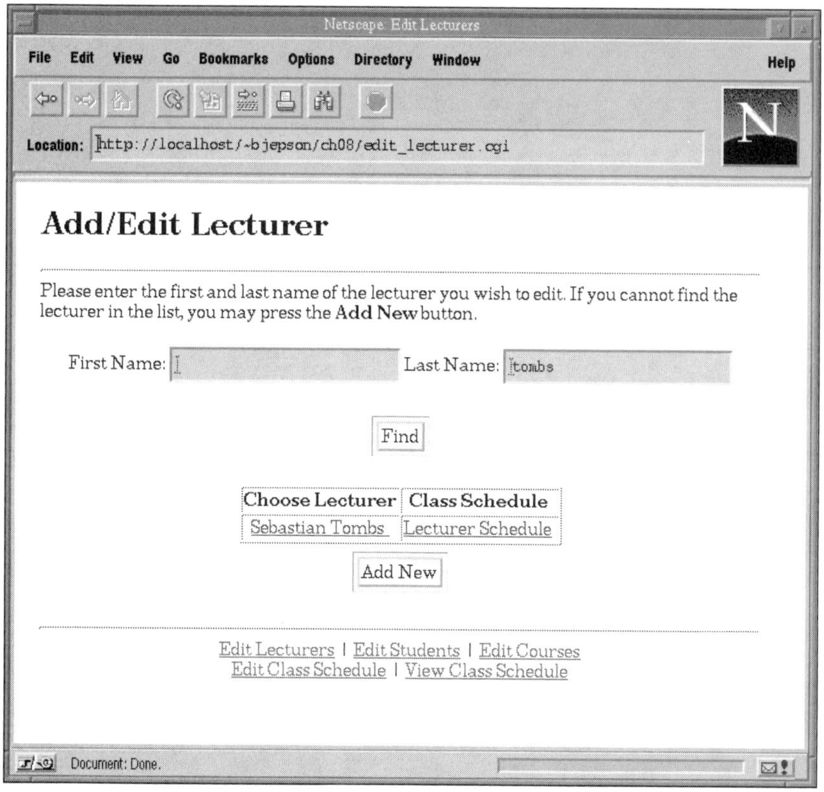

FIGURE C.2 The Add/Edit Lecturer search page.

```
use MsqlSourceBook::Courses;
@ISA = ("MsqlSourceBook::Courses");
use strict 'vars';
```

The `init()` method takes care of selecting the database, starting the form, calling `save_data()`, `load_data()`, and `create_form()`, and finally calling `end_form()`. Basically, it orchestrates all of the actions of this program, governing the invocation of each method.

```
sub init {

    my $self = shift;

    # Select the msql_sourcebook database. You should
    # have created this with the msqladmin utility.
    # Also, you should feed the \eg\ch08\tables.sql
    # script into the msql monitor; this will create
    # all the tables.
```

```
#
$self->{dbh}->selectdb("msql_sourcebook");

# Set up some day-of-week lookup arrays.
#
# The first, dow_array, is a simple array that
# contains a numeric range of all the days in
# the week, starting with 0 and ending with 6.
# The schedule.dow_string column is simply
# a concatenation of these numbers. If the class
# meets on Monday, Wednesday, and Friday,
# the $dow string will be '135'.
#
# The dow_hash is a hash that maps the numeric
# day value to a three-letter day name. We could
# easily have used a regular array here, but this
# works very well with the hash expected by the
# labels parameter of CGI.pm's checkbox_group()
# method, as we'll see later.
#
@{$self->{dow_array}} = (0..6);
```

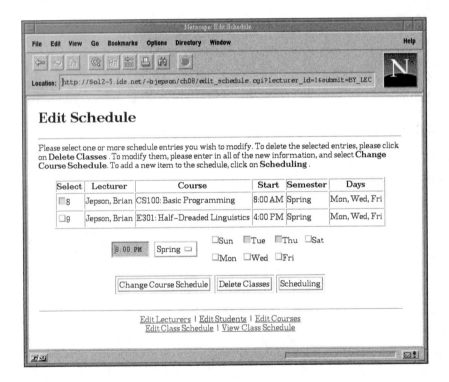

FIGURE C.3 The Edit Schedule form.

```
%{$self->{dow_hash}} = (0 => 'Sun', 1 => 'Mon',
                        2 => 'Tue', 3 => 'Wed',
                        4 => 'Thu', 5 => 'Fri',
                        6 => 'Sat');

# Remember that the CGI object is hidden behind
# the Framework's ->{query} property. Here, we'll
# invoke CGI.pm's startform() method.
#
$self->printbuff( $self->{query}->startform );

# Each of these methods performs critical
# functions for this module, and must be
# invoked in this order.
#
$self->save_data;
$self->load_data;
$self->create_form;

# Invoke CGI.pm's endform() method.
#
$self->printbuff( $self->{query}->endform );

# Invoke the superclass' init() method, just
# in case it does anything important.
#
$self->SUPER::init;

}
```

The `save_data()` method is responsible for processing updates to the database. This includes deletions, additions, and changes. This method actually delegates the execution of each type of update to a different method, which generates the SQL needed to perform the update, and sends it to the mSQL server.

```
sub save_data {

    my $self = shift;

    # The submit query parameter is set, appropriately,
    # by the submit buttons. We're using it here to
    # determine what action the user wants to perform.
    # It can be any of the following:
    #
    #     Delete Classes
    #     Add to Schedule
    #     Change Course Schedule
    #
    # Although the following cases are not handled in this
    # method, submit can also be equal to any of the
    # following:
```

```
#
#    BY_LECTURER
#    BY_COURSE
#    BY_SCHEDULE
#
# Those cases are handled in the create_form()
# method.
#
my $submit = $self->{query}->param("submit");

# Get the course and lecturer id from the query
# parameters.
#
my $course_id   = $self->{query}->param("course_id");
my $lecturer_id = $self->{query}->param("lecturer_id");

# If the user has elected to modify one or more
# scheduled class, the id value will return an
# array holding all of the classes the user chose
# to modify.
#
my @id           = $self->{query}->param("id");

# The user chose to delete a schedule entry. Note
# that the match is case-forgiving, but it must
# match the entire string.
#
if ($submit =~ /^DELETE CLASSES$/i) {

    # If the user didn't select one or more classes
    # to delete, they are given a warning, and no
    # action is performed.
    #
    unless (@id) {

        $self->error(
            "You must choose at least one class.");

        # Reset the value of submit to what it was
        # before they pressed the Delete Classes
        # button.
        #
        $self->{query}->param("submit",
            $self->{query}->param("currentform"));

        return;
    }

    # If they chose one or more classes, delete each
    # one in turn by sending a DELETE statement
    # for each schedule id.
    #
```

```perl
    foreach (@id) {

        my $sql = "DELETE FROM schedule WHERE id = $_";
        $self->{dbh}->query($sql);

        # In the event of an error, stop processing
        # the delete statements and return.
        #
        return if $self->error;

    }
    return;

}

# If the user elected to add a new class to
# the schedule, we'll invoke the save_schedule()
# method to take care of saving the information.
#
if ($submit =~ /^ADD TO SCHEDULE$/i) {
    $self->save_schedule();
}

# If the user chose to modify one or more
# scheduled class, we'll invoke save_schedule()
# to save the changes.
#
if ($submit =~ /^CHANGE COURSE SCHEDULE$/i) {

    # If the user didn't select one or more classes
    # to change, they are given a warning, and no
    # action is performed.
    #
    unless (@id) {

        $self->error(
            "You must choose at least one class." );

        # Reset the value of submit to what it was
        # before they pressed the Change Course
        # Schedule button.
        #
        $self->{query}->param("submit",
            $self->{query}->param("currentform"));

        return;

    } else {

        # Call save_schedule() to take care of
        # updating the schedule.
        #
```

```
        $self->save_schedule(@id);

    }
}

}
```

The `save_schedule()` method generates an SQL statement that will take care of the
meaty part of either updating one or more course schedule entries or inserting a new one. It needs
to examine the state of the id values in order to make a determination. If this method was given
an array of id values, then each row that corresponds to each id in the array needs to be updated
with the information in the form. Otherwise, it is understood that this method is to insert a new
row with the information provided in the form.

```
sub save_schedule {

    my $self = shift;

    # In cases where we are saving more than one record,
    # this will contain all of the ids (one or more)
    # that are to be updated. We'll get the updated
    # information from the CGI query.
    #
    # In cases where we are saving a new class to
    # the schedule, this will be blank.
    #
    my @id = @_;

    # Get the start time from the query, and use
    # Msql's quote() method to prepare the string
    # before sending it to the database. This takes
    # care of wrapping it in quotes, since it's a
    # character string.
    #
    my $start_time = $self->{dbh}->quote(
        $self->{query}->param("start_time"));

    # Ditto for the semester id.
    #
    my $semester    = $self->{dbh}->quote(
        $self->{query}->param("semester"));

    # Ditto for the day-of-week string.
    #
    my $dow_string = $self->{dbh}->quote(
        join("", $self->{query}->param('dow')));

    # If the @id array is set, then it contains a list of
    # schedule ids that we are to update with the
    # information that we just got from the CGI query.
    #
    if (@id) {
```

```perl
# For each of the ids, update the start time,
# semester, and day of week string.
#
foreach (@id) {

    my $sql = qq[UPDATE schedule ] .
              qq[SET start_time = $start_time, ] .
              qq[    semester    = $semester,   ] .
              qq[    dow_string  = $dow_string  ] .
              qq[WHERE id = $_];

    $self->{dbh}->query($sql);

    # check for errors
    #
    $self->error;

}

# Reset the submit value to whatever id was before
# the user chose "Change Course Schedule."
#
$self->{query}->param("submit",
    $self->{query}->param("currentform"));

# If @id wasn't set, we need to insert a new class
# into the schedule, rather than update existing entries.
#
} else {

    # Get the lecturer and course id from the CGI
    # query. Since these are integer values, we
    # don't need to put them through the quote()
    # method.
    #
    my $lecturer_id =
        $self->{query}->param("lecturer_id");
    my $course_id   =
        $self->{query}->param("course_id");

    # Don't let them save unless there's at least a
    # lecturer and a course selected.
    #
    unless ($lecturer_id && $course_id) {

        $self->error(
            "You must choose a lecturer and a course.");
        $self->{query}->param("submit", "SCHEDULE");
        return;

    }

    # Get the next sequence from the schedule table
```

```
    #
    my $sql = qq[SELECT _seq FROM schedule];
    my $sth = $self->{dbh}->query($sql);
return if $self->error;
    my %result_hash = $sth->fetchhash;
    my $seq = $result_hash{_seq};

    # Insert the new scheduled class into the
    # schedule table.
    #
    $sql = qq[INSERT INTO schedule
                (id, lecturer_id, course_id,
                 semester, start_time, dow_string)
                VALUES
                ($seq, $lecturer_id, $course_id,
                 $semester, $start_time, $dow_string)];
    $self->{dbh}->query($sql);

    # check for errors
    #
    $self->error;
}

}
```

This method is simply a helper method that creates picklist data for lecturers and courses. The data is stored in arrays that are properties of this class. These arrays will be used as the values and labels arrays for a `scrolling_list` or `popup_menu` item.

```
sub load_data {

    my $self = shift;

    my $sth;

    ####
    # This section of code is used to generate an array
    # and a hash. The array and hash are stored as
    # properties of this object, and will be used later
    # to generate a popup menu or scrolling list of
    # lecturers, using CGI.pm.
    #

    # Issue a query to get the ids, first names, and last
    # names of *every* lecturer.
    #
    $sth = $self->{dbh}->query(qq[SELECT id, first_name,
                                         last_name
                              FROM lecturer
                              ORDER BY last_name,
                                       first_name]);

    # Set the scope of this array and hash to be local
```

```perl
# to this method.
#
my (@le_values, %le_labels);

# Only process this if the statement handle ($sth)
# is defined. If it's not, there's a problem.
#
if (defined $sth) {

    my %hash;
    my $rowcount = $sth->numrows;
    my $i;

    # Process each row.
    #
    for ($i = 0; $i < $rowcount; $i++) {

        # Get each row as a hash, keyed by the
        # column name.
        #
        my %hash = $sth->fetchhash;

        # Add the lecturer id to the @le_values
        # array.
        #
        push @le_values, $hash{id};

        # Add the lecturer's name to the %le_labels
        # hash, and key it by the lecturer id.
        #
        $le_labels{$hash{id}} =
            qq[$hash{last_name}, $hash{first_name}];
    }
}

# Copy the values of the @le_values array and the
# %le_labels hash into corresponding properties of
# this object.
#
# Note that the members 'le_values' and 'le_labels'
# contain scalar values. However, the value they
# contain is a reference to an array and a hash,
# respectively. This is why you see the funny @{}
# and %{} notation.
#
@{$self->{le_values}} = @le_values;
%{$self->{le_labels}} = %le_labels;
#
####

####
# This section of code is used to generate an array
```

```
# and a hash. The array and hash are stored as
# properties of this object, and will be used later
# to generate a popup menu or scrolling list of
# courses, using CGI.pm.
#

# Issue a query to get the ids, course names,
# and course codes of *every* course.
#
$sth = $self->{dbh}->query(qq[SELECT id, course_code,
                                         course_name
                              FROM course
                              ORDER BY course_code]);

# Set the scope of this array and hash to be local
# to this method.
#
my (@co_values, %co_labels);

# Only process this if the statement handle ($sth)
# is defined. If it's not, there's a problem.
#
if (defined $sth) {

    my %hash;
    my $rowcount = $sth->numrows;
    my $i;

    # Process each row.
    #
    for ($i = 0; $i < $rowcount; $i++) {

        # Get each row as a hash, keyed by the
        # column name.
        #
        my %hash = $sth->fetchhash;

        # Add the course id to the @co_values
        # array.
        #
        push @co_values, $hash{id};

        # Add the course's name and code to the
        # %co_labels hash, and key it by the
        # course id.
        #
        $co_labels{$hash{id}} =
            qq[$hash{course_code}: $hash{course_name}];
    }
}

# Copy the values of the @co_values array and the
# %co_labels hash into corresponding properties of
```

```
    # this object.
    #
    @{$self->{co_values}} = @co_values;
    %{$self->{co_labels}} = %co_labels;
    #
    ####

}
```

Depending upon whether this CGI form was called with the BY_LECTURER, BY_COURSE, or BY_SCHEDULE parameter, this will either call up a form for viewing course schedules by lecturer, by course, or it will call up the schedule form, which lets the user add a new schedule entry.

```
sub create_form {

    my $self = shift;

    # The submit query parameter is set, appropriately,
    # by the submit buttons. We're using it here to
    # determine what action the user wants to perform.
    # It can be any of the following:
    #
    #     BY_LECTURER
    #         (view all of the classes scheduled for a
    #          particular lecturer)
    #     BY_COURSE
    #         (view all of the classes scheduled for a
    #          particular course)
    #     BY_SCHEDULE
    #         (view a particular scheduled class)
    #
    # Although the following cases are not handled in this
    # method, submit can also be equal to any of the
    # following:
    #
    #     Delete Classes
    #     Add to Schedule
    #     Change Course Schedule
    #
    # Those cases are handled in the save_data()
    # method.
    #
    my $submit = $self->{query}->param('submit');

    if ($submit =~ /^BY_LECTURER$/i) {

        $self->edit_schedule("LECTURER");

    } elsif ($submit =~ /^BY_COURSE$/i) {

        $self->edit_schedule("COURSE");

    } elsif ($submit =~ /^BY_SCHEDULE$/i) {
```

```
        $self->edit_schedule("SCHEDULE");

    } else {

        # If the user didn't select one of the other
        # options, the default behavior of this
        # module is to display a form to add new
        # classes to the schedule.
        #
        $self->schedule;

    }

}
```

The `lecturer_chooser()` and `course_chooser()` methods simply generate a scrolling list for lecturers and courses, respectively. These methods use the data that was fetched in the `load_data()` method.

```
sub lecturer_chooser {

    my $self = shift;

    # If the lecturer values array and labels hash are
    # defined, we'll create a scrolling list which
    # displays the names of the lecturers, but yields
    # the lecturer id as the CGI query variable
    # 'lecturer_id'.
    #
    # If no lecturer values array and labels hash are
    # defined, we'll simply display the fact that there
    # are no lecturers in a soothing green color.
    #
    if (@{$self->{le_values}}) {

        $self->printbuff(
            $self->{query}->scrolling_list (
                    -name    => 'lecturer_id',
                    -values  => \@{$self->{le_values}},
                    -labels  => \%{$self->{le_labels}},
                    -size    => 4));
    } else {
        $self->printbuff(
            qq[<font color="green">No Lecturers Defined
                </font>]);
    }

}

sub course_chooser {

    my $self = shift;
```

```perl
# If the course values array and labels hash are
# defined, we'll create a scrolling list which
# displays the names of the courses, but yields
# the course id as the CGI query variable
# 'course_id'.
#
# If no course values array and labels hash are
# defined, we'll simply display the fact that there
# are no courses in a soothing green color.
#
if (@{$self->{co_values}}) {

    $self->printbuff(
        $self->{query}->scrolling_list (
                    -name    => 'course_id',
                    -values => \@{$self->{co_values}},
                    -labels => \%{$self->{co_labels}},
                    -size    => 4));
} else {
    $self->printbuff(
        qq[<font color="green">No Courses Defined
            </font>]);
}

}
```

The `schedule()` method displays an entry form for adding a new class schedule entry. This allows the user to add courses to the schedule, and to choose all the necessary information for those classes.

```perl
sub schedule {

    my $self = shift;

    # This hash allows us to resolve the semester codes,
    # 'S' and 'F', into the values 'Spring' and 'Fall'.
    # This is used later in a call to the CGI.pm
    # method popup_menu(), which is very similar to the
    # scrolling_list() method.
    #
    my %semester = ('S' => 'Spring', 'F' => 'Fall');

    # Set the title of the page, and display a
    # prompt.
    #
    $self->set_title("Create Class Schedule");
    $self->printbuff(qq[<h1>Create Class Schedule</h1><hr>
                    Please select the combination of
                    lecturer and course; then, you must
                    select a starting time, semester,
                    and the days of the week upon which
                    the class falls. When you are
```

```
                        finished, select <strong>Add to
                        Schedule</strong>.<p>]);

# In order to precisely position items within the
# page, I often use a table. I'm also using the
# border option, which looks nice in some cases.
#
$self->printbuff( qq[<center>] );
$self->printbuff( qq[<table border>] );

# Display headers for each of the the data entry
# components.
#
$self->printbuff( qq[<th>Choose Lecturer</th>] );
$self->printbuff( qq[<th>Choose Course</th>] );
$self->printbuff( qq[<th>Start Time</th>] );
$self->printbuff( qq[<th>Semester</th>] );
$self->printbuff( qq[<th>Days</th>] );

# Invoke the lecturer_chooser() and course_chooser()
# methods to get picklists for lecturers and courses,
# respectively. Notice that these are embedded in
# table cells.
#
$self->printbuff( qq[<tr><td>] );
$self->lecturer_chooser;
$self->printbuff( qq[</td><td>] );
$self->course_chooser;

# Display a text input field for the class'
# start time.
#
$self->printbuff( qq[</td><td>] );
$self->printbuff(
    $self->{query}->textfield( -name => 'start_time',
                               -size => 8));

# Display a popup menu to allow the user to pick
# a semester. Although they see the long names
# (Spring and Fall), the semester CGI query
# parameter is set to 'S' or 'F'.
#
$self->printbuff( qq[</td><td>] );
$self->printbuff(
    $self->{query}->popup_menu ( -name   => 'semester',
                                 -values => ['S', 'F'],
                                 -labels => \%semester));
$self->printbuff( qq[</td><td>] );

# Put up a set of checkboxes for each day of the
# week. The labels that are displayed are the
# names of the day (three letter abbreviations),
```

```perl
# but the value that gets put in the CGI
# parameter (actually an array of values) is the
# numeric values, 0-6.
#
$self->printbuff(
    $self->{query}->checkbox_group(
                        -name   => 'dow',
                        -values => \@{$self->{dow_array}},
                        -labels => \%{$self->{dow_hash}},
                        -rows   => 2, -columns => 4 ));

# Finish the table
#
$self->printbuff( qq[</td><tr>] );
$self->printbuff( qq[</table>] );

# Display a button to add this class to the schedule.
#
$self->printbuff(
    $self->{query}->submit(-name => 'submit',
                            -value => 'Add to Schedule'));
$self->printbuff( qq[</center>] );

}
```

The `edit_schedule()` method will display the class schedule associated with a given course or lecturer, and allow the user to modify one or more of the schedule entries in the list.

```perl
sub edit_schedule {

    my $self = shift;

    # The edit_schedule() method is invoked by the
    # create_form() method. The mode can be any one
    # of LECTURER, COURSE, or SCHEDULE.
    #
    my $mode = shift;

    # Set the title of the page, and display a
    # prompt.
    #
    $self->{title} = "Edit Schedule";
    $self->printbuff(qq[<h1>Edit Schedule</h1><hr>
                        Please select one or more schedule
                        entries you wish to modify. To
                        delete the selected entries, please
                        click on <strong>Delete Classes
                        </strong>. To modify them, please
                        enter in all of the new
                        information, and select <strong>
                        Change Course Schedule</strong>.
                        To add a new item to the schedule,
```

```
                     click on <strong>Scheduling
                     </strong>.<p>]);

# This hash allows us to resolve the semester codes,
# 'S' and 'F', into the values 'Spring' and 'Fall'.
# This is used later in a call to the CGI.pm
# method popup_menu(), which is very similar to the
# scrolling_list() method.
#
my %semester = ('S' => 'Spring', 'F' => 'Fall');

# Set the currentform variable to the value of
# submit. This can be used in subsequent calls
# to this form to backtrack in the case of errors.
#
$self->{query}->param("currentform",
    $self->{query}->param("submit"));

# The join condition $where_condition will be used
# in the SELECT statement to fetch all of the course
# entries; depending on the mode, that SELECT will
# either be filtered by a lecturer, course or
# single scheduled class.
#
my $where_condition;

# If the mode is set to 'SCHEDULE,' then the user wants
# to see the information for a particular scheduled
# class, which will always result in only one record
# being brought up.
#
if ($mode eq 'SCHEDULE') {

    # Get the id from the CGI query parameter.
    #
    my $schedule_id =
        $self->{query}->param("schedule_id");

    # The join condition $where_condition will bind
    # the column schedule.id to the schedule_id
    # value that came in from the query.
    #
    $where_condition = " schedule.id = $schedule_id ";

    # Force the checkbox to default to being checked,
    # since there will only be one row.
    #
    $self->{query}->param("id", $schedule_id);

}

# If the mode is set to 'LECTURER,' then the user wants
```

```
# to see all of the classes scheduled for a particular
# lecturer, which can result in more than one record
# being displayed.
#
if ($mode eq 'LECTURER') {

    # Get the id from the CGI query parameter.
    #
    my $lecturer_id =
        $self->{query}->param("lecturer_id");

    # The join condition $where_condition will bind
    # the column schedule.lecturer_id to the
    # lecturer_id value that came in from the query.
    #
    $where_condition =
        " schedule.lecturer_id = $lecturer_id ";
}

# If the mode is set to 'COURSE,' then the user wants
# to see all of the classes scheduled for a particular
# course, which can result in more than one record
# being displayed.
#
if ($mode eq 'COURSE') {

    # Get the id from the CGI query parameter.
    #
    my $course_id =
        $self->{query}->param("course_id");

    # The join condition $where_condition will bind
    # the column schedule.course_id to the
    # course_id value that came in from the query.
    #
    $where_condition =
        " schedule.course_id = $course_id ";
}

# Issue the SQL SELECT statement, interpolating
# the where condition that we just created.
#
my $sql = qq[SELECT lecturer.first_name,
                    lecturer.last_name,
                    course.course_code,
                    course.course_name,
                    schedule.start_time,
                    schedule.semester,
                    schedule.dow_string,
                    schedule.id
             FROM lecturer, course, schedule
             WHERE lecturer.id = schedule.lecturer_id
```

```
            AND    course.id   = schedule.course_id
            AND    $where_condition];

# If there was an error, display the page (this
# automatically displays errors) and exit this
# program.
#
my $sth = $self->{dbh}->query($sql);
unless (defined $sth) {
    $self->error( $self->{dbh}->errmsg );
    $self->display_page;
    exit;
}

# Process the results of the query.
#
my $rowcount = $sth->numrows;

# The @td array will contain an array of table
# cells that have all of the information about
# the scheduled class. This will be reunited
# with the @id array, which holds the id of
# the scheduled class. That way, we can build
# checkboxes next to each row, and the user can
# choose which classes to update with the changes
# they'll be able to make in the data entry
# region below the list of classes.
#
my ($i, @td, @id);
for ($i = 0; $i < $rowcount; $i++) {

    my %hash = $sth->fetchhash;

    # Retrieve the id, lecturer name, course name,
    # start time, semester, and days that the class
    # meets.
    #
    my $id         = $hash{id};
    my $lecturer   =
        qq[$hash{last_name}, $hash{first_name}];
    my $course     =
        qq[$hash{course_code}: $hash{course_name}];
    my $start_time =
        $hash{start_time} || (" " x 5);
    my $semester   = $semester{$hash{semester}};
    my $dow        = $hash{dow_string};

    # Convert the day-of-week string into human-readable
    # form, using comma-separated three-letter day names.
    #
    my @dow;
```

```perl
    # The $dow string is a concatenation of the
    # numbers 0-6, in some permutation - if the class
    # meets on Monday, Wednesday, and Friday,
    # the $dow string will be '135'.
    #
    # This next bit first splits the string into
    # a list, and iterates over that list with
    # the grep() function.
    #
    # For each element that it processes, it
    # gets the corresponding three letter day
    # name from the %self->{dow_hash}, and pushes
    # it onto the @dow array.
    #
    # After it's done that, it joins the @dow array
    # into a comma-separated list; if, for some
    # reason, the @dow array is empty, then five
    # non-breaking spaces are displayed instead
    # of the list.
    #
    grep( push (@dow, $self->{dow_hash}->{$_}),
            sort split(//, $dow) );
    my $dow = join(", ", @dow) || (" " x 5);

    # build a table row with the information, but save
    # the row (@td) and the schedule id (@id) in separate
    # arrays.
    #
    my $td  = qq[<td>$lecturer</td>];
    $td .= qq[<td>$course</td>];
    $td .= qq[<td>$start_time</td>];
    $td .= qq[<td>$semester</td>];
    $td .= qq[<td>$dow</td>];
    push @td, $td;
    push @id, $id;
}

# get an array of checkboxes for each schedule id
#
my @checkboxes =
    $self->{query}->checkbox_group( -name    => 'id',
                                    -values => \@id );

# put up headers for each matching row.
#
$self->printbuff( qq[<center>] );
$self->printbuff( qq[<table border>] );
$self->printbuff( qq[<th>Select</th><th>Lecturer</th>
                    <th>Course</th><th>Start</th>
                    <th>Semester</th><th>Days</th>]);

# display each detail row, along with the corresponding
```

```
# checkbox for the schedule entry id. Since the @id
# and @td values were pushed on the array in the same
# order, this is safe.
#
foreach (@td) {

    # Pull a checkbox off the list of checkboxes,
    # shortening the list from the top.
    #
    my $checkbox = shift @checkboxes;
    $self->printbuff(
        qq[<tr><td>$checkbox</td>$_</tr>\n] );

}
$self->printbuff( qq[</table>] );

# display entry fields for start time, semester, and
# day of week.
#
$self->printbuff( qq[<table>] );
$self->printbuff( qq[</td><td>] );

# Display a text input field for the class'
# start time.
#
$self->printbuff(
    $self->{query}->textfield(-name => 'start_time',
                              -size => 8) );

# Display a popup menu to allow the user to pick
# a semester. Although they see the long names
# (Spring and Fall), the semester CGI query
# parameter is set to 'S' or 'F'.
#
$self->printbuff( qq[</td><td>] );
$self->printbuff(
    $self->{query}->popup_menu (-name   => 'semester',
                                -values => ['S', 'F'],
                                -labels => \%semester));

$self->printbuff( qq[</td><td>] );

# Put up a set of checkboxes for each day of the
# week. The labels that are displayed are the
# names of the day (three letter abbreviations),
# but the value that gets put in the CGI
# parameter (actually an array of values) is the
# numeric values, 0-6.
#
$self->printbuff(
```

```
        $self->{query}->checkbox_group(
            -name   => 'dow',
            -values => \@{$self->{dow_array}},
            -labels => \%{$self->{dow_hash}},
            -rows   => 2, -columns => 4 ));

    # Finish the table
    #
    $self->printbuff( qq[</td><tr>] );
    $self->printbuff( qq[</table>] );

    # Add a submit button to change all the selected
    # classes.
    #
    $self->printbuff($self->{query}->submit(
                        -name   => 'submit',
                        -value => 'Change Course Schedule'));

    # Add a submit button to delete all the selected
    # classes.
    #
    $self->printbuff(
        $self->{query}->submit( -name => 'submit',
                                -value => 'Delete Classes'));

    # This button will take the user to the "Create Class
    # Schedule" form, also handled by this script.
    #
    $self->printbuff(
        $self->{query}->submit( -name => 'submit',
                                -value => 'Scheduling' ));

    # Here, we preserve certain CGI parameters as
    # hidden fields so they will persist between
    # invocations of this form.
    #
    $self->printbuff(
        $self->{query}->hidden( -name => 'currentform'));
    $self->printbuff(
        $self->{query}->hidden( -name => 'lecturer_id'));
    $self->printbuff(
        $self->{query}->hidden( -name => 'course_id'));
    $self->printbuff(
        $self->{query}->hidden( -name => 'schedule_id'));
    $self->printbuff( qq[</center>] );

}

####################
#
```

```perl
# Instantiate a new edit_schedule
# object, and put it through its paces.
#
package main;
my $f = new edit_schedule;
$f->init;
$f->display_page;
```

Annotated Source for the MsqlSourceBook:: MsqlFramework Module

The following listing contains all of the source code to the `MsqlSource-Book::MsqlFramework` module. It has been reformatted so that the inline documentation stands out; after you install the module, this documentation may also be viewed on line, using Perl's documentation system. After you install it, you can view it at any time by typing

```
perldoc MsqlSourceBook::MsqlFramework
```

This framework is designed to offer some simple features when developing applications for the Web using the Perl DBI. It offers features that include user-authentication against database tables, error handling, binding of CGI variables to tables and columns, and others . The present incarnation relies on private metadata functions for Mini SQL. As a result, it is nonportable, but future releases will track the DBI in a portable manner once the DBI offers more metadata functions.

```
package MsqlSourceBook::MsqlFramework;

use CGI;
```

The `new()` method constructs a new instance of the `MsqlSourceBook::MsqlFramework` object. This method requires a DBI connection (database handle) object as an argument.

```
sub new {

    # standard Perl object construction.
    # (see the perltoot manpage)
    #
```

```
my $proto = shift;
my $class = ref($proto) || $proto;
my $self = {};
bless ($self, $class);

# Store the database handle as one of this object's
# properties.
#
my $dbh      = shift;
$self->{dbh} = $dbh;

# construct a new CGI object and store it as a property.
#
$self->{query} = new CGI;

# Give this object a default title. This can be changed
# with the set_title() method.
#
$self->{title} = "NO TITLE";

# Initialize the buffer; this is where all the HTML
# goes before being displayed.
#
$self->{buffer} = "";

# Initialize the tag; this is printed at the bottom
# of each document.
#
$self->{tag} = "";

# Return the object to whoever called this constructor.
#
return $self;

}
```

Although the init() method is empty, it is possible that it may do something in the future, so any subclasses *should* explicitly invoke the superclass method using the $self->SUPER::init statement.

```
sub init {

}
```

The display_page() method empties out the HTML buffer, and includes a header and title before it does so; you shouldn't put anything but the document body into the HTML buffer (see the printbuff() method for a means of adding to the HTML buffer). This method will also display a "tag line" at the bottom of each page, which you can set with set_tag(). If you override this method, either ensure that you duplicate its functionality (bad) or invoke it using the superclass method ($self->SUPER::display_page) at the end of your method (better). This method will also display errors at the top of the form by calling the errors() method.

```perl
sub display_page {

    my $self = shift;

    # Print out the HTTP header and the start of the HTML
    # The title can be set with set_title().
    #
    print $self->{query}->header;
    print $self->{query}->start_html(
        -BGCOLOR=> "#FFFFFF",
        -title => $self->{title});

    # Display any errors.
    #
    $self->errors;

    # Add the contents of the tag to the buffer.
    #
    $self->printbuff($self->{tag});

    # Empty the html buffer.
    #
    print $self->{buffer};

    # End the html.
    #
    print $self->{query}->end_html;

}
```

This next method, the error-handling method, can be invoked in two ways. The first is to pass it no values whatsoever; it will check the DBI connection for errors, and register any error that is found with the list of errors for this form. The second way to use this is to pass in a user-defined error message that will be registered in the list of errors. The second way will not check the DBI connection for errors. This is a good method to invoke after any SQL call; it returns True if there was an error, and all errors will get displayed when you invoke `display_page()`.

```perl
sub error {

    my $self = shift;

    # If the caller passed in an error, use that
    # message, or look for one in the DBI connection.
    #
    my $error = shift || $self->{dbh}->errstr;

    # if there was an error, add it to the list of errors,
    # and return 1.
    #
    if ($error) {
        push @{$self->{errors}}, $error;
```

```
        return 1;
    }
}
```

This method displays all of the errors in the list of errors. Each error is displayed in a threatening red color. This is normally called by `display_page()`, but if you want to annoy your users, you should call it as often as possible.

```
sub errors {

    my $self = shift;
    my @errors = @{$self->{errors}};

    # Iterate over the list of errors, and display each
    # in a big red font.
    #
    foreach (@errors) {
        print qq[<font size="+2" color="red">];
        print;
        print qq[</font><p>];
    }

}
```

The `printbuff()` method simply adds some text to the buffer that holds the HTML page. It is followed by the `set_tag()` method, which sets an optional tag line that is displayed at the bottom of each form. The `set_title()` method also follows, which sets the HTML title for the page.

```
sub printbuff {

    my $self = shift;
    my @data = @_;
    $self->{buffer} .= join("\n", @data);

}
sub set_tag {

    my $self = shift;
    $self->{tag} = shift;

}
sub set_title {

    my $self = shift;
    $self->{title} = shift;

}
```

The `bind_param()` method binds a parameter to a column in the specified table. This does a lot of stuff behind the scenes. The mechanism can be used to build data entry forms that are tied directly to a table row; in conjunction with the update_table() method and the fetch_data() method, this can be used to implement reads and writes to the table with no extra programming. You'll need to use the set_key() method to control which key column/CGI parameter to use for updates.

```perl
sub bind_param {

    my $self = shift;

    # Fetch the CGI object into a local variable.
    #
    my $query = $self->{query};

    my $cgi_parm = shift; # The CGI parameter name.
    my $table    = shift; # The table name.
    my $column   = shift; # The column name.

    # If there is a binding for this table, it will be
    # stored in the CGI query as the parameter _$table.
    # A binding is stored in the CGI query as a list of
    # values, and this list is represented in Perl as a
    # hash. The keys of the hash are the column names, and
    # the values of the hash are the CGI parameter names.
    #
    my %binding = $query->param("_bind_$table");

    # Set the binding for this column/parameter.
    #
    $binding{$column} = $cgi_parm;

    # I'll delete the binding here (just to be on the safe
    # side), and then add it back in.
    #
    $query->delete("_bind_$table");
    $query->param("_bind_$table", %binding);

    # Add this table to the master list of bindings, so we
    # can find out about it later.
    #
    my @binding_list = $query->param('_bindings');

    # If this table is not already listed in the list of
    # bindings, add it to that list. The list of bindings
    # is simply a list of table names preceded by the text
    # '_bind_'
    #
    if (! grep /^_bind_$table$/, @binding_list) {
        push @binding_list, "_bind_$table";
        $query->delete('_bindings');
        $query->param('_bindings', @binding_list);
    }

}
```

For a given table, the set_key() method sets the primary key column for updates, inserts and selects.

```
sub set_key {

    my $self = shift;

    # Fetch the CGI object into a local variable.
    #
    my $query = $self->{query};

    my $table    = shift; # The table name.
    my $column   = shift; # The column name.

    # Get the hash of key/table pairs.
    #
    my %keys = $query->param('_keys');

    # Set the key for this table.
    #
    $keys{$table} = $column;

    # Return the hash to the query.
    #
    $query->delete('_keys');
    $query->param('_keys', %keys);

}
```

For a given table, the fetch_data() method will fetch data for all bound columns. You must have set a key for this table or it will fail, reporting an error. This method constructs an SQL statement using that key to limit the result set. Since each value for the primary corresponds to one and only one row, this method will only expect to get one row in the result set.

```
sub fetch_data {

    my $self  = shift;
    my $table = shift; # The table we are fetching.

    # Fetch the CGI object into a local variable.
    #
    my $query = $self->{query};

    # Get the database handle.
    #
    my $dbh = $self->{dbh};

    # Try to fetch a binding for this table.
    #
    my %binding;
    unless (%binding = $query->param("_bind_$table")) {
        $self->error(
```

```
                "No columns are bound for the $table table.");
        return;
    }

    # Try to fetch the primary key for this table.
    #
    my %keys = $query->param('_keys');
    my $key;
    unless ($key = $keys{$table}) {
        $self->error(
            "No key is defined for the $table table.");
        return;
    }

    # Build the select statement. It is expected to only
    # return one row, since we are selecting based on the
    # primary key. The column list in the SELECT statement
    # is based on the keys of the binding hash. The binding
    # hash's keys are the column names, and the values are
    # the CGI parameter names.
    #
    my $columns = join(", ", keys %binding);
    my $row_id = $query->param($key);
    return unless $row_id;

    my $sql = "SELECT $columns FROM $table " .
              "WHERE $key = $row_id";

    # Issue the SELECT statement, and return if there was an
    # error.
    #
    my $sth = $dbh->prepare($sql);
    unless ($sth->execute) {
        $self->error;
        return;
    }
    my @row = $sth->fetchrow; # Fetch the row.
    $sth->finish;

    # Populate each CGI parameter with the results of the
    # SQL query.
    #
    my $column;
    foreach $column (keys %binding) {

        # Find out the name of the parameter from the
        # hash that contains all the binding information.
        #
        my $parm = $binding{$column};

        # The columns in the select statement appear in the
        # same order as the columns we are populating, so we
        # can just use shift to pull array elements off the
```

```
        # top.
        #
        $query->param($parm, shift @row)
    }


}
```

Attempt to update the given table, using all of the CGI parameters that are bound to that table. This will be an INSERT if the primary key is NULL, otherwise it will be an UPDATE statement. You must have set a key for this table using the set_key() method.

```
sub update_table {

    my $self   = shift;
    my $dbh    = $self->{dbh};     # The database handle.
    my $query  = $self->{query};   # The CGI object.

    my $table = shift;

    # Try to fetch a binding for this table.
    #
    my %binding;
    unless (%binding = $query->param("_bind_$table")) {
        $self->error(
            "No columns are bound for the $table table.");
        return;
    }

    # Try to fetch the primary key for this table.
    #
    my %keys = $query->param('_keys');
    my $key;
    unless ($key = $keys{$table}) {
        $self->error(
            "No key is defined for the $table table.");
        return;
    }

    # Get metadata for the table that is to be updated.
    # Here's where things become non-portable :-(
    #
    my $met = $dbh->func( $table, '_ListFields' );
    my @flds  = @{ $met->{NAME} };
    my @types = @{ $met->{TYPE} };

    # Create a hash that contains the data types, keyed by
    # the column name.
    #
    my %types;
    @types{ @flds } = @types;

    # Get the value of the primary key.
```

```perl
#
my $row_id = $query->param($key);

# Build the first part of the SQL statement. In order to
# keep the code simple, and only include one main loop,
# this method builds a valid INSERT and UPDATE
# statement, but only issues one of them. The INSERT is
# issued if the primary key is blank or NULL, and the
# UPDATE is issued if the primary key has a value.
#
my $insert = "INSERT INTO $table ";
my $update = "UPDATE $table SET ";
my (@set_list, @col_list, @val_list, $where_clause);

# Process each row in the binding.
#
my $column;
foreach $column (keys %binding) {

    # Fetch the column value from the CGI parameters.
    #
    my $parm = $binding{$column};
    my $val  = $query->param($parm);

    # If this is a character data type, then the
    # value needs to be quoted.
    #
    if (defined $val && $types{$column} == 2) {
        $val = $dbh->quote($val);
    }

    # If the value is undefined, then it should be NULL.
    #
    if (!defined $val) {
        $val = 'NULL';
    }

    # If the column is the primary key, and it's NULL,
    # then we need to fetch a new id value. This implies
    # that we're going to be building an INSERT
    # statement rather than an UPDATE.
    #
    if ($column eq $key && $val eq 'NULL') {

        # More non-portable stuff. This fetches the next
        # unique id from the table's sequence.
        #
        my $sth = $dbh->prepare(
            "SELECT _seq FROM $table");
        $sth->execute;
        return if $self->error;
        @row = $sth->fetchrow;
```

```
        $val = $row[0];
        $sth->finish;

        # Since a new key has been obtained, we can
        # add it to the CGI parameters and have it
        # come up in edit mode after we save it.
        #
        $query->delete($parm);
        $query->param($parm, $val);

    }

    # Add the column name to the array of columns, and
    # the value to the array of values. These are only
    # used by the INSERT statement.
    #
    push @col_list, $column;
    push @val_list, $val;

    # If the column name that we're currently processing
    # is the primary key, then add it to the WHERE
    # clause as a comparison. This is only used for the
    # UPDATE statement, and is used to only update the
    # row that matches the current value of the primary
    # key; otherwise, the statement would update every
    # row, which is not what you want!
    #
    # If the column is not the primary key, then it will
    # be added to the list of values for the SET clause
    # in the UPDATE statement.
    #
    if ($column eq $key) {
        $where_clause = " WHERE $column = $val";
    } else {
        push @set_list, "$column = $val";
    }

}


# If the primary key is NULL or blank, then this should
# be processed as an INSERT. Otherwise, it should be
# handled as an UPDATE.
#
if (!$row_id || $row_id =~ /NULL/i) {

    # Generate the INSERT statement.
    #
    $sql = $insert;
    $sql .= ' (' . join(', ', @col_list) . ')';
    $sql .= ' VALUES (' . join(', ', @val_list) . ')';

} else {
```

```
        # Generate the UPDATE statement.
        #
        $sql = $update;
        $sql .= join(', ', @set_list);
        $sql .= $where_clause;

    }

    # Execute the SQL statement, whether it be an INSERT or
    # an UPDATE.
    #
    my $sth = $dbh->prepare($sql);
    $sth->execute;
    $self->error;
    $sth->finish;

}
```

This method inserts hidden fields for keys and bindings at the point at which this is called. This should be invoked once for each form on the page, preferably before the call to CGI::end_form().

```
sub hidden_fields {

    my $self = shift;

    my $query = $self->{query}; # The CGI object.

    # print out a hidden field for the binding list.
    #
    $self->printbuff( $query->hidden('_bindings') );
    $self->printbuff( "\n" );

    # There can be more than one table binding. Fortunately,
    # the _bindings parameter knows all about them.
    #
    my @binding_list = $query->param('_bindings');
    my $binding;
    $self->printbuff( "\n" );
    foreach $binding (@binding_list) {

        # Print out a hidden field for each binding.
        #
        $self->printbuff( $query->hidden($binding) );

    }
    $self->printbuff( "\n" );

    # Print out a hidden field for the primary key list.
    #
    $self->printbuff( $query->hidden('_keys') );
```

```
    # Print out a hidden field for the session id,
    # username, and user id. The username may consist of
    # more than one column.
    #
    $self->printbuff( $query->hidden('_session') );
    $self->printbuff( $query->hidden('_uid') );

    foreach (@{ $self->{username_hidden} }) {
        $self->printbuff( $query->hidden($_) );
    }

    $self->printbuff( "\n" );

}
```

This method generates an HTML scrolling list. It derives its values from an SQL query. The SQL query is generated using parameters that are passed into this method, shown and explained in detail here:

```
sub db_scroll_list {

    my $self = shift;

    # Fetch the CGI object into a local variable.
    #
    my $query = $self->{query};

    # Fetch the database handle into a local variable.
    #
    my $dbh = $self->{dbh};

    my %parms = @_;

    # These parameters are required to construct the
    # scrolling list.
    #
    # $parms{table}          The table name
    # $parms{row_id}         The name of the primary key column.
    # $parms{row_label}      This is a template that is used to
    #                        generate the label for each list
    #                        element. It should consist of any
    #                        column names and other characters
    #                        you wish to use as the label.
    # $parms{order_by}       The order by clause, without the
    #                        ORDER BY part - it should just be a
    #                        comma-delimited list of columns.
    # $parms{cgi_parm}       The name of the CGI parameter to use
    #                        for this scrolling list.
    # $parms{size}           The height of the list. Use 1 to
    #                        have it appear as a popup menu.
    #
```

```perl
# $parms{none_option} This should be non-zero to have a
#                     '[ None ]' choice in the list that
#                     has zero as its value.
#
my $table     = $parms{table};
my $row_id    = $parms{row_id};
my $row_label = $parms{row_label};
my $order_by  = $parms{order_by};
my $cgi_parm  = $parms{cgi_parm};
my $size      = $parms{size} || 5;
my $none_option = $parms{none_option};

# @values - the row ids, used by the scrolling_list
#           method as the list values.
# %labels - a hash that correlates values to label
#           columns.
#
my (@values, %labels);

# If the caller requested that we put a '[ None ]'
# option in the list, then do so now.
#
if ($none_option) {
    push @values, 0;
    $labels{0} = " [ None ] ";
}

# Generate an SQL Statement to retrieve the row ids and
# row labels from the table.
#
my $sql = "SELECT * FROM $table";
if ($order_by) {
    $sql .= " ORDER BY $order_by";
}

# Prepare the statement for execution, and execute it.
#
my $sth = $dbh->prepare($sql);
if ($sth->execute) {

    # If the statement executed without a problem, then
    # fetch each row with the fetchrow_hashref() method,
    # which returns the row as a reference to a hash,
    # keyed by column name.
    #
    my $row;
    while ($row = $sth->fetchrow_hashref) {

        # Get the hash that the $row scalar refers to.
        #
        my %row = %$row;
```

```perl
        # Get the row id and row label from the array.
        # The row label is basically a template, into
        # which columns will be interpolated.
        #
        my $label = $row_label;
        my $rowindex = 0;

        # Assume that the column name will consist of
        # alphanumerics (including underscore). That
        # way, we can do a simple substitution for each
        # word in the row_label; simply substitute each
        # column name with the value of the column in
        # the %row hash.
        #
        foreach ($row_label =~ /(\w+)/g) {
            if (defined $row{$_}) {
                $label =~ s/$_/$row{$_}/g;
            }
        }

        # Get the value of the row id.
        #
        my $id    = $row{$row_id}; # row id

        # Populate the @values array with the row id
        # value.
        #
        push @values, $id;

        # Populate the %labels hash - add the label,
        # and key it by the row id.
        $labels{ $id } = $label;
    }
    $sth->finish;

} else {
    $self->error; # check for error messages
    return;
}
$sth->finish;

# Now, create a scrolling list object and return it to
# the caller.
#
my $sl = $query->scrolling_list( -name   => $cgi_parm,
                                 -values => \@values,
                                 -labels => \%labels,
                                 -size   => $size);
return qq[\n$sl\n];

}
```

The login() method is a rather powerful piece of this module. It allows you to use any table as an authentication table, and will prompt the user for a user id and password using an HTML form. If the user is not presently logged in, or if authentication fails, the method returns undef. After the user is authenticated, this state is maintained within each subsequent form. A hidden field is kept for each component of the userid, and a special value is generated to authenticate the user. For this purpose, the password is used to encrypt the user's IP address. This value is carried from form to form; on the next form the user visits within an application, the userid is used to retrieve the password. Then the password is used to encrypt the remote user's IP address, and that value is compared to the value stored in the CGI query as the _session parameter. At present, the module only permits comparison against clear text passwords, so the passwords must be stored unencrypted in a database table. This is an extremely lightweight security scheme, and should not be used where users have access to the table being used for authentication, and should certainly not be used to protect sensitive data.

This method requires a hash of parameters, which includes $parms{table}, the name of the table to use for authentication. This also includes $parms{username_col}, which is a reference to a list of columns that comprise the username. This can be useful when you want to use multiple columns, such as a first name and a last name as a user id. The $parms{username_label} parameter is a reference to a list of string values that should be used as a prompt for the respective user id column.

The $param{uid_col} value is usually the name of the primary key column in the table, and the $param{pwd_col} value is the name of the column to be used as a password. The $param{cleartext} parameter is currently unused.

```
sub login {

    my $self = shift;
    my %parms = @_;

    # Get the database handle.
    #
    my $dbh = $self->{dbh};

    # Get the CGI query object.
    #
    my $query = $self->{query};

    my $table          = $parms{table};
    my @username_col   = @{ $parms{username_col}   };
    my @username_label = @{ $parms{username_label} };
    my $uid_col        = $parms{uid_col};
    my $pwd_col        = $parms{pwd_col};
    my $cleartext      = $parms{cleartext};

    # Look for a session id in the query.
    #
    my $session= $query->param('_session');
```

```perl
# Get the userid column(s) from the query.
#
my ($where_clause, @username, @quoted_username,
    @where_clause, @input_prompt, @input_field);
foreach (@username_col) {

    my $username = $query->param(qq[_username_$_]);
    my $quoted_username = $dbh->quote($username);

    push @username, $username;
    push @quoted_username, $quoted_username;
    push @where_clause, qq[$_ = $quoted_username];
    push @input_prompt, shift @username_label;
    push @input_field,
        $query->textfield( -name => qq[_username_$_] );
    push @{ $self->{username_hidden} }, qq[_username_$_];

}

# Get the password from the table.
#
my ($pwd, $uid);
if (@username) {
    my $where_clause = join(" AND ", @where_clause);
    my $sql = "SELECT $pwd_col, $uid_col FROM $table " .
              "WHERE $where_clause";
    my $sth = $dbh->prepare($sql);
    unless ($sth->execute) {
        $self->error;
        return
    }
    my @row = $sth->fetchrow;
    $pwd = $row[0];
    $uid = $row[1];
    $sth->finish;
}

# Figure out the valid session id for this user. It
# should be the user's IP address crypted with the
# password as salt.
#
my $session_id = crypt($ENV{REMOTE_ADDR}, $pwd);

# If there was a session id amongst the CGI parameters,
# then it's assumed that the user has actually logged
# in at some point. Let's check the valid session id
# that was just generated against the one that's in the
# CGI query.
#
if ($session) {

    if ($session eq $session_id) {
```

```
        return 1;
    } else {
        $self->error("Access denied.");
        return undef;
    }

} else {

    # If there was no session id, look for a password
    # amongst the CGI parameters. This indicats that the
    # user has just come from the login screen.
    #
    if ($pwd && $pwd eq $query->param('_pwd')) {

        # Add the session id to the query and let them
        # in.
        #
        $query->param("_session", $session_id);
        $query->param("_uid", $uid);
        return 1;

    } else {

        # Display the login screen. If there is a
        # password amongst the CGI parameters, it must
        # have been a bad one to get this far.
        #
        if ($query->param('_pwd')) {
            $self->error("Login Failed.");
        }

        $self->printbuff( $query->startform );

        $self->printbuff( qq[<h2>Please Log In</h2><hr>] );
        $self->printbuff( qq[<center>] );
        $self->printbuff( qq[<table>] );

        foreach (@input_prompt) {
            my $textfield = shift @input_field;
            $self->printbuff( qq[<tr>] );
            $self->printbuff( qq[<td>$_</td>] );
            $self->printbuff( qq[<td>$textfield</td>] );
            $self->printbuff( qq[</tr>] );
        }

        $self->printbuff( qq[<tr><td>] );
        $self->printbuff( qq[<strong>Password</strong>] );
        $self->printbuff( qq[</td><td>] );
        $self->printbuff(
            $query->password_field( -name => '_pwd' ));
        $self->printbuff( qq[</td></tr>] );
        $self->printbuff( qq[</table>] );
```

```
        $self->printbuff(
            $query->submit( -name  => 'submit',
                            -value => 'Log In'));
        $self->printbuff( qq[</center>] );

        $self->printbuff( $query->endform );
        return undef;
    }
  }

}

=head1 AUTHOR

Brian Jepson - bjepson@ids.net

Copyright (c) 1997 Brian Jepson. All rights reserved.

This program is free software; you can redistribute it
and/or modify it under the same terms as Perl itself.

=head1 SEE ALSO

DBD::mSQL, CGI.pm

=cut

1;
```

What's on the CD-ROM?

The CD-ROM includes chapter examples from the book, a developer's version of Mini SQL 2.0, past versions of Mini SQL, and other related pieces of software. The chapter examples are included in the eg/ directory, and Mini SQL source code is included in the src/ directory. Older versions of Mini SQL are included in the old_versions/ directory, and other programs, such as Win32 and OS/2 versions of Mini SQL, and the PHP/FI package, are included in the contrib/ directory.

What Is Freeware/Shareware?

Freeware is software that is distributed by disk, through BBS systems, and the Internet, free. There is no charge for using it, and it can be distributed freely as long as the use it is put to follows the license agreement included with it.

Shareware (also known as user supported software) is a revolutionary means of distributing software created by individuals or companies too small to make inroads into the more conventional retail distribution networks. The authors of Shareware retain all rights to the software under the copyright laws while still allowing free distribution. This gives the user the chance to freely obtain and try out software to see if it fits his or her needs. Shareware should not be confused with Public Domain software even though they are often obtained from the same sources.

If you continue to use Shareware after trying it out, you are expected to register your use with the author and pay a registration fee. What you get in return depends on the author, but may include a printed manual, free updates, telephone support, and so on.

Hardware and Software Requirements

Source code for Mini SQL 1.0 and 2.0 is included on the CD-ROM. This source code can be compiled on most machines running Unix or a Unix variant. The contrib/Win32 directory contains versions of Mini SQL for Win32 (Windows NT, and Windows 95), and the contrib/OS2 directory includes versions for OS/2. The amount of memory needed by Mini SQL is fairly minimal—you should be able to run it on a machine with as little as eight megabytes. The compilation of Mini SQL requires about three megabytes initially, which will grow during compilation. The base installation of Mini SQL requires approximately two megabytes, but this will grow as you create tables and add data to them.

Installing the Software

Installation instructions for Mini SQL 2.0 are included in Chapter 1. The distribution that you should unpack depends upon whether you are a qualified non-commercial user (see the Introduction for more information). If you are a qualified non-commercial user, you can use the standard distribution of Mini SQL without restriction. This is included on the CD in src/msql-2.0.4.tar.gz. The limited developer's version is included on the CD in src/msql-2.0.4-dev.tar.gz.

You should copy the chapter examples to a locally accessible filesystem. These examples are included on the CD-ROM in the eg/ directory.

User Assistance and Information

The software accompanying this book is being provided as is without warranty or support of any kind. Should you require basic installation assistance, or if your media is defective, please call our product support number at (212) 850-6194 weekdays between 9 AM and 4 PM Eastern Standard Time. Or, we can be reached via e-mail at: wprtusw@wiley.com.

To place additional orders or to request information about other Wiley products, please call (800) 879-4539.

Index

A

CUSTOMER NOTE: IF THIS BOOK IS ACCOMPANIED BY SOFTWARE, PLEASE READ THE FOLLOWING BEFORE OPENING THE PACKAGE.

This software contains files to help you utilize the models described in the accompanying book. By opening the package, you are agreeing to be bound by the following agreement:

To use this CD-ROM, your system must meet the following requirements:

Platform/Operating System: MiniSQL is written primarily for UNIX. If you are running Windows NT, Windows 95, or OS/2, please refer to the .lsm files in the contrib/Win32 and contrib/Os2 folders for system compatibilities and requirements. Windows 3.1 and Macintosh systems are not supported.

Hard drive space: MiniSQL requires between 3 MB and 6 MB hard drive space, depending on your operating system.

Peripherals: CD-ROM Drive.